Understanding, Assessing, & Counseling the Criminal Justice Client

Anthony Walsh

Boise State University

Brooks/Cole Publishing Company
Pacific Grove, California

Brooks/Cole Publishing Company
A Division of Wadsworth, Inc.

Printed in the United States of America

10   9   8   7   6   5   4   3   2   1

Library of Congress Cataloging-in-Publication Data

Walsh, Anthony, [date]
  Understanding, assessing, and counseling the criminal justice client.

  Includes bibliographies and index.
  1. Social work with delinquents and criminals—United States.   2. Delinquents—Counseling of—United States.   3. Prisoners—Counseling of—United States.
  4. Criminal behavior.   I. Title.
HV7921.W34   1987   365′.66   87-25002
ISBN 0-534-08652-7

Sponsoring Editor: *Claire Verduin*
Editorial Assistant: *Linda Ruth Wright*
Production Editor: *Fiorella Ljunggren*
Manuscript Editor: *Meredy Amyx*
Permissions Editor: *Carline Haga*
Interior and Cover Design: *Lisa Thompson*
Cover Photo: *Lee Hocker*
Art Coordinator: *Sue C. Howard*
Interior Illustration: *Judith L. Macdonald*
Typesetting: *Carlisle Graphics, Dubuque, Iowa*
Printing and Binding: *Diversified Printing & Publishing Services, Brea, California*

CREDITS:

Chapter 6: Pages 108–109, "Felony Sentencing Worksheet," copyright The Ohio State Bar Foundation, with permission.

Chapter 9: Page 163, Table 9-3, from "Managing Adult Inmates: Classification for Housing and Program Assignments," by the American Correctional Association. Reprinted by permission. APPENDIX, pages 169–174, from *Prison Classification: A Model System Approach*, developed under federal sponsorship by the National Institute of Corrections in cooperation with the Federal Bureau of Prisons. APPENDIX, pages 179–184, all from "Managing Adult Inmates: Classification for Housing and Program Assignments," by the American Correctional Association. Reprinted by permission.

Chapter 11: Pages 224–225, "The Michigan Alcoholism Screening Test: The Quest for a New Diagnostic Instrument," by Melvin L. Selzer, *American Journal of Psychiatry*, 1971, *127*, 1653–1658. Revised 1980. Reprinted by permission.

Understanding, Assessing, & Counseling the Criminal Justice Client

*Dedicated to all my students in
criminal justice interviewing and counseling:
"Go gently into the winds, loved ones."*

Preface

Having taught, as a professor of criminal justice, introductory and advanced interviewing and counseling and having practiced what I preach for several years as a probation officer, I realized that there was a critical need for a text that meets the unique needs of criminal justice students. To meet these needs in my classes, I found that I had to use a variety of texts drawn from fields other than criminal justice.

To introduce students to interviewing and counseling, for example, I had to rely on social work or psychology texts, which did not fit in too well with the special needs and circumstances of criminal justice clients. By and large, these texts largely proceed on the assumption that clients are self-selected and motivated to explore their problems, whereas criminal justice clients are more often than not extremely reluctant to be in any interviewing and counseling relationship and frequently impervious to the problems that led them to it. This book assesses the special requirements associated with interviewing and counseling under these conditions.

The professional assessment of criminal justice clients has been a central part of my courses. To teach this crucial aspect of my discipline, I have depended on case material I had accumulated in my days as a field practitioner—presentence reports, sentencing guidelines, classification scales, and risk and needs scales—which made the courses more realistic for my students. But not many instructors have access to this kind of real-world material, and this is why I have reproduced in the book the various forms and scales used in the field. This material will allow students to write their own presentence reports, as well as assess and classify their fictitious clients, and can also be used as a basis for counseling exercises.

The realistic assessment of criminal justice clients is based on an understanding of criminal behavior, both in general terms and in terms of specific offender types. Although criminal justice students are required to take courses in criminology, these courses rarely relate theory to the problems involved in dealing with real flesh-and-blood clients. Therefore, I have included two chapters on theoretical criminology addressed from a practical point of view. In writing these chapters, I constantly kept before me the question "How does this theoretical discussion enhance students' understanding of criminal behavior as they will be confronting it in practice?" It goes without saying that understanding is a requisite for proper assessment and that meaningful counseling has to proceed from proper assessment.

The chapters on interviewing and counseling are also geared exclusively to the criminal justice client. The chapter on interviewing contains a section on interrogation, and the material on counseling addresses individual and group counseling in both community and institutional settings. Unlike most counseling texts, this one maintains that proper assessment prior to counseling is of the utmost importance. Therefore, there is a chapter on assessment as it applies to community corrections and a chapter on institutional assessment and classification.

Two chapters are devoted to those clients in criminal justice who are either most frequently encountered or the most difficult to supervise and help. These are the alcoholic, the drug addict, the sex offender, the schizophrenic, and the mentally deficient. The closing chapter deals with the resources available in the community to aid the corrections worker in the task of turning clients' lives around. These vital resources are often overlooked in conventional counseling texts.

The subject of this book encompasses a tremendous amount of material, all of which is available elsewhere in more detail. As I indicate in the section on presentence writing, the secret of successful professional report writing is the ability to glean from voluminous and diverse sources that which is necessary to know, as opposed to that which is merely nice to know. However, I also hope that this book will whet the appetites of students contemplating a career in correctional counseling and encourage them to read much further on the topics they will encounter herein.

Acknowledgments

I wish to express my gratitude to the reviewers of the manuscript for their constructive criticism and helpful suggestions. They are Steven G. Cox of Illinois State University, Lynne Goodstein of Pennsylvania State University, Peter C. Kratcoski of Kent State University, and Anna Kuhl of San Jose State University. Special thanks go to my editors at Brooks/Cole—Claire Verduin and Fiorella Ljunggren—for their support, encouragement, and outstanding professional guidance in the production of this book and to Meredy Amyx, the manuscript editor, for her skillful editing job.

Thanks also to my wife, and sometimes research associate, Patricia Ann Walsh, for her patience and understanding during the time it took to write this book. Her love and support during the last 24 years have helped me in more ways than she knows. Thanks, Pat.

Anthony Walsh

Contents

Chapter 1
Introduction and Theories of Crime Causation

Introduction

The purpose of this book is to introduce students to the process of "correcting" the antisocial behavior of correctional clients. There is a great deal of skepticism and cynicism surrounding this corrective process. Such attitudes have some basis in reality, but often they are not warranted. If we believe that "nothing works," then we in the criminal justice field will operate consistently with this belief, and the outcome will justify our beliefs. If we believe that people can change, and that many do so every day, then we will act in accordance with that belief and will also find it vindicated—prophecies tend to be self-fulfilling. Of course, you will run into some people for whom it is true that nothing works. Realize also that no one thing works for everybody. But some things work for some people some of the time, and other things work for other people at other times.

Counseling and Criminal Justice

Counseling is a process in which clients are led to explore their feelings and concerns; in the case of criminal justice clients, many of those feelings and concerns have led the person to behave irresponsibly. We hope that the counseling process will lead clients to an increased awareness of the self-destructive nature of their behavior and of alternative behavior choices. Counseling is aimed at removing barriers to personal growth and un-covering resources that clients can use to forge a prosocial lifestyle.

Criminal justice counseling is different from general counseling in three important ways: (1) criminal justice clients do not generally seek counseling voluntarily, and so you are more likely to encounter reluctance and resistance to the counseling process than you would in other counseling settings; (2) criminal justice clients in general have fewer coping resources on which to draw than do clients in other counseling set-tings; and (3) criminal justice clients often have a psychological and economic investment in re-taining their current lifestyle. It was these differ-ences that led to the writing of this book, because few general counseling texts address the special problems of dealing with clients of this type or with their special needs.

On the other hand, we also enjoy an advantage in criminal justice that counselors in other areas don't have. This advantage is that we often pos-sess a wealth of verified information about our clients' background and past behavior from a va-riety of sources, such as juvenile files, police re-ports, and social and psychological evaluations. This information allows us to assess our clients more readily than counselors can in many other settings. Assessment is the process of subjecting a client to a formal evaluation and analysis of his or her deficiencies and needs, as well as the risks he or she poses to the community, so that realistic counseling plans and strategies can be worked out. Assessment is accomplished with the use of well-researched and tested instruments (which are included in this book). Attempting to counsel a criminal justice client without a thorough as-sessment is somewhat like a physician's perform-ing surgery without first conducting a thorough diagnostic workup of a patient.

But even before a physician conducts a diag-nostic workup, he or she must have a grounding in the disease or condition that could account for the patient's complaint. Similarly, you should have a grounding in the causes of the kind of behavior you are trying to correct. Hence the ordering of the title of this book: (1) understand-ing, (2) assessing, and (3) counseling. *Criminol-ogy* is the study of the causes of crime. It is, or should be, an interdisciplinary study, encom-passing biology, physiology, psychology, eco-nomics, and sociology. Yet much of what passes as criminology is limited to sociological analysis. Individual differences are often ignored, and one gets the impression from sociological criminol-ogy that everything is responsible for crime except the criminal. Not that sociological variables are not useful in understanding crime. Indeed, they are of tremendous importance, but they don't exhaust the causal possibilities.

This is not a textbook on criminological theory, and no effort has been made to make it compre-hensive. The theories of criminology that are briefly presented should help you understand more fully the counseling theories addressed later, as well as enhancing the quality of your applica-tion of them in practice. In other words, we are interested in criminological theories here only in-sofar as they provide a foundation on which coun-seling techniques can be grounded. I make no apologies for centering my discussion of these theories on the unifying theme of this book: crime, as well as most other forms of destructive behav-ior, can often be traced to the problem of depri-vation of love. This idea derives from many of the giants of the human sciences (Comte, Marx, So-rokin, Maslow, Fromm, Montagu), as well as from the originators of the counseling theories we will encounter (Freud, Rogers, Berne, Glasser). Thus, we begin with a discussion of the usefulness of theory in general and then go on to examine five theories of the *etiology* (cause) of crime.

The Usefulness of Theory

Workers in any field must understand the nature of the phenomena with which they work. As a correctional practitioner, or as a student aspiring to be a practitioner, you must understand the phenomenon of crime and its causation so that you may more effectively deal with your clients. Theories of crime seek to offer plausible explanations of how the known correlates of crime are linked together. Empirically generated facts are silent in themselves. Only theories of their inter-relationships give voice to what would otherwise be a babble of unintelligible static. A theory is an intellectual scaffold around which is constructed an edifice of useful knowledge. Empirical facts are the bricks of the edifice, each one slotted into its proper place to form a coherent whole.

Given the numerous competing theories of crime causation, you may be forgiven for asking which one is "true." Physicians don't ask which theory of disease is the true one, because they know that there are many different kinds of disease for which there are many different causes. Like disease, crime is not a unitary phenomenon explicable in terms of a single cause or set of causes. Even in context-specific instances, theories are never considered true in any absolute sense. Truth for the scientist is tentative, relative, and open to qualification and falsification. If a theory generates useful empirical research and provides order and consistency within the domain of interest, we are more faithful to the spirit of science if we call it adequate than if we call it true.

An adequate theory must conform to the pragmatic, correspondence, and coherence theories of truth as outlined by philosophers of science. That is, a theory is "true" to the extent that it (1) provides useful guidance for the further exploration of the phenomena of interest, (2) corresponds with the factual data already known about the phenomena of interest, and (3) fits those data into propositions to form a logically connected and coherent whole.

The usefulness of a given theory is context-specific. It would be of little help to a sociologist seeking to explain fluctuations in the crime rate, for instance, to learn that neurophysiologists have discovered that a certain category of criminals have a higher-than-expected frequency of dysfunction involving certain regions of the brain. Likewise, the neurophysiologist is little interested in the sociocultural variables alleged by the sociologists to account for differentials in the crime rate. The sociologists and the neurophysiologists

are simply dealing with different units of analysis: societies and brains, respectively. The criminologist and the criminal justice practitioner seeking to understand his or her clients, however, must be sensitive to the *macro* (large-scale) analyses of the sociologist and the *micro* (small-scale) analyses of the physiologist, as well as to all the disciplines in between that attempt to understand the phenomenon of crime at their particular levels of analysis.

As a correctional worker dealing with individuals, you will quite naturally find theories dealing with individuals' behavior and their immediate environment to be the most suitable for your purposes. After all, these are the areas most accessible to perception and most amenable to change within the context of the correctional worker/client relationship. Nevertheless, when you are engaged in interviewing, assessing, and counseling criminal clients, you will be able to perform the task more professionally if you have an adequate understanding of crime causation at all levels of analysis. Therefore, we shall briefly examine five theories of criminality dealing with different levels of analysis ranging from the macrosociological to the psychophysiological.

Figure 1–1 is a schematic diagram representing the route or routes that may have led your clients to you. It begins with the forces in the larger sociocultural environment that are considered to be *criminogenic* (crime generating). This aspect of crime causation is addressed in *anomie* theory. A "lower" level of analysis is the subcultural theory of *differential association*. Whereas all Americans share the larger sociocultural environment of the United States, only a portion of them share in those subcultures declared criminogenic by differential association theory. Even those individuals within a criminogenic subculture experience differential socialization within the context of the family environment. These experiences are the subject matter of control theory. Finally, it is widely recognized that similar environmental experiences can produce both saints and sinners. By nature, some individuals socialize more easily than others for a variety of

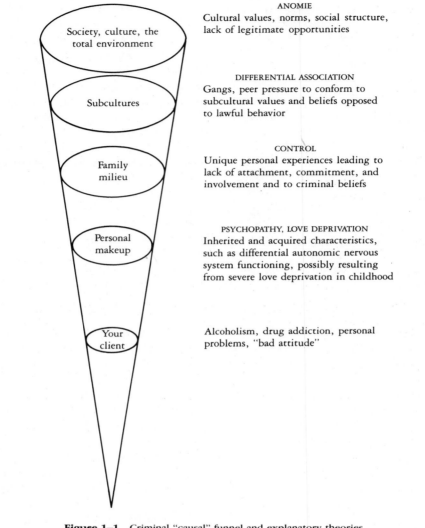

ANOMIE
Cultural values, norms, social structure,
lack of legitimate opportunities

Society, culture, the
total environment

DIFFERENTIAL ASSOCIATION
Gangs, peer pressure to conform to
subcultural values and beliefs opposed
to lawful behavior

Subcultures

CONTROL
Unique personal experiences leading to
lack of attachment, commitment, and
involvement and to criminal beliefs

Family
milieu

PSYCHOPATHY, LOVE DEPRIVATION
Inherited and acquired characteristics,
such as differential autonomic nervous
system functioning, possibly resulting
from severe love deprivation in childhood

Personal
makeup

Alcoholism, drug addiction, personal
problems, "bad attitude"

Your
client

Figure 1–1   Criminal "causal" funnel and explanatory theories

complex reasons. Chapter 2 addresses those reasons in the context of psychopathy and love deprivation.

Please note that the diagram implies intimate connections among all levels of analysis. This doesn't mean that each of the theories can't stand alone as a plausible explanation of crime at its respective level of analysis. Neither does it mean that a person who commits a crime because he or she lacks legitimate opportunity (as anomie theory sets forth) necessarily belongs to a gang (as differential association theory describes) or lacks family attachments (as control theory proposes). It simply means that the development of the individual cannot be viewed in isolation from the micro or macro environments that constitute his or her reality. Nor can the effects of those environments be separated from the effects of the personal attributes and unique experiences brought to them by individuals.

Sociological-Psychological Theories

Criminological theories are often not so much proven wrong as simply pushed to one side in favor of newer interpretations. The hope of the social sciences, of course, is to achieve an elegant simplicity, and perhaps in time the explanation of crime will form a coherent whole.

Gresham Sykes

Anomie Theory

The term *anomie* is a French word meaning "lacking in rules" or "normlessness." It is a relative term, for no society is completely lacking in rules for the regulation of social life. French sociologist Emile Durkheim first used this term in his book *The Division of Labor in Society* (1951a). His basic idea was that as societies become increasingly complex, the problem of maintaining social cohesion becomes more difficult. Crime (as well as other forms of deviance) grows in proportion to the loss of social cohesion. A loss of social cohesion means that there will be considerable ambiguity and many contradictions regarding the rules and standards of moral behavior. Durkheim did not, however, view crime as abnormal. He argued that because crime is found at all times and in all societies, it is a normal and inevitable phenomenon. What needs to be examined, according to Durkheim, is the social-structural conditions and contradictions that result in different levels of criminal activity in different nations and at different times (Durkheim, 1950:chap. 3).

American sociologist Robert Merton used Durkheim's concept of anomie to develop a popular sociocultural explanation of crime. Like all other macrosociological theories of crime, Merton's anomie theory uses a frame of reference that involves three major elements: social structure, social values, and social norms. This theory views crime not as a symptom of personal inadequacies but as a "normal" response to the various ways that these sociocultural elements impinge on and limit the responses of certain groups of individuals. According to anomie theory, the basic cause of crime is not to be found within individuals. Rather, it is structural contradictions within society that place what anomie theorists term *strain* on individuals, which, in turn, may engender criminal behavior in those most affected by the alleged contradictions.

The structural contradiction identified by Merton as the most important in terms of generating criminal behavior is the disjunction, or contradiction, between the cultural value of material success and the lack of equal access to legitimate means of accomplishing it. As Merton (1957:146) put it:

> It is only when a system of cultural values extols, virtually above all else, certain common success goals for the population at large while the social structure rigorously restricts or completely closes access to approved modes of reaching these goals for a considerable part of the same population, that deviant behavior ensues on a large scale.

It must be emphasized that although the theories presented here were formulated in an American context, they also apply to other societies that share to one degree or another similar values and social arrangements.

American society has taken what morality has traditionally considered to be base and evil—acquisitiveness and usury—and elevated them to the status of prescriptive (required or recommended) goals. Material things (two cars in the driveway, home entertainment centers, electric carving knives, the latest popular recordings, and mink belly-button brushes) equal happiness, prestige, and self-worth in the American equation. If you don't possess at least a modicum of these visible trappings of self-worth, it is obvious to all that something is remiss in your character—you are not a participant in the "American dream." Pause and reflect a moment: is this not the constant message you receive from all quarters on a daily basis? Are not the most popular heroes of the "soaps" and the prime-time series on television rich and powerful men and women playing with a lot of expensive toys?

To maintain a sense of self-worth, then, individuals are exhorted to strive to achieve culturally approved goals. However, certain groups of individuals are systematically denied access to the competition because of various structural impediments such as race and class. In other words, we are all encouraged to develop champagne tastes, even if we have only beer budgets. It is not the beer budget per se that generates the sort of dissatisfaction that may lead to crime, it is the size of one's budget relative to the size of one's culturally defined wants and needs. It is difficult to be happy, as Eastern philosophers have long maintained, if expectations exceed accomplishments or if wants and needs are not proportionate to means. As Durkheim himself dramatically put it (1951b:246), "No living being can be happy or even exist unless his needs are sufficiently proportioned to his means."

Modes of adaptation. Happiness, then, could be viewed as an equation:

$$happiness = \frac{accomplishments}{expectations \ or \ goals}$$

To bring this equation into balance, individuals have either to increase their accomplishments or to decrease their expectations. In other words, people have to adapt. Merton identifies five modes or methods of adaptation to a social structure that exhorts us all to strive for accomplishments but that denies some persons legitimate access to the means by which these accomplishments can be realized: conformity, ritualism, retreatism, rebellion, and innovation.

• The *conformist* is the individual who accepts the validity of the cultural goals and the socially approved methods of achieving them. Conformists quietly live out their lives and will probably never get themselves into any serious trouble with the law.

• The *ritualist* is the nine-to-five slugger who has long given up on ever achieving the cultural goals but who nevertheless continues to work ritually within the boundaries set forth as legitimate. This sort of person also is rarely in legal trouble.

• The *retreatist* rejects both the cultural goals and the institutionalized means of attaining them.

People in this category drop out of society and often take refuge in drugs, alcohol, and transiency. They are frequently in trouble with the law because of crimes committed to support a drug and/or alcohol habit. It is this type of individual who often presents the greatest challenge to the criminal justice worker.

• The *rebel* rejects both the goals and the means of capitalist American society but, unlike the retreatist, wishes to substitute alternative goals and alternative means. He or she is committed to some form of sociopolitical ideal, such as socialism, that aims for a more just and equitable society. You will rarely have to deal with this type of individual unless he or she becomes radicalized to the point of putting ideology into actions that break the law.

• Finally, we have the *innovator.* This individual fully accepts the validity of the cultural goals of monetary success but rejects (possibly because of having been denied access to them) the legitimate means of attaining them. Crime is an innovative avenue to success—a method by which deprived people get what they have been taught by their culture to want.

Lessons and concerns. As useful as this theory may or may not be to the macrosociologist, it has little practical utility for the correctional worker dealing with individual retreatists or innovators. There are no policy recommendations logically derived from it that could be implemented by the corrections worker. The "cure" for crime logically derived from this theory is the expansion of legitimate opportunities and equal access to them. Every correctional worker can recount numerous instances in which he or she has shed blood, sweat, and tears to obtain employment for clients only to see them "blow it" for one reason or another in short order. It is not enough simply to provide jobs for some clients who may have come to prefer taking advantage of illegitimate opportunities. As a criminal justice worker, you must convince such people of the ultimate futility of their short-run hedonism and the necessity of becoming responsible human beings.

Further, you must not be seduced into accepting the propositions of anomie theory as excuses for criminal behavior. Being a criminal does not necessarily mean that legitimate opportunities have not been made available. In fact, one of the flaws in anomie theory is that it is tautologous (arguing circuitously). That is, it poses a cause of crime (lack of legitimate opportunity) and then uses the alleged effects of that cause (crime) as a measure of the opportunities one has not had (Nettler, 1978:252).

A lesson of anomie theory that is worth the attention of corrections workers is the notion that crime can be a highly rational response to social conditions as they are perceived by the offender. Here the term *rational* means having a logical fit between a desired goal and the means used to attain it. Rational action in pursuit of a goal does not imply that the action is "right" or "moral." It merely means that the actors have sought a goal at a price they feel they can afford. A criminal who risks life and limb in the illegitimate pursuit of legitimate cultural goals is certainly behaving irrationally from the point of view of a middle-class observer. But rationality must be defined in terms of the actor, not the observer. The innovator simply has more to gain and less to lose than does the middle-class observer. Perhaps realization of this point will lead you to develop a *deficiency* definition, rather than a *pathological* definition, of criminal behavior: criminals should be viewed as being deficient in the attributes that are productive of lawful behavior rather than as being somehow psychologically defective.

Differential Association Theory

Differential association theory, first formulated by sociologist Edwin Sutherland, focuses on subcultural elements that may predispose an individual to one or another of Merton's methods of adaptation. This theory stresses the potency of group pressures. It asserts that we all, like chameleons, take on the hues and colors of our environments. We blend in, we conform. We tend to like baseball, hot dogs, apple pie, and Chevrolets, as the commercial would have it, rather than soccer, bratwurst, strudel, and Volkswagens, not because

the former are demonstrably superior to the latter but because we are born Americans and not Germans. We view the world differentially according to the attitudes, beliefs, and expectations of the groups around which our lives revolve.

Assumptions. There are nine propositions or components of differential association theory, but, for brevity, they can be compressed into four general principles:

1. Criminal behavior is learned in interaction with other people. Criminal behavior, therefore, is not biologically inherited, the result of psychological abnormalities, or invented anew by each criminal.
2. For the most part, the learning of criminal behavior occurs within intimate personal groups. This learning includes specific techniques, motives, rationalizations, justifications, and attitudes.
3. The direction of the cognitive components of learned criminal behavior is derived from definitions of the legal code (the law) as favorable or unfavorable to violations of the law. Thus, a person becomes a criminal because he or she holds an excess of definitions favorable to the violation of the law over definitions unfavorable to violations of the law.
4. Associations with others holding definitions favorable to violation of the law vary in frequency, duration, priority, and intensity. That is, the earlier in life one is exposed to criminal norms of conduct, the more often one is exposed to them, the longer those exposures last, and the more strongly one is attached to one's mentors, the more one is likely to become a criminal.

The general validity of this line of thinking has been supported by a number of empirical studies (see Matsueda, 1982, for a brief review). However, the theory has been described as both "true and trivial" (Nettler, 1978:265). It can be applied as a causal explanation to all sorts of values, attitudes, tastes, and behaviors as a general theory of socialization within subcultures. "Culture" explains everything in a global sense and therefore explains nothing in a specific sense. The commission of crime is a specific behavior engaged in by a few individuals within a cultural setting, and in no sense is it a cultural expectation.

Differential association theory is a variation on the old social pathology theme. Criminal behavior is cooked up in the simmering caldron of pathological neighborhoods; stirred by morally bankrupt companions; spiced by trouble, toughness, and excitement; and dished up with a jungle philosophy of "do unto others as they would do unto you—but do it first!"

Lessons and concerns. Although we can't deny the cogency of the line of thought presented to us by differential association theory, it contains little practical leavening to lighten the dense dough of theory. As a correctional worker, you will be able to do nothing to mitigate the pernicious effects of poor neighborhoods. You can merely help clients to act responsibly within them. Nonetheless, you must be sensitive to the burden of peer pressures felt by criminal justice clients. An awareness of those pressures will enable you to formulate realistic goals for treatment rather than moralizing with clients about the company they keep. Life in the steaming ghettoes of the United States often requires—literally requires—belonging to a gang and participating in its attitudes and behaviors for survival. A young man, and sometimes a young woman, living in a ghetto who does not take advantage of the comradeship and protection of the local gang is certainly not acting in his or her best interests. Nonparticipation in such groups leaves one naked to the preying designs of those more in tune with the reality of their existence. Quite often the simple acts of getting married and/or obtaining legitimate employment will distance clients from their former companions and place them in the company of others with a more prosocial set of values.

Control Theory

Whereas anomie and differential association theories focus on causes said to propel us into crime, control theory focuses on those conditions of our environment that restrain us from it. Control theory assumes that the criminological need is not so much to explain why some of us behave badly but, rather, why most of us behave well most of the time.

Control theory implicitly agrees with the Freudians that self-interest is innate, that we are born antisocial (or, perhaps, asocial), and that we must learn painful lessons. We must learn that civilization is bought at the cost of the repression of natural urges and that our wants and needs are inextricably linked to the wants and needs of others. If we don't learn these lessons, we're heading for trouble.

Identifying the "typical" criminal. The version of control theory examined here—that of Travis Hirschi (1977)—is compelling. It is consistent with what we are reasonably certain we know about the personal and demographic characteristics of those who commit crimes, as well as with the perceptions of crime causation held by most workers in the field of criminal justice. Hirschi starts with the correlates of the "typical" criminal and finds him to be a young male who grew up in a fatherless home in an urban slum, who has a history of difficulty in school, and who is unemployed. Of course, there are also female criminals. But in the following discussion the masculine pronoun emphasizes that we are talking about Hirschi's typical criminal.

Having defined the typical criminal, Hirschi makes a series of logical deductions flowing from the nature of crime. First, he observes that criminal activity is contrary to the wishes and expectations of others. From this observation he deduces that those most likely to commit crimes are least likely to be concerned with the wishes and expectations of others. Criminal activity is contrary to the law and involves the risk of punishment. Therefore, those who commit crimes are least likely to accept the moral beliefs underlying the law and are least likely to concern themselves with the risk of punishment. Finally, criminal acts take time and are, therefore, most likely to be engaged in by those who have the time that the act requires (they are unemployed).

What demands explanation are the conditions of the typical criminal's life that lead him to run roughshod over the wishes and expectations of others, his lack of belief in the moral order, his relative lack of concern for punishment, and his possession of the excess time that criminal activity requires. To state the question in terms more consistent with the theory: What controls, which are present in the environments of noncriminals and restrain them from criminal activity, are absent in the environments of criminals? These restraining controls are attachment, commitment, involvement, and belief.

The four controls. *Attachment* refers to one's psychological and emotional closeness to others. It implies a reciprocal love relationship in which one feels valued, respected, and admired and in which one values the favorable judgments of the person or persons to whom one is attached. Sociologists use the concept of *significant others* (close family members and friends) and *reference groups* (those groups of people we admire and seek to emulate) to refer to the people we consider important to us and whose good opinions we value. These are the people to whom we look for guidance in our behavior, values and attitudes. Much of our behavior can be seen as attempts to gain favorable judgments from our reference groups and significant others. Parents are for many years the most important behavior-orienting significant others.

It follows that those who don't care about parental reactions are those who are most likely to behave in ways contrary to their parents' wishes. Risking the good opinion of another is of minor concern when that good opinion is not valued. Why that good opinion is not valued is a question that need not concern us at this point. In general, however, we may state that it is a function of the lack of a reciprocal love relationship between parent and child.

Lack of attachment to parents and the attending lack of respect for their wishes easily spill over into a lack of attachment and respect for the broader social groupings of which the child is a part. Much of the controlling power of others outside the immediate family lies in the threat of reporting juvenile misbehavior to parents. If the child has little fear of parental sanctions, the control exercised by others has limited effect simply because parental control has limited effect. The family is the nursery of human nature. If the family is in disarray, if there is little love, concern, or attachment within it, then the product will be defective. The child of such a family will fail to form a conscience, he will lack the ability to sympathize and empathize with others. He will learn that the world for him is a cold and heartless place and will act toward it accordingly.

Commitment refers to a lifestyle in which one has invested considerable time and energy in the pursuit of a lawful career. The pursuit of such a lifestyle is assumed to be highly rewarding to the individual, who, therefore, has a valuable stake in conforming to the moral standards of his society. The person who has made this considerable investment, or who aspires to, is not likely to risk it by engaging in criminal activity. The cost/benefit ratio (what the individual stands to benefit from crime contrasted with what he stands to lose if caught) renders the cost of crime prohibitive for such a person. However, the lower the stake with which one enters the criminal game, the more appealing are the possible prizes. The poor student, the truant, the dropout, the unemployed person, has very little investment in conventional behavior and risks less in the cost/benefit comparison. For example, although the bank president and the casual laborer may equally desire to engage the services of an underage prostitute, the bank president is more likely to restrain the urge because he stands to lose far more than the laborer if caught and exposed.

The successful acquisition of a stake in prosocial conformity, of course, requires success in school. Success in school requires disciplined application to tasks that children don't particularly relish but that they nevertheless complete in order to gain the valued approval of significant others, especially parents. Again, if approval is not forthcoming or is not valued, children will busy themselves in tasks more congenial to their natural inclinations, inclinations that almost certainly don't include business math or the principles of grammar. Attachment, then, would appear to be an essential prerequisite of any genuine commitment to a prosocial lifestyle.

Involvement, a direct consequence of commitment, is a part of a conventional pattern of existence. Essentially, involvement is expressed in terms of the time and energy we devote to our commitments. Involvement in lawful activities reduces exposure to illegal activities. Conversely, the lack of involvement in lawful activities increases the possibility of exposure to illegal activities: "The devil finds work for idle hands." Puritanical considerations aside, it is a cogent statement.

Belief refers to the ready acceptance of the social prescriptions and proscriptions regulating conduct. Those individuals who are free of the constraints imposed on their behavior by attachment, commitment, and involvement evolve a belief system shorn of conventional morality. It is a system of belief containing narrowly focused images of self-interest justified by a jungle philosophy.

Unlike differential association theory, control theory does not view the criminal belief system as causative in the sense that it generates criminal behavior. Rather, criminals act according to their urges and then justify or rationalize their behavior with a set of instrumental statements such as "Suckers deserve what they get," "Everybody does it—why not me?" and "Do unto others as they would do unto you, only do it first." These are the statements of alienated individuals—Merton's innovators—reflecting and rationalizing the lifestyle of the unattached. For the control theorist, the behavior gives birth to the belief rather than vice versa.

Control theory agrees with differential association theory that criminals gain reinforcement of their beliefs in the company of like-minded individuals. However, it strongly disagrees with the proposition that such peer groups are intimately connected, loyal to one another, and bound by a prescriptive code of conduct. Criminal ties reflect more the criminals' weak bond with conventional society than their attraction to one an-

other. Any worker in the criminal justice field will attest to the fact that, when in a legal bind, criminals will trip over one another in the race to be the first to "cut a deal" favorable to themselves, to the detriment of their "friends."

Let me now make a point of importance to the criminal justice worker seeking to understand criminal behavior. The lack of attachment, commitment, and involvement with regard to conventional others does not constitute a motive for crime as an "excess of definitions favorable to the violation of the law" is alleged to provide in differential association theory. The lack of these controls represents social deficiencies that result in a reduction of the potential costs of engaging in criminal activity. Nor is a criminal belief system a motive for crime; it is merely an after-the-fact justification for antisocial behavior. The criminal justice worker should, of course, consider both the behavior and the alleged justification for it totally unacceptable.

Lessons and concerns. The utility of control theory for the criminal justice worker is that it provides meaningful guidance in working with criminal justice clients. Obviously, nothing can be done about your clients' levels of attachment to their families. You can't visit the past and interfere with pathological family dynamics, unfortunate though that may be. You can take steps in your role as an advocate and a broker of community resources to involve your client in a conventional lifestyle. The criminal justice worker has considerable power over the activities of his or her clients. That is to say, you can lead the horse to water, and, with a little judicious use of authority, persuade your client to sip. Perhaps he or she may even acquire a taste for it. Contrary to the belief of the currently fashionable nihilistic "nothing works" philosophy, I have witnessed many remarkable turnarounds by clients who have had the guidance of caring criminal justice professionals.

Although control theory has much in the way of practical guidance to commend it over the other two theories examined, it is certainly not the final word in the understanding of criminal behavior. It does not account for those who simply appear to prefer a criminal lifestyle despite having been afforded numerous opportunities to forge a conventional lifestyle. It sees criminal activity simply as a poor second choice made by unhappy individuals whose socialization has rendered them largely unfit to pursue conventional avenues to success. In the vast majority of cases, I believe this to be an accurate assessment. Most individuals caught up in criminal activity might well prefer acceptance into the "moral community," $50,000 a year from a straight job, a house with a white picket fence, and membership at the country club. Unfortunately, their experiences during their formative years have not prepared them psychologically, emotionally, or intellectually to accept the possibility that such a lifestyle could be a reality for them. They have a tremendous burden of inertia that prevents them from taking that first step on the long journey to social respectability, a stifling orientation to the here and now.

However, control theory does not address that small percentage of criminals who have genuine contempt for the "straight life," those who, by their nature, find it extremely difficult to function in a conventionally acceptable way. These are the people who enjoy hurting people and who crave the danger, excitement, and adventure provided by a life of crime. Life without the opportunity to hurt and dominate others, without drugs and alcohol, without violence and predation, without fast cars and faster women, would be quite meaningless to them. We call such people *psychopaths, sociopaths,* or *antisocial personalities.* Although they constitute a small minority of the criminal population with which you will have contact, it is important to have an understanding of them because they are engaged in a level of criminal activity out of all proportion to their numbers.

Summary

The sociological theories outlined in this chapter, especially anomie and differential association theories, locate the causes of crime in the criminal's environment. Both of these theories would agree with the proposition that societies get the kind of criminals they deserve. Anomie theorists believe we manufacture criminals by the socioeconomic conditions that, while emphasizing monetary success, keep a significant number of people from having access to legitimate avenues toward this goal. The retreatist and innovator modes of adaptation to the social structure are the modes that generate criminal behavior. The conformist and the ritualist modes of adaptation produce individuals who are, in the main, law abiding. Only under certain circumstances does the rebellious mode generate illegal behavior.

Differential association theory concentrates on specific subcultural environments that predispose individuals to adopt specific modes of adaptation. This theory emphasizes that criminal behavior is learned within subcultures where criminal behavior is more or less "normal" behavior. Differing levels of criminal behavior depend on the frequency, duration, priority, and intensity of association with criminals and criminal values and attitudes. Thus, for these two theories, criminal behavior can be a quite rational adaptation to the conditions people find themselves in. In short, theorists in both of these camps tend to give the impression that everyone is guilty of crime—except the criminal.

Although these theories offer no policy recommendations that could be put into practice by the criminal justice worker, they do illuminate the relationship between criminality and the social arrangements in which it exists. Their main value to you should be that they lead you to a deficiency rather than a pathological interpretation of criminal behavior.

Control theory differs from the other two theories in that, rather than looking at conditions that may lead people to commit crimes, it looks at the conditions that isolate people from it. Those conditions, or controls, are attachment, commitment, involvement, and belief. The presence of the latter three controls depends to a large extent on the initial presence of attachment. Criminal beliefs do not "cause" one to commit crimes. They merely serve as rationalizations for those who do commit crimes.

Control theory fits well with most criminal justice practitioners' perceptions of why individuals commit crimes. It recognizes that an individual's lack of controls is not entirely his or her own fault, but it does not attempt to justify irresponsible behavior by pointing to this lack as a cause. Control theory offers some useful practical guidance for criminal justice workers, both in terms of understanding criminal behavior and in terms of pointing to conditions that can be rectified in the counseling and supervision process.

References and Suggested Readings

Durkheim, E. (1950). *The Rules of the Sociological Method.* Glencoe, IL: Free Press.

Durkheim, E. (1951a). *The Division of Labor in Society.* Glencoe, IL: Free Press.

Durkheim, E. (1951b). *Suicide: A Study in Sociology.* Glencoe, IL: Free Press.

Hirschi, T. (1977). "Causes and prevention of juvenile delinquency." *Sociological Inquiry,* 47:322–341.

Matsueda, R. (1982). "Testing control theory and differential association: A causal modeling approach." *American Sociological Review,* 47:489–504.

Merton, R. (1957). *Social Theory and Social Structure.* New York: Free Press.

Nettler, G. (1978). *Explaining Crime.* New York: McGraw-Hill.

Reid, S. (1976). *Crime and Criminology.* Hinsdale, IL: Dryden Press.

Sutherland, E., and D. Cressey (1978). *Principles of Criminology.* Philadelphia: Lippincott.

Chapter 2
Psychophysiological Theories

Two traits—lovelessness and guiltlessness— distinguish the psychopath from other human beings, for he is neither "normal," "neurotic," "psychotic," nor a usual criminal.

William McCord

Psychopathy

Ever since French psychiatrist Phillipe Pinel introduced the concept of psychopathy to the world in the eighteenth century, it has had a checkered career. Conceptual and ideological arguments associated with the psychopathic syndrome moved Gibbons (1973:171) to state: "We regard any attempt to proceed further with the psychopathy/ criminality line of inquiry a futile business." Numerous studies prior and subsequent to Gibbons's cavalier dismissal of the usefulness of the concept of psychopathy strongly suggest that his opinion was extremely ill considered. Such studies have shown rather convincingly that psychopaths can be distinguished from nonpsychopaths physiologically, psychologically, and sociologically (Allen, Linder, Goldman, & Dinitz, 1971; Goldman, Linder, Dinitz, & Allen, 1971; Walsh, 1987). A similar claim cannot be made for the anomic, the alienated, or, for that matter, any other of the conceptual types (including race) said to be causally related to levels of criminal activity.

It is well known that a small number of recidivists account for the lion's share of all crime. Marvin Wolfgang's (Wolfgang, Figlio, & Sellin, 1972) classic study of a birth cohort of 10,000 males in Philadelphia over a period of 20 years found that 35% of them were arrested one or more times. However, a mere 6.3% of those arrested (2.2% of the total cohort) accounted for

52% of all offenses and 66% of all violent offenses known to have been committed by arrested members of the cohort! Other cohort studies in various countries have shown essentially the same results; that is, approximately 6% to 8% of offenders are responsible for roughly two-thirds of all serious crimes. Although the studies were interested in identifying recidivists, and not psychopaths per se, it is reasonable to assume that many of those chronic and violent recidivists possessed many of the descriptive features of psychopaths. Interestingly, the percentage figures for chronic recidivists match almost exactly the percentage figures for those criminals diagnosed as psychopaths (7% to 10%) in a review of nine studies conducted since 1918, as reported by Bennett, Rosenbaum, and McCullough (1978:76).

Descriptive Features of Psychopaths

What are the descriptive features of psychopaths? In an effort to find out, Gray and Hutchinson (1964) obtained data from 677 Canadian psychiatrists. The psychiatrists rank-ordered ten descriptive items that they considered to be most characteristic of psychopaths. The results were as follows:

1. inability to profit from experience
2. lack of a sense of responsibility
3. inability to form meaningful relationships
4. lack of impulse control
5. lack of moral sense
6. consistent antisocial behavior
7. ineffectiveness of punishment in changing behavior
8. emotional immaturity
9. inability to experience feelings of guilt
10. extreme self-centeredness

The majority of these psychiatrists (43.9%) felt that psychopathy has its origins in the interplay of hereditary and environmental influences; 38.2% felt that the problem was mostly environmental; and 14.4% felt that the problem was primarily one of heredity. We shall explore studies relevant to the majority view.

Psychopathy and the Autonomic Nervous System

Operating on the premise that the primary defining characteristic of psychopaths is their inability to foresee the negative consequences of their behavior, a number of studies have focused on the autonomic nervous system (ANS). The ANS is part of the central nervous system and consists of two branches: the sympathetic and the parasympathetic. The sympathetic branch functions to increase the organism's potential for action. It prepares the body to react to fearful and stressful stimuli by pumping hormones into the blood stream to make possible a more energetic response to threat (the "fight or flight" response). Individuals differ considerably in the reactivity of their ANSs. In general, the greater a person's reactivity to fear and anxiety-generating stimuli, the more likely the person is to avoid the stimuli that bring on the unpleasantness of autonomic upheaval. A person with a hyperreactive (overreactive) ANS is highly conditionable and compliant and has a strong fear of any sort of punishment or social displeasure.

A number of studies have shown that psychopaths exhibit abnormally diminished ANS responses to stimuli that would be threatening to individuals with normal or hyperactive autonomic nervous systems. Hare and Quinn (1971) found significant differences between psychopaths and nonpsychopaths in various physical indicators of ANS arousal such as electrodermal, cardiac, and vascomotor activity. Shalling (1978) found significantly lower levels of catecholamines in the urine of psychopaths awaiting criminal sentencing than in nonpsychopaths awaiting the same anxiety-generating experience. Catecholamines are stress-related hormones. The levels of such hormones in the urine or blood stream serve as a strong indicator of the level of stress being experienced. Since psychopaths had significantly lower levels of these hormones in their urine than did nonpsychopaths, we have evidence that their ANSs were not "turned on," or activated, to pump the catecholamines into the blood stream. It follows that they were not unduly anxious or afraid about an impending event that might terrify most of us.

Similarly, Ferguson (1973) reports that a number of different studies have found distinctly different brain wave patterns between psychopaths and nonpsychopaths in response to anticipation of some event. A normal subject's electroencephalogram (EEG) response to the anticipation of a stimulus—such as a flash of light, a noise, or a puff of air—is referred to as the *contingency negative variation* (CNV). Significantly, psychopaths show no CNV at all, indicating that they simply do not relate what went before to what will happen later. Such studies provide strong physiological explanations for the psychopath's inability to learn from experience and for the inability of punishment to alter his or her behavior.

Psychopathy and the Wechsler P > V Test

A rather readily available and frequently used marker of psychopathy is the Wechsler P > V test. In his studies of the sociopathic phenomenon, Wechsler (1958:176) noted: "The most outstanding feature of the sociopath's test profile is the systematic high score on the performance as compared with the verbal part of the scale." The scales to which Wechsler refers are the Wechsler Intelligence Scale for Children (WISC) and the Wechsler Adult Intelligence Scale (WAIS).

The performance section of the WISC/WAIS is a test of short-term memory and is more productive of anxiety than is the verbal section. We have already pointed to the hyporeactivity (low reactivity) of psychopaths to anxiety-evoking stimuli, and some authorities suggest that this functions to prevent the disruption of short-term memory (Mednick & Hutchings, 1978; Andrew, 1982; Mednick & Finello, 1983). Keiser (1975:306) interprets the relationship between ANS hyporeactivity and memory disruption thus: "An interference hypothesis might suggest that when affective [emotional] processes are underreactive there will be less distortion of immediate memory traces within the same anatomical structures; for example, the hippocampal circuits that

are thought to play a role in short-term memory systems." What this rather difficult sentence means is that a person who doesn't become nervous in a short-term memory testing situation will tend to score much better than he or she will on tests of long-term memory, such as the verbal portion of the WISC or WAIS.

Psychopaths, then, tend to have higher performance IQ scores relative both to their own verbal IQ scores and to the performance/verbal discrepancy scores of nonpsychopaths. A recent study determined that this difference was not a function of either low verbal scores or lower overall intelligence. In fact, this study showed that those subjects designated as psychopaths had significantly higher overall intelligence than nonpsychopaths on the full-scale IQ test and did not differ significantly on scores obtained on the verbal section (Walsh & Beyer, 1986). This is a potentially useful piece of information in the assessment of your clients because IQ subscores are often reported in juvenile probation psychological reports. However, you should tread lightly and not be too anxious to pin the psychopathic label on a client on the sole basis of his or her performance/verbal discrepancy score.

Psychopathy and the Reticular Activating System

Other investigators into the psychopathic syndrome have studied cortical arousal mechanisms to explore the possibility that psychopaths' apparent need for intense stimulation (a need that gets them into a lot of trouble) could be a function of their reticular activating systems' (RAS) proneness to inhibition. The RAS is a finger-sized network of cells located in the brain stem that regulates the brain's alertness. Those with a RAS prone to inhibition (sluggishness) easily lose interest in people and things; as a consequence, they constantly seek new excitement to alleviate their boredom. Their brains just seem to "turn off." Studies indicating this proneness (by such methods as noting electrically recorded involuntary pauses when subjects are asked to tap a metal stylus) can be found in Hare (1970) and Eysenck (1970).

Stimulant drugs such as amphetamines function to increase cortical arousal, thus increasing responsiveness to environmental stimuli. The heavy use of psychoactive drugs, as well as a demonstrated lack of protracted interest in hobbies, vocations, or other people, may provide you with valuable diagnostic clues in identifying possible psychopathy.

Lessons and Concerns

Psychopathy theories are more an interesting set of interrelated propositions drawn from many fields of inquiry than they are theories in any strict sense. The data presented here have not been formally linked together to present a fully coherent picture. This is a pity because the data appear to be solidly grounded in empiricism and harder than data presented in strictly sociological theories. Nevertheless, the challenge to society presented by the type of individuals described here makes an understanding of them imperative. What follows is an attempt to link the empirical findings just described, as well as the clinical insights provided by the major theories of counseling, into a coherent theory of psychopathy.

Love Deprivation

What follows is my own interpretation of the etiology of psychopathy, which is based on many years of experience dealing with loveless clients and on my own published research on psychopathy and love deprivation. Like psychopathy "theory" itself, love deprivation "theory" does not conform to the strict definition of theory and is an attempt to integrate data from a wide variety of disciplines. You may at times find it somewhat difficult reading, but this knowledge will provide you with a firmer grounding for understanding and applying the counseling theories you will encounter later. It will help you to see why love is emphasized so much in these theories, and you will have a firmer grasp on the underlying mechanisms.

Many giants of the human sciences have written eloquently of the ennobling power of love in human affairs (Comte, 1896; Freud, 1924; Maslow, 1953; Sorokin, 1954; Fromm, 1965; Montagu, 1978). To this list of venerable theorists we add Marx and Engels, who wrote (1956:119): "Love not only makes the man an object, but love makes the object a man."* If this is true, it would seem incumbent on us to discover what kind of beings are wrought by its absence.

I employ the following conceptual definition of love: "Love, then, can be defined as the need to receive and bestow affection and nurturance, to be given and to give assurances of value, respect, and appreciation, and to offer and accept the warm symbiosis that nature herself decrees" (Walsh, 1981:96). Having perused thousands of criminal histories filed in juvenile and adult probation departments and at a state penitentiary, I am led to agree with Glasser (1976:187) that the vast majority (Glasser estimates about 85%) of those in constant and violent conflict with the law have not had these needs met.

Love Deprivation and the Brain

Love deprivation is seen as a physical-emotional privation that begins in infancy and adversely affects the biochemical and neuronal (nerve-cell) structuring of the brain. It may also affect the way that the ANS functions in responses to stimuli. The brain is a marvelously plastic organ, the functioning and even the structure of which are highly sensitive to early environmental input. The experiences that cultivate our beings are perceived, processed, and acted upon via intricate electrochemical interactions among a conservatively estimated one hundred billion brain cells (neurons). At birth, the neurons are largely unpatterned, unorganized, and undifferentiated. The patterning and organization of the brain cells is a function of habituated synaptic connections (a synapse is the interface between neighboring neurons).

---

*Marx and Engels were using the term *object* in the sociological sense; that is, the child has to develop the ability to "stand outside" himself or herself to view the self through the eyes of others.

Interneuronal communication occurs with greater facility the more often the electrochemical synapses have been made. It has consistently been shown since the work of Bennett, Diamond, Kretch, and Rosenzwig (1964) that organisms raised in stimulus-enriched environments develop greater cortical density and greater quantities of essential neurotransmitter chemicals than organisms raised under less stimulating conditions.

The stimuli with which we are concerned are acts of cutaneous (skin) stimulation—affectionate touching, kissing, and cuddling—tactile assurances for the infant that it is loved and secure. The neural effects of a lack of tactile stimulation have been aptly described by Rutter (1972:57): "It has been well shown that neural metabolism varies with the rate of stimulation, and recent work has demonstrated ganglionic atrophy and the reduction in dendritic growth following light privation during the stage of active cell growth." (Basically, dendrites are short fibers that extend from neurons and receive the electronic impulses. Glial cells cover the dendrites, except at the synaptic terminals, and serve, it is thought, to amplify impulses). The effects of tactile stimulation on the brain can be understood with the realization that the skin is almost an external extension of the brain, formed as it is from the same layer of embryonic tissue (Taylor, 1979:136). In a quite literal sense, we are talking about the "wiring" of the neuronal circuits for love.

Experimental evidence for these effects includes the oft-quoted series of love deprivation studies with monkeys conducted by Harry Harlow and his colleagues (1958, 1962). Harlow raised a number of monkeys in isolation from their mothers and other monkeys. These unfortunate simians, deprived of normal stimulation, especially of their mothers' tactile stimulation, never exhibited the normal behavior patterns of their nondeprived peers. When introduced to other monkeys, they responded either with fearful withdrawal or with excessive aggression, sometimes with a combination of both. The aggression was obviously not learned, since they hadn't had the opportunity to learn anything from other monkeys.

When female isolates were introduced to normally raised males, they insisted on remaining chaste. Harlow, however, devised "rape racks" in order that they might be impregnated. When the offspring of those rapacious unions were born, their mothers did not display normal maternal behavior but, instead, ignored, attacked, and even killed them. We tend to call similar noncaring and violent behavior psychopathic when displayed by human beings. Subsequent deprivation experiments involved the sacrificing of deprived monkeys in order to examine their brains. Predictably, the brains of deprived monkeys showed abnormal dendritic wiring. It is important to note that the observed aberrant behavior was the direct result of abnormal brain structuring, which was in turn the direct result of deprivation of love (Suomi, 1980).

A plausible neurophysiological explanation for the behavior of Harlow's monkeys is that the circuits to the septum pellucidum (the brain's pleasure center) had not been wired, thus allowing the uninhibited expression of the impulses emanating from the primitive amygdala (the brain's violence center). Both of these neurological structures are part of the limbic system, the area of the brain that regulates emotional reactions. As Heath (cited in Restak, 1979:150) put it: "Aberrant electrophysiological activity occurs in deep cerebellar nuclei, as well as other deep-brain structures—most pronounced in the limbic system—in association with severely disturbed behavior resulting from maternal-social deprivation." Further, Mark and Ervin (1970) and Surwillo (1980) have demonstrated that violent criminals, many of whom were diagnosed psychopaths, show abnormal brain waves from the limbic system on an EEG. Recent studies by Walsh and Beyer (1986) and Walsh and Petee (forthcoming) have demonstrated a firm link between love deprivation, psychopathy, and violent crime among juvenile probationers in two different jurisdictions. Violent crime is the kind of crime that disturbs us most deeply. Although it must be said that the great majority of criminals are not psychopaths, psychopaths commit a disproportionate share of violent crime (Blair, 1975; Andrew, 1982).

The connection between the elements in the love deprivation-psychopathy-violence triangle appears to be a tight one, with evidence coming from a variety of sources. For instance, criminologist C. Ray Jeffery (1979:109) notes that psychopaths "come from homes without love or security, where beatings are everyday occurrences, where brutality is a way of life." Anthropologist Ashley Montagu (1978:178) writes: "Take any violent individual and inquire into his history as a child, and it can be predicted with confidence that he will be discovered to have had a lacklove childhood, to have suffered a failure of tender, loving care." Neuropsychologist James Prescott (1975:65) goes even further to state that deprivation of tactile manifestations of what he called "tender loving care" is responsible for "a number of emotional disturbances which include depressive and autistic behaviors, hyperactivity, sexual aberration, drug abuse, violence and aggression." A more comprehensive review of the literature on this subject is contained in Haynie (1978).

Love Deprivation and ANS Responsiveness

The ideas we have examined thus far would appear to indicate that neural dysfunction—specifically, limbic system dysfunction—is the intermediate step between love deprivation and violent behavior. That is, love deprivation adversely affects neural structure and function, and those effects lead to many of the aberrant behaviors displayed by the psychopath. The question we now ask ourselves is: Could the hyporeactivity of the psychopath's ANS also be a function of love deprivation? Although the published research indicates a clear hereditary mechanism determining ANS response activity, the work of DiCara (1970), for one, has shown conclusively that ANS responses can be conditioned to an amazing degree.

Wadsworth has suggested that the stress associated with an unloving family background may contribute to ANS hyporeactivity. He states (1976:246): "Certainly from the published work it would be reasonable to speculate that children who in early life lived in surroundings of stress and emotional disturbance are more likely to develop some kind of mechanism for handling the effects of stress, and that may be reflected in later autonomic reactions to stressful situations." Wadsworth's own research cautiously supports his reasonable speculation, as do the findings of Walsh, Beyer, and Petee (forthcoming).

Love Deprivation and the Violence-Predictive Triad

A triad of early childhood and adolescent behaviors long considered to be predictive of violence may also be examined in the light of the kind of variables we have been discussing. These three behaviors—enuresis (bed wetting), fire setting, and cruelty to animals—are often addressed in psychological reports. However, the reports don't explain the specific mechanisms of how this triad translates into future violent behavior. The lack of connection confuses and frustrates judges and criminal justice workers who must act on this information. I have challenged, without much success, examining psychiatrists and psychologists to explain the hows and whys of the predictive use of this triad. The usual response is, "We don't know how or why; we only know that taken together they are a fairly reliable predictor." If explanations are forthcoming, they are couched in misty psychoanalytic terms such as "urethral eroticism" for enuresis, "a destructive wish for close object relationships" for fire setting, and "the acting out of aggressive sexual sadism with a nonthreatening object" for cruelty to animals. Although any or all of these unconscious sexual motivations may be true, I believe that such behaviors can be better explained with reference to the kind of physiological variables we have been discussing.

The response to the necessity to void our bladders during sleep usually results in waking up and doing so, or holding the urine until we get up. This response is under the control of our autonomic nervous systems, which have been conditioned to it by rewards and punishments. An ANS that conditions poorly may not alert us to void in the appropriate place. It would appear that in the absence of any organic pathology, enuresis can be seen as a function of a hyporeactive ANS. Since a hyporeactive ANS is a defining characteristic of the psychopath, enuresis beyond early childhood, if seen in conjunction with the other components of the triad, can also be viewed as a possible marker of psychopathy.

Setting fires and watching them burn is an exciting activity. Most of us limit this kind of activity to burning leaves and garbage. Some find that setting fires to buildings is intensely stimulating, a real "turn-on." Could this be a particularly destructive variation of the psychopath's need for intense emotional stimulation? Since psychopaths lack that attribute we call a conscience, there is little difficulty in accepting that they may have few qualms about sacrificing someone's home in the pursuit of the visceral excitement they crave. Recall that this need for excessive excitement has been viewed as a function of an overly sluggish reticular formation, which inclines the psychopath to consider what we find exciting to be eminently boring.

The third behavior in the triad, cruelty to animals, is indicative of the lack of love and sympathy psychopaths have for other living things and their lack of empathy for the suffering of others. The violent adult psychopath would prefer torturing humans, but the child finds cats and hamsters to be a safe substitute. Not having had love, sympathy, and empathy wired into their neural circuits by their early experiences, psychopaths cannot be expected to display behavior for which they have not been adequately programmed.

Any one of these three behaviors taken alone requires a variety of interpretations that don't concern us. Taken together, they constitute an excellent diagnostic tool. The pertinent observation for us is that studies inquiring into the backgrounds of individuals with a history of violent behavior have consistently unraveled histories of severe love deprivation (Hellman & Blackman, 1966; Wax & Haddox, 1972). It is important to emphasize that there are many other variables besides these three that are predictive of violent behavior. This triad has been included because, unlike many other predictors, it is almost routinely included in the psychiatric and psychological reports that you will be reading as corrections practitioners.

Lessons and Concerns

What are the implications of love deprivation theory for you as a criminal justice worker beyond an increased understanding of the problem of violence and the pernicious effects of love deprivation? Certainly, you can do nothing about the early developmental history of your clients. The answer to the problem, if there is one, lies in social engineering with respect to child-rearing practices on a massive scale. We have thus returned to sociology and to the same sort of practical difficulties we encountered when examining sociological theories. Canadian theorist Blaine Harvey (1980) suggests that we begin with hospital maternity practices (mother/infant bonding and tactile stimulation). He also suggests, citing recommendations made by a Canadian senate committee on the matter, that we offer paid maternal leaves for women and family allowances (1980:8). However, given the American ethic (we are still one of the few industrial nations without such programs), these recommendations are not likely to be implemented in the United States. As corrections practitioners, we can only say that it would be nice, but we have to adapt ourselves to conditions as they exist.

The psychopath is a particularly poor candidate for rehabilitation. Hare states (1970:113): "The psychopath is apparently incapable of the empathy, warmth, and sincerity needed to develop the type of emotional relationship required for effective therapy." Hare does relate studies that have reported limited success with psychopaths when very strict and authoritarian methods were used (1970:113). A corrections worker who is to achieve any success at all with such individuals must be prepared to set strict limits on their behavior and stand doggedly by them. He or she must also be to some extent an authority figure, albeit a warm "parental" authority figure. Reality therapy (to be discussed later) may prove to be the most effective method of dealing with the psychopath in a correctional setting.

Perspectives from the Field

Dr. Foraker-Thompson is a professor of criminal justice at Boise State University. She has held a variety of positions in the field, including college teaching in Soledad and Deuel Prisons in California. She has been the chief planner for the New Mexico State Police, a correctional mental health liaison person, project director of a state-wide restitution project, and a prison reform worker. She has been actively involved in victims' rights issues since 1974.

Is Theory Useful in the Criminal Justice Field?

Dr. Jane Foraker-Thompson

Is theory useful in the CJ field? Definitely yes! It was my experience to work with offenders in two major prisons in California, one in New Mexico, and a well-rounded offender community treatment program before I got around to really studying criminology. When I finally began to study the theories seriously, I picked and chose among them for those that spoke to me in the sense that they described some of the hundreds of offenders that I had personally known and dealt with over the years. This is not the preferred or the normal way toward scholarship in this area. For me it was practice first and then meet the theories. However, it was a good way to test the theories for their reality value. I began in the criminal justice field as a practitioner with no thought of ever becoming a scholar.

My approach is eclectic. I don't believe that any one theory can explain all offenders, or even one offender. When one speaks of offenders as a category of people, one cannot classify them as a single type. All they have in common is that they have offended against the law. They have done so for a variety of personal, environmental, psychological, and sociological reasons. The mix is different for each person. I see merit and find help in Merton's theory of anomie, especially in his "retreatist" and "innovator" categories. The differential theory of Sutherland is also useful and contains some accurate descriptions of the

experiences of some offenders in some circumstances, but by no means all offenders.

Judging by my interpretation of reality, Hirshi's control theory comes closer to being more specific and reality-based. As he puts it, the gathering of like delinquents together is not a matter of "birds of a feather flocking together; the birds have already been flocked." That is, they have already been deprived by their early childhood and lack the ties of attachment, commitment, involvement, and belief. They are not part of the so-called middle-class mainstream. So like seeks like for comfort and security, but not really friendship or caring.

The recent findings from a variety of fields regarding psychopathy bring together a fascinating combination of empirical data that the field has not yet dared to put together into a coherent theory. We (psychiatrists, psychologists, criminologists, social workers, and corrections personnel) have been talking about psychopaths for years, with some doubt that such a category actually exists. But those of us who have personally dealt with hundreds of offenders over a number of years know that such a category exists. The psychopathy concept explains a group of people and their behaviors in a way that no other concept does. Certainly not all offenders are psychopaths, and not all psychopaths are offenders. Some are our neighbors, or our uncles or cousins, or a business person down the street. Whoever they may be, we do know that they exist.

Thanks to recent physiological studies, we now have indications that there are physical reasons for what seems to be the inexplicable, nonrational, and self-destructive behavior of people who may otherwise be intelligent, talented, and often charming. We who are privileged to have been well nurtured as children, to be trained and educated, and to have rational and responsible behavior patterns have difficulty understanding why some people don't turn out like us. This is especially true if such people are one of several children in a family and the other children seemed to "turn out OK." Perhaps their bodies do function differently, thereby causing criminal behavior.

Because the early biologically based writings of theorists such as Lombroso were found to be primitive and outrageous, we have been embarrassed ever since to return to the thought that there may be physiological explanations for some types of criminal behavior. Take the recent findings about the effects of nutrition as well as vitamin and mineral imbalances on the behavior of delinquents, for instance. These physiological variables are definitely worth exploring in an earnest, rigorous, and scientific manner. In fact, it is probably overdue that we make a serious attempt to weave the bits and pieces together to generate a respectable theory of psychopathy.

Walsh's love deprivation theory is an attempt to do just that. Given what we know about psychopaths and violent people in general, it makes sense. It is another piece of the puzzle in our attempts to figure out why some offenders behave the way they do. This knowledge can be used both by presentence investigators when making recommendations to the judge and by the judges themselves in their evaluations of the possible dangerousness of leaving certain offenders in society.

All the theories addressed here provide useful information for corrections workers that will enable them to assist and monitor their clients more effectively. The more they learn and assimilate these theories into their everyday operating practices, the better correctional workers they will be. As Lewin said, "There is nothing so practical as a good theory."

Summary

From the two perspectives presented in this chapter, the tendency toward crime is located in the individual. This doesn't mean that people are born criminals or that crime is "in the genes." We have looked at psychopathy in terms of ANS and RAS functioning. A person with a hyporeactive ANS doesn't feel the same level of fear and anxiety that people with more normally functioning ANSs feel. Not being overly concerned with the punitive consequences of criminal activity, lacking a sense of guilt, and lacking sympathy for their victims, psychopathic criminals tend to engage in crime with alarming frequency. We looked at the various physiological markers of psychopathy, with emphasis on the Wechsler $P > V$ test. This is not necessarily the "best" marker, but it is usually readily available to the criminal justice worker.

A person with a sluggish RAS is prone to boredom. He or she seeks higher levels of excitement than do most of us, a search that often ends in trouble. A person who is quickly bored is also not very likely to spend much time in academic pursuits that lead to a rewarding legitimate career. Such a person is also quite likely to seek artificial stimulation through the use of drugs.

Love deprivation was examined as an explanatory variable in the etiology of psychopathy. The experiences that we undergo during the phases of rapid brain cell growth influence the structure and function of our brains. Positive experiences in the form of plentiful stimuli, especially tactile stimuli, have the effect of wiring the brain for love. Negative early experiences have the opposite effect. Extremely negative experiences during infancy and childhood may lead to future violent behavior of psychopathic proportions.

We looked at the possibilities that love deprivation could result in later hyporeactive ANS functioning and that ANS functioning might be able to explain the triad of violence-predictive behavior: enuresis, fire setting, and cruelty to animals.

The chapter has emphasized the awesome importance of tender, loving care for the development of wholesome individuals and pointed to the interaction of environmental influences and physiological functioning in the production of criminal behavior, especially violent criminal behavior.

References and Suggested Readings

Allen, H., L. Linder, H. Goldman, and S. Dinitz (1971). "Hostile and simple sociopaths: An empirical typology." *Criminology,* 6:27–47.

Andrew, J. (1982). "Memory and violent crime among delinquents." *Criminal Justice and Behavior,* 9:364–371.

Bennett, E., M. Diamond, D. Kretch, and M. Rosenzwig (1964). "Chemical and anatomical plasticity of the brain." *Science,* 146:610–619.

Bennett, L., T. Rosenbaum, and W. McCullough (1978). *Counseling in Correctional Environments.* New York: Human Sciences Press.

Blair, D. (1975). "Medicolegal implications of the terms 'psychopath,' 'psychopathic,' and 'psychopathic disorder.'" *Medicine and Science,* 15:110–123.

Comte, A. (1896). *The Positive Philosophy of Auguste Comte.* Trans. and ed. H. Martinue. London: Bell.

DiCara, L. (1970). "Learning in the autonomic nervous system." *Scientific American,* 222:30–39.

Eysenck, H. (1970). *Crime and Personality.* London: Palladin.

Ferguson, M. (1973). *The Brain Revolution.* New York: Bantam.

Freud, S. (1924). *A General Introduction to Psychoanalysis.* New York: Washington Square.

Fromm, E. (1965). *The Art of Loving.* New York: Bantam.

Gibbons, D. (1973). *Society, Crime, and Criminal Careers.* Englewood Cliffs, NJ: Prentice-Hall.

Glasser, W. (1976). *The Identity Society.* New York: Harper & Row.

Goldman, H., L. Linder, S. Dinitz, and H. Allen (1971). "The simple sociopath: Physiological and sociological characteristics." *Biological Psychiatry,* 3:77–83.

Gray, K., and H. Hutchinson (1964). "The psychopathic personality: A survey of Canadian psychiatrists' opinions." *Canadian Psychiatric Association Journal,* 9:452–461.

Hare, R. (1970). *Psychopathy.* New York: Wiley.

Hare, R., and M. Quinn (1971). "Psychopathy and autonomic conditioning." *Journal of Abnormal Psychology,* 77:223–235.

Harlow, H. (1958). "The nature of love." *American Psychologist,* 13:673–685.

Harlow, H. (1962). "Social deprivation in monkeys." *Scientific American,* 206:137–144.

Harvey, B. (1980). "Searching for the roots of violence." *Liaison: A Monthly Journal for the Criminal Justice System,* 6:3–8.

Haynie, R. (1978). "Deprivation of body pleasure: Origin of violence? A survey of the literature." *Child Welfare,* 59:287–297.

Hellman, D., and N. Blackman (1966). "Enuresis, firesetting, and cruelty to animals: A triad predictive of adult crime." *American Journal of Psychiatry,* 132:1431–1435.

Jeffery, C. (1979). "Punishment and deterrence: A psychobiological statement." In C. Jeffery (Ed.), *Biology and Crime.* Beverly Hills, CA: Sage.

Keiser, T. (1975). "Schizotype and the Wechsler digit span test." *Journal of Clinical Psychology,* 31:303–306.

Mark, V., and F. Ervin (1970). *Violence and the Brain.* New York: Harper & Row.

Marx, K., and F. Engels (1956). *The Holy Family, or Critique of Critical Critique.* London: Foreign Language Publishing House.

Maslow, A. (1953). "Love in healthy people." In A. Montagu (Ed.), *The Meaning of Love.* New York: Julian Press.

Mednick, S., and K. Finello (1983). "Biological factors and crime: Implications for forensic psychiatry." *International Journal of Law and Psychiatry,* 6:1–15.

Mednick, S., and B. Hutchings (1978). "Genetic and psychophysiological factors in asocial behavior." *American Journal of Child Psychiatry,* 17:209–223.

Montagu, A. (1978). *Touching: The Human Significance of the Skin.* New York: Harper & Row.

Prescott, J. (1975). Body pleasure and the origins of violence. *The Futurist,* April:64–65.

Restak, R. (1979). *The Brain: The Last Frontier.* New York: Warner.

Rutter, M. (1972). *Maternal Deprivation Reassessed.* Middlesex, England: Penguin.

Shalling, D. (1978). "Psychopathy-related personality variables and the psychophysiology of socialization." In R. Hare and D. Shalling (Eds.), *Psychopathic Behavior.* New York: Wiley.

Sorokin, P. (1954). *The Ways and Power of Love.* Boston: Beacon Press.

Suomi, S. (1980). *A Touch of Sensitivity.* Boston: WGBH Foundation.

Surwillo, W. (1980). "The electroencephalogram and childhood aggression." *Aggressive Behavior,* 6:9–18.

Taylor, G. (1979). *The Natural History of the Mind.* New York: Dutton.

Wadsworth, M. (1976). "Delinquency, pulse rates and early emotional deprivation." *British Journal of Criminology,* 16:245–246.

Walsh, A. (1981). *Human Nature and Love: Biological, Intrapsychic and Social-Behavioral Perspectives.* Lanham, MD: University Press of America.

Walsh, A. (1983). "Neurophysiology, motherhood, and the growth of love." *Human Mosaic,* 17:51–62.

Walsh, A. (1987). "Distinguishing features of diagnosed psychopaths among convicted sex criminals." *Free Inquiry in Creative Sociology.* 15:40–42.

Walsh, A., and J. Beyer (1986). "Wechsler performance-verbal discrepancy and juvenile delinquency." *Journal of Social Psychology,* 126:419–420.

Walsh, A., and T. Petee (forthcoming). "Love deprivation and violent delinquency." *Journal of Crime and Justice.*

Walsh, A., J. Beyer, and T. Petee (forthcoming). "Violent delinquency: An examination of psychopathic typologies." *Journal of Genetic Psychology.*

Wax, D., and V. Haddox (1972). "Enuresis, fire setting and cruelty to animals in male adolescent delinquents: A triad predictive of violent behavior. *Journal of Psychiatry and Law,* 2:45–71.

Wechsler, D. (1958). *The Measurement and Appraisal of Adult Intelligence.* Baltimore: Williams & Wilkins.

Wolfgang, M. E., R. M. Figlio, and T. Sellin (1972). *Delinquency in a Birth Cohort.* Chicago: University of Chicago Press.

Chapter 3

The Self: Principal Tool of the Criminal Justice Helper

The most important factor affecting behavior is the self-concept. . . . The self is the star of every performance, the central figure in every act. Persons engaging in the helping professions, therefore, need the broadest possible understanding of the nature, origins, and functions of the self-concept.

Arthur Combs, Donald Avila, and William Purkey

As Garrett points out, it is important that the professional interviewer have more than a casual knowledge of human behavior and motivation, and that "They should apply this knowledge, not only to an understanding of their clients' personalities, needs, prejudices, and emotions, but also to an understanding of their own. The wise maxim of the ancient Greeks, 'Know thyself,' applies especially to interviewers" (1982:5).

Knowing Yourself

There are many tools available to criminal justice (CJ) workers to modify the behavior of their clients, but the worker's self-concept is the most important. A person can decline the use of other tools, but corrections work demands the use of the self. Effective helping behavior involves interaction between two selves. The offender's self, almost by definition, is deficient in some important aspects. His or her involvement in the criminal justice system demonstrates some degree of difficulty in behaving in a responsible manner. In order to compensate for the deficiencies of one half of the interacting dyad, the other half must possess some extraordinary qualities if the relationship is to be an effective one. Before we proceed to discuss the interviewing process, then, it is a good idea to examine briefly the primary tool used in that process.

The Self-Concept

The importance of self-concept in understanding your behavior and that of your clients is of the utmost importance. Your self-concept is who and what you believe that unique individual you refer to as "me" is all about. It is the central core of your existence, your focus of reality, from which the world around you is experienced, understood, and evaluated. Your self-concept is both the product and producer of your experiences. If you are capable of giving and receiving love, if you consider yourself to be a worthwhile person, if you are confident in yourself and if you behave responsibly, you will be able to bring positive feelings about yourself to the helping relationship. You have developed these ideas about yourself through a lifetime of interacting with others and incorporating both their attitudes and feelings about you and their evaluations and expectations of you. This is what it means to say that your self-concept is the product of your experience. Since you do have a positive self-concept derived from the positive beliefs about you held by significant others, your behavior will tend to confirm their beliefs and yours in a kind of psychological version of the "rich get richer" spiral. This is what it means to say that the self-concept is a producer of your behavior.

Now, consider individuals whose experiences have resulted in a negative self-concept. Their behavior will also tend to confirm their self-perceptions derived from those unhappy experiences. If their experiences are such that they develop negative self-concepts, they are likely to view the world as an unfriendly place and to engage in behavior not likely to endear them to others. Such people may feel trapped in a way of life without much hope of improvement, being in effect victims of their own self-perceptions. The psychological spiral now swirls in the opposite direction: "The poor get poorer." "I'm no good. I can't be—nobody loves me, wants me, or cares for me." "Who cares anyway? Not me. They can all go to hell!" "I can't get a job because I'm not very smart—everyone says so." "I'll just get

what I need by taking it from all those suckers out there, and just let them try to stop me." This is the mind-set of many clients caught up in the criminal justice system, and this is the mind-set that the CJ helper must wrestle with and overcome.

However, in order to accomplish this task, and it is an arduous and lengthy one, your own self-concept must be up to it. As Combs, Avila, and Purkey (1971:56–57) so well put it:

> Since new concepts of self are learned as a consequence of interactions with the helper, effective helpers must be significant people. They cannot be nonentities. One cannot interact with a shadow. The helping relationship is an active one, and a passive helper is unlikely to teach his [or her] client anything but his [or her] own futility. The personality of the helper must play a vital part in any helping relationship. It is the helper's use of his [or her] self which makes the interaction whatever it is to become.

Qualities of an Effective CJ Worker

CJ helpers must possess some extraordinary qualities if they are to have a meaningful part in changing the deficient self-concepts of so many of their clients. We will now take a brief look at what those qualities are and at some potential problems associated with unidentified areas of the CJ worker's self that may detract from the helping process.

The criminal justice worker must possess a thorough knowledge of criminal behavior and its correlates. You should develop the interest and the patience to conduct an ongoing study of the forces and events affecting the lives of your clients. Knowledge of criminological theories and theories about substance abuse and of abnormal psychology enables you to view more objectively your clients' frame of reference and lessens the impulse toward moralizing about their behavior from your own. The subject matter of your field is people with problems that cause them to act irresponsibly. Individuals who aspire to be professionals must know their subject matter.

The criminal justice worker must be realistic, neither a Pollyanna nor a Cassandra. A Pollyanna is one whose irrespressible optimism finds good in everything. Such a person often fails to see, or discounts, danger signals. He or she avoids or discourages negative feedback and is extremely reluctant to confront resistant or reluctant clients. Pollyannas allow manipulative clients to get away with too many minor infractions. They believe that this leniency marks them as nonauthoritarian and nondirective counselors. What they really are, however, is individuals who, lacking in self-confidence, provide no meaningful guidance or supervision to clients whose personal and legal needs require it.

The Cassandra is one who sees negativism in everything. He or she also lacks a sense of competence and feeds such lack by discounting positive feedback. Cassandras don't trust their clients at all and attempt to avoid positive interactions with them. They also tend to set their goals and expectations impossibly high, thus ensuring failure. Whereas Pollyannas tend to provide unwarranted positive feedback when confrontation is required, Cassandras give feedback only when the client has not lived up to expectations and will not reinforce positive behavior with positive feedback.

Both of these working styles are unrealistic and reflect attitudes about the self as well as toward clients. The Pollyanna sees corrections work solely as social work; the Cassandra views it as police work. The realistic corrections worker views his or her task as both and has sufficient self-understanding and self-confidence to know when the use of either role is appropriate.

The criminal justice helper does not use clients to satisfy his or her needs. If the criminal justice worker has unresolved needs, the counselor/client relationship is not the place to attempt to satisfy them. The insecure worker who needs to feel powerful, for instance, will overcontrol interactions. He or she will dominate the direction of counseling sessions, pose as an expert, and try to convert clients by preaching at them. Power-hungry counselors feel safe in pursuing their needs in this way with a captive clientele, but it is a counterproductive misuse of authority.

Other criminal justice workers may attempt to satisfy their needs for warmth and acceptance through clients. Their interactions with their clients are designed to elicit cues that they are liked and accepted. Like Pollyannas, they will blind themselves to negative cues because they fear rejection, and they are opening themselves to manipulation.

In contrast, there are those unresourceful counselors who are fearful of control or who are fearful of closeness. Whereas the power-hungry and the acceptance needers suffocate their clients with attention, the weak and the distance needers avoid contact as much as possible. Those who fear control will neglect to offer clients advice and direction when needed and will generally be passive onlookers. Those counselors who fear closeness will act distant with their clients, will avoid addressing clients' positive feelings, and will not develop the involvement necessary to the helping process.

The criminal justice worker inspires trust, confidence, and credibility in clients. Effective helping requires that clients feel confident that they can share themselves with the helper. If they are to share their feelings, hopes, fears, and concerns openly, they must first sense a nonjudgmental acceptance on your part. They must come to view you as a credible professional, have confidence in your abilities and motives, and trust you to accept their feelings and concerns without criticizing, shaming, or ridiculing them. To be perceived this way you must be this way. You cannot long feign openness, honesty, concern, and acceptance. You must work on these self-attributes.

The criminal justice helper reaches inward as well as outward. You should develop a commitment to nondefensive self-examination and awareness: "Who am I, what am I like as a person?" "Am I almost always honest, trustworthy, likable, accepting?" "Am I the kind of person who inspires confidence and trust?" "Do I really make an effort to understand my clients and their environments?" "Am I a competent person?" "Do I find myself using people to satisfy my needs for power or for acceptance?" "Do I have the courage to change those aspects of myself that I don't like?"

As a criminal justice helper, you will often have clients who are different from you. What are your attitudes about people who are different? Do you harbor racist or sexist attitudes and stereotypes? Can you accept and interact with individuals of a different race, sex, or socioeconomic background as easily as with individuals with whom you have these things in common? Do you value, or are you fearful of, diversity of attitudes and values? Do you accept different religions, political ideologies, and sexual lifestyles as being alternatives rather than regarding them as deviant?

The more you learn about the various types of people with whom you will come into contact, and the more you explore your attitudes toward them and toward yourself with an open mind, the more you will become the sort of person who is an effective helper. Let's now examine the benefits of looking inward.

Benefits of Self-Disclosure

One of the most important qualities that criminal justice workers should possess is the willingness to share their selves with others, including their clients, through self-disclosure. *Self-disclosure* refers to the communicating of personal information to another who would not normally have that information. One may reasonably inquire what use it is for the CJ helper to communicate personal information to a client: isn't the client's self the focus of the client/helper relationship— indeed, the reason for its existence? Yes, it is, and it was not until the advent of humanistic psychology that self-disclosure was considered appropriate and beneficial (Okun, 1987:261; Ivey, in press). However, the willingness of the CJ helper to share his or her self serves some very useful functions. First, it is a form of modeling behavior that encourages reluctant clients to reveal intimate facts about themselves. The diffi-

culty that clients doubtless experience in revealing their most intimate feelings, thoughts, and valuations may well be lessened by the helper's example. Remember, reciprocal self-disclosure is the basis of the success of various self-help groups such as Alcoholics Anonymous. Confession is good for the soul, and it yields an abundance of needed information for the assessment of the client to boot.

Second, self-disclosure gives the client a new perspective on things derived from your personal experiences. Again, the sharing of personal experiences, the implanting of possibilities for alternative frames of reference in the minds of others, is part of the modus operandi of self-help groups. This process of self-disclosure should, of course, be free of value judgments, moral exhortations, and self-serving and boastful exhibitionism. Besides being bad practice, it is not considered good taste to advertise what a great person you are. If the contrast between the client's experience and yours is too great, he or she will not view your revealed frame of reference as being realistic. If you moralize and pass judgment, the client is not likely to reveal any further personal information to you that could invite further denigration.

You must always be aware of the feelings and humanity of your clients. If, for example, Bob reveals that he has experienced great difficulty obtaining employment because of his lack of a high school diploma and the vagaries of his lower-class upbringing, you may reply with sensitivity, revealing your own class origins, the possibility of obtaining a general education diploma (GED), and how you managed to acquire an education despite acknowledged early deficiencies. Rendered in this nonthreatening manner, your experience may strike a responsive chord of the possible within the client. If you couch it in terms designed to emphasize your moral superiority ("I did it, why can't you?" "It takes guts, buddy." "You can get a job if you get off your lazy ass and start looking."), Bob is very likely to react negatively to such an assault on his self-concept, either by becoming hostile or by clamming up. Either way, you have lost the opportunity to further the meaningful interaction so necessary for an adequate assessment of your client. You have also reinforced Bob's sense of hopelessness and his feeling that "nobody cares" and revealed your own inadequacies as a helper. If such an exchange takes place during the initial interview, and if Bob is subsequently placed under your supervision as a probationer, parolee, or inmate, efforts to counsel him will meet with resistance because you have communicated to him that he is not worth much and that you are not really interested in him or his problems.

Some caveats about self-disclosure to a client are in order at this point. The client's problems must be the focus of any interview or counseling session. The worker's self-disclosure should therefore be infrequent, relevant, and focused and should not give the client the impression that you are working out your own problems with him or her. Chatty and unstructured conversations are inappropriate during a session designed to gather information about the client, although they may have use in later counseling sessions if your motives are consistent with establishing a genuine atmosphere of informality. Egan's advice (1986:231) is instructive here: "Helpers should be willing and able to disclose themselves, even deeply, in reasonable ways, *but should actually do so only if it is clear that it will contribute to the client's progress*" (emphasis added).

Improving Your Self-Concept through Self-Disclosure

Training exercises in self-disclosure, such as those given at the end of this chapter, should be an integral part of the CJ helper's training. They are necessary for two reasons. First, they provide the helper with a gut-level understanding of the feelings of his or her clients as they are asked to reveal intimate information. Disclosing intimate information can be highly embarrassing and intimidating to the client. Imagine the embarrassment of a 55-year-old minister who has been found guilty of molesting a child as he is being asked to reveal details of his sex life to a probation officer young enough to be his grandson or granddaughter! The probation officer (or any other CJ officer, for that matter) must be highly sensitive to this embarrassment if he or she is to conduct a successful interview and make an adequate assessment. One of the best ways to learn this sensitivity is to experience the same sort of discomfort by self-disclosure in a classroom setting.

However, the classroom setting will not be as threatening to the student as the real-life setting is for the client. Students can easily role-play rather than dealing with real concerns. That is, they can manufacture fictitious problems that do not threaten them rather than exploring real problems that they may have. Only by realistically exploring problems can you gain insight into what it is like to be a client. Remember, all prospective psychoanalysts have to undergo intensive psychoanalysis before they are allowed to practice their skills on others.

The second reason for engaging in realistic self-disclosure is to improve your greatest asset—your self-concept. It is important for us to assess ourselves, to know what kind of people we are, to know our strengths, weaknesses, potentials, and problem areas so that we can operate effectively in our environment. Some authorities consider wholesome self-disclosure to be as necessary for mental health as proper exercise and nutrition are for physical health. Fromm (1955) has written that in order to reduce our alienation from ourselves and from others we must open ourselves to ourselves by disclosing ourselves to others; and Mowrer (1964) feels that an unwillingness to disclose oneself is a major factor in many areas of behavioral pathology. The more we know about ourselves, the better able we will be to understand others. Self-knowledge is desirable for all people, but it is vital for those in the helping professions because understanding others is a prerequisite to helping them. How can you help your clients come to terms with feelings that are hindering their functioning if you have not confronted and dealt with similar feelings in yourself?

We must not harbor static images of ourselves. If we do, we will have unrealistic pictures of the world and our relationship to it. A static self-concept cuts us off from the fullness of the experiences that the world offers us, thus stunting our emotional and intellectual growth. Rather than building walls and defenses against life's fullness, we should accept all experiences and fit them into our self-concepts. We must adapt positively to the environment as it changes. To accomplish this successfully, we must receive information about ourselves from concerned others and use it for positive change. To receive information about ourselves from others, however, we must be strong enough to be willing to share ourselves with others. Both the receiving of information about ourselves and the sharing of ourselves is accomplished by meaningful self-disclosure. You will, after all, be asking your clients to do all these things: adapt positively to their environments, experience lifestyles different from the one they have grown accustomed to, share themselves through disclosure, and receive information from you that you will expect them to employ fruitfully. If this is not a part of your personal operating philosophy, you will not be successful in imparting it to your clients.

The Johari Window

An Aid to Self-Understanding

A useful framework for viewing self-concept and understanding how self-disclosure is valuable in improving it is the Johari Window (Luft, 1963), reproduced as Figure 3–1. This device divides the self into four components or "cells," representing aspects of the self ranging from those known to almost everyone to aspects of which you yourself are not aware. Positive self-disclosure should have the effect of enlarging cell I (the public self) while shrinking the other three cells correspondingly. The following is a general discussion of the principles of self-disclosure. It should not be viewed within the context of the counselor/client relationship. You certainly will not be asking clients to help you explore your intimate concerns.

	Known to self	Unknown to self
Known to others	I Public self	II Blind self
Unknown to others	III Private self	IV Unknown self

Figure 3–1   The Johari Window   (*Adapted from Luft, 1963.*)

The *public self* is the self as it is habitually shared with others. It is an area of self-knowledge that you can reveal without qualms.

The *private self* obviously has relevance to self-disclosure. You need not, or even should not, burden others with excessive and exhibitionist disclosure of the private self: "If only you knew what I've accomplished in my life, and against what odds, you too would realize what a great person I really am." The idea is to disclose only those aspects of the private self that others can help with in the exploration of those aspects that are of concern to you, such as values, weaknesses, and social and sexual identities.

The *blind self* is that part of the self that others see but we don't. It is involved in self-disclosure only if others bring their images of you to your attention and if you are willing to acknowledge the validity of the transmitted information. The transmitted information may not be an accurate assessment of you, but it may be beneficial to you at least to recognize the possibility that it is. If the revealed information is negative, do not throw up fences and retreat from it. Instead, work with that aspect of the self to see how it can be improved. Never ignore traits or characteristics that others perceive and that may be negatively affecting your effectiveness as a helper or as a person.

The *unknown self* is the area of latent, inchoate, subconscious, and preconscious facets of the self. It is an area of shadowy fears and weaknesses, but also a reservoir of great untapped potential and talents that we all, including our clients, have. An unwillingness to explore unknown areas of the self is indicative of a frozen self-concept. In the process of exploring the blind self, it is possible that aspects of the unknown self will become accessible to you so that you may confront them and develop those that are desirable or deal constructively with those that are not.

Whereas it is generally agreed that self-disclosure (moving information contained in cells II, III, and IV into cell I) facilitates personal growth, it may result in growth-inhibiting outcomes. Whether self-disclosure is beneficial or harmful depends on the state of the receiver and the quality of the relationship shared by the receiver and the transmitter. Inevitably, self-disclosure involves a certain amount of risk taking. A turtle never moves forward until it sticks its neck out.

Self-disclosure demands trusting and making an investment in the other person. As a professional CJ worker, you will be asking clients to trust you and invest in you. If you are to perform your task in an effective and efficient manner, you must prove worthy of that trust and investment by responding to clients in a sensitive, empathetic, and fully involved way. Furthermore, you must also be secure enough in yourself to be completely honest with your client. Your honesty, openness, and acceptance do not guarantee that your client will act likewise, but they certainly make it more probable.

Application to the Client

Although the Johari Window was conceived as a strategy for self-exploration, it can be fruitfully adapted to serve as a model for the officer/client relationship. For instance, the situation representing the immediate state of your "knowledge" of your clients on your first meeting with them is presented in Figure 3–2. The major difference between exercises in voluntary self-disclosure for the purpose of self-growth and the officer/client encounter is that the public self in this case is the self that the client chooses to present to you, not the public self that he or she habitually shares with family, friends, and acquaintances. Your knowledge of his or her public self is, for the moment, limited to information written down in various official documents. Therefore, even getting to know the client as others know him or her may prove to be an exacting assignment, for at this point you know only the *official client.* Your initial task is the melding of the two subsections of cell I to form a unified picture of the client as he or she normally presents himself or herself to others. Clients may have a number of aspects of the public self that they are unwilling to share with you. Consequently, they will erect barriers to protect those areas. The barriers can be scaled by an effectively conducted interview with the client and by collateral interviews with others acquainted with him or her.

The *private client* is that part of the client's self that he or she wishes to keep unscrutinized by others, especially by the corrections worker. It represents the behaviors, feelings, and motivations that the client habitually hides but that may be revealed when he or she chooses. These behaviors, feelings, and motivations, since the client is aware of them, will most probably be the first target areas for mutual exploration. They are not necessarily problem areas. They may just as well be growth-promoting areas that, with a little support and encouragement, the client could actualize. If aspects of the private client are of

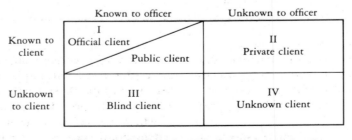

Figure 3–2 The Johari Window applied to the client

This essay by an anonymous writer is an anguished cry for understanding and acceptance. It illustrates our discussion of self-disclosure, as well as the discussion of listening still to come. Notice how the writer has built a false self-image and erected barriers to protect it, and how painful the writer finds his or her inauthenticity. We all want to be accepted and loved, but many of us fight against what we so desperately need. The writer wants to be authentic by disclosing his or her true self and true feeling but is so terribly afraid of rejection. This could have been written by any of your future clients, perhaps even by some of your classmates (or even you). Remember it when you do your exercises in self-disclosure. Above all, remember it when you are working with real clients.

The Mask: Please Hear What I'm Not Saying

Author Unknown

Don't be fooled by me. Don't be fooled by the face I wear. For I wear a mask. I wear a thousand masks, masks that I'm afraid to take off, and none of them are me. Pretending is an art that's second nature to me, but don't be fooled, for God's sake don't be fooled. I give you the impression that I'm secure, that all is sunny and unruffled with me, within as well as without. That confidence is my name and coolness is my game, and that I need no one.

But don't believe me. My surface is my mask. Beneath dwells the real me in confusion, in fear, in aloneness. But I hide this. I don't want anybody to know it. I panic at the thought of my weakness and fear being exposed. That's why I frantically create a mask to hide behind, to shield me from the glance that knows. But such a glance is precisely my salvation—that is, if it's followed by acceptance, by love. It's the only thing that can liberate me from my own self-built prison walls. It is the only thing that will assure me of what I can't assure myself—that I'm really worth something.

But I'm afraid to tell you this; I'm afraid that your glance will not be followed by acceptance and love. I'm afraid you'll laugh, and that laugh will kill me. I idly chatter to you in the suave tones of surface talk. I tell you everything that's really nothing, and nothing of what's everything, of what's crying within me.

Please listen carefully and try to hear what I'm not saying, what I'd like to be able to say, what for survival I need to say. I'd really like to be genuine and spontaneous, and me, but you've got to help me. You alone can release me from my shadow-world of panic and uncertainty, from my lonely prison. It will not be easy for you. A long conviction of worthlessness builds strong walls. The nearer you approach me, the blinder I may strike back. I am irrational—I fight against the very thing that I cry out for. But I am told that love is stronger than strong walls. Please try to beat down those walls with firms hands, but with gentle hands—for I am very sensitive. Who am I, you may wonder. I am someone you "know" very well, I am every man you meet and I am every woman you meet.

this kind, he or she may possibly be more disposed to relating them to a relative stranger who is perceived as caring and accepting than to more familiar others from whom he or she may fear ridicule.

The *blind client* represents those aspects of the self of which the client is unaware but that the officer perceives and is sensitive to. Just as the corrections worker is able to enhance the self by feedback in an atmosphere of openness and trust, so may the client. Emphasis should be placed initially on the positive aspects of the client's self of which the officer is aware, such as positive statements by others. If, for instance, an officer has access to school records indicating that the client scored well on IQ tests, the officer may discuss the nature of IQ and the potential and possibilities open to the client with such scores. This kind of information, needless to say, is most welcome and tends to spill over into congenial discussions of other aspects of the client's blind self that he or she might not be so readily willing to accept.

The *unknown client* represents those aspects of the client's self that are unknown to officer and client alike. Realistically, we know that many facets of the client's unknown self will remain unknown. The initial interview, for whatever reason it is conducted, is not the place to attempt to probe into this area. Under supervision, however, the client should be encouraged to explore it in order to discover the unknown potential that we surely all possess. You must have faith in this proposition if you are to be an effective correctional worker.

The Johari Window is, then, a useful framework for conceptualizing the process and purpose of interviewing. However, we should never forget that our criminal justice clients come to the interviewing process with vastly different biographies, motives, and attitudes. Each interview is a unique process between human beings who are far too individualized to be reduced to precise formulas. Interviewing is an art rather than a science. However, certain basic principles exist that enable the helper to conduct a successful interview. They are discussed in the next chapter.

Summary

This chapter emphasizes the primacy of the self in the helping process. Nothing is more important to the success or failure of a counseling relationship than the quality of the helper's self. The self-concept is the product and producer of experience. Positive experiences lead to a positive self-concept, and a positive self-concept leads to further positive experiences. The opposite progression, often found in criminal justice clients, is also true.

We looked at the various attributes that characterize the professional criminal justice worker. You should examine these attributes closely to determine how you measure up. Deficiencies and weaknesses in any of the areas can be explored in the process of self-disclosure.

To improve the self-concept, a person must accept a wide variety of experiences and integrate them into his or her self-concept. One way of doing this is through meaningful self-disclosure. Self-disclosure helps us to gain knowledge about ourselves by receiving feedback about ourselves from others. Every prospective counselor should experience self-disclosure in a number of sessions before actually practicing counseling, not only to gain valuable self-insight but also to experience the process in which he or she will be asking clients to engage. The Johari Window is an excellent device for guiding self-disclosure of this type. There are few bits of advice more useful than the ancient injunction to "know thyself."

◑ Exercises in Self-Exploration through Disclosure

The purpose of this activity is twofold: (1) to facilitate self-exploration by disclosing to a partner various aspects of yourself and (2) to give you some experience of what it is like to reveal oneself to a relative stranger. During the initial session, you may, out of fear, anxiety, or embarrassment, decide upon some relatively nonthreatening topic. Or you may possess the self-assurance to pick a topic that is of real concern to you. It is preferable, of course, to choose aspects of the private self, especially those of an interpersonal nature, for exploration. The section asking you to explore values and attitudes toward various kinds of individuals will prove to be valuable in developing an empathetic understanding of them if both disclosure and feedback are open and honest.

Exercises should be done in pairs, with frequent changes of partner. If your instructor chooses not to assign partners, it is preferable that you do not sit with the same person too often. Make an effort to sit with someone of a different race, sex, or ethnic background. You will find this to be a good learning experience and very rewarding. Each student should take turns in disclosing the chosen issue to the other. Remember, you are not engaging in a conventional conversation. The disclosing person should have control of the communication. The listener should listen, paying attention to the techniques of active listening as outlined in the next chapter. The listener should speak only for the purposes of clarification and of prompting further disclosure by the use of probes. Each of the following suggested topics is suitable for a discussion of about five to ten minutes.

Topic 1: Generalities

The kinds of people I like best are_____

_____

The kinds of people I like least are_____

_____

I try to avoid thinking about_____

_____

I think that the most important thing in life is

_____

I feel most competent when I_____

_____

I feel least competent when I_____

_____

My career goals are_____

_____

I would really like to be able to_____

_____

Topic 2: Values and Attitudes

My values are important to me because

_____

Here's how I *really* feel that the relationship between the sexes should be_____

_____

Here's how I *really* feel about blacks/whites

_____

Here's how I feel about alcoholics_____

_____

Here's how I feel about drug abusers_____

_____

Here's how I *really* feel about homosexuals

_____

Here's how I *really* feel about criminals

_____

An open mind is desirable because_____

_____

Topic 3: Feelings

I am happiest when_____

_____

I get the most depressed when_____

_____

I get embarrassed when_____

_____

I get very angry when_____

_____

I feel guilty when_____

_____

I am sometimes ashamed of_____

_____

I feel very hurt when_____

_____

I feel anxious when_____

_____

Topic 4: Identity

Who are you, what kind of person are you? Odds are that you have never really thought too much about your identity. Try writing out ten separate answers to the question "Who am I?" Next, eliminate those answers that simply signify your various ascribed and achieved statuses, such as "American," "student," "male," or "19 years old." With your partners, explore those aspects of the self that you have left on your lists. You may have written, for example, "I am a shy person." Explore this aspect with your partner. Why do you think you are shy? What does your shyness do to your social life? How much more successful do you think you would be in life if you were not shy? How do you feel about your shyness? What do you think you can do about it?

Topic 5: Strengths and Weaknesses

Make a list of your five greatest strengths and five greatest weaknesses and discuss each one with

your partner. These strengths and weaknesses should be developmental "feeling" topics rather than statements like "I'm a good/poor tennis player." For instance, how do you relate to other people, especially those close to you? Are you secure in your sexual identity? Are you a leader or a follower? Do you respect the feelings of others? Are you an autonomous person? Can you take constructive criticism?

Topic 6: Effectiveness as a Criminal Justice Helper

Go back to the description of an effective criminal justice helper and rate yourself according to those attributes. Where are you weak, and where are you strong? What personal attribute do you possess that will aid you in becoming a more effective helper, and what personal attribute do you think will most detract from your ability to become an effective helper? Discuss these strengths and weaknesses with a partner.

References and Suggested Readings

Combs, A., D. Avila, and W. Purkey (1971). *Helping Relationships: Basic Concepts for the Helping Professions.* Boston: Allyn & Bacon.

Egan, G. (1986). *The Skilled Helper.* Pacific Grove, CA: Brooks/Cole.

Fromm, E. (1955). *The Sane Society.* New York: Holt, Rinehart & Winston.

Garrett, A. (1982). *Interviewing: Its Principles and Methods.* New York: Family Services Association of America.

Hartman, H. (1978). *Basic Psychiatry for Corrections Workers.* Springfield, IL: Charles C Thomas

Ivey, A. (in press). *Intentional Interviewing and Counseling.* Pacific Grove, CA: Brooks/Cole.

Luft, J. (1963). *Group Process: An Introduction to Group Dynamics.* Palo Alto, CA: National Press.

Mowrer, O. (1964). *The New Group Theory.* Princeton, NJ: Van Nostrand Reinhold.

Okun, B. (1987). *Effective Helping.* Pacific Grove, CA: Brooks/Cole.

Chapter 4
Interviewing
and Interrogating

It is not easy to achieve the ideal balance between relieving a client of the unbearable burden of what seem to be insurmountable difficulties and leaving him with essential responsibility for working out his own destiny.... One of the most important skills of the interviewer is a knowledge of his own limitations.

Annette Garrett

The interview is a focused process of communication by which you gather information for the purpose of assessing the interviewee. It is a structured and purposeful method of getting to know another person. Any interview, regardless of the context in which it takes place, is designed to help the interviewer make decisions, usually about the interviewee (for example, is he or she suitable for the job, eligible for benefits, serious about this task, a good candidate for treatment?). Corrections workers spend the major portion of their time conducting interviews with clients, victims, police officers, and many other people involved in some way with their clients' activities. Thus, it is necessary that you become informed about the basic principles of effective interviewing.

also   Interrogation is also part of the corrections worker's task sometimes. Like interviewing, interrogation involves information gathering, but the focus is more sharply delimited. As Wicks (1974:133) describes it, "Interrogation is conducted either to get an admission of guilt from a person who has been involved in a crime or to obtain clarification and elaboration of certain facts from someone who is innocent." The ability to conduct an effective interrogation is an important and necessary part of your professional development.

Purpose of the Criminal Justice Interview

The Client

Applied to the criminal justice client, interviewing is a diagnostic tool that will enable you to arrive at a preliminary understanding of clients and their problems and to recommend and implement effective treatment modalities. A well-conducted interview may also be considered the first step in the counseling process if it creates an arena in which clients can formulate an honest picture of their problems, and if they gain an understanding of the motives and resources of the helping person. Criminologist and prominent correctional administrator Paul Keve put it this way: "The most important step in the investigation process is the first interview with the defendant, and if you handle it skillfully, you not only have the basis for a truly competent report, but you also have gone a long way toward launching the treatment job that must develop later" (quoted in Hartman, 1978:309). The implication is that the interview can be the beginning of the rehabilitative process, or it can be merely a ritual in which uninterpreted demographic data are gathered and reported.

The principles of interviewing are the same regardless of the specific purpose of the interview: preparing a presentence investigation (PSI) report, meeting a newly assigned probationer or parolee, or conducting an intake interview for a new arrival at an institution.

The Victim

A growing, but long-overdue, awareness of the victim as the "forgotten party" in the criminal justice system has prompted a number of states to require that victims have a more active part in the sentencing process. Ohio, for instance, requires that a "victim impact statement" be included in each PSI, and this same statute mandates that the judge must consider statements contained therein when making the sentencing decision. This requirement demands something more than the perfunctory telephone call to as-

certain financial losses that used to be the norm. A telephone call will suffice, however, when the victim in a case of theft, burglary, or forgery is a business establishment (where no one individual has been personally victimized) and you merely wish to determine restitution figures.

In the case of personal victimization, victims should be given the courtesy of a face-to-face meeting with you. Both you and the victim benefit from such an interview. You gather information that will help you to evaluate your client; the victim can receive assurances of safety and a feeling that he or she has not been forgotten or ignored by the criminal justice system.

Techniques of Interviewing

The goal of interviewing is to gather information given voluntarily. It is not really as difficult as you may think to obtain voluntary information from clients, even criminal justice clients. Most people like nothing better than to talk about themselves. Even reluctant, angry, or embarrassed clients will probably succumb to the temptation if they perceive that you are genuinely interested in them. It is for this reason that in my interviewing and counseling classes I stress the development of genuineness, caring, and empathy over technique. Too much emphasis on technique has a way of detracting from the humanness of the interviewing process and can be painfully transparent if not developed properly in a training situation.

Active Listening

This doesn't mean that techniques aren't valuable; they are extremely valuable. The most valuable of these techniques is active listening. Active listening (the opposite of passive listening) is the key to effective communication. It means paying complete attention to the information being offered by the client and conveying that attention to the client both verbally and nonverbally.

To communicate to the client that you are actively listening, you should maintain eye contact. In addition to expressing interest, eye contact enables you to observe your client's nonverbal responses to uncomfortable questions. When does the client avert his or her eyes? When does the client flush, smile, or sneer? You cannot determine this if you are not watching. There are, however, certain subcultural differences attached to the meaning of eye contact. Middle-class people tend to view frequent eye contact as a sign of honesty and the averting of the eyes as indicative of furtiveness. Inner-city residents, especially blacks, feel that too much eye contact is a non-verbal challenge, so it may provoke hostility. Be very careful that your efforts to maintain eye contact do not inadvertently turn into an attempt to stare the client down.

When you are listening to your client you should be sitting about two arm's lengths apart (don't have a desk or other physical objects between you), and you should maintain a slightly forward-leaning posture. Leaning forward at certain points during the interview conveys an intensification of interest. Don't get so close to the client as to make him or her feel uncomfortable—that is, so that he or she feels an invasion of personal space. This is particularly important if the client is of the opposite sex. It is all too easy to convey unintended messages of a sexual nature this way. I once had a female client who started to cry during the PSI interview. I offered her a tissue and placed a comforting hand on hers. She took immediate advantage of this gesture of sympathy to grasp my hand and state, "I'll do anything to get out of this." This obvious sexual invitation was disquieting to me. Clients who make such offers expect something in return (a favorable sentencing recommendation, easy supervision conditions, a blind eye to certain violations, and so on). Had I succumbed to her invitation I might well have found myself paying the $700 in restitution she owed, violated my professional code of ethics, and, not the least, opened myself to a criminal charge. Needless to say, you must be very careful that your behavior is not open to this kind of misinterpretation.

Questioning and Probing

Although the purpose of the interview is to listen to what the client has to say, you have to guide the communication toward relevant topics. You are interested in gathering information about the client's background and lifestyle, about his or her attitudes toward the offense, and about concerns and problems that may have led to it. To get this information you have to ask questions. We will discuss two types of questioning here: *open* and *closed.* According to Ivey (1983:41), "Open questions are those that can't be answered in a few short words. They encourage others to talk and provide you with maximum information. Closed questions can be answered in a few short words or sentences. They have the advantage of focusing the interview and obtaining information, but the burden of talk remains with the interviewer." *Probes* are indirect open-ended questions that encourage the client to explore some point to which he or she has alluded.

Criminal justice clients will often be unwilling to explore their personal lives and feelings with you. It is rare, however, that they will outright refuse to answer your questions. With reluctant clients, it is necessary to encourage sharing through the use of probes. Probes are verbal tactics for prompting clients to talk about themselves and to share their thoughts, feelings, and concerns with you in a specific and concrete way. For example, if Debbie indicates to you that her marriage is an unhappy one and that she "wants out," don't be content with that raw datum. Explore. Say something like: "So you feel terrible about your marriage and feel trapped. What exactly is it that you feel worst about?" You are encouraging Debbie to clarify her general statement by relating specific and concrete instances that give rise to her generalized feelings of dissatisfaction. Your probing may give Debbie the first real opportunity she has ever had to really explore and vent her feelings with regard to her marriage. Furthermore, Debbie's trouble with the law may be a direct or indirect consequence of her poor marital relationship. If this turns out to be the case, you will have discovered a starting point for your later counseling sessions with her if she is placed on probation.

Probing questions should be open-ended, meaning that they can't be answered by a simple yes or no. Questions should be of the type: "Now that you know what the problem is between you and your husband, what do you plan to do about it?" They should not be of the type: "Now that you know what the problem is between you and your husband, do you plan to do anything about it?" A response of yes or no to this question will lead to further questions, giving Debbie the impression that she is being grilled. Using open-ended questions reduces the number of questions you ask and gives the client some sense of control.

It is obviously desirable in some cases to use closed questions, which require simple answers, such as "What was the last school you attended?" Closed questions will probably be used most often in your follow-up to client responses to open questions and in dealing with factual information such as whether a client is married. Closed questions sometimes have to be used when open-ended questions would be preferable, such as when working with adolescents and with mildly retarded clients who verbalize poorly. Sometimes you will run into street-wise clients who make it a practice of not volunteering any information that is not specifically requested, which means that in order to get the information you want, you will have to rephrase your open question as a closed one. You should never stop trying, how-ever, to get the client to speak freely about him-self or herself by the use of open questions.

Regardless of the type of question used, you shouldn't rush your clients by throwing questions at them in staccato fashion. Your tone of voice and rate of speech indicate clearly how you feel about another person and whether or not you have been really listening to previous replies. Think of the many ways that you can say, "I'm really interested in you." Give clients ample time to think through their answers to your questions. Don't be embarrassed by silence or attempt to fill it in with small talk. The client may be groping for ideas during such breaks in the conversation, and small talk will interrupt the flow of thought. If the silence becomes overly long, continue the interview by asking the client to tell you some more about the last point you covered. Don't attempt to break the silence by putting words into your clients' mouths. They may grasp at your

idea and agree with it in an effort to please you or in order to avoid saying what was really on their minds. Either way, you will be recording and evaluating your clients' responses as theirs when they are actually your own.

Listening

The third ear. Evaluating responses to ques-tions requires active listening. Active listening requires a lot of practice. Some people are easy to listen to, and some are difficult to listen to. Prejudices and biases on the part of the officer will interfere with active listening to the client, as will poor communications skills on the part of the client. When either of these conditions is present, it is especially important to make an ex-tra effort to really listen to what the client is saying. Active listening requires a great deal of alertness and flexibility. Be especially alert to any recurring thoughts or concepts the client pre-sents and mentally flag them so that you can raise them later for further and deeper discussion. Be flexible enough to deal with issues as the client presents them. If you insist on dealing with topics only when you are ready for them, you may miss some vital information because the client may no longer feel as disposed to discuss it as he or she was at first mention. In short, active listening im-plies what psychologist Theodor Reik (1956) calls "listening with the third ear." This does not re-quire the mere auditory recording of the client's actual words so much as listening to what he or she is trying to tell you.

Clients may be telling you things that they have no conscious intention of revealing. Does the client reveal self-centeredness by the overuse of personal pronouns? Does the client reveal over-dependence or a lack of responsibility by con-stantly blaming others for every little misfortune? Does the client bemoan his or her sins as vig-orously as they are committed, thus perhaps re-vealing false remorse? What do the adjectives the client uses to describe significant others reveal about the state of his or her interpersonal rela-tionships? What kind of defense mechanisms (to be discussed later), such as rationalization, projection, and displacement, does the client use to distort reality? This third-ear listening will tell you a lot more about your client than face-value responses of the "what he did to me and what I said to her" type.

However, you must restrain the urge to play Dr. Freud by reading too much into nonspecific responses at this stage. You simply don't yet have sufficient knowledge of the client to make unsupported speculations in a report that has so much importance to his or her future. Third-ear insights should be noted for your future use, but they should not be relayed to the sentencing judge as facts. When you begin to develop an empathetic understanding of your client, and when a positive relationship has formed between you, then you may broach such issues. Of course, if you perceive something about a client's response that has direct applicability to the present offense (such as rationalizing or intellectualizing about the crime) and that has implications for sentencing and supervision, such responses should be explored with the client then and there.

Resisting the temptation to interrupt. Have you ever noticed while conversing with someone that instead of really attending to what the other person was saying, you were thinking of the next thing you wanted to say, or that you interrupted that person in midsentence? And have you ever noticed how annoying this can be when others do it to you and how it causes you to lose your train of thought? When you are interviewing a client, you are not engaged in a debate in which your objective is to score points. It is all too easy to interrupt clients when you perceive their verbal responses to your inquiries to be off the track. Don't let yourself become irritated and impatient with clients' digressions. They may be approaching the topic you brought up in the most direct way they know how. There are limits, of course, to the amount of digression that you may tolerate, but an interruption made too soon may prevent the emergence of significant information. Some people simply need more time to arrive at their destination. Although side excursions can be time-

consuming, a little extra time allowed during the initial interview can actually conserve time when you are attempting to establish a working relationship with a client.

Keeping the client in the foreground. Give the client the lion's share of the "air time" during the interview. Goyer, Redding, and Rickey (1968:14) have suggested that if you find yourself talking uninterruptedly even for as little as two minutes during an interview, you are failing to get through to your client. It follows that it is a good idea to reduce interviewer talk time as much as possible. After all, we have agreed that the time is theirs. You must resist the temptation to thrust your opinions and advice onto clients and talk them into a coma. Many clients will be only too happy to allow the interviewer to babble on as a tactic to avoid exploring their own problems. Talk only when necessary to elicit information or to refocus or channel the interview in fruitful directions.

Some further impediments to active listening. There are certain other impediments to active listening against which you should guard: daydreaming, detouring, arguing, and rehearsing. We are all guilty of each of these errors at one time or another. It is important in your chosen field to be aware of them and to take steps to reorient yourself to the content of your clients' communication when you perceive yourself to be drifting away from it.

Daydreaming occurs when you are bored with what you are hearing or when you have pressing needs unrelated to the present concerns. You veer off on your own personal track and leave the client behind, forgetting that the interview time belongs to the client. You must never daydream while interviewing clients. It soon becomes apparent to clients that you are not interested in their problems, and you will experience failure in your efforts to establish a firm relationship. Frequent daydreamers are out of touch with their present reality. They fail in many tasks because they focus more on a future "could be" than on what is actually going on now.

Detouring occurs when some piece of communicated information reminds you of something not immediately relevant. You may then tend to let your thoughts wander off on tangents, coming back now and again to touch the actual line of communication. By the time your thoughts once more make contact with the client's, you can never be sure that the track you are on accurately corresponds to the client's track. More often than not, it won't. Whether on the highway or in an interview, detours can get you lost. Frequent detourers are inclined to be scatterbrained; they have difficulty focusing on the problem at hand.

Arguing occurs when a client makes a statement that rankles you in some fashion and you cut off the client's line of communication to present your opinions. You are forgetting that it is the client's opinion and not yours that is the present concern. Allow clients to express and explore their feelings fully without debating them. It is important not to argue with clients, either by actually voicing your opinions or just by debating the client in your mind. Arguers tend to be either self-righteous or contentious individuals who are overly concerned with their own viewpoints.

Rehearsing occurs when, instead of continuing to attend to the client, you pause to consider how you will respond to an earlier statement. Rehearsers tend to be either unsure of themselves or perfectionists. They feel that responses are never adequate if they are not well formulated before delivery. They seek just the right word or example to make a point. The trouble is that, while you are thinking of that perfect response, you will have missed what else the client says, including things that might make your response irrelevant.

Responding: Guiding the Client's Disclosure

No matter how hard you have been listening, it is often necessary to verify a client's message so that you don't jump to wrong conclusions. When you perceive a response to be somewhat ambiguous, you should ask for *clarification*. Clarification involves a question of the type: "Are you

saying that . . . ?" or "Do you mean that . . . ?" Your request for clarification gives the client the opportunity to confirm or disconfirm your understanding. *Paraphrasing,* a simple restatement of the client's message in the interviewer's words, is similar to clarification. Paraphrasing is used to restate a message with factual content, such as a description of a person, place, event, or situation, to clarify the message, to let clients know that you've been attending, and to encourage them to focus on the content more deeply.

In contrast, *reflection* is a rephrasing of the emotional content of the client's message. Reflection is useful when you want to identify the client's feelings about the factual message presented to you. Feelings are not always expressed verbally but may be identified by nonverbal cues such as rigid body posture, reddening of the face, pursed lips, tone of voice, and so forth. The purpose of reflection is to help clients to become fully aware of their feelings and to encourage them to explore them.

A hypothetical dialogue illustrates these techniques. A 30-year-old single mother of three children, Betty has been found guilty of child endangering. Her oldest son, Jason, age 9, was hospitalized with a broken arm. A physical examination revealed that he had frequently been physically abused. You ask her to explain why she abuses Jason. Some possible interviewer responses follow her reply. Try to think of some of your own replies by imagining what it would be like in Betty's shoes.

CLIENT: I don't really know why I do these things to Jason. I do love him. I'd do anything to change things. I'm not proud of what I did. He's a beautiful boy. I guess I just get so frustrated having to bring three children up on what the welfare pays you. You know, it's no easy task trying to raise three kids. I can't get work because the kids are all so young. I just sit at home thinking about the future. I find myself drinking more heavily as time goes on. All that sitting and drinking hasn't done much for my figure. I weigh about 210 right now. Who would want to hire a slob like me? If only I could get a job, I know things would be better for us all.

INTERVIEWER: Are you saying that one of the hardest things facing you right now is your inability to get work, which would enable you to make a better life for yourself and your children? Do you mean that your situation leads you to do these things to Jason? (*Clarification.*)

INTERVIEWER: You love Jason, but your responsibility for raising your family by yourself is very difficult for you. You are having a tough time of it. (*Paraphrase.*)

INTERVIEWER: You feel frustrated and angry about your inability to take care of your children as you would like. You feel terribly guilty about doing what you did to Jason. You feel embarrassed about your weight. (*Reflection.*)

In summarizing this section on listening and questioning, I think it accurate to say that regardless of counseling orientation or the purposes of an interview, the most crucial skill of all is listening. It is the prerequisite to all other skills. After all, if you have not really listened to what your client has been saying, you cannot formulate meaningful follow-up questions, you cannot develop rapport, you cannot even begin to understand the client, and your assessment will be sloppy at best. Poor listening will frustrate and alienate clients, and you may become part of their problem rather than part of the solution.

Interviewing the Client

Preparation

The physical setting. The results of your interview will probably have a significant impact on your client's future. Recognizing the importance of this process, it is vital that you give the client your undivided attention during the time you are together. Although the physical facilities in many CJ agencies may not be ideal, it is important that the interview setting be as private and free of distractions as possible. The receptionist should be instructed to hold all nonemergency telephone calls, and a "do not disturb" sign should be displayed on your office door. Some interruptions may be inevitable, but they must never be of the personal or frivolous kind. You must convey to your clients that this time belongs to them and that they are the only topic of importance to you during this period.

Familiarity with the case. Before interviewing the client, you must thoroughly familiarize yourself with the case materials obtained from police and prosecutor's files. On the basis of these materials, you should formulate the questions that you plan to ask. A comprehensive semistructured interview schedule that is being used in probation and parole agencies nationwide is included in Chapter 6. It is an excellent tool for the beginning interviewer because it covers everything of importance for the interviewing of the typical client. The schedule will be discussed in greater depth in Chapter 6, but one point is worth mentioning now. Although the schedule begins with questions regarding clients' attitudes toward the offense and offense patterns, I very strongly feel that questions pertinent to the crime and to the client's criminal history are best left until last. These are the questions most likely to threaten the client, and they may require the use of interrogation rather than interviewing techniques. Clients will more easily answer questions about the offense and about prior offenses after friendly rapport has been established and they feel less threatened by the situation in which they find themselves.

Most probation departments use an intake form, which the client fills out prior to meeting the probation officer. This form should request basic demographic data such as name, place and date of birth, current address and telephone number, names and addresses of family members and places of work, schools attended, and the client's financial situation. It should also ask clients for pertinent medical information and a recitation of prior involvements with the law and should include a section that asks them to write out their version of the offense.

The use of such a form serves a number of functions: (1) it gives structure to the interview, (2) it sensitizes the client to the kind of questions you will be asking in more detail, (3) it provides the client with an opportunity to decide in private if he or she is going to be honest with you, (4) it gives you the opportunity to decide if the client has indeed been honest with you by checking the written statement with "the record," (5) it gives you some insight into the client's level of communications skills, and (6) it minimizes the recording of factual information (age, phone numbers, addresses, and so on) during the interview, which would detract from its smooth flow. A typical social history questionnaire is included in Chapter 6.

Initiating the Interview

A criminal justice client's first contact with a community corrections agency is usually the result of a referral to a probation department for a presentence investigation report after being adjudicated guilty of a crime. Because the presentence investigation interview is perhaps the most important interview the client will experience, we will assume in the following discussion that we are conducting such an interview. Given the circumstances of the presentence referral, it is necessary to realize that the client may probably view it as being punitive rather than as an opportunity to receive help and guidance. In light of the involuntary nature of the client's presence, and in light of the client's possible ingrained mistrust and disregard for authority, it is particularly important that the interview get off to a good start.

Meeting the client: Respect and rapport. Your first meeting with the client, who may be anxious and nervous, should convey your respect and concern. I cannot overemphasize the importance of the first contact with the client. First impressions will certainly color much of what will follow between you and your client. It is essential, then, that positive rapport be established at this time. You should greet your client by looking him or her straight in the eye and offering a smile and a firm handshake. First names should not be used at the first meeting, especially with older clients. Traditionally, the superordinate individual addressed the subordinate individual by first name, whereas the person in the inferior position was expected to use the presumed superior's full title and last name. This convention was designed to emphasize social distance, something you definitely wish to avoid. However, a more informal first-name relationship should be established as soon as you perceive that the client is amenable to it. Your initial statement should be something like "Good morning, Mr. Smith. My name is Joyce Williams. I will be your probation officer."

You have now introduced yourself and your role. Although your client is a troubled individual whom you are seeing because he or she has committed some crime of which he or she may be deeply ashamed, there must not be any hint of a patronizing, condescending, or judgmental attitude in either your voice or your nonverbal behavior. You may have extremely negative feelings about the kind of behavior that has brought the client to you. Any attempts to deny to yourself that your client's behavior elicits those feelings in you will result in an artificial, stilted, and unproductive interview. You should acknowledge to yourself that these feelings exist and that they are normal and to be expected. You should, however, also recognize that their expression in a professional goal-oriented setting is inappropriate. If you reveal your anger or embarrassment, even subtly or unconsciously, the client will pick up on your cues and perhaps respond with his or her own anger or embarrassment. Negative emotions, either yours or the client's, are not conducive to an effective interview. Professional recognition and control of personal feelings rather than denial and repression of them is a goal you should strive for.

Early in my career I had a client whose appearance and whose crime had a very negative effect on me. She had paid a number of neighborhood boys to have sex with her over a period of several months. Although I had struggled to rid myself of the sexist attitudes acquired through my socialization, I couldn't free myself of the notion that women were "simply not supposed to act that way." Consequently, I perceived her crime as being somehow much more odious than I would have if she had been a man convicted of similar behavior. Furthermore, when I met her, her physical appearance made matters worse. She was an extremely obese woman with multiple chins thickly folded upon an expansive bosom, and she had a body odor too strong to ignore.

I tried hard to respond positively to her, but, on later reflection, I realized how completely artificial I must have seemed to her. I ran through the interview and approached the embarrassing (both to her and to myself) question of her offense with insensitivity. In other words, I let my attitudes and feelings about my client obscure her basic humanity. The interview was a simple ritual. She was placed on probation to me, but our relationship never did manage to overcome our disastrous first encounter. First impressions are indeed vital! I did learn a lot about myself and my attitudes through that encounter, and I don't think I ever made the same mistake again.

My experience with this woman underscores the desirability of examining your attitudes and prejudices relating to various kinds of people and their behavior before ever having to actually deal with them in a field situation. Treat each person as a unique individual, not as a member of some larger group from whom you expect or don't expect certain ways of behaving. A colleague of mine used to have a saying on her office wall, which she said she read at the beginning of every day "to keep me honest." It said: "There is so much good in the worst of us, and so much bad in the best of us, that it ill behooves any one of us to find any fault with the rest of us."

Explaining the purpose of the interview. The actual interview should begin by asking your clients if they know the purpose of the interview. If a client doesn't know—and many don't—then the purpose should be fully explained. You should inform the client of the kind of information you wish to obtain, what it will be used for, and who will have access to it. Although an explanation of the uses to which a presentence investigation report will be put (to aid in sentencing decisions, and, if the client is incarcerated, in prison classification and parole hearings) can raise the anxiety level of a client, I have found that the honesty is appreciated.

It is a good idea at this point to ask clients if they understand what they have been told so far and if they have any questions. It is very important, however, not to respond with any opinion to such questions as "What do you think I'll get?" or "What are my chances?" Remember, you do not make the final sentencing decision, and you do not wish to raise false hopes or to generate needless anxiety. If you tell a client that you are "sure" that he or she will receive probation, and the client is incarcerated instead, that person will surely feel bitter and betrayed. One such incident may have a lasting negative effect on any subsequent dealings that client may have with you or with any other correctional worker. Conversely, if you tell a client that he or she is as good as on the bus to prison, but the client is actually placed on probation, his or her attitude toward you could be one of smug contempt: "The judge didn't buy your recommendation. Just goes to show how valuable your opinion is, doesn't it?"

Some authorities would disagree with me on this point, feeling that if incarceration seems probable, it is a humanitarian gesture to prepare the client for it. This is rather like the physician's dilemma when asked, "How long have I got?" An honest appraisal in either case, so the argument goes, gives the individual the opportunity to prepare for it by saying good-byes and putting personal affairs in order. However, in the case of a client told that he or she will probably be sent to prison, the good-byes may well be said to the jurisdiction of your state. If you do offer your client an opinion that turns out to be wrong, or if it leads the client to abscond, you have only yourself to blame for the consequences. Instead, I believe you should politely reply that you don't engage in second-guessing judges and that it is not your place to speculate. You are now ready to begin the interview proper.

Conducting the Interview

The interviewer's language and demeanor.
If you are using a client intake form, the interview is for the purpose of clarifying and elaborating on the information the client has written down. When questioning a client, you are making contact with another human being. Questions must be geared both to the client's vocabulary and to his or her pace. Legalistic or sociological jargon, street "jive talk," and ten-dollar words should be avoioided. The use of fancy phraseology will serve to embarrass the client whose vocabulary is limited and won't impress one who is as articulate as you are. Either way, it will distance your client from you. Similarly, the use of street jive is unprofessional and will give the client the idea that you are either being patronizing or playing buddy-buddy. Use conventional and easily understandable English. Just as important, do not adopt street mannerisms such as an artificially laid-back posture or the latest fad in handshakes. Don't say or do anything that is artificial to you; it will be blatantly visible to those used to being treated dishonestly.

The use of authority. A final concern is the officer's proper use of authority. Some experts in the counseling field feel that the use, or even the possession, of authority is detrimental to the helping process. I don't agree. Authority and helping can be incompatible, however, if you use and abuse authority to emphasize the moral distance between you and your client and to puff yourself up with your own importance. The bombastic "big stick" approach will serve only to alienate clients. They will immediately type you as "just another cop in social worker's threads" and will scoff at your insistence that you only want to "help" them.

Yet authority comes with the job and it cannot be denied. The failure to use your authority when appropriate will be viewed as weakness by clients who value strength and who are adept at manipulating perceived weakness. Like feelings, officers' authority must be recognized and accepted but used with professional restraint. Needless to say, the accoutrements of force, such as guns or handcuffs, should not be on display at the first meeting with the client.

Dealing with awkward clients. Some of your clients will be fearful or angry and thus will act hostile or refuse to answer certain questions. It may be that they are just trying to maintain a sense of dignity and control in the only way they know. When such an attitude becomes apparent to you, you should not continue with the interview as if you hoped that ignoring it would make it go away. Say something like "Mr. Jones, I know that this is unpleasant for you and that you must be feeling a little uptight. It's quite natural for you to feel that way, lots of people do. Why don't we agree to be civil to one another? What do you say?" This lets Mr. Jones know that you are aware of his feelings, that others have felt that way, that you accept his feelings as natural, and that you are willing to start over again on a new footing.

In those rare instances when clients continue to refuse to answer questions, or when they continue to respond in a sarcastic, rude, or abrupt manner, you must let them know in no uncertain terms that this kind of attitude is simply unacceptable. You must inform them that if they continue in such a way, then the interview will be terminated and that it will be necessary for them to return to the department to try again after they have rethought their approach. You may also indicate that such an attitude will be conveyed to the sentencing judge if it continues. If this tactic doesn't work, try a phone call to the client's attorney outlining the problem; I have found that it never fails to bring about a change in the client's demeanor.

Most often, however, clients are anxious to be cooperative and to convey a positive impression during the initial interview. They are feeling you out just as surely as you are feeling them out. Most clients are aware that their attitudes will be reported to the judge and that they may influence your recommendation. Reluctance and uncooperativeness are much more common among clients under actual supervision than they are prior to formal supervision. The presentence investigator and the parole board usually see clients at their best. It is the supervising probation and parole officers who are most frequently confronted with uncooperative clients. For this reason, it is of the utmost importance that the groundwork be laid for the development of a trusting relationship at the initial interview, a period in which the client's frame of mind is most conducive to it. (The problem of the reluctant client is addressed in more detail in Chapter 8.)

Regardless of the client's level of cooperation, his or her overall demeanor will provide you with valuable clues for your assessment. Someone who comes to the interview smelling of alcohol or under the influence of drugs isn't exactly taking the process very seriously and will obviously be difficult to supervise if placed on probation. A servile or arrogant manner will also provide clues to assessment of character and possible supervision strategies.

Such observations will assist you in designing a preliminary plan of treatment and will help you to decide if a referral to a specialized agency, such as those listed and described in Chapter 13, is in order. When you decide that a referral is advisable, you should discuss the matter with the client and explain your reasoning. Don't antagonize the client or put the client on the defensive by flatly stating that he or she has a problem. Try to steer clients toward that conclusion themselves by asking them how the problem you perceive them as having affects their relationships with others and how they would feel if they could find support in controlling the problem. You may then discuss the services provided by the agency in question and the benefits clients may derive from talking with a counselor there. Again, I cannot emphasize enough that the initial interview is positively your best opportunity to get your foot in the door to obtain a client's cooperation and compliance.

Terminating the Interview

At the end of the interview, summarize what has gone on during it. Your summary provides the opportunity to determine if anything important has been overlooked and gives the client the chance to change, clarify, or add to transmitted information. Ask the client if he or she has anything to add or anything else to ask. If not, you may conclude the interview, shake the client's hand, inform the client that you will be in touch in the near future, and walk him or her to the door. Back in your office again, you should immediately go over your notes and write down additional impressions while they are fresh in your mind. The results of your interview should also decide for you what collateral interviews will be necessary.

Interviewing the Victim

Preparation

Your first approach to the victim should be a phone call to make an appointment. You should explain the reason for your wish to meet personally with the victim and set up a time at his or her convenience. In order to relieve victims of any further inconvenience, and as a courtesy, the meeting should take place in the victim's home unless he or she wishes otherwise. When you meet with the victim, you should identify yourself as an officer of the court by presenting your credentials. You may then restate the purpose of the interview. Some victims welcome the opportunity to speak about the crime again in the informal and familiar setting of their own homes. But for some it is a nuisance that they would rather avoid. Make an effort to let the victim know that your presence indicates the concern of the legal system about his or her experience and that it is an opportunity to have some input into the sentencing process. This assurance tends to ease some of the pain and anger of all except the most cynical, and it returns a sense of control to those victims who feel that they have lost much of it by their victimization.

Personal criminal victimization is an intensely negative experience. Even if the crime was a nonviolent one in which the victim never had to confront the offender, the experience can leave a person with feelings of complete helplessness and violation. These feelings quite naturally tend to generate anger and a certain measure of self-blame, the latter especially among victims of sexual assault. The typical experience of the victim as the case progresses through the courts, sometimes involving interminable delays and postponements, does nothing to mitigate these feelings. Some of that anger and self-blame may be displaced onto the presentence investigator. You should be prepared to encounter such a natural reaction and to deal with it in a sensitive manner.

Your most trying experiences in the field may be to conduct interviews with parents who have lost a child to a drunken driver or with relatives of loved ones who have been brutally raped or murdered. Extreme sensitivity and understanding are absolute musts in such instances. In no case should you imply sympathy for the offender or any suggestion that the victim may have contributed to his or her own victimization even if the thoughts are in your mind, and never argue with a victim or the victim's survivors. An investigator should possess a self-concept strong enough to allow victims or their survivors to vent their anger on him or her without retaliation.

When Not to Interview

The matter of interviewing child victims of sexual abuse is entirely different. I learned early in my career to avoid absolutely any contact with such victims. It is not merely uncomfortable for a child to recount the episode; it may add to the psychological damage the child suffers. Henry Hartman, a criminal psychiatrist of many years' experience, puts it this way (1978:217): "Intense emotional reactions on the part of the parents, repeated questioning by police, unpleasant appearances and cross-examination in courtrooms may all be as traumatic or even more traumatic than the offense itself." There is no point in risking further trauma for the sake of a little additional insight into the offense. I have seen children who, even after long-term sexual victimization by adults, have suffered no ill effects until the relationships were discovered and the children subjected to

responses like those Hartman names. Such social reactions lead children to believe that much or all of the blame for what transpired belongs to them. Certainly it does not, and the investigating officer should not call up the child's residual feelings of guilt and shame in the pursuit of a "complete" PSI. Parents of the children should, of course, be interviewed and allowed to discuss the effects of the offense on their children.

Conducting the Interview

Asking for details of the offense. It is not advisable to request the details of the offense from victims in all cases. They have already recounted them numerous times to other officials, and the retelling may be quite painful for them. You should, however, offer them the opportunity to speak about the offense if they want to. You might say something like "I know this has been an awful experience for you and you would probably like to forget it, but is there anything at all that you would like to add that you didn't tell the police or the prosecutor?" In posing the question this way you have conveyed to the victim your recognition of his or her ordeal, and you have given the victim the option of elaborating. The decision must be entirely the victim's, and the officer should not press the issue in the face of obvious reluctance.

Reassuring the victim. One of the things that crime victims need most is reassurance of their safety. Many victims fear retaliation or worry that a burglar will come back. In my experience as a police officer and as a probation officer, I have never known a perpetrator to retaliate against the victim after the case had been adjudicated or a burglar to hit the same house twice. This is not to say that such things don't happen, but they are extremely rare. You should make a clear statement to this effect to frightened victims. In the event that the victim and offender are known to each other, you may even indicate that in the event that the perpetrator is placed on probation, you will make it a condition of probation that he or she is to have no contact of any sort with the victim. Victims need to hear such reassurances.

Promises to the victim.   It is important that you not make any promises to the victim that you cannot keep or make statements regarding the defendant's probable sentence. Some states have made provisions for victims to have input into the sentencing of those who have offended against them. If your state has a statutory provision for a victim's recommendation for sentencing, you should, of course, request one. Whether these recommendations actually have an impact on sentencing decisions is a question awaiting a body of research. My own recent research indicated a statistically significant relationship between victim's recommendations and sentences imposed in sexual assault cases. But the relationship disappeared when I controlled for the effects of seriousness of crime and offender's prior record (Walsh, 1986). Future research may show different results. Whatever the case may be, don't lead the victim into the belief that his or her recommendation will necessarily be heeded. Be as honest with victims as you are with offenders. Don't risk victims' future anger and disrespect for the sake of their momentary peace of mind and satisfaction. Specific questions that you should ask the victim are listed in the next chapter on the PSI report.

Terminating the Interview

You should terminate the interview with the victim by reiterating your assurances and thanking the victim for his or her cooperation. You should give the victim your card and invite him or her to call you with further concerns at any time in the future. This invitation will probably be viewed by the victim as a further indication that he or she is not the forgotten party in the criminal justice process. Finally, if it is not the practice of the prosecutor's office in your jurisdiction to apprise victims of sentencing dates, you might tell victims that you will notify them personally. At the very least, you should inform the victim of the final disposition of the case.

Interrogating the Client

Reasons for Interrogation

When clients break the law or some condition of their supervision, or are suspected of doing so, it is your duty to question them. Your questioning under such circumstances will require a different strategy from that of interviewing. We call this type of questioning *interrogation.*

Most jurisdictions legally define their probation and parole officers as law enforcement officers. As a law enforcement officer, you will be responsible for monitoring the behavior of your clients. To those who enter the community corrections field with the notion that their only role is that of a helper, this definition is sometimes distasteful, probably because they associate interrogation with the third-degree tactics of yesteryear. You must not lose sight of the fact that you are functioning both as a law enforcement officer and as a counselor, but those two roles do not necessarily conflict. As a law enforcement officer, you may sometimes have to use the techniques of interrogation. For instance, you may need to learn the truth about acts committed by your clients that place them in violation of their probation or parole. Clients do not readily admit to violations. You are not doing justice to your role, or ultimately to your clients, if you don't learn and deal with details of their violations.

You may also need to interrogate a client during a PSI interview if the client flatly denies having committed the crime of which he or she has just been convicted. This is not as unusual as one might expect. An unpublished study at the department in which I worked found that 18% of a sample of 416 clients denied their crimes during the PSI interview. Since denial has implications for decisions about sentencing and treatment, it behooves the investigating officer not to report simply that the client denies the crime and leave it at that. Many clients will tell you that they are innocent and that they pled guilty on their lawyer's advice, or that they did so in order to obtain a plea-bargain agreement. Although it is not unknown for innocent clients to plead guilty because their lawyers have considered the case against them to be too strong, the fact that the case is now before you makes the possibility rather remote. Given the legal restraints on police questioning (restraints that you do not have in the PSI situation) and the defendant's privilege of silence in court, your interrogation may be the first opportunity to get to the truth of the matter. In my own experience, I would estimate that about one out of every four clients who initially denied their guilt finally admitted it under questioning and at least two of the others made statements that were sufficient to dispel doubts of guilt in my mind.

Interrogation is a thorough investigation of a specific allegation brought against a suspect through the use of systematic and formal questioning. There are two basic differences between interviewing and interrogation. The first concerns your relationship with the client. You have temporarily discarded the helping attitude of the counselor and adopted the skeptical manner of the law enforcement officer. The second concerns purpose. Interviewing has the broad goal of gathering general information, whereas interrogation involves the drawing out of quite specific information, which the client may be highly motivated to keep hidden—namely, whether your client did or did not commit the act you, the police, or some other party accuses him or her of committing.

The interrogation is also different from the interviewing process in that it requires that the interrogator, not the client, control the flow of activity. You must control the timing, content, and wording of your questioning with your singular purpose in mind. Suspect clients must be given only enough initiative and control to allow them to relate their stories. They must come to understand that you mean business and that for the moment you are not interested in anything else but the question at hand.

Preparation

Preparing yourself for an interrogation is both different from and similar to preparing for an interview. The major difference is that an interrogation is often a battle of wits, and the atmosphere can be highly charged because the client is aware of that fact. If you are to conduct an effective interrogation, by which I mean one that will lead you to the truth regarding the matter at hand, you have to approach the task with confidence. You must also convey an impression of confidence to the client. To achieve this level of confidence, you must be fully prepared: you must be completely familiar with all the evidence supporting the client's guilt, as well as any evidence that might indicate otherwise. Depending on the situation, such evidence might include police reports, victim statements, or information from an informant. Not having all the information that is available to you will put you at a serious disadvantage once the interrogation begins.

Conducting the Interrogation

The interrogation may take place in your office or it may take place in a cell at the county jail. In any case, as the client's supervising officer you will, unlike a police officer, have had an ongoing relationship with him or her. Consequently, you are able to dispense with the usual police lead-ins to interrogation, such as requests for demographic information (name, address, place of employment, and so on). You should greet the client in a friendly but businesslike manner and inform him or her of your purpose by saying something like "Jim, I've asked you to come to see me (or, I've come to see you) to get to the bottom of this matter that has come to my attention." You may then begin your questioning.

Confidence. Confidence in your professionalism and in your preparation is of the utmost importance. A lack of confidence, reflected by frequently referring back to reports, hemming and hawing around, squirming in your chair, acting impatient, and so forth, will convey the impression to the client that perhaps the evidence against him or her is not very strong. You should demonstrate to the client that the evidence that is in your possession leads you to the firm conviction that he or she is guilty. This conviction should be stated in a nonemotional and clinical manner. The credibility of the interrogator depends on these two points: the interrogator's thorough knowledge of the matter under discussion and the client's perceptions of him or her as a competent professional. Do not jeopardize the positive relationship that you have worked so hard to gain with your client by becoming frustrated and angry because you feel that you cannot break down his or her defenses.

Style. Despite the goal differences between interviewing and interrogation, much that we have said about interviewing also applies to the process of interrogation. First and foremost, you must approach the task in a completely professional manner. Any attempts to borrow the techniques of the movie detective will prove disastrous. Don't put up a "tough guy" front. The typical criminal will see through this and match you verbal blow for verbal blow, a competition that could well end up being decided in favor of clients who rely on such tactics to survive every day of their lives. If this happens, you reveal yourself as a phoney, and you can kiss any respect that your client may have had for you good-bye.

Neither should you adopt the attitude of "NIGYSOB" ("Now I've got you, you son-of-a-bitch") described by Eric Berne (1964) in his book *Games People Play.* If you project such an obviously self-satisfied attitude to clients undergoing interrogation, you are in effect issuing a challenge and inviting resistance. You also imply that your objective all along has been to "get" your client rather than to help your client.

Ask leading questions. Within the context of an interrogation your questions will often be of the *leading* type. A leading question is one in which the wording strongly encourages a specific answer (this kind of question should never be used in an interview). For example, you receive a complaint from Jim's estranged wife that he was drinking last night and that he went over to her home and slapped her around. Jim's parole conditions include maintaining sobriety and staying away from his wife. You may confront Jim with "You were in the Western Bar drinking last night, weren't you? Isn't it also true that you became drunk and went over to your wife's home and beat her up?" Such questions, asked in a businesslike tone, have the psychological effect of making it more difficult to deny than a simple "Were you drinking last night?"

Reveal a little information. You should reinforce both your confidence and the client's anxiety by revealing some of the evidence you have that is indicative of guilt or, in a PSI situation, some of the evidence gathered by police agencies, taking careful note of how the client deals with the information. However, you should not reveal all evidence in one giant salvo. If the client successfully weathers the initial attack, you have nothing left in reserve with which to surprise him or her. Always keep clients on the defensive by letting them guess at the extent of the evidence in your possession. Point out inconsistencies in their stories and ask them to account for them (you cannot do this if you have not thoroughly assimilated the "official" version and paid complete attention to the client's version).

Some clients will respond to a straightforward statement from you indicating that alibis or protestations of innocence are "bullshit." On more than one occasion I have been confronted with a knowing smile, followed by the real story, after such a remark. This usually works with a client who has been through the system before and who tends to regard what is going on between you as some sort of game. This, of course, depends on the seriousness of the consequences to the client of making such an admission. Other clients will react defensively to this kind of direct statement. With such clients, it is preferable to state, "You haven't told me the whole truth," rather than saying, "You've been lying to me." The difference is a subtle one, but a real one nevertheless. Only experience will tell you when each approach is preferable. Usually, however, the latter method works best with the more "respectable" and less street-wise clients.

Let clients damn themselves. It is often a good ploy to allow the client to make statements that you know are lies and to give the impression that you are accepting them at face value. The awkward thing about a lie is that it requires additional lies to support it. Eventually, this compounding of falsehoods should paint the client into a very uncomfortable corner from which the only out is the truth. If you allow clients to get themselves into such a psychologically untenable position and then point out a series of inconsistencies, you have created a strong motive (the removal of psychological discomfort) for clients to "come clean."

Take advantage of client discomfort. If the tactic of trapping clients in their own falsehoods does not provide the desired admission, you should point out signs of guilt, such as confusion, stammering, nervous sweating, and other emotional reactions, interpreting them as indications of guilt. You should take advantage of such signs of physiological discomfort by looking the client squarely in the eye and repeating some of your most threatening questions. You may also ask the client to repeat his or her story three or four times at different points in the interrogation. It is easy to be consistent if the story is true, but it is very difficult to remember little details that are used to support a falsehood. That is, you can tell the truth in four different ways, but it is hard to do the same with a lie. Knowing that you are aware of their discomfort often prompts clients to unburden themselves by making a confession.

Bluffing. Bluffing is a weak form of interrogation. *Bluffing* means conveying to clients the impression that you have access to information that is damaging to them when, in fact, you do not. For instance, you may be interrogating Jack on the basis of police information that he has been trafficking in drugs. You may indicate to him that you have "accurate" information from "confidential informants" that he has been selling drugs. Bluffs such as this may pay off in large dividends, but they are more likely to be called. If Jack calls your bluff, all you can do is withdraw as gracefully

as possible. What if he really is not guilty of trafficking? Your crude "poker" tactics will sorely offend him and perhaps do irreparable damage to the supportive relationship you have been seeking to develop with him. The cost/benefit ratio of such tactics does not recommend their use. Be honest with your clients; it's always the best policy.

The "back door" approach. Some authorities on police interrogation advocate a "back door" approach to interrogation; that is, prompting a confession from a suspect by downplaying the seriousness of the offense the individual is suspected of committing, conveying sympathy and "understanding" of why such a crime would be committed under the circumstances, placing the burden of blame on victims or accomplices, or intimating that the act was perhaps accidental. Although I have used such an approach as a police officer, I do not advocate it for the corrections worker. Using this psychological ploy obtains confessions by reducing the suspects' feeling of guilt. It tells them that their actions were not really so bad, that others would do the same thing in their shoes, and that they can share the blame. Although this device suits police purposes by clearing crimes, it is counterproductive to the correctional goal. Rehabilitation is not accomplished by providing offenders with easy rationales for their actions. The correctional worker must always be aware of his or her dual role and should not compromise one part of it to satisfy the immediate requirements of the other.

Terminating the Interrogation

The way you terminate the interrogation will depend on the circumstances. If the interrogation was necessitated by a technical violation of conditions of supervision, such as associating with known criminals, continued substance abuse, or failing to report to you, you may take discretionary action. You may feel it necessary to initiate formal proceedings for the revocation of probation or parole, or you may decide to resume your helping relationship. If the interrogation resulted from an arrest for a new crime, any further action on your part has to await formal adjudication.

You should inform the client of your next step as soon as you have decided what it is to be. You may be able to notify the client of your decision then and there, or you may feel it necessary to investigate further and think the matter over before declaring your intentions. In any case, you should explain your decision to the client and your reasons for making it. Regardless of what that decision might be, you should make every effort to reestablish your working relationship with the client. Even if you have decided to initiate revocation proceedings, most clients realize that you are only doing your job and will not permanently alienate themselves from you if you have dealt fairly, honestly, and professionally with them.

◑ Exercise in Listening and Interviewing

This is an exercise in listening using the CMC (Client Management Classification) semistructured interview schedule, which is reproduced in Chapter 6. Although this exercise will serve to familiarize you with the type of questions asked in a typical PSI interview, the main purpose for the present is to provide experience in listening. Did you ever buy a lottery ticket or bet on a ball game and then listen for the results on the radio? Think back to that time and how you listened to the results. If you are like me, you sat close to the radio and faced it with intense interest. You leaned toward it, and you were impervious to all other stimuli surrounding you. That's how you should proceed with this exercise—with intensity and interest.

Students should be divided into groups of two, with one student taking the part of the interviewer and the other the interviewee. Rather than role playing, the interviewee should relate to the interviewer actual aspects of his or her life. For instance, when asked "How do (did) you get along with your father?" the interviewee should respond accurately with reference to his or her own father. You should ask the questions provided in the schedule, but you should, when appropriate, use probes, ask open-ended questions, request clarification, paraphrase responses, and reflect feelings.

On the basis of the interview, you should write a brief social history of your partner (a PSI without offense, criminal history, and evaluation and recommendation material) based on the information obtained from him or her. After writing this history, give it to the interviewee for evaluation. The interviewee should evaluate the history and your interviewing performance according to the following criteria:

1. Eye contact was maintained without gazing or staring. Yes ___ No ___

2. Body posture was appropriate (relaxed, slight forward lean). Yes ___ No ___

3. He/she made me feel comfortable and relaxed. Yes ___ No ___

4. By the use of probes, he/she made me really think about things that I haven't thought about for some time. Yes ___ No ___

5. He/she seemed to be genuinely interested in me. Yes ___ No ___

6. He/she delivered questions without hesitations. Yes ___ No ___

7. He/she often asked for clarification and often paraphrased. Yes ___ No ___

8. He/she accurately reflected my feelings. Yes ___ No ___

9. I felt that I could tell him/her just about anything he/she asked about my personal life. Yes ___ No ___

10. On a scale of 1 to 10, I would rate his/her reported accuracy of my social history as 1 2 3 4 5 6 7 8 9 10 (circle one).

After each student has taken a turn at being both the interviewer and interviewee, you should share ratings with one another. Ratings should be the honest evaluations of the rater and not excuse poor technique with false compliments. The interviewer should accept constructive feedback for what it is. Think of it as another exercise in self-disclosure in which your partner has revealed something of your "blind self"—in this case, your ability to conduct an effective interview. The benefits of these exercises will be greatly enhanced if you have access to a video recorder so that you can receive visual and audio feedback of your interview behavior. Don't forget that this is your first attempt, but do learn from it.

Summary

This chapter has introduced you to the techniques of interviewing and interrogation—two skills that must be a part of your repertoire. You should prepare for both tasks by thoroughly familiarizing yourself with all the pertinent information available. An effective interview must begin by establishing rapport. This is particularly important in criminal justice, for clients are not exactly enthusiastic about being in your office. Your clients are convicted criminals, but they are also human beings who are deserving of consideration and respect. Make them as comfortable as possible, and show that you are concerned and are willing to listen to them.

Listening, really listening, is the most important aspect of an effective interview. Give the client the "air time," and resist interruptions and debates—the interview time belongs to the client. Clients must be encouraged to explore themselves and their behavior. You can encourage exploration through the frequent use of probes and open-ended questions. Make sure that you understand what your clients are trying to tell you by using paraphrasing, clarification, and reflective techniques. Even the most awkward of clients will settle down and provide lots of valuable information for your assessment if you treat them with patience and respect, but also with firmness when it is required.

Interviewing victims requires a special sensitivity to their victimization. Any reluctance on their part to be interviewed or to approach certain subjects should be respected absolutely. Do not dig for details of sexual offenses. I also consider it extremely unadvisable to interview child victims of sexual assault. Never argue with victims about anything, and don't upset yourself if they sometimes use you as a convenient target for their verbal anger. Reassure victims as much as possible, but don't make any promises that are not within your power to keep.

Sometimes interrogation techniques are required. Any interrogation should be approached in a calm, clinical, and professional manner. Unlike the interview, in which the purpose is to gather large amounts of general information, the interrogation is geared to one specific aim: answering the question "Did you do it?" Furthermore, you rather than the client will control the content and pace of the interrogation. Know the evidence supportive of your client's guilt, but don't jeopardize your relationship with your client by coming on like the movie detective. Useful interrogation techniques include letting clients damn themselves and taking advantage of client discomfort. Use these recommended techniques when it is necessary for you to interrogate, but above all, be honest and fair with the client, and be yourself.

References and Suggested Readings

Aubry, A., and R. Caputo (1965). *Criminal Interrogation*. Springfield, IL: Charles C Thomas.

Benjamin, A. (1981). *The Helping Interview*. Boston: Houghton Mifflin.

Berne, E. (1964). *Games People Play.* New York: Grove Press.

Egan, G. (1986). *The Skilled Helper.* Pacific Grove, CA: Brooks/Cole.

Garrett, A. (1982). *Interviewing: Its Principles and Methods.* New York: Family Services Association of America.

Goyer, R., C. Redding, and J. Rickey (1968). *Interviewing Principles and Techniques.* Dubuque, IA: William C. Brown.

Hartman, H. (1963). "Interviewing techniques in probation and parole." *Federal Probation* (series of four articles: March, June, September, and December).

Hartman, H. (1978). *Basic Psychiatry for Corrections Workers.* Springfield, IL: Charles C Thomas.

Ivey, A. (1983). *Intentional Interviewing and Counseling.* Pacific Grove, CA: Brooks/Cole.

Kleinke, C. (1975). *First Impressions: The Psychology of Encountering Others.* Englewood Cliffs, NJ: Prentice-Hall.

Reik, T. (1956). *Listening with the Third Ear.* New York: Grove Press.

Walsh, A. (1986). "Placebo justice: Victim recommendations and offender sentences in sexual assault cases." *Journal of Criminal Law and Criminology,* 77:1126–1141.

Wicks, R. (1974). *Applied Psychology for Law Enforcement Officers and Correctional Officers.* New York: McGraw-Hill.

Chapter 5
The Presentence Investigation Report

The presentence investigation is the first step in the attempt to correct the offender's behavior. . . . It requires great skill in the study, evaluation, and supervision of offenders; familiarity with community resources; and an understanding of their subculture.

Harvey Treger

The presentence investigation report is the end product of the interviews you have completed with the offender, the victim, arresting police officers, and other interested parties. The quality and usefulness of the report depend on how well you have conducted your interviews and how well you can summarize and communicate a voluminous amount of material, making a reasoned selection of pertinent information from the mass available to you. You must learn to discriminate between information that is necessary to know and information that is merely nice to know. Too much unnecessary material will clutter the report and confuse the reader. I have seen reports liberally padded with trivia that add nothing to the understanding of the client and cloud the issue of sentencing decisions. Studies exploring the decision-making process have shown an inverse relationship between the sheer weight of data and appropriate or useful decisions (Nettler, 1970). Would you, if you were the sentencing judge, want to read a 15-page report full of irrelevancies when you had perhaps ten other reports to read?

Good report writing is an art that flows from practice and feedback from classroom instructors, co-workers, supervisors, and judges. There is no easy substitute for the twin processes of practice and feedback. However, a discussion of specific content areas of the PSI report should lay the groundwork for the writing of thorough, factual, concise, readable, and useful PSI reports.

Uses of the PSI Report

A brief review of the uses to which a PSI report is put will underline the importance of making sure that your reports exhibit those attributes. Functions they fulfill fall within the general areas of decision-making aids and treatment aids.

• *Judicial sentencing decisions.* Presentence investigations for the purpose of aiding the judge in the selection of appropriate case dispositions serve the positivist philosophy of individualized justice. Probation officers are charged with the task of putting this philosophy into practice by presenting to the courts their assessments of "individualized" offenders and making sentencing recommendations consistent with those assessments. Numerous studies have shown that probation officers have been spectacularly successful in gaining judicial compliance with their recommendations (Hagan, 1975; Myers, 1979; Walsh, 1984, 1985a). Given that these recommendations, which should flow naturally from the information contained in the PSI report, can have a profound effect on an individual's life, it is imperative that they accurately reflect the facts.

• *Departmental and institutional classification.* Diagnostic information contained in the PSI report is used by probation departments to determine the supervision level of clients placed on probation. Information such as prior supervisions, arrest record, attitude, needs and risk assessments, and the nature of the crime are quantified on a scale (such as the risk and needs scales to be examined later) to determine the type and frequency of supervision. If the client is incarcerated, his or her medical, psychological, and criminal history, as well as vocational and educational information, are used by the institution as an aid in determining security level, work assignments, and vocational, educational, and counseling needs.

• *Parole decisions.* The PSI report accompanies the client to the institution and, in addition to classification, is used as an aid to parole-release decisions. The parole officer to whom the client is released also uses information contained in the PSI report in formulating initial treatment and supervision plans. In the case of parole revocation decisions, PSI information is used as a baseline to gauge the offender's progress (or lack of it) since his or her initial assessment.

• *Counseling plans and community agency referrals.* The treatment plans outlined in the PSI report are used for the guidance of the probation officer who is supervising the client (it may or may not be the officer who wrote the report). They also aid the officer in making appropriate referrals to agencies that deal with any specific problems of the client that are beyond the officer's purview or expertise. The information contained in the PSI report is then used by the receiving agency as a planning guide, relieving the agency of the necessity of gathering duplicate information. Such information should not be provided to the agency, however, without the written consent of the client.

Sample PSI Report

An actual PSI report is presented on pp. 56–61 to illustrate its areas of content. Bear its uses in mind as you examine it. Names, locations, and circumstances have been altered sufficiently to protect anonymity. This particular report was selected because of its excellent quality and because it illustrates some interesting applications of the theories we have examined or will examine. Please realize that I am not using this report to validate these theories in any way but, rather, to illustrate them.

Discussion of Sample Report

We will explain, section by section, the kind of information required in each section of the PSI report. Then we will comment on each content area using examples from the Bloggs PSI.

Circumstances of Offense

It has been estimated that approximately 90% of all felony cases are disposed of through plea negotiations rather than by trial. Consequently, the sentencing judge is often quite unaware of the

THE ADRIAN COUNTY ADULT PROBATION DEPARTMENT
LOWMAN, IDAHO
PRESENCE REPORT

NAME: William (Bill) Bloggs
ADDRESS: Currently in Adrian County Jail
   Formerly: 780 N 30th, Lowman, ID
AGE: 26; DOB 7-25-58
SEX: male
RACE: white
PENDING CASES/DETAINERS: none
OFFENSE:
Aggravated Robbery
IRC # 2911.01
Attempted Murder
IRC # 2923.02

JUDGE: Joseph B. Lynch

INDICTMENT # 84-3457

ATTORNEY: S. Bonnetti

MARITAL STATUS: married
DEPENDENTS: none

DATE: October 19, 1984
PROBATION
   OFFICER: Paul Corrick

CIRCUMSTANCES OF OFFENSE

On 6-13-84, at approximately 1:30 A.M., the defendant entered the Big Man Restaurant, located at 1324 Main St., through an open rear door and announced his intention of robbing said establishment. Armed with a .38 caliber pistol, the defendant ordered the manager to fill a bag embossed with the Lowman College seal, which he had brought with him, with the day's takings. The manager, Barry Harbourne, complied with the demand and filled the bag with cash totaling $1,203.32. The defendant then picked up the bag and exited through the back door. As soon as he left the restaurant, Mr. Harbourne called the police to the scene. Upon leaving the scene, the defendant stopped to remove his sweater, gloves, and the face mask he was wearing. The police arrived as he was doing this and spotted him. At this point, the defendant saw them and started to run. The police ordered him to stop. He did not heed this warning and kept on running. The police were firing at him as he ran. The defendant returned the fire with two rounds, one shot hitting Patrolman Williams in the leg. The defendant was able to elude the pursuing officers at this time. However, the police found a 1976 Buick Special parked three buildings east of the Big Man registered to the defendant. In making good his escape, the defendant dropped the bag containing the money and a number of personal artifacts. The bag was the aforementioned Lowman College bag containing a man's wallet with the defendant's driver's license and other identification inside. The gun was found in the grass in a storm ditch across from Ray's Auto Supply Store, located at 1200 Main.

The defendant, accompanied by his attorney, turned himself in to the Lowman police the next morning and made a full confession. He confessed to the present offense, as well as to two previous robberies of the same establishment, and one at the Big Man Restaurant at State and Glover on 4–12–84.

STATEMENT OF THE DEFENDANT

The defendant wrote out his statement for this officer. It was decided that it should be reproduced verbatim in order to preserve its flavor.

"On the morning of June 13, 1984, I robbed the Big Man Restaurant. In order to understand why I needed the money, first we should examine my childhood in order to find some underlying reason(s) for my behavior. Our family had a farm and a dog food processing business. The family hobby was hunting and trapping, totally our father's idea. The family businesses left very little time for our parents to be parents, they were most always in the position of boss.

"During the years previous to meeting the woman who became my wife (she was not my first girlfriend), I did not see myself in any real one-to-one loving relationships. Even the pets I had would be taken from me, eventually I learned not to become attached to anything for fear it would be taken away. Death of something which I had compassion for never received mourning—the family was conditioned against it. The dog food processing experience also made me cold in the need for caring relationships with anything. The horses I saw were many times slaughtered, shot before my very eyes, then we as a family would skin, bone, grind up and package the meat. We even killed and trapped animals for "sport." The business would have been great if adults did all the work.

"I never became close friends with any girls until after I graduated from high school. Never really finding anyone who cared as much for me as I cared for them until I met Susan, it became an obsession for me to please her, at times I probably ran her life. I hated her to work so she quit a good job as a secretary. I don't think she ever asked for anything that she didn't get. Now we both admit that our direction was wrong, and we have done something about it. We have sold many of our possessions and she has a job. She still does not want to work and I don't like the idea but it's part of reality—Bill cannot make enough money! Never again will I work third shift and regular weekends, I was so busy working I did not know what was happening to my brain. The more money I made the more I spent and the more I felt the need for money, which was not real but imagined.

"Since my imprisonment, we have sadly learned the need for Susan to lose Bill, if not through imprisonment then through death. Shortly after I was arrested, Susan had a life reading, and one of the results has been this realization that she would lose Bill. In a past life she lost me through death very early, and has past Karma to overcome. I am sure of the need for Bill's punishment to correct the Karma he has for his crimes. I also know that Bill had the choice to do what he did or not to do it. What Bill does not know is this, how would Susan correct her Karma if I were not imprisoned. Would I die? This is a good question. What I have done is not easily forgivable, but I know that when I'm free, Bill will grow and hopefully will still have Susan to grow with him. I have been saved from a terrible future, no one was killed but many were hurt and hurt seriously and it will take a lot of hard work to correct the mistakes, I hope I have the chance to correct them—in this life."

It will be gleaned from the above statement that the defendant is interested in mysticism and paranormal phenomena. The "life reading" to which he refers is retrogressive hypnosis. This technique supposedly takes the client back into his or her past to elicit memories buried in the subconscious. The true initiate apparently believes that this even extends to prior existences in other times and places. The defendant believes that he lived before in what he called the "horse and buggy" days. In that life, he and his wife reversed sex roles; i.e., the defendant was the female and his wife was the male. The defendant stated that he died of a brain tumor at the age of 35 on his last sojourn on earth. He/"she" was also a robber in that life. The combination of his early death and his antisocial career drove his wife/"husband" to alcoholism (I wonder if he is not projecting his perceptions of his wife's possible reactions to his current predicament into this story). He feels that the "bad Karma" built up by their actions in the former life has to be worked out in this one.

Karma is an ethereal "something" which automatically adheres to the perpetrator of an evil act (something akin to sin). It must be canceled or "worked off" by a positive act which has a measure of good proportionate to the evil of the negative act. If this is not accomplished, the self is caught up in an endless cycle of birth and death. This belief, so the defendant states, enables him to tie everything he has done in this life to past lives of himself and his wife. He says that prison is necessary for him to equilibrate his "bad Karma." He wants to do volunteer work in the prison and upon his release to build up his reserve of "good Karma."

Although the defendant has a teleological view of life, he does not claim that he was "fated" to commit his crimes. He stated that "Bill has the free will that he was blessed with" (it is interesting to note that he often referred to himself in the third person. It is as though he disassociates himself and views himself as an object apart from himself). He did occasionally lapse into fatalistic explanations. For instance, when asked how he was able to elude capture and avoid getting hit by police

(continued)

fire, his eyes turned heavenward, and he replied with a cryptic "them." Who "them" are was not made clear.

Notwithstanding the interesting story he tells, at bottom, the reason he committed the robberies was simply that he "needed" more money than he was making in order to indulge his wife's expensive tastes.

STATEMENT OF VICTIM (Patrolman Fredrick Williams)
Patrolman Williams stated that he and his partner responded to a robbery call at the Big Man Restaurant at about 1:30 A.M. on the morning of 6–13–84. As they came upon the scene, he noticed the defendant in a field taking off his sweater. The defendant fled as he and his partner approached, and he refused to stop when ordered to do so. Williams was chasing the defendant on foot when the defendant turned and fired two shots, one of which struck Williams in the leg. Patrolman Williams stated that his wound required six weeks off work and two weeks' light duty. When asked his opinion of the defendant, and what he thought should happen to him, Williams replied: "The guy's sick; he needs help. As far as I'm concerned, you can put him away for 80 years."

PRIOR RECORD   BIR # 234569   FBI # 356 953 V1
Juvenile:
Adrian County juvenile authorities report no juvenile record.
Adult:
    6–14–84 LPD (a) Attempted Murder (b) Aggravated Robbery—present offenses.
            Two other counts of Aggravated Robbery nolled in CR84-4357.
            One count of Aggravated Robbery nolled in CR84-4358
    LCPD, BCI, FBI and Juvenile record checks made and received.

FAMILY AND MARITAL HISTORY
The defendant is the youngest of four children born to James and Mary Bloggs. The defendant, up until his marriage, lived his entire life on the family farm located at Box 3123, Rural Route 10, 4Elko, ID. Information received from the defendant's wife and certain of his siblings revealed that his childhood was characterized by excessive work demands, physical abuse, and forced incestuous relationships with his sisters. Details of the above are contained elsewhere in this report. It is quite clear that the entire Bloggs family was under the strict and uncompromising figure of Mr. Bloggs. The defendant had very little time to pursue any personal interests that he may have had, always having to acquiesce to the wishes of his father. His whole life evidently revolved around the family business, which he despised.

The defendant's older sister related that her father was "absolutely livid" when he found out that her mother was pregnant with the defendant. He did not even visit his wife in the hospital during her confinement. She further stated that the defendant would often get blamed for things he did not do, and was made to feel unwanted. She went on to relate how both the defendant and his older brother were bed-wetters up to a relatively late age, and that her father would "hog-tie" them and keep them lying in bed in their urine all day. Interestingly, the defendant denied a history of enuresis to court psychologists as if to block out all memory of these extremely unpleasant occurrences.

The defendant left home at the age of 22 to take up residence with his girlfriend, now his wife, Susan Overton. This marriage took place on 9–15–84 in the Adrian County Jail. In an interview with Susan at this office, she described herself as an "old fashioned" type who did not wish to go out to work. She described the defendant as being "jealous and possessive," adding that he is prone to "snap in and out of an explosive temper." She stated that he felt like he owned her, and that he once hung and killed a kitten of hers when he suspected that she was seeing another man.

When I inquired, in light of the above negative statements, and in light of the prison sentence that the defendant is facing, that she would marry him, she replied that they are "fated" to be together. She said that she could not cope with his death in their previous existence, and that she must now learn to cope with his absence in this one.

When asked why she thought that the defendant committed his crimes, she indicated the aberrant family situation previously mentioned. She stated that Mr. Bloggs slept with both of his daughters and had on numerous occasions forced them to instruct the defendant and his brother in sexual matters while he watched. On a second interview with the defendant I questioned him about this. He felt that this was no "big deal," and stated that he was about 10 when these incestuous encounters began.

While Susan believes that this sexual deviance may have been a distinct influence, she felt that the more proximate cause for the defendant's criminal behavior was his desire to satisfy her request for a big wedding, which he could not afford. It is ironic that their desire for a conspicuous and grandiose wedding may have led them to nuptials in a barren jail cell with a corrections officer as a witness. Her final statement to me was "Don't send him to prison, he won't come back."

The defendant's father and mother were interviewed at their family farm. Mr. Bloggs is 54 years old, has two years of college, and is a self-employed farmer. He is an impressive professorial-looking person who is obviously accustomed to being in control of any situation. He spoke slowly and deliberately, and appeared to take great pains to use just the right word. He stated that he is at a loss to explain his son's behavior, that he loved him, and will continue to support him. He denied any mistreatment of the defendant beyond what he called "normal chastisement." I did not feel it appropriate to raise the issue of the alleged incest with him in front of his wife.

The defendant's mother is 53 years old, has one year of college, and describes her occupation as "housewife." She is a timid-looking soul who complements her husband's personality with a passivity which approaches sycophantic proportions. She was never able to complete two successive sentences without her husband finishing them for her. She profusely praised her husband as a father and a provider, and also denied that he was excessively punitive. One wonders if she has any knowledge of her husband's sexual abuse of their children. A computer record check revealed no criminal history for either parent.

The defendant's oldest sister, Patricia Knowles, is a high school graduate who currently drives a cab for Black and White. Pat has been married and divorced twice, and has a ten-year-old daughter and a nine-year-old son. Pat has a criminal history of child endangering and drug abuse. Pat does not presently associate with her father, stating that "He f---ed all of us kids up. He's the one that should be in jail."

Ann, the defendant's second sister, has similar feelings about her father. She is a high school graduate. She stated that she ran away from home right after graduation, and openly admits that she went to Los Angeles to become a call girl. She eventually quit that occupation after becoming pregnant (she kept her child). She is currently on welfare in Los Angeles. A check with LAPD revealed numerous soliciting arrests for Ann.

Fredrick Bloggs, the defendant's older brother, could not be reached. However, Pat indicated that Fred dropped out of high school at the age of 16, has been married and divorced, and is now an "alcoholic bum" in Omaha, Nebraska. It would appear that the defendant is not the only victim of Mr. Bloggs' highly distasteful personality.

EMPLOYMENT HISTORY (Social Security #302-42-9988)
At the time of his arrest, the defendant was working for Lowman Cascade as a press operator. He has been employed there since 4–14–76. He works all the overtime that he can get and frequently brings home in excess of $400 per week. The defendant's immediate supervisor characterized him as "a good and dependable worker who gave us no trouble."

The defendant had taken the entrance examination to become a Lowman City police officer. Lt. Murdock of LCPD indicated that the defendant was to be called to the next class at the academy.

The defendant relates no other employment except at his family business.

(*continued*)

PHYSICAL HEALTH
The defendant is a white male, 26 years of age, 6′ tall, and weighs 155 lbs. He has dark blonde hair, blue eyes, and a fair complexion. He describes his current physical health as "excellent." He has suffered no hospitalizations or serious diseases, and relates no defects of hearing, speech, or vision. There is a family history of hypertension, and he feels that he is disposed to it himself. He is an infrequent consumer of alcohol, stating that the last time that he was drunk was over two years ago. He smoked marijuana rather heavily while in college, and stated that he frequently used amphetamines while working the night shift at Lowman Cascade in order to stay awake. He did not feel that he was addicted to them, however.

MENTAL HEALTH
The defendant graduated from Capital High School in 1978. He graduated 31st out of a class of 63, with a GPA of 2.27 on a 4.0 scale. School IQ testing saw the defendant obtain a full-scale IQ of 113, placing him in the 85th percentile of U.S. population IQ scores. Were his educational attainments commensurate with his IQ percentile ranking, the defendant would have placed 9th in his class. The defendant stated that he was too busy working on the farm to do justice to his studies.

Upon graduation from high school, the defendant entered Boise State University. He majored in, of all things, criminal justice. He was still attending BSU at the time of his arrest. He has obtained a cumulative GPA at BSU of 2.49. His criminal justice advisor stated that he was a "quiet student who participated very little in class, but his written work showed evidence of real independent thinking."

The Court Diagnostic and Treatment Center report indicates that their testing saw the defendant obtain a full-scale IQ score of 114, indicating a certain consistency in mental ability. It is noted that he scored significantly above average in tasks requiring nonverbal and short-term memory skills.

It is too easy to ascribe some form of mental abnormality to one who subscribes to the world view described by the defendant. It should be remembered, however, that his views are a valid discourse for millions of people in the world. I am more inclined to view his neurotic materialism as indicative of mental instability than his new-found religious eclecticism. He himself views his seemingly insatiable acquisitiveness as being responsible for his criminal actions. He was socialized in a family seemingly obsessed with making money. Neither can we discount the incestuous behavior he was forced into as a generating factor. It is clear that love was not a prevalent quality in this man's life. This deficiency may explain his clinging, jealous, and paranoid attraction to the one person (Susan) who showed a loving interest in him.

Although the CD&TC [Court Diagnostic and Treatment Center] report states that he is experiencing high levels of anxiety and depression, he now states to me that he is "more at peace" with himself. He spends much of his time in his cell these days reading the Bible and esoteric literature. He describes himself as "driven to achieve," and feels that he is very aggressive in a nonviolent way. Given his crime, the hanging of the kitten, and Susan's statement about his "explosive temper," one might well dispute this description. The CD&TC report also describes him as being "in the early stages of a schizophrenic reaction, specifically of a paranoid type." His frequent reference to himself in the third person perhaps augments the impression of disassociation. Overall, this officer gained the impression that the defendant is a very bright, knowledgeable, and articulate person. He has been completely cooperative, and was a pleasure to talk with.

EVALUATIVE SUMMARY
Before the Court is a 26-year-old married male facing his first criminal conviction. He is an extremely bright, articulate, and personable young man. He evidently had a childhood in which he wanted for nothing materially, but which was characterized by excessive labor, harsh punitive treatment, and forced incestuous episodes. It is evident from the defendant's own statements, and from information uncovered in the course of this investigation, that he was severely deprived of close and loving interpersonal relationships. His father was viewed by family members as the great

patriarch, or as the defendant put it: "as a boss, not a father." His father bestowed praise and approval only when the defendant met his excessive demands. Love, if there indeed was any, was withdrawn on the slightest pretext. His mother was viewed as a good person, but also as a pusillanimous alter-ego to the father.

The defendant's lack of experience of loving relationships rendered him ill-equipped to function well within one when Susan came into his life. He was obviously obsessed with making good this deficit. His relationship with Susan, now his wife, appears to have been a clinging obsession with him. He was paranoid about the possibility of losing her, and hypersensitive to her "needs," which everyone concerned agree were considerable. He wanted only the best for her, and often worked seven days a week, even while attending college, to get it for her. Even his considerable income was not sufficient to purchase all of the things he felt were necessary to ingratiate himself.

Nonetheless, we cannot overlook a string of armed robberies and the shooting of a police officer. It is evident that the robberies were well-planned and executed. In any objective sense, he was not in any desperate need of money, as he was earning a wage well in excess of average. He needed love, and his materialistic background told him that love was just another expensive commodity to be purchased with cash.

His intelligence, desire to learn, and intensity of purpose will stand him in good stead upon his release from the institution. His new-found spirituality, coupled with psychological counseling, will, I believe, function to prevent any further criminality in the future. He is well aware of the terrible crimes he has committed, and stands ready to accept the consequences. The extreme seriousness of his crimes point to the necessity of imposing consecutive sentences.

STATUTORY PENALTY

| IRC #2911.01
Aggravated Robbery | ". . . shall be imprisoned for a period of 4, 5, 6, or 7 to 25 years and/or fined up to $10,000." |
| IRC #2911.01
Attempted Aggravated Murder | ". . . shall be imprisoned for a period of 4, 5, 6, or 7 to 25 years and/or fined up to $10,000." |

RECOMMENDATION

Regarding 80–1234, Aggravated Robbery, it is respectfully recommended that the defendant be sentenced to 4 to 25 years at the Idaho State Penitentiary and ordered to pay the costs of prosecution.

Regarding 80–3456, Attempted Aggravated Murder, it is respectfully recommended that the defendant be sentenced to 5 to 25 years at the Idaho State Penitentiary, and that he be first conveyed to the Idaho Medical and Reception Center for evaluation and classification. It is further recommended that said sentences be served consecutively, and that the defendant be ordered to pay the costs of prosecution.

Respectfully submitted,

pc/kk

Paul E. Corrick, Probation & Parole Officer

circumstances that brought the offender before the bench for sentencing until he or she has read the PSI. This section, then, should lay out the official (police) version of all pertinent details of the offense. It should contain basic information such as the place and time of the offense, the names of any codefendants, whether or not any weapons were involved, and the name and address of the victim, and it should report injuries or financial loss suffered by the victim. Additionally, you should report the circumstances surrounding the defendant's arrest: How was the defendant discovered? What was the defendant's condition at the time of arrest (drunk, high)? Did he or she resist arrest, or did the person voluntarily surrender to the police? Be concise but thorough.

Statement of the Defendant

A recitation of the client's version of the offense assists you in filling in gaps in the official version. It is quite likely that the PSI interview is the client's first occasion to really tell his or her side of the story. The police are usually concerned only with the question of commission and couldn't care less about the whys and wherefores of the case. As for defense attorneys, clients often seem to think that their only interest is to "sell" them the plea agreement.

Nevertheless, you must never allow a client's sob story to distract you from the facts contained in the official version. Your job is not to retry the case in your PSI. Judges don't take too kindly to such efforts. Some interrogation techniques may be necessary, however, in order to attempt to reconcile any major discrepancies between the client's story and the official version. Interrogation should not be carried out until you have listened objectively to the entirety of the client's story. You must note discrepancies and go over them one at a time with the client until you are satisfied that they are resolved.

Don't let your humanitarian impulses get in the way if you believe that the client is trying to snow you. Note how the story is told. Is it just too slick and obviously memorized? Are there claims of memory loss (a favorite ploy with child molesters)? Are there major inconsistencies within the client's own version of the offense? If you think the story is untrue, come right out and say so. This may be all that is needed to get the real story. You can be burned badly if you succumb to the natural impulse to put your unconditional faith in the poor troubled human being sitting beside you. Not only will you be putting your credibility with the judge and your colleagues in jeopardy but you will also be compromising it with the client. Worse yet, you could be opening

yourself up for a lawsuit if, as a result of your report, a dangerous client is released on probation and subsequently harms someone else. Dig hard and dig deep. If you cannot reconcile the different versions, simply note them in your report. If you believe that unresolved discrepancies are the result of deliberate attempts at deception, you should report this in the PSI and fully support your reasoning behind the belief.

An important variable to assess is your client's attitude about the offense. Is there remorse? Is the remorse apparently genuine, or is it just sorrow for getting caught? Experience will sensitize you to signs of genuine remorse. Shame, as an indication of remorse, is signaled by blushing and sighing when the crime is discussed, attempts to avoid discussing embarrassing details of the offense, stuttering, stammering, apparent confusion, and the avoidance of eye contact previously established.

Similarly, guilty feelings are good indicators of genuine remorse. Behaviors consistent with a sense of guilt include voluntary confessions and the acceptance of complete blame, surrender to the police, a tendency to dwell on details of the offense, and the expression of a willingness to make amends in any way necessary. Clients who display some or all of these indicators of shame and guilt are usually individuals who normally conduct themselves according to conventional moral standards. The interviewer should be sensitive to the inclination toward depressive states, and even suicidal ideation, among clients of this type.

Such clients are rare, however. Most will try to claim some sort of mitigation, such as bad company, victim precipitation, or alcohol. In my unpublished study of 416 probation clients, 52.7% of them tried to shift the blame for the offense in directions other than themselves. Victim precipitation is a favorite in assaultive crimes, alcohol or drug abuse in property crimes. In those cases involving multiple defendants, fully 92% placed the blame on bad company, neglecting to realize that each was the whipping boy of the other. This is not to assert that all claims of mitigation lack any substance. It is your good judgment that will decide what degree of credence you will give to such claims.

You should also discuss victims' losses with your clients and inquire as to their attitudes about making restitution and their ability to do so. Restitution may include victims' medical bills, time lost from work, or replacement costs for property lost or damaged. The court may order payment of restitution either directly to the victim or to his or her insurance company. The client's willingness and realistic ability to pay restitution will probably be an important factor in both your recommended disposition of the case and in its actual disposition. Remember, however, that restitution can't legally be ordered if the client's plea was "no contest" rather than "guilty." This limitation displays a total disregard for victim's rights and is one of the major injustices of the criminal justice system.

Application to sample PSI report. Bill's version of the offense exactly mirrors the official one, and he doesn't attempt to deny any aspects of it. His statement written "in order to understand why I needed the money," however, is most instructive and interesting. His story is a psychiatric delight, illustrating for us many of the ego-defense mechanisms that we will be discussing later. Constant themes throughout his statement are severe deprivation of love and the pressures of life with an authoritarian father. His love for Susan was a clinging, cloying, jealous one. He was willing to go to any lengths to buy from her the love he so desperately needed. He was painfully aware that he had grown up in a loveless environment, so much so that he "learned not to become attached to anything for fear it would be taken away." Susan was inadequately filling his desperate need for love, his deeply felt deficiency. His jealousy, and indeed his crimes, can be viewed as stemming from his unrealistic attempts to cling to someone toward whom he had finally developed a form of attachment. He had convinced himself (apparently genuinely) that this attachment extended back to a prior existence. We note that the processing probation officer didn't disparage Bill's bizarre story but tried, instead, to under-

stand it and fit it into the client's frame of reference for the readers of the report. However, he correctly didn't let this factor sway him from consideration of the extremely serious nature of Bill's crimes. To understand is not to excuse. The probation officer also perceptively picked up on Bill's use of the third person when discussing himself and nicely tied it in with evidence from the examining psychiatrist, who indicated that Bill may have been in the "early stages of a schizophrenic reaction."

Was Bill remorseful, and if so, was his remorse genuine? He did turn himself in to the police, and he did make a full confession. However, given that he left behind so much identifying evidence at the scene of the crime, we can hardly assume that his cooperation was indicative of remorse. Further damaging to any interpretation of genuine remorse is the fact that the present offense was his fourth such robbery within a short period of time. But he did accept full responsibility for his crimes ("Bill has the free will that he was blessed with"), and he did accept the legitimacy of his impending punishment. The overall impression one gains is that Bill would have continued his crime spree had he not been caught. His apparently genuine remorse was late in coming, was related to the situation he was in at the time of the interview, and couldn't be viewed as a mitigating factor when considering sentencing.

Statement of Victim

As we have noted, many jurisdictions require that a "victim impact statement" be included in the PSI report. Such a statement is worth including even in the absence of a legal requirement. The statement should include the victim's version of the offense and the physical, psychological, and financial impact of the crime on him or her. You should also obtain an itemized statement of any financial losses from the victim or the victim's insurance company. It is not unusual, although it is understandable, for victims to inflate the extent of their losses. I always made it a point to solicit a statement of the victim's feelings and a recommendation regarding the disposition of the case.

Application to sample PSI report. Given the seriousness of this client's crimes, it was obvious from the onset that incarceration had to be the recommended disposition. Therefore, no attempt was made to ascertain financial losses to Patrolman Williams or the police department (aside from the defendant's inability to pay restitution if incarcerated, the courts can't monitor payments if the defendant is under the jurisdiction of the Department of Corrections). Since Officer Williams's version of the offense was an integral part of the official version, his additional statement throws no more light on it. His understandably negative response to "his opinion of the defendant, and what he thought should happen to him," was of no value in the formulation of a sentencing recommendation.

Prior Record

Before you interview your client, a complete criminal history should be available to you. This should include juvenile, local police, state Bureau of Criminal Investigation (BCI), and Federal Bureau of Investigation (FBI) arrest sheets ("rap sheets"). Most of these records should be included in the prosecutor's case file. Immediately upon receiving the case, however, you should run your own computer check for an updated history. A computer check will also reveal any outstanding warrants for the client. If you discover that the client is wanted, you should make inquiries with the issuing clerk of courts concerning the particulars of the warrant. It is your duty to place the client under arrest if the warrant indicates a serious crime. For obvious reasons, you should not reveal your knowledge of the warrant until after you have conducted the interview. Telling a client that he or she will be arrested at the conclusion of the interview will not make for a very productive interview. If the warrant was issued for something as innocuous as nonpayment of traffic fines, it is probably a better idea to tell the client to take care of them before you see him or her again rather than making an arrest. At this point it is wise to avoid confrontation about relatively unimportant matters.

Having gathered arrest records as well as any previous PSI reports and records, you should review this history of criminal activity with the client. Ask the client to explain any particularly serious prior arrest and conviction, and try to discern any pattern among the arrests. For instance, are the crimes all of a similar type (property, sex, violent), or is the record one of a polymorphous deviant? Do they reveal a pattern of increasing seriousness? At what point in life did the client start acquiring a criminal record? Are any or most of the crimes related to alcohol and/or drug abuse? Is the pattern one of planned criminality, or do the crimes seem mostly those of opportunistic spontaneity? Finally, does the client readily admit all crimes to you, or does the client attempt to rationalize the majority of them away?

Application to sample PSI report. The lessons to be learned from a perusal of your client's criminal history are many and valuable. In Bill's case, it is very instructive to see that he had no previous arrests, either as a juvenile or as an adult. Yet his offenses were of an extremely serious kind. In the normal progress of a criminal career, one graduates over a period of years from committing far less serious crimes to the kind of crimes Bill committed. It is so extremely rare to find a client who, at the age of 26, begins a criminal career with armed robbery that you should be immediately alerted to the fact that there are some very special circumstances involved.

Family and Marital History

A family history should contain the names and addresses of parents, siblings, children, spouse, and any former spouses and indicate the current status of each family member (deceased, divorced, retired, imprisoned, whereabouts unknown). These data will yield important information about the client's family dynamics. You should inquire into the client's relationship with his or her parents during the formative years. Were they divorced early? With whom did the client live? Did either or both of the parents remarry, and what was the relationship with step-parents like? What are the client's current relationships with his or her parents and significant others like—supportive or rejecting? An exploration of parental reactions to the present predicament will gain you access to the kind of moral environment in which the client was raised. Collateral interviews with parents, if time allows and the seriousness of the case warrants, can be used to validate and expand upon the client's perceptions.

It may be instructive to inquire into clients' friendship networks. Do they associate with known criminals? If so, ask why. How is leisure time spent with friends—in productive or nonproductive ways?

You should then obtain the client's marital history, if any. How many times has the client been married? Frequent marriages, common-law or otherwise, indicate an inability to form lasting relationships and a certain lack of responsibility. If the client has been married more than once, what was the reason for divorce? Placing the blame on the spouse may reflect an overall pattern of blaming others for negative outcomes. You should find out if the client has any children from former relationships. If the client is a male, is he living up to his support obligations?

The quality of the relationship with the current spouse should be examined next. If there are any major difficulties, explore their nature and extent. Is the client responsibly supporting dependents, or does his or her lifestyle demonstrate neglect? Again, a collateral interview with the spouse may prove useful. You may conduct a collateral interview by telephone, although you lose much of the flavor if you do. You would certainly want to find out the spouse's attitudes about your client's criminal activity and how he or she would cope if the client were to be imprisoned.

Application to sample PSI report. Officer Corrick's collateral interviews with Bill's wife, his parents, and selected siblings certainly paid off in terms of insight into the origins of Bill's criminal behavior. Although Bill's family was comfortably middle class and demonstrated commitment to, involvement in, and belief in typical American success values, beneath the veneer of respectability lay an abominable family situation. Attachment, genuine reciprocal love, was obviously absent. Bill appeared to have tried very hard to gain his father's love and approval. His father, however, seems to have been a patriarchal, sadistic, sexually perverted, and over-demanding individual. His absolute control over the family is quite in evidence in the report. His mother "complements her husband's personality with a passivity which approaches sycophantic proportions." Note that she never mentioned anything to Corrick regarding the incestuous behavior that went on for so many years. It is not at all unusual for wives to deny, even to themselves, that such behavior is taking place. This behavior first came to light during the collateral interview with Susan. It was then incumbent on Officer Corrick to verify the information, which he did with Bill himself and with two of his siblings. Such potentially damaging information should never be included in a report on the basis of one individual's statement.

The effects of growing up under the conditions that existed in the Bloggs family have resulted in many negative outcomes for Bill's siblings as well. Pat has had two broken marriages in four years and has a record of child abuse and drug abuse. Ann has one illegitimate child and was a prostitute for a period of time, with numerous soliciting arrests. Fred is a high school dropout, was divorced after one year of marriage, and is an admitted alcoholic. All this, in spite of having access to all the "objective" advantages of a white, middle-class status, supports Officer Corrick's analysis of the origin of Bill's behavior as presented in the evaluation section of the PSI report.

Susan's statements indicate that she shared Bill's unusual interpretation of their relationship ("they are 'fated' to be together"). She quit her job when she and Bill started living together, and she was evidently quite happy to allow Bill to work all hours of the day and night to satisfy her considerable material wants. Her comments about Bill's "explosive temper" and his hanging of her kitten provide all those who will use the PSI report in the future with valuable insight not gleaned from either Corrick's or the diagnostic center's interviews with Bill.

Very few collateral interviews will ever be as valuable to you as the ones presented here. Further, for less serious cases, time constraints will usually prohibit going to the extraordinary lengths to which Corrick went here. Nor would it be especially productive if the offender fit the profile of the typical armed robber. The typical armed robber would fit a certain profile which, by definition, is associated with most others who commit such crimes (lower-class, poorly educated, from a broken home, unemployed, and so on). It was the atypicality of Bill's criminal profile that led Corrick to dig as deeply into Bill's past as he did.

Employment History

The section covering employment history explores the client's employment or other sources of income, such as welfare, social security, or disability income. A complete and verified employment history is a vital part of any client assessment. As the theories we have examined inform us, a steady work history, evidence of prosocial commitment, involvement, and access to a legitimate avenue of success are incompatible with serious criminal involvement. Of the 416 offenders in my unpublished (1983) study, only 55.8% were working at the time of the PSI interview. Of those working, fully 86.6% of them were in unskilled dead-end occupations. Only 2.8% were in managerial, technical, or professional occupations, and all of those were first-time offenders.

The name, address, and telephone number of the client's current place of employment is the first item on the agenda. To avoid putting your clients' jobs in jeopardy, you can verify employment by having them bring in their most recent paycheck stubs. Length of employment can be verified through the clients' tax records. Ask clients what type of work they do and if they enjoy it. Are there opportunities to move up in the company? Do they feel that their present in-

come is sufficient to meet their basic needs? Do they criticize the company excessively? Why?

Former employment must be verified directly. A standard form should be sent to former employers asking them to indicate type of work, length of service, reason for leaving, and an evaluation of a client's work performance and of his or her general character. What is the client's pattern of movement in the work force? Does the client work steadily and quit employment only to obtain a better position, or does the client quit on any pretext after minimal periods? This information will give you a general picture of your client's level of responsibility, his or her ability to get along with others, and his or her general persistence. You should fully explore all gaps in employment history. You should also ask the military for a copy of the client's service record, if any, although you may not receive it until long after sentencing.

Application to sample PSI report. Bill's employment history is an atypically good one. At the time of his arrest he had been working for more than two years for the same company. He worked hard and earned a good income. Management at his place of employment was very positive toward him, even to the extent of planning to promote him to supervisor. He also worked part time on the family farm and had passed the examination to become a police officer. Bill's exemplary work history obviously impressed Officer Corrick and further alerted him to dig beyond surface demographics to explain Bill's behavior.

Physical Health

An assessment of clients' physical health (self-reported, or, if necessary, verified by a physician), noting how their social and vocational functioning could be affected by it, should be included. Recent hospitalizations and diseases, use of medications or prosthetic devices, and drinking habits and drug abuse should be noted in this section. Substance abuse should be the central concern of this section because of its association with many criminal acts. Drugs and alcohol are chemical substitutes for the lack of love and meaning in many clients' lives—a method of temporarily shutting out the cruelties and responsibilities of life. You should inquire into the extent and frequency of clients' drinking, noting if they have any alcohol-related offenses, such as drunk driving, on the rap sheet. A useful assessment scale for alcohol use is included in Chapter 11.

The extent, frequency, and type of drug abuse should be addressed next. Not all clients will be willing to admit abuse, but with careful observation you will know when to probe. Physical indicators of drug abuse are examined in Chapter 11. A word of warning here: some clients will exaggerate the extent of their substance abuse in the hope that blame will be shifted from them to the substance and that they will touch a sympathetic chord in the officer. My (1983) study found that 13.5% blamed substance abuse for their crimes. If clients claim drug dependency, or if you suspect it, they should be immediately referred to a drug dependency clinic for a complete workup and evaluation.

Application to sample PSI report. Nothing unusual was uncovered in Bill's physical health history that is pertinent to decisions of sentencing, classification, or treatment. He did report heavy use of marijuana while in college and current use of amphetamines. However, given the ubiquity of marijuana use among the young and his stated reason for taking amphetamines, there is no cause for undue alarm. We do note that the use of amphetamines is favored by those seeking intensified stimulation.

Mental Health

The first item for consideration under the heading of mental health is the client's education. Names and locations of all schools attended, including dates of attendance, should be listed and records requested from the client's last high school or college. From school records you should note grade point average, class standing, IQ and vocational testing, and attendance and behavioral history. If the client dropped out of high school,

inquire about the reason. If you feel that your sentencing recommendation will be probation, you might explore the possibility of the client's attending GED classes. Clients' responses to this and similar suggestions will give you some idea of their motivation to better themselves. IQ and vocational testing results will provide you with a client's range of possibilities, but don't be misled by low scores to dismiss a client as a hopeless case. A recent study showed that probationers attending GED classes at a probation department had significantly fewer arrests, and committed significantly less serious crimes, than a matched group of dropout probationers not attending classes (Walsh, 1985b).

Any psychiatric or psychological workups done on clients should be discussed with them and integrated into your own assessment. Discuss any discrepancies that may exist between the stories they have told you and those they have related to mental health professionals. Lies told have an awkward tendency to be soon forgotten. Do not be afraid to disagree with or add your own opinions to those of the mental health professionals— you are a professional in your own right. Studies have shown that when the recommendations of probation officers conflict with those of mental health professionals, judges are somewhat more apt to agree with the officers (Morash, 1982). Remember, the training and role expectations of mental health workers lead them to see mental pathology in nearly all cases they review. Although real mental illness does exist, I believe that a deficiency view rather than a pathological view of criminal behavior is both more productive and less stigmatizing. You should never contend with mental health professionals, however, if they advise psychiatric hospitalization. Such recommendations are not rendered lightly, and you must respect boundaries of expertise.

When discussing aspects of their mental functioning with your clients, you should concentrate on how they feel about themselves, their aspirations, their goals, and their usual ways of coping with stress and adversity. If you feel that a particular client has some special problems that require the assistance of mental health professionals, you should refer him or her for a workup, indicating the areas you wish the diagnostic center to explore.

Application to sample PSI report. We have already addressed many of the possible underlying reasons for Bill's criminal behavior. It is interesting to see how Officer Corrick added and integrated his own findings into those of the court diagnostic and treatment center. However, he didn't step beyond the boundaries of his professional expertise to contest the findings and opinions of the center's personnel. He merely added to their insights and provided additional light. His collateral interviews with family members made him privy to information unavailable to court diagnostic personnel. We know that enuresis and cruelty to animals are two of the childhood and adolescent behaviors predictive of violent behavior and that Bill exhibited these behaviors. We don't know if Bill also liked to set fires, so perhaps we shouldn't make too much of this; it is the three behaviors taken together that are considered predictive. Nevertheless, Corrick was aware of Bill's late enuresis (we note that Bill denied it to the examining psychiatrist) and his hanging of Susan's pet kitten; court diagnostic personnel were not. Would they have labeled Bill *passive aggressive* (shooting a police officer and hanging a kitten are certainly aggressive, but hardly passive) had they known? Nor were they aware of the sexual perversities into which Bill's father forced him and his siblings. This case is an excellent example of the use of collateral interviewing when appropriate. The court diagnostic center's other diagnosis of Bill as being "in the early stages of a schizophrenic reaction" was supported by Officer Corrick's observation that Bill often spoke about himself in the third person.

Other revealing pieces of information contained in this section help us gain a clearer picture of Bill. Whereas Bill's high school GPA of 2.27 is respectable, it, as well as his class standing, is considerably below what one would expect from someone with an IQ in the bright-normal range. Is this indicative of an underachiever or of someone kept too busy working for his father to do

justice to his studies, as Bill claimed? The consistency of IQ test scores taken seven years apart reveals that regardless of what other mental problems Bill may have had, he suffered no deterioration of intellectual functioning.

Alert students will have noted an important piece of information that Officer Corrick reported but did not comment on: Bill "scored significantly above average in tasks requiring nonverbal and short-term memory skills." We noted in the section on psychopathy that the performance IQ is determined by performance on such tasks, and that a performance IQ that is clearly in excess of a verbal IQ has been considered by many authorities as a clear marker of psychopathy. Unfortunately, Officer Corrick did not report the performance and verbal IQ subscales but only the full-scale score. We don't know, therefore, if Bill's performance IQ was "clearly in excess" of his verbal IQ. However, this piece of information, in conjunction with Bill's enuresis, cruelty to animals, apparent inability to form close loving relationships, and history of love deprivation renders the application of the psychopathic label plausible. Had Corrick picked up on this (assuming that he was aware of the theory behind it), he might have been led to investigate further along those lines. This observation again underscores the necessity for criminal justice workers to be conversant with criminological theory.

Finally, it is clear that Officer Corrick was very much impressed with Bill, but he did not let that reaction cloud his judgment when he made his sentencing recommendation.

Evaluative Summary

The evaluative summary is the most challenging section of the PSI report to write. You are summarizing the facts contained in your report and drawing reasoned conclusions from them. This section represents the distilled wisdom of the investigator and separates the true professional from the data gatherer. It is the product of a disciplined effort to organize, synthesize, and analyze your collected data. No new data should be included in this section; your sole task here is to draw meaning from what you have already reported.

Since this section requires the inclusion of value judgments, every effort must be made to minimize any emotional feelings you may have for or against clients and/or their behavior. You must fully appraise your subjective feelings by asking yourself, "Why do I feel this way?" The tone of your report can convey impressions of the offender to the reader that may have a major impact on the offender's future. Emotion-laden terms such as "morally bankrupt" or "a picture of womanly virtue" reveal more about the investigator's attitudes than the client's and should not be a part of a professional report. If you find that your client evokes this kind of heavy emotional response, it is a good idea to consult with your supervisor or your colleagues before writing this section in order to clarify and objectify your thoughts.

This doesn't mean that you should not take a firm and positive stand. Indeed, as a professional this is your duty. Ambiguous, wishy-washy, hedging statements are indicative of an investigator who is uncomfortable in his or her role and uncertain of his or her expertise. Such beating around the bush undermines the authority of the entire report and causes the reader to have doubts about the advised plan of action.

All strong statements should, of course, be firmly grounded in the information uncovered and set down in other sections of the report. Of the utmost importance is your evaluation of your clients' strengths and weaknesses, their patterns of criminal behavior, their potential for reform, and their amenability to various kinds of treatment and training. Evaluation requires a thorough knowledge of available community resources as well as of the offender. This knowledge serves as the basis for a treatment plan, which is the logical conclusion of the evaluative summary. The treatment plan should be realistic and rendered with full knowledge of the possible. The recommendation of a treatment plan that cannot be implemented is frustrating to the person who must act on your recommendations. One client with a string of armed robberies to his name had been released on parole after serving ten years and was

in jail for a parole violation for yet another robbery. He received a recommendation from his officer that he be allowed to go to another state under the care of a Christian youth camp. The officer had been convinced by the client and by the client's spiritual counselor that he was a "born-again Christian." The officer skillfully sold his recommendation to the sentencing judge, who allowed the client to go. After this 53-year-old man found himself surrounded only by youths and discovered that he was expected to work for his daily bread, he left the camp and committed further crimes before he was apprehended. Needless to say, that officer found his credibility seriously compromised.

In formulating a treatment plan, you must give the threat that your client poses to the community equal consideration with the client's rehabilitative needs. Clues to this threat are provided by the nature of the present offense and by the length and seriousness of the person's criminal record. You should weigh various alternative plans in terms of their advantages and disadvantages for the client and the community. Give the reasons that made you decide to reject plans, and show complete justification for the accepted plan in terms of both client and community concerns. Treatment plans that involve other agencies should be formulated in concert with them. Their special expertise may uncover deficiencies in a client's character or motivation that in their opinion render him or her unsuitable for the plan you have in mind. If this be the case, you should respect their professional evaluation and concentrate on an alternative plan.

Application to sample PSI report. Officer Corrick begins his evaluative summary by reiterating the fact that the present offense is Bill's first conviction and by rendering his positive feelings about the client based on objective criteria and on his dealings with him. He then launches into a thoughtful examination of the possible origins of Bill's behavior. He emphasizes the lack of love, the punitive and incestuous milieu in which Bill grew up, and the excessive acquisitiveness of both Bill and Susan. After reading this evaluation, one

Perspectives from the Field

Marilyn West is a presentence investigator with the Fourth District (felony) Court, Ada County, Idaho, and a member of the Fourth Judicial District Sexual Abuse Task Force. A graduate of Northwest Nazarene College, she is active in many community organizations aimed at criminal rehabilitation.

Interviewing in Presentence Investigations
Marilyn West

In most jurisdictions presentence investigations are prepared by probation officers. In some jurisdictions there are people whose work consists solely of doing presentence investigations reports (PSI's). I am one of those people.

A PSI is a necessary and vital function of the criminal justice system, but due to its confidential nature, few people outside of the criminal justice system know that these reports exist. This makes being a presentence investigator a real conversation starter. People are intrigued to hear that someone is in charge of gathering all sorts of background information on felony criminals and presenting it to the court. People who have served on juries often express concern that the criminal histories of defendants are not made known to juries. Former jurors are relieved to learn that there is a point in the process where these histories are taken into consideration.

Because our PSI reports make sentencing recommendations, we have to make sure that our information is factual and our conclusions well grounded. This involves interviewing large numbers of people who know the defendant, including friends, relatives, and professional contacts. PSI reports are also a conduit for defendants and victims to express their feelings to the court.

Normally, the investigator has contact with the defendant for about three weeks following a

guilty verdict or guilty plea. The goal of the presentence process is not to conduct actual rehabilitation; it is to do a diagnostic workup. Of course, a good workup can go a very long way toward a beginning in the ultimate goal of rehabilitation. Good interviewing skills are an absolute necessity if you are to perform a good diagnostic workup. You can't simply "ask questions" and expect to get meaningfgful answers in criminal justice settings. You'll always get answers to your questions regardless of how they are asked, but they won't necessarily be helpful or truthful. You must establish a relationship in which the defendant can feel comfortable in revealing intimate information to you. That's quite a challenge.

We are obliged to be objective in our reports. This requires a special effort because a lot of emotions can surface during the investigation. The victim's side of the story often arouses our feelings, and oftentimes we discover traumatic or tragic circumstances in the defendant's past which stir our sympathies as well. This type of emotional information rarely comes to light in police or prosecutor's investigations, and is of little concern to them. But we have to decide how much of this information is necessary to us in the formulation of our recommendations to the court. Overall, our goal in constructing the recommendation is the same as that of the sentencing judge: to protect society.

Perhaps one of the most valuable functions the presentence investigator performs is that of making specific recommendations. It is not enough to simply recommend that a person be treated for some problem. We have to recommend the specific resource, keeping in mind such practical matters as the appropriateness of treatment, cost, and availability. In order to make these recommendations we must keep ourselves current on what is available in the treatment community. This means that we have to become "quasi-experts" in many treatment fields. Several people in our office are active in community treatment organizations for such problems as alcohol and drug abuse or sexual abuse. We are also charged with offering our opinion to the court as to whether an individual is capable of being rehabilitated. As you can imagine, this is sometimes a tough question. We have to supply ample information to show what our opinions are based on. Again, this underscores the absolute necessity of good interviewing techniques.

It is a challenge to obtain a valid profile of an individual's life in the space of a few weeks. It makes me feel good when my recommendations are confirmed by judges, or when probation officers come up to me and say something like, "Your report on so-and-so was right on the money. Now maybe we can draw his attention to some of the things he's doing to get himself in trouble, and maybe we can show him some of the ways to stay out of trouble." That's what this business is all about.

feels that one "knows" Bill fairly well without ever having seen him. This is the ideal for which you should strive.

Officer Corrick did not outline a treatment plan for Bill because he felt that the seriousness of Bill's crimes warranted incarceration in spite of Bill's "first offender" status. He seemed to feel that the experience of being caught, incarcerated, and having the opportunity to examine his behavior would deter Bill from future criminality.

Recommendation

Like the denouement of a mystery novel, the recommendation should flow logically from all the information preceding it. It also should be consistent with the legal requirement of the state. Certain crimes, such as murder, rape, and aggravated robbery, are not probationable, and certain crimes outside that category may contain elements that render them nonprobationable. The officer must be aware of the penal codes of his or her jurisdiction.

The recommendation should concisely state the number of years the client is to spend in prison or on probation. If you recommend probation, you should state special conditions of probation, such as amount of restitution and the name and address of payee, attendance at alcohol or drug centers, fines to be paid, amount of time that you feel the defendant should serve locally (in jail or a work release program), and so forth.

Application to sample PSI report. Corrick's estimation of community feelings, the possible threat Bill posed to the community, and the extreme seriousness of the offense led him to recommend that Bill serve two consecutive prison sentences of 4 to 25 years and 5 to 25 years. The judge imposed those sentences. What would you have recommended?

PSI Checklist

The most useful summary of this chapter takes the form of a checklist of factors that should be considered in any presentence investigation. Styles and formats of PSI reports vary from department to department, and some areas we have discussed (such as victim's statement and officer's recommendation) may be optional inclusions at your department. Remember one thing above all: the PSI will have a significant impact on your client's future. Accuracy is of the utmost importance.

1. *Circumstances of present offense(s).* A concise summary of all the relevant details of the offense(s) for which the client is to be sentenced.
2. *Client's version.* How does the client's version differ from the official version? What is

the client's attitude about the offense, and what is his or her overall attitude like? The officer should evaluate and make judgments about these questions.

3. *Prior record.* A complete and verified criminal history of your client. Patterns of criminality should be noted.

4. *Family history.* Family demographics, characteristics, conflicts, migrations, child-rearing practices, marital history, and so on.

5. *Employment history.* A complete and verified history of the client's employment and financial situation.

6. *Physical and mental health.* Recent hospitalizations and diseases. Drug and/or alcohol abuse. Level of intellectual functioning (school grade completed, GPA, IQ). Vocational training, psychological information.

7. *Evaluative summary.* A capsulated version of the entire report, evaluating its overall meaning. The officer's professional assessment of what is to be done to amend the client's behavior.

References and Suggested Readings

Division of Probation, Administrative Office of the United States Courts (1978). *Presentence Investigation Report.*

Hagan, J. (1975). "The social and legal construction of criminal justice: A study of the presentence process." *Social Problems,* 22:620–637.

Mangrum, C. (1975). *The Professional Practitioner in Probation.* Springfield, IL: Charles C Thomas.

Morash, M. (1982). "A case study of mental health professionals' input into juvenile court decision making. *Criminal Justice Review,* 7:48–56.

Myers, M. (1979). "Offended parties and official reactions: Victims and the sentencing of criminal defendants." *Sociological Quarterly,* 20:529–540.

Nettler, G. (1970). *Explanations.* New York: Harper & Row.

Walsh, A. (1983). *Differential Sentencing Patterns among Felony Sex Offenders and Non-Sex Offenders.* Ann Arbor, MI: University Microfilms International.

Walsh, A. (1984). "Gender-based differences: A study of probation officers' attitudes about, and recommendations for, felony sexual assault cases." *Criminology,* 22:371–387.

Walsh, A. (1985a). "The role of the probation officer in the sentencing process: Independent professional or judicial hack?" *Criminal Justice and Behavior,* 12:289–303.

Walsh, A. (1985b). "An evaluation of the effects of adult basic education on rearrest rates among probationers." *Journal of Offender Counseling, Services & Rehabilitation,* 9:69–76.

Chapter 6

Practice Cases and Assessment Tools

Justice consists of treating equals equally and unequals unequally according to relevant differences.

Aristotle

Aristotle's epigraph to this chapter signifies the philosophy of individualized justice underlying the effort to operationalize justice by assigning numeric scores on assessment scales. These tools attempt to determine Aristotle's "relevant differences" so that justice can be done as equitably as possible.

This chapter provides instruction on the various assessment tools used in many probation and parole agencies. These forms and scales are filled out by the processing officer on the basis of his or her evaluation of the offender. If your instructor assigns PSI interviews, he or she will provide you with actual cases for practice interviews and assessments. If you are role-playing the offender, you will have access to information supplied by the offender. It is the "officer's" task to elicit this information from the "offender" using the interviewing techniques described in Chapter 4.

If you are role-playing the interviewing officer, you will be presented only with the case materials that are normally provided by sources other than the offender, such as a statement of circumstances of the offense, criminal record, victim statements, and school records. Drawing on the information provided by the client and other sources, you should make an evaluation of the client, make a realistic recommendation, and formulate a treatment plan. There are no "correct answers." There are only good or poor evaluations, realistic or unrealistic recommendations, and workable or unworkable treatment plans.

When considering each section in the practice PSI reports, reread the appropriate section of Chapter 5 to determine if you have considered everything pertinent before deciding on an evaluation and recommendation. Don't hesitate to recommend imprisonment if you feel that the case warrants such a disposition. However, for the purposes of formulating a treatment program, assume probation placement even if you recommended imprisonment. All the assessment tools covered in the following discussion appear in the Appendix at the end of this chapter.

The forms and scales in this chapter are presented in the sequential order that they are encountered by officers in the field. Clients fill out the Social History Questionnaire before meeting the officer assigned to the case. The officer may then make use of the structured interview schedule, after which he or she will complete the sentencing guideline. The risk and needs scales are completed after the client is sentenced to probation or granted parole, as are the treatment plans. Thus, we begin with the Social History Questionnaire.

Social History Questionnaire

The first tool you should become familiar with is the Social History Questionnaire (SHQ). An intake officer or the agency receptionist hands this questionnaire to the client referred for a presentence investigation. Clients are requested to fill it out completely before they meet with the presentence investigator. For the purpose of conducting presentence exercises, students role-playing offenders should complete copies of the form using the data provided by their "offender" PSI reports. Each item is self-explanatory.

Client Management Classification Assessment Instrument

The second tool is the Client Management Classification Assessment Instrument (referred to as CMC in the Appendix). This semistructured interview schedule is reproduced in its entirety

in the chapter Appendix. Developed for the Wisconsin Bureau of Community Corrections, the tool is the end product of much study and research. Whereas the SHQ deals primarily with factual demographic data, the CMC offers guidance for your exploration of clients' attitudes and feelings and for supervision and treatment planning. When using this schedule, don't feel bound to repeat the questions exactly as they are printed on the page. There is sufficient leeway to incorporate your own style into the questions and to allow for unusual situations. However, the meaning of each question should be preserved in the translation into your own words. Also, and with all due respect to the architects of the CMC, I strongly suggest that the issues addressing the crime and criminal history should be left until the end of the schedule, at which time sufficient rapport should have been achieved to make these questions less threatening to clients.

In actual practice the CMC is scored so that probation and parole officers can assign clients to one of four treatment modalities (selective intervention, environmental structure, casework/control, and limit setting). This scoring, a rather complicated procedure for the uninitiated, is accomplished by using eight templates (cardboard sheets with holes punched in them that fit over a scoring guide). Probation and parole officers attend three-day workshops and receive extensive follow-up training before they are considered to be able to use this system to its fullest. To attempt to explain the system in its entirety is well beyond the scope of this book. In fact, the training material used in these training sessions constitutes a book in itself. Thus, you should consider the interview schedule included here simply as a guide to the kind of questions you should be asking your clients and as an introduction to the CMC system of client classification. The classifications obtained from scoring the CMC are highly correlated with the classification scheme obtained from the far more succinct risk and needs scales to be explained later in this chapter.

Nevertheless, it is useful to gain some idea of the characteristics of the clients who fall into each of the four classifications. The following descriptions are paraphrased and considerably shortened from those that appear in the CMC training manuals.

Selective Intervention

Clients in the selective-intervention category require the least time and present the fewest supervision problems. As the term implies, the supervising officer will intervene in the client's life only on an as-needed basis. Clients in this category almost always fall into the low-risk category as determined by the risk and needs scales. They generally have relatively stable and prosocial lifestyles, and their current offense is frequently their first involvement with the law. Their offenses can be viewed as a temporary lapse or suspension of an otherwise normal value system. They often show strong indications of guilt and embarrassment. You should avoid increasing guilt and criminal identification in these clients without allowing them to intellectualize or minimize their criminal acts.

These clients respond best to a warm, supportive relationship with their officers and to the use of rational problem-solving approaches to counseling. Avoid giving the impression to such clients that you are trying to run their lives for them or that you lack trust in them. If your agency uses a system of minimal contact, such as allowing low-risk clients to report in to the agency by mail or by telephone, make sure clients know that you are available to help them through temporary crisis situations or emotional problems that may prompt further criminal activity. These clients should not be put on minimal supervision or write-in status until any needs for treatment are dealt with satisfactorily.

Environmental Structure

Clients who need environmental structure generally fall into the low end of the medium-risk category and require regular supervision. Intellectual, vocational, and social deficits contribute considerably to their criminal activities. They tend to lack foresight, to have difficulty learning from past mistakes, and to be overly dependent on like-minded individuals for acceptance and approval. They are not usually committed to a criminal career, and malice as a motivation for criminal activity is rare.

The typical goals to seek with these clients are to develop and/or improve intellectual, social, and work skills, to find alternatives to associations with criminal peers, and to increase control of impulses. You should be more directive and concrete with these individuals than with your selective-intervention clients. You must move slowly to build a success identity for your clients by balancing your expectations of them with their present coping resources (this theme is taken up in the next chapter). You may often have to do things with and/or for them initially (such as taking them job hunting), but take care that you don't foster overdependence. Many of the clients in this category can, with a warm and accepting officer who knows the available community resources, become productive citizens.

Casework/Control

Casework/control clients are those who require more intensive casework and whose activities should be more tightly controlled. Clients in this category are at the high end of the medium risk and needs scale. They evidence a generalized instability in their lifestyles. They lack goals in their lives and have difficulty with interpersonal relationships and in finding and keeping employment. They tend to have had chaotic and abusive childhoods, which they repeat with their own families. Alcohol and drug abuse is frequently found among these offenders, and many of their criminal convictions reflect this abuse.

The basic goals to be achieved with this group are much the same as those outlined for the environmental-structure clients but are more difficult to achieve because of their substance abuse and greater emotional problems. These clients require a great deal of your time, as well as considerable coordination of auxiliary programs. Attendance and involvement with outside programs must be strictly monitored, and they should be allowed to suffer the consequences of noncompliance, such as short periods in the county jail. In short, you should use all the leverage at your disposal to promote client compliance. These clients will severely try your patience and professional competence, but they can be turned around by a knowledgeable, caring, and no-nonsense officer.

Limit Setting

Clients who need strict limits set for them by their officers are those at high risk on the risk and needs scale. They are quite comfortable in their criminal lifestyles and demonstrate a pattern of long-term involvement with criminal activities. They delight in their ability to beat the system and tend to minimize or deny any personal problems. They see themselves as being normal individuals who have simply chosen a criminal lifestyle for themselves. Indeed, in comparison with the structured-environment and casework/control clients, they often show quite superior ability to function normally (if not morally) in society.

Clients in the limit-setting category are typically assigned to a special intensive-supervision officer. Intensive-supervision officers usually enjoy small caseloads, enabling them to devote the time necessary to supervise high-risk clients. Protection of the community through surveillance and strict control (often with the aid and cooperation of the police) of the clients is of primary concern. Such clients are extremely manipulative and will frequently test your resolve. Any failure on your part to act assertively will be interpreted as weakness. Thus, you must always be prepared to confront them with even minor infractions of the rules. If you do not, you will not be respected, and you can be sure that they will escalate their violations.

These clients respond best to the techniques of reality therapy, as described in Chapter 8, and to rational discussion because their criminal behavior is often more a function of choice than of emotional or intellectual deficiencies. The exercise in figuring the cost/benefit ratio of crime

(Chapter 10) may be beneficial to these clients. Since they also tend to be quite energetic and to possess adequate native intelligence, they have the capabilities that can be channeled into profitable and legal endeavors. Attempt to develop challenging and innovative opportunities to provide them with satisfying alternatives to a criminal lifestyle.

For clients who have defeated all your best efforts, who have repeatedly sabotaged treatment plans and exhausted existing programs, and who plainly lack any sort of motivation to change, it may be appropriate to discontinue major efforts to restructure their lives. When all else has failed, but you have not initiated formal legal action against them, expect nothing more than legal conformity from them. Make it crystal clear, however, that any legal violation, no matter how minor, will result in official action.

Felony Sentencing Worksheet

The Felony Sentencing Worksheet (FSW) is one of several sentencing guidelines used throughout the nation. The FSW is a sentencing guideline that has been used by the courts in Ohio. Sentencing guidelines were developed as a kind of compromise between factions in criminal justice who believe either that the punishment received by an offender should "fit the crime" or that punishment should fit the offender and be appropriate to rehabilitation. Both of these positions are addressed in the guideline, with seriousness of offense being weighted more than the offender in the consideration of sentence.

Guidelines were also developed to attempt to minimize wide disparities in sentencing for similar crimes and similarly situated individuals. They are aimed at structuring judicial discretion in sentencing and promoting consistency by providing judges with sentencing norms based on the past practices of their peers when confronted with similar cases. Implicit in the idea of guidelines is the notion that disparity flowing from legitimate variation among different crimes and different offenders is acceptable, but disparity shorn of just or coherent reason is not. It may be useful to view sentencing guidelines as an application of Aristotle's definition of justice as stated in the epigraph to this chapter.

The processing probation officer scores the FSW by assigning the indicated numerical scores on the basis of the legal and social factors addressed in each subsection. Some sections simply require the recording of factual data, such as the degree of offense, multiple offenses, prior convictions, and repeat offenses. Other sections, covering culpability, mitigation, and credits, require a great deal of interpretation. Don't be confused if you and your classmates arrive at different FSW scores. Since judgments are called for, the FSW allows for the intrusion of ideology in its scoring. A recent study showed that the FSW is differentially scored by practicing probation officers according to their ideological convictions, with conservative officers assigning significantly higher scores (Walsh, 1985). Sentencing by arithmetic is not impervious to ideological intrusion, but it does constitute an improvement on unstructured sentencing. An earlier study of the effects of the guideline on sentencing found it to have a predictive accuracy of 85%; that is, judges imposed the suggested sentence in 85% of the cases, with 8% being harsher than indicated and 7% being more lenient than indicated (Swisher, 1978). This study was carried out a year after implementation of the guidelines. Judges may have been more willing to abide by them initially because of the novelty effect. I am among those individuals who believe that it is of utmost importance to develop value-free guidelines and to make it mandatory that sentences suggested by them be heeded except under special circumstances that are fully justified in writing.

After scores have been assigned and added for both the offense and the offender categories, they are applied to a grid on the reverse side of the FSW at the point at which they intersect. The grid indicates a suitable sentence for offenders whose crimes and whose criminal histories fall into it. These are suggested sentences only. Don't be hesitant to recommend sentences that are not consistent with the grid if you feel there should be alternatives and can justify them. In fact, it is

probably a good idea for practice purposes to ignore the scoring of the FSW until after you have decided on a recommendation. You may then score the FSW and see how close your decision comes to the suggested sentence.

As a quick exercise, let's score Bill Bloggs on the FSW. He was a first offender and thus is scored 0 on the "offender rating" section of the sheet. In the "degree of offense" subsection, Bill would receive the maximum points (4) because both of his crimes were first-degree felonies. In the "multiple offenses" category he would receive 2 points because he was convicted of aggravated robbery and attempted aggravated murder. In the "actual or potential harm" category he would receive 2 points for his wounding of the police officer. His 8 points thus far already put him beyond the FSW's range for probation. I believe that I would also assess 2 points against Bill in the "culpability" section for "shocking and deliberate cruelty," but I don't think I could justify deducting any points in the "mitigation" category. Bill therefore would get 10 offense-rating points assessed against him, a score that places him in the upper left-hand square of the grid.

Risk and Needs Assessment Scales

The risk and needs assessment scales to be discussed are part of the Client Management Classification System and are designed to be used in conjunction with the CMC interview schedule. The system consists of two separate scales that assess the client's "risk" and "needs." Client *risk* refers to the probability of reoffending and/or the threat the client poses to the community. Assessment is accomplished by assigning numerical scores on variables known to correlate with recidivism. The earlier one begins a criminal career, the more involved one is in it, the more one turns to chemical substances, the less one is legitimately employed, and the more negative one's attitude is, the more likely one is to reoffend. The more likely clients are to reoffend, the more they represent a risk to the community and the more closely they must be supervised. It is the practice in many jurisdictions to move clients up one level of supervision higher than the score indicates if they have a history of assaultive offenses. Risk and needs scales, and a complete scoring guide, are reproduced in the Appendix to this chapter.

Client *need* refers to deficiencies in clients' personal repertoires and lifestyles that may be preventing them from making any commitment to a conventional moral pattern of behavior. Scores on the risk and on the needs sections of the scale tend to be highly correlated. That is, a client who is high risk tends to have high needs, and clients with few needs are not high risk. The needs section constitutes the area in which the probation and parole officer's counseling skills and knowledge of community resources are of great value.

You should complete a risk and needs scale for each of the "clients" for whom you write a practice PSI. As you are doing this, be mindful of the need for complete accuracy. The safety of the people of the community and the rehabilitative needs of your client depend on your accurate assessment. Read the instructions carefully before you assess any points. Place your client at the appropriate level of supervision.

Let's see how Bill Bloggs would do on the risk and needs scales. Going over the risk scale, we note that Bill would be assessed only 3 points (he was between the ages of 18 and 29 at the time of the current offense). However, the "assault factor" would automatically place him up one level of supervision in most departments.

In the "emotional stability" section of the needs scale, I would have to assign Bill 2 points. On the one hand, given some of his weird behavior and statements, I would be uncomfortable assessing him only 2. On the other hand, his symptoms don't prohibit adequate functioning. I would also assess 3 points against him in the "living arrangements" category. The only other assessment that I could justify against him is 1 point for "situational or minor difficulties" under "financial status," but I think I would assess 5 points under "agent's impression," for a total of 11 points.

If we turn to the supervision level matrix (Figure 6-1), we discover that Bill's level of supervision, without the assault override, would have been minimum. That supervision level is clearly

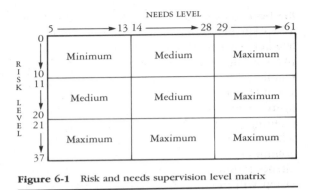

Figure 6-1 Risk and needs supervision level matrix

untenable for someone who committed the kind of crimes that Bill did (this level might be fine if he were being classified for parole rather than probation and if information from prison authorities justified it). Such a possible classification problem underscores two points: (1) that Bill was clearly an atypical case and (2) that the suggestions of these scales, based as they are on the "typical" criminal, are not cast in concrete. In the extremely unlikely event that Bill had been placed on probation, you would have been seriously remiss if you had followed these guidelines unquestioningly.

Supervision Level Matrix

On the basis of scores obtained in both sections of the assessment scale, clients are placed under minimum, medium, or maximum supervision. These levels of supervision closely correlate with the case management classification system derived from the CMC. Correct assessment of clients at this point contributes greatly to the efficient use of officers' time. The time not wasted in "overservicing" low-risk and low-needs clients can be fruitfully spent with those who require more attention.

Five cells of the supervision level matrix represent maximum supervision, three represent medium, and only one cell represents minimum supervision. Only clients with 10 or fewer risk points and 13 or fewer needs points fall into this minimum category. Don't be alarmed by the number of cells calling for maximum supervision. It has been empirically determined that only about 15% of probation and parole clients fall into these five cells. About 50% of the clients will fall into the medium level of supervision, and the remaining 35% will require only minimal supervision (Idaho Dept. of Corrections, n.d.:19). These figures will vary according to the probation/parole-granting practices of a given jurisdiction. If, for whatever reasons, a jurisdiction relies heavily on community-based corrections, the number of clients requiring maximum and medium supervision will be a lot greater than in jurisdictions that only reluctantly grant probation/parole. In the latter type of jurisdiction one might expect the number of clients requiring minimum supervision to be perhaps 60% to 70%.

Supervision Planning

Having placed the offender in the appropriate supervision level, you now have to formulate a plan aimed at his or her rehabilitation. The first thing you must remember when formulating a treatment plan is that plans must represent a balance between the client's treatment needs and the client's present coping resources, as outlined in Chapter 8. You have identified the client's needs, so the next task is to prioritize them according to their importance relative to his or her legal difficulties. The supervision planning form is an aid in this endeavor. It asks the officer to list the client's strengths/resources and problems/weaknesses. In rank-ordering problem areas, the officer should give extra weight to the problems most amenable to speedy change so that the client can begin to develop a success identity.

The officer should be particularly alert to what may be a primary or "master" problem, a particularly debilitating one that may be the source of most of the client's other problems. For instance, lack of education and employment, poor financial status, and poor spousal relationships are highly interdependent areas that may possibly be mitigated by meaningful vocational training and subsequent employment. Perhaps all these areas, as well as others such as the influence of criminal companions, are themselves dependent on some

form of substance abuse. If an evaluation of the client's problems leads the officer to believe that most of them are secondary to substance abuse, then the obvious plan is to rank substance abuse as top priority for change.

With the client's rehabilitative needs identified and prioritized, you are ready to draw up a tentative supervision plan according to the form reproduced in the Appendix. The tentative supervision plan includes a problem statement, long-range goal, short-range objectives, probationer/parolee action plan, and officer/referral plan.

For instance, the officer may identify alcoholism/problem drinking and vocational training as the problems needing immediate attention. Alcoholism can be identified by the client's score on the MAST scale (see Chapter 11) and by alcohol-related legal problems on record. A second problem that may be identified is a client's lack of marketable skills, which keeps him or her from obtaining worthwhile full-time employment.

The long-range goals, therefore, would be to maintain sobriety and to complete vocational training, respectively. As we will see in Chapter 8, a good plan should be simple, should identify something to do and not something to stop doing, should call for something to be done as soon as possible, and should be specific. Accordingly, the officer may state the short-range goal to be two days of sobriety and attendance at the next Alcoholics Anonymous (AA) meeting for alcoholism. The officer will then formulate a probationer action plan and request that the client indicate commitment to it by signing it. The officer/referral action plan may state the officer's commitment to the plan by indicating that he or she will attend the first AA meeting with the client and that the client is to be referred to an alcohol treatment facility for further evaluation of the extent of his or her drinking problem and for treatment recommendations. The procedure for the second problem area is likewise simple and focused.

The reassessment plan is implemented after the outcomes of the tentative plans have been determined. For instance, the information received from the alcohol treatment facility may have advised more intensive treatment or concluded that the client's drinking problem had perhaps been overemphasized by the officer. In either case, the officer will plan the next supervision phase accordingly. Assuming that the client had been referred for vocational training, and that this training was successfully completed, the long-range plan may now be to secure and maintain full-time employment, and the short-range plan may be for the client to file a designated number of applications for employment every day until he or she has secured a job. Supervision plans must be frequently reassessed and changed as circumstances dictate.

After six months, and semiannually thereafter, there should be a reassessment of the client's risk and needs. Reassessment may result in a higher or lower supervision category on the basis of the client's progress or lack of progress in the preceding six months.

A Final Word about the CMC System

It is important that neither the seasoned officer nor the student see the CMC system as just bureaucratic paper-pushing. It does seem like a lot of extra work to the officer used to supervising clients in accordance with his or her "intuition" or "experience." I must confess that I was one of those who complained about filling out forms when the system first came out. Once I got used to it, however, I became a committed convert. I soon realized that the CMC system is actually an efficiency-enhancing device that will ultimately save time. A recent study (Lerner, Arling, and Baird, 1986) found that high-risk clients on CMC supervision experienced 8% fewer parole revocations than regularly supervised ("seat of the pants") high-risk clients. Medium-risk CMC clients experienced 6% fewer revocations than non-CMC medium-risk clients. Both these differences were statistically significant. The substantive difference represented by these percentages was 95 fewer parole violation reports, and that's a lot of time saved. More important, it meant that 95 clients were saved from the futility of the revolving prison door because their needs had been identified and efficiently serviced. CMC supervision of low-risk clients resulted in only 1% fewer (6% versus 7%) revocations than the regularly supervised low-risk clients. This seemingly insignificant difference is more a function of the generally good performance of low-risk clients than the inapplicability of the CMC system to them.

What do other field practitioners think of the system? Let me quote from a recent enthusiastic paper by Michael Schumacher, Ph.D., Chief Probation Officer of Orange County, California:

> Probation programs ... can no longer rely upon the assertions of "doing good" for people based upon a subjective model of human behavior. The risk/needs approach provides an objective look at offenders based on characteristics that have been shown to have some predictive value for the success or failure of other probationers. It supports a healthy balance between the peace officer role [and the] social work role. It is a tool that has been a long time coming and shows promise for probation supervision as a major factor in the resocialization of offenders. Longitudinal research conducted in jurisdictions where this system has been fully implemented has shown encouraging results in the reduction of criminal behavior by probationers. If this system is properly implemented, I am convinced reductions in recidivism rates will result (1985:454–455).

Summary

The proper assessment of correctional clients has become increasingly important in criminal justice. The various scales, forms, and questionnaires found in this chapter constitute efforts to classify and treat clients in a more rational and equitable way.

The Social History Questionnaire and the Client Management Classification Interview Schedule are interviewing and assessment aids. They are used prior to sentencing. The felony sentencing worksheet assists you in making sentencing recommendations by providing you with sentencing norms based on past experience.

The risk and needs assessment scales are supervision aids. These scales provide you with information relating to the risk your clients pose to the community and the needs they have in order to lead a more productive life. They also provide you with the information you need to develop treatment plans for your clients. Treatment plans begin by identifying major problem areas and devising a tentative treatment plan based on the need to alleviate them. These plans should be reassessed as frequently as necessary, or at least every six months. The use of the tools contained in this chapter has resulted in a remarkable improvement in corrections supervision over the old "seat of the pants" methods of supervision.

References and Suggested Readings

Idaho Department of Corrections, Adult Probation and Parole (n.d.). *Client Management Classification Training Manual.* Boise: Author.

Lerner, K., G. Arling, and C. Baird (1986). "Client management classification: Strategies for case supervision." *Crime and Delinquency,* 32:254–271.

Schumacher, M. (1985). "Implementation of a client classification and case management system: A practitioner's view." *Crime and Delinquency,* 31:445–455.

Swisher, T. (1978). *Sentencing in Ohio.* Columbus: Ohio State Bar Research Foundation.

Walsh, A. (1985). "Ideology and arithmetic: The hidden agenda of sentencing guidelines." *Journal of Crime and Justice,* 8:41–63.

Chapter 6 Appendix

SOCIAL HISTORY QUESTIONNAIRE

Prior to your next appearance in court for final disposition, the Adult Probation Department must complete a presentence investigation for the judge. This presentence investigation includes information about your background that the judge will take into consideration when deciding whether to place you on probation or not. Please completely fill out this questionnaire, and if you have any questions concerning the questionnaire, feel free to ask. The information that you provide will be confidential in that only the Probation Department and the judge will be allowed to see it. Upon completion of this questionnaire, please return it to the person who gave it to you.

GENERAL INFORMATION:

FULL NAME: _____

PRESENT ADDRESS: _____

TELEPHONE #: _____

PLACE OF BIRTH: _____

DATE OF BIRTH: _____

SOCIAL SECURITY NO.: _____

SOCIAL HISTORY QUESTIONNAIRE

FAMILY:

Please list the members of your family, including parents, brothers, sisters, spouse and children.

NAME	RELATIONSHIP	AGE	ADDRESS
PARENTS			
BROTHERS & SISTERS			
WIFE/HUSBAND			
CHILDREN			

Have you ever been married before?

Date of wedding:

Date of divorce:

SOCIAL HISTORY QUESTIONNAIRE

EDUCATION:

Please list what schools you have attended (elementary, secondary, college and job training programs).

School	Dates Attended	Highest Grade Completed

EMPLOYMENT:

Please list in order your job history. If employed at the present time, please note where and the name of your supervisor.

Employer	Address	Date Started	Date Left	Reason

Spouse's Current Employer:

SOCIAL HISTORY QUESTIONNARIE

MILITARY HISTORY:

Please note the following information:

Branch of Service:_____

Date of Entry:_____

Date of Discharge:_____

Type of Discharge: _____ _____

Location of Service:_____

_____

HEALTH:

Please make a statement as to your general state of health. Do you have any medical
problems, are you under a doctor's care, or are you on medication? Please note below:

PRIOR RECORD: SIR #   FBI #

If you have been arrested before, either as a juvenile or adult, please list these
arrests. Also, please note what happened in court after these arrests. Please note
if you have been on probation or parole before, or if you are under any supervision
at the present time.

SOCIAL HISTORY QUESTIONNAIRE

Please fill in the following list of information:

1. Housing costs: Weekly:_____ or monthly_____

2. Food costs: Weekly:_____ or monthly_____

3. Utilities:

    A. Telephone_____

    B. Gas_____

    C. Water_____

    D. Electric_____

4. Loan Payments:

    A.

    B.

    C.

    D.

    E.

5. Other Miscellaneous Costs:

    A.

    B.

    C.

    D.

    E.

SOCIAL HISTORY QUESTIONNAIRE

Print in your own words a statement concerning the offense. What did you do, when, who was involved, why, did you repay the victim?, etc.

_____

_____

_____

_____

_____

_____

_____

_____

_____

_____

_____

_____

_____

_____

_____

_____

_____

_____

_____

_____

_____

_____

_____

STRATEGIES FOR CASE SUPERVISION

The purpose of CMC is to provide the probation professional with an efficient and effective case management system. CMC includes procedures for developing individualized strategies for the quality supervision of *adult* offenders. This process is accomplished through the completion of the three system components: an assessment procedure, a supervision planning process and supervision according to one of five distinct strategies, depending on individualized case needs. It is not to be used with juveniles nor for any other than its stated purpose.

CMC INSTRUCTIONS

There are four parts to the CMC assessment instrument. Whenever possible, the following sequence (A to D) should be followed.

- A. *Attitude interview (45 items)*
- B. *Objective history (11 items)*
- C. *Behavioral observations (8 items)*
- D. *Officer impressions of contributing factors (7 items)*

The Attitude Section

Column One:

A SEMI-STRUCTURED INTERVIEW with suggested questions has been developed to elicit attitude information about the offense, the offender's background, and about present plans and problems. The average interview takes about forty-five minutes and the scoring about five minutes.

Use a natural, open, conversational style of interviewing which is comfortable for both you and the probationer. If the probationer presents some important or interesting information requiring follow-up, feel free to do so before returning to the structured sequence. While stressing free-flowing communication, some structuring is required to insure the reliability and validity of the instrument. Therefore, make every effort to preserve the meaning of the questions when transposing them into your own words.

In the interview, each section is introduced by one or two open-ended questions which are intended to encourage discussion on a particular subject. If the information needed to score the items is not obtained from the open-ended questions, one or two specific questions are provided for each item. If those questions fail to elicit the needed information, continue to inquire with increasingly direct questions unless you see the word –STOP–. "–STOP–" means to discontinue inquiry (except to repeat or clarify a misunderstood question).

For some items, "a" and "b" questions are included. If the "b" question is asterisked (*), always ask it unless the answer to the "a" makes the "b" questions meaningless (e.g., "no" to question 10a). If question "b" is not asterisked, ask it if the needed information was not elicited from question "a".

Column Two:

THE ITEM OBJECTIVES AND RESPONSES are listed in column two. Many times the suggested questions will approach the item objective in an indirect manner in order to elicit the most valid response.

Column Three:

A SCORING GUIDE is included to provide criteria and assistance in scoring ambiguous responses. When scoring, you must choose only one alternative for each item. If you cannot choose an alternative, do not rate the item.

ATTITUDES ABOUT OFFENSE

Could you tell me about the offense that got you into trouble?

QUESTIONS	RESPONSES	SCORING GUIDE
1a. How did you get involved in this offense? 1b. *(If denied)* What did the police say that you did?	1. Motivation for committing the offense (a) emotional motivation (e.g., anger, sex offense, etc.) (b) material (monetary) motivation (c) both emotional and material motivation	*1. a.* - *Using drugs.* - *Assault (not for robbery).* *b.* - *Prostitution.* - *Car theft (except for joy riding).* - *Selling drugs (including to support a habit).* *c.* - *Stealing from parents for revenge.* - *Stealing primarily for peer acceptance.* - *Man who won't pay alimony primarily because he's angry with his ex-wife.*
2a. How did you decide to commit the offense? 2b. Could you tell me more about the circumstances that led up to the offense?	2. Acceptance of responsibility for current offense (a) admits committing the offense and doesn't attempt excuses (b) admits committing the offense, but emphasizes excuses (e.g., drinking, influence by friends, family problems, etc.) (c) denies committing the offense	*2. a.* *Explains circumstances but* **takes responsibility.** *b.* **Blames** *circumstances and does* **not** *take responsibility.* *c.* *Probationers who deny any significant aspect of the offense are scored "c" (e.g., the probationer admits that he helped to jimmy a car window but denies responsibility for removing valuables because his friends removed them).*
3. Looking back at the offense, what is your general feeling about it? **-STOP-**	3. Expression of guilt about **current** offense (a) expresses guilt feelings or spontaneous empathy toward victim (b) expresses superficial or no guilt (c) victimless crime	*3. a.* *Probationer must feel some personal shame and regret (***not*** just verbalization to impress the officer).* *b.* - *"I feel bad because now I have a record."* - *"People are disappointed in me." (Indicates some regret but not necessarily guilt.)* - *"I know it was wrong." (Emphasis is on having done wrong, but not on feeling bad because one has done wrong.)* *c.* - *Using drugs.* - *Sexual activities between* **consenting** *adults.*

OFFENSE PATTERN

I'd like to talk to you about your prior offenses. Have you been in trouble before? *(Obtain a complete picture of probationer's offense style, including current offense, when scoring items 5 - 8.)*

QUESTIONS	RESPONSES	SCORING GUIDE

4a. What prior offenses have you been convicted of?
*4b. Were you ever in trouble as a juvenile?
(List on grid below)
	4. Offense and severity
	(a) no prior offenses *(Skip items 5, 6, 7 and 8.)*
	(b) mainly misdemeanors
	(c) no consistent pattern
	(d) mainly felonies
		4 - 8. Include juvenile and serious traffic offenses (e.g., drunk driving). Don't count dismissals.
		
		4. Use only prior offenses.
		  b. Should **not** be used if probationer has more than two serious felonies. (Use choice "c" or "d".)
		  d. Over 50% of probationer's offenses are felonies.

5a. Have you ever been armed or hurt someone during these offenses? * 5b. Did you ever threaten anyone?	5. Was probationer ever involved in an offense where he (she) was armed, assaultive, or threatened injury to someone? (a) yes (b) no	5 - 8 Use current and prior offense factors to score 5 - 8.

6a. How did you decide to commit these offenses?
6b. Did you plan these offenses beforehand? (Discuss offenses individually until a clear pattern emerges).
	6. Offenses were *generally*
	(a) planned
	(b) no consistent pattern
	(c) impulsive
		6. Officer's judgement based on all factors.
		  a. - Exhibitionist who drives around in a car looking for a girl to which to expose himself.
		  - Person who decides to commit an offense, then drinks to build courage.
		  c. - Exhibitionist who is driving to work, suddenly sees a girl, and pulls over and exposes himself.
		  - Person gets drunk and into a bar fight.

7. Were you drinking or on drugs when you committed this offense?	7. Percent of offenses committed while drinking or on drugs (a) never (b) 50% or less (c) over 50%	7. Count offenses where there was **any** chemical use regardless of whether person was intoxicated or not.

8. Did you do the offense alone or
    with others?

8. Offenses were *generally* commit-
    ted
    (a) alone
    (b) no consistent pattern
    (c) with accomplices

Offense	(Item 4) Fel./Misd.	(Item 5) Assaultive?	Circumstances of Offense	(Item 6) Planned?	(Item 7) Chemicals?	(Item 8) Accomplices?

SCHOOL AND VOCATIONAL ADJUSTMENT

Now, I'd like to find out some things about your background. Let's begin with school. How did you like school?

QUESTIONS	RESPONSES	SCORING GUIDE
9. What was your favorite subject in school? -STOP-	9. Favorite subject (a) vocational (b) academic (c) gym (d) no favorite subject	9. *a. - Business courses.* *b. - Music or art.*
10a. Did you have a favorite teacher in high school? 10b. What did you like about him (her)?	10. Attitude toward teachers (a) no favorite teacher (b) teacher chosen because of certain qualities that the probationer admired (c) teacher chosen because of close personal relationship with the teacher	10. *b. - "She would help kids."* *c. - "She would help me."*
11a. How far did you go in school? 11b. Did you have any problems with schoolwork? *(If probationer did not graduate from high school, find out why not.)*	11. Probationer's school performance (a) no problems (b) learning problems (difficulty performing schoolwork) (c) lack of interest, behavior, or other problems	11. *a. Don't use for probationer who didn't complete high school.* *b For probationer whose learning problems result from a **lack of capacity** (not just from lack of interest or behavioral problems). If probationer has both a lack of capacity **and** behavioral problems, score "b". **Lack of capacity** takes precedence when scoring.*
12. Now, I'd like to know about your work history. What kinds of jobs have you had? *(Find out actual job responsibilities. Use grid on page 5.)*	12. Primary vocation (a) unskilled labor (b) semi-skilled (c) skilled labor or white collar (d) no employment history (homemaker) *(Skip 13 & 14)* (e) student or recent graduate *(Skip 13 & 14)*	12. *a. - Average person could do job without training.* *- Probationer's been in the job market for over six months, but has no employment history. (Also score items 13 and 14.)* *c. Job requires some training and/or experience.* *d. For homemaker, use prior vocational history, if any. If none, check "d" and skip items 13 and 14.* *e. Probationer was recently (within 6 months) a student and hasn't had the opportunity to establish an employment pattern. (Skip items 13 and 14.)*

QUESTIONS	RESPONSES	SCORING GUIDE
13a. How long did you work on your most recent job? 13b. How long between that job and your previous job? *(Start with most recent job and go backwards until a clear pattern emerges. Use grid below for 12 - 14.)*	13. Percent of working life where probationer was employed full time (a) over 90% (b) over 50% to 90% (c) 50% or less	13. - *"Working Life...", i.e. time period society would expect one to be working. Subtract time in school, institutions, etc.*
14a. What was the reason for leaving your most recent job? 14b. Have you had any trouble getting jobs?	14. Primary vocational problem (a) none *(Can be used only if item 13 is scored "a".)* (b) problems due to lack of skills or capacity (c) attitude or other problems	14. *a.* **Don't use "a" if working less than 90%.** *c.* - *"Because of my drinking problem."*

(Item 12) *(Start with most recent)* Jobs and Job Responsibilities	(Item 13a) Duration	(Item 14a) Reason for Leaving
(Item 13b) Unemployment Interval ⟶		
(Item 13b) Unemployment Interval ⟶		
(Item 13b) Unemployment Interval ⟶		

94

QUESTIONS	RESPONSES	SCORING GUIDE
15a. Where do you live now? 15b. Have you moved around much? *(Deal with time period after probationer turned 18.)*	15. Living stability background (a) essentially stable living arrangements (b) some unstable periods (c) essentially unstable living arrangements	15. *Consider what is stable for the probationer's age group.*
16a. Have you had any trouble supporting yourself or received welfare? 16b. *(If applicable)* How did you support yourself when you were unemployed?	16. History of being self-supporting (a) probationer has usually been self-supporting (b) probationer has had several periods where he (she) wasn't self-supporting (c) probationer has essentially not been self-supporting	16. *Illegal activities and welfare are not counted as self-supporting. For probationer who has not had the opportunity to support (her) himself (e.g., homemaker or person living with relatives), estimate the likelihood of (her) his being able to support (her) himself.*

FAMILY ATTITUDES

Now I'd like to know about your childhood. Can you tell me what it was like?

QUESTIONS	RESPONSES	SCORING GUIDE
17a. How do (did) you get along with your father? 17b. How do you feel about your father?	17. Present **feelings** toward father (a) close (b) mixed or neutral (c) hostile	17. *In multi-father families, use the person whom the probationer identifies as father.* *b. - "We get along" (without implication of closeness).*
18a. If you did something wrong as a **teenager**, how did your father handle it? 18b. What kind of discipline did he use?	18. Type of discipline father used (during probationer's **teenage** years) (a) verbal or privilege withdrawal (b) permissive (generally let probationer do as he (she) pleased) (c) physical	18. *If the probationer didn't live with father or father figure during at least part of his (her) adolescent years, do not rate item 18.* *b. - "He always left it to Mom."*
19a. How do (did) you get along with your mother? 19b. How do you feel about your mother?	19. Present **feelings** toward mother (a) close (b) mixed or neutral (c) hostile	19. *In multi-mother families, use the person whom the probationer identifies as mother.* *b. - "We get along" (without implication of closeness).*

QUESTIONS	RESPONSES	SCORING GUIDE

20a. If you did something wrong as a **teenager**, how did your mother handle it?
20b. What kind of discipline did she use?

20. Type of discipline mother used (during probationer's **teenage** years)
(a) verbal or privilege withdrawal
(b) permissive (generally let probationer do as he (she) pleased)
(c) physical

20. If the probationer didn't live with mother or mother figure during at least part of his (her) adolescent years, do not rate item 20.
 b. - "She always left it to Dad."

21a. Were you ever abused by either of your parents?
21b. Did either of them ever go overboard on the punishment?
-STOP-

21. Was probationer ever physically abused by a biological, step or adoptive parent
(a) yes
(b) no

21. Item 21 should be based on facts described and not whether the client felt abused.
 a. - cuts on face
 - severe body bruises
 - sexual abuse
 - locked in closet or starved for unusual periods of time

22a. How would your parents have described you **as a child (before you were a teenager)**?
*22b. Did both of your parents see you the same way?

22. Parental view of probationer (prior to adolescence)
(a) good child
(b) problem child
(c) parents differed

22. a. - No special problems.
 - "Like anybody else."
 b. - "My parents were always complaining about me."
 - Seen as "strange kid."

23. How would you describe yourself as a child **(before you were a teenager)**?

23. As a child, probationer describes self as
(a) good child (normal or average)
(b) problem child

23. Accept what the probationer says even if his (her) behavior does not match his (her) perception. (Examples from item 22 also apply here.)

24a. How do you get along with your brothers and sisters?
24b. How do you feel about them?

24. General **feelings** toward siblings
(a) close
(b) neutral or mixed
(c) hostile
(d) no siblings

24. Include half-siblings; exclude step-siblings.
 b. - "Like some, not others."

25. Would you describe your early childhood **(before you were a teenager)** as happy or unhappy?
-STOP-

25. General attitude toward childhood
(a) happy
(b) not happy

25. Accept the probationer's view.

26. If you could change anything about your childhood, what would you change?

26. Satisfaction with childhood
(a) basically satisfied (would change little)
(b) dissatisfied with material aspect
(c) dissatisfied with self, family, or emotional climate

26. c. - "I should've gone to school."

QUESTIONS	RESPONSES	SCORING GUIDE
27. Can you describe your father's personality? *(If answer is unclear, ask probationer to describe another person he (she) knows well.)*	27. Probationer's description of personality (a) multi-faceted (b) superficial (e.g., "good", "bad", "nice", etc.)	27. *The focus of this item is the complexity with which the probationer views people. The ability to describe attributes, or explain the reasons for behavior, is being measured. "Superficial" indicates a lack of capacity to perceive depth in personality and not just an evasion of the question. One or two complex statements are sufficient for an "a" score.* *a. - "Ambitious and honest."* *- "Sensitive to others."* *- "Dad was strict because that is the way he was brought up."* *b. - "No-good drunk" (with no further elaboration).* *- "Kind."* *- "Don't know."*

INTERPERSONAL RELATIONS

Let's talk about your friends. Do you spend much time with them?

QUESTIONS	RESPONSES	SCORING GUIDE
28a. What are your friends (associates) like? *28b. Have any of them been in trouble with the law? *(If probationer has no current associates, use prior associates.)*	28. Probationer's associates are (a) essentially non-criminal (b) mixed (c) mostly criminal	28. *Don't count marijuana use (alone) as criminal.* *a. Don't use "a" if probationer committed offense(s) with accomplices.*
29a. How do you get along with your friends? *29b. How do they act towards you?	29. In interaction with friends, probationer is (a) used by others (b) withdrawn (c) other problems (d) normal	29. *This item should be based on officer's judgement of the quality of the probationer's interactions. If the officer thinks the probationer is used by friends even though the probationer thinks he (she) gets along "ok", check choice "a".*
30a. Do you have a closest friend? *30b. What do you like best about him (her)? -STOP-	30. Description of probationer's relationship with his (her) closest friend (a) talk (share feelings) or help each other (b) do things together (less emphasis on talking or sharing feelings) (c) has none	30. *a. - "We do things for each other."* *- "We're like brothers."* *b. - "He's a hunter too."*

QUESTIONS	RESPONSES	SCORING GUIDE
31. Are you satisfied with the way you get along with people?	31. Satisfaction with interpersonal relationships (a) feels satisfied (b) feels dissatisfied	31. Accept the probationer's statement.
32. In general, do you tend to trust or to mistrust people? -STOP-	32. General outlook toward others (a) basically trusting (b) mixed or complex view (c) basically mistrusting	32. b. A complex view of people (e.g., trusts in some situations and not in others). - "I trust people too much." - "It takes awhile to get to know them."
33a. Can you tell me about your relationship with women (men)? *33b. Do you generally go out with a lot of women (men) or date the same person for long periods?	33. Probationer's opposite sex relationship pattern generally is (a) long term (over 6 months) or serious relationships (b) short and long term relationships (c) short term, less emotionally involved relationships, or little dating experience	33. c. Short-term relationships with no solid commitments to persons of the opposite sex.
34. In your relationship with your wife/girlfriend (husband/boyfriend), who tends to make the decisions?	34. In opposite sex interactions, probationer generally (a) dominates (b) is average or adequate (c) is nonassertive or dominated	34. Officer's judgement. Do not accept the probationer's response without exploring his (her) relationships or seeing how some specific decisions are made (e.g., who decides what to do or with whom to socialize; or who controls the money).

FEELINGS

Now, I'd like to ask you about your feelings. Have you had any problems handling your feelings?

QUESTIONS	RESPONSES	SCORING GUIDE
35. Do you consider yourself to be a nervous (or anxious) person? -STOP-	35. Does probationer view self as a nervous person? (a) yes (b) no	35. Accept the probationer's statement. a. - "I worry a lot." - "I'm hyperactive."

36a. What kinds of things get you depressed?

36b. What do you do when you're feeling depressed? *(If denies, find out how he (she) keeps from getting depressed.)*

36. What does probationer do when feeling depressed?
    (a) seeks someone to talk to, or tries to figure it out
    (b) seeks an activity to distract self
    (c) drinks or uses drugs
    (d) isolates self

36. *b. - "Forget about them."*
    - "Watch T.V."
    d. - "I pray."
    - "I go to sleep."

37a. Have you ever thought seriously about hurting or killing yourself?

37b. *(If probationer says yes to above)* Have you ever tried it?

37. Self destructive behavior
    (a) never seriously contemplated suicide
    (b) has had definite thoughts of suicide
    (c) has attempted it

37. *c. Requires overt action which resulted in self-harm or clear intent toward suicide.*

38a. What do you do when you are feeling angry with people?

38b. Have you ever hurt anybody when you were angry?

38. In handling anger, probationer
    (a) is physically aggressive
    (b) avoids expression to others or has trouble expressing anger appropriately
    (c) responds appropriately

38. **Based on all sources** *of reliable information (e.g., offense history) and not just on probationer's statement. Physically aggressive problems should take precedence in scoring. If probationer says, "I leave," find out if/how he (she) deals with the anger later.*
    b. - "I break things."

39a. Can you describe your personality?

39b. What do you like and what do you dislike about yourself?
    -STOP-

39. In describing self, probationer
    (a) emphasizes strength
    (b) emphasizes inadequacy (probationer tends to downgrade self)
    (c) can't describe self

39. *If the probationer gives both positive and negative statements about (him) herself,* **choose the one emphasized most.** *If the positive and negative have equal emphasis, choose the first response given.*
    c. Choice "c" is designed to identify the probationer who is incapable of showing **insight** *or* **complexity** *into (him) herself; (e.g., "I'm okay." (and can't elaborate); "I'm nice"; "I get into too much trouble"; etc.*

40. *(No question asked. Rate your impression of probationer's openness in discussing feelings.)*

40. Openness in discussing feelings
    (a) discusses as openly as able
    (b) is evasive or superficial

40. *a. If the officer felt that the probationer was fairly straightforward in talking about his (her) feelings.*
    b. If the officer thought the probationer was evasive or superficial.

PLANS AND PROBLEMS

QUESTIONS	RESPONSES	SCORING GUIDE
41. Aside from your legal problems, what is the biggest problem in your life right now? -STOP-	41. What does the probationer view as his (her) most important problem area right now? (a) personal (b) relationships (c) vocational-educational (including employment) (d) financial (e) no big problems presently *(Score item 42 as "a")*	41. a. *Probationer names several important problems.* *- Drinking or drugs.* *- "Get my head together."* b. *- "Get things straightened out with my fiancee."* *- "Try to get along better with my parents."*
42. How do you expect this problem (from item 41) to work out?	42. Attitude toward solving problems (a) optimistic; expects to succeed *(Include 41.e.)* (b) unclear (c) pessimistic; expects to fail	42. a. *- "O.K., because I've got a better paying job."* b. *- "O.K., I hope."* *- "I'll be O.K. if I get a better paying job."* c. *Probationer is pessimistic about outcome or can't figure out a solution.*
43a. What goals do you have for the future? *43b. What are your plans for achieving your goals? -STOP-	43. Future plans (a) short-term goals (most goals can be fulfilled within about 6 months) or no goals (b) unrealistic goals (c) realistic, long-term goals (most .goals are well developed and extend beyond 6 months)	43. a. *- "Just live day to day."* *Poorly developed goals with no plans for achieving them.* b. *- Strange, way out, or impossible to achieve goals.* c. *Probationer is able to, 1) set a goal within the realm of possibility and, 2) lists the steps necessary to achieve the goal.*
44. *(No question asked. Rate the item based on follow-through on jobs, education, training programs, treatment programs, etc., based on all sources.)*	44. Probationer usually sticks with, or completes, things he (she) begins (a) yes (b) no	44. *Compare to the average probationer.*
45a. How will being on probation affect your life? 45b. What do you expect to get from being on probation? -STOP-	45. Probationer's general expectations about supervision (a) no effect (b) monetary, counseling, or program help (c) hopes supervision will keep him (her) out of trouble (d) negative expectations (e) mixed or unclear expectations	

OBJECTIVE BACKGROUND ITEMS

Instructions: *Ask direct questions to obtain the following information.*

QUESTIONS	SCORING GUIDE

Legal History

1. Age of earliest court appearance:
   - (a) 14 or younger
   - (b) 15 - 17
   - (c) 18 - 22
   - (d) 23 or older

   46. Include juvenile offenses and serious traffic offenses (e.g., drunk driving, hit and run). Exclude divorce, custody proceedings, etc.

2. Number of prior offenses:
   - (a) none
   - (b) 1 - 3
   - (c) 4 - 7
   - (d) 8 or more

   47. Exclude the probationer's present offense in rating this item. Include juvenile and serious traffic offenses.

3. Number of commitments to state or federal correctional institutions:
   - (a) none
   - (b) 1
   - (c) 2 or more

   48. Include juvenile commitments.

4. Time spent under probation or parole supervision:
   - (a) none
   - (b) 1 year or less
   - (c) over 1 year; up to 3 years
   - (d) over 3 years

   49. Include juvenile supervision.
   a.   Use "a" for new probationer

Medical History

5. *(Circle all applicable choices.)*
   - (a) frequent headaches, back or stomach problems
   - (b) serious head injuries
   - (c) prior psychiatric hospitalization
   - (d) out-patient pyschotherapy
   - (e) none of the above

   50. a.   Vague complaints not diagnosed by a physician
   b.   Skull fractures
   Head injuries which required treatment (beyond X-ray)
   d.   Professional in-patient or out-patient drug/alcohol treatment

School History

6. Highest grade completed:
    (a) 9th or below
    (b) 10th to 12th
    (c) high school graduate (exclude GED)
    (d) some post high school training leading toward a degree

7. Did probationer ever receive special education or remedial help
    in school?
    (a) yes
    (b) no

52. *Include special programs for learning deficiencies (rather than behavior problems). Do **not** include English-as-a-second-language.*

Family History

8. Probationer was raised primarily by:
    (a) intact biological family
    (b) other

53. *Choice "a" requires **both natural parents** in an **intact** home until probationer reached about 16 years of age.*

9. Did either parent have a history of:
    (Circle all applicable choices.)
    (a) being on welfare
    (b) criminal behavior
    (c) psychiatric hospitalization
    (d) suicide attempts
    (e) drinking problems
    (f) none of the above

54. *Includes step and adoptive parents.*

10. Have siblings (including half and step siblings) ever been
    arrested?
    (a) none
    (b) some
    (c) most
    (d) not applicable

Marital Status

11. Currently probationer is:
    (a) single (never married)
    (b) single (separated or divorced)
    (c) married (including common-law)

———————————— END INTERVIEW ————————————

BEHAVIORAL PATTERNS

Instructions: *Rate the following behaviors as observed during the interview. Use (b) for the average probationer. Use (a) and (c) for distinct exceptions to the average.*

1   Grooming and Dress

    (a)   Below Average   (b)   Average   (c)   Above Average

2.   Self-Confidence

    (a)   Lacks Confidence   (b)   Average   (c)   Overly Confident

3.   Attention Span

    (a)   Easily Distractable   (b)   Average   (c)   Very Attentive

4.   Comprehension

    (a)   Below Average   (b)   Average   (c)   Above Average

5.   Thought Processes

    (a)   Sluggish   (b)   Average   (c)   Driven (Accelerated)

6.   Affect

    (a)   Depressed   (b)   Average   (c)   Elated

7.   Self Disclosure

    (a)   Evasive   (b)   Average   (c)   Very Open

8.   Cooperation

    (a)   Negativistic   (b)   Average   (c)   Eager to Please

IMPRESSIONS

Instructions: *On the continuum below, rate the significance of each factor with regard to the probationer. Did (does) this problem contribute to the probationer's legal difficulties? At least one item must be rated a "1" and at least one item must be rated a "5".*

A.   SOCIAL INADEQUACY

Socially inept. **Unable** to perceive the motives and concerns of others. **Unable** to survive in society and care for self.   (1)   (2)   (3)   (4)   (5)   Socially adept. **Able** to assert self and to perceive the motives and concerns of others. **Able** to survive in society and care for self.

Do not merely rate performance in social situations. Rate ABILITY.

B.   VOCATIONAL INADEQUACY

Lacks the capacity to obtain and maintain relatively permanent and reasonably paying employment.   (1)   (2)   (3)   (4)   (5)   **Has the capacity** to obtain and maintain relatively permanent and reasonably paying employment.

Do not merely rate job performance. Rate CAPACITY.

C.   CRIMINAL ORIENTATION

Criminal behavior is an acceptable and common part of the probationer's life **and** s/he attempts to live off of crime without trying to make it in a pro-social way.   (1)   (2)   (3)   (4)   (5)   Criminal behavior is **not** an acceptable **nor** common part of his/her life, **nor** does s/he attempt to live off of crime without trying to make it in a pro-social way.

Do not merely rate the frequency of offenses. Rate VALUES and ORIENTATION.

D.   EMOTIONAL FACTORS

Emotional problems (e.g., chemical dependency, sex, fear, depression, low self-esteem, anxiety, self-destructiveness) contributed highly to the offense (pattern).   (1)   (2)   (3)   (4)   (5)   Emotional factors did **not** contribute significantly to the offense (pattern).

E.   FAMILY HISTORY PROBLEMS

Parental family problems childhood and adolescence contributed significantly to the offense (pattern).   (1)   (2)   (3)   (4)   (5)   Parental family problems of childhood and adolescence did **not** contribute significantly to the offense (pattern).

F.   ISOLATED SITUATIONAL (TEMPORARY CIRCUMSTANCES)

Unusual or temporary circumstances in the probationer's life, which are unlikely to be repeated, contributed significantly to the offense.   (1)   (2)   (3)   (4)   (5)   Offense is **not** a result of unusual or temporary circumstances (i.e., offense is part of a continuing pattern).

Do not merely rate infrequency of offenses. Rate OVERALL PATTERN.

G.   INTERPERSONAL MANIPULATION

Uses, controls, and/or manipulates others to gain his/her own ends with little regard for the welfare of others.   (1)   (2)   (3)   (4)   (5)   Misuse of others, manipulation, and control, did **not** contribute significantly to offense (pattern).

SUPERVISION PLANNING

STEP 1: FORCE FIELD ANALYSIS: *Using all resources available, identify the strengths/resources and problems/weaknesses, if any, that pertain to each area in reference to the probationer and his (her) primary environment.*

Area	Rank	Strength/Resource	Problem/Weakness	Rank
Present Offense				
Offense pattern				
Correctional History				
Education				
Mental Ability				
Employment Record				
Vocational Skills				
Finances				
Residential Stability				
Family History				
Interpersonal Skills				
Companions				
Intimate Relationships				
Emotional Stability				
Drugs & Alcohol				
Plans & Goals				
Probation Expectations				
Sexual Behavior				
Health				
Values & Attitudes				

STEP 2: PRIORITIZATION: *Apply the following criteria to the above in order to rank the four most important areas relative to the probationer's legal difficulties: the relative strength, the alterability, the relative speed with which change can occur, and the interdependency with other areas.*

STEP 3: TENTATIVE SUPERVISION PLAN: *Using the priority areas from step B, "pencil in" tentative goals, objectives, and action plans. Use Supervision Guidelines as a resource.*

1. Problem Statement: _____

    Long-range Goal: _____

    Short-range Objectives: _____

    _____ Date Achieved: _____

    _____ Date Achieved: _____

    Probationer Action Plan: _____

    _____

    _____

    _____

    _____

    Officer/Referral Action Plan: _____

    _____

    _____

2. Problem Statement: _____

    Long-range Goal: _____

    Short-range Objectives: _____

    _____ Date Achieved: _____

    _____ Date Achieved: _____

    Probationer Action Plan: _____

    _____

    _____

    _____

    Officer/Referral Action Plan: _____

    _____

STEP 4: FINAL PLAN: *Negotiate the above with the probationer and modify accordingly.*

REASSESSMENT PLAN: *Revise at routine intervals or when special circumstances so indicate.*

1. Problem Statement: _____

    Long-range Goal: _____

    Short-range Objectives: _____

    _____ Date Achieved: _____

    _____ Date Achieved: _____

    Probationer Action Plan: _____

    _____

    _____

    _____

    _____

    Officer/Referral Action Plan: _____

    _____

    _____

2. Problem Statement: _____

    Long-range Goal: _____

    Short-range Objectives: _____

    _____ Date Achieved: _____

    _____ Date Achieved: _____

    Probationer Action Plan: _____

    _____

    _____

    Officer/Referral Action Plan. _____

    _____

    _____

Ohio State Bar Foundation
2nd rev. 3-1-79

FELONY SENTENCING WORKSHEET

Defendant's Name _____ Case No. _____

OFFENSE RATING

1. Degree of Offense

Assess points for the **one** most serious offense or its equivalent for which offender is being sentenced, as follows: 1st° felony = 4 points; 2nd° felony = 3 points; 3rd° felony = 2 points; 4th° felony = 1 point. _____

2. Multiple Offenses

Assess 2 points if one or more of the following applies: (A) offender is being sentenced for two or more offenses committed in different incidents; (B) offender is currently under a misdemeanor or felony sentence imposed by any court; or (C) present offense was committed while offender on probation or parole. _____

3. Actual or Potential Harm

Assess 2 points if one or more of the following applies: (A) serious physical harm to a person was caused; (B) property damage or loss of $300 or more was caused; (C) there was a high risk of any such harm, damage or loss, though not caused; (D) the gain or potential gain from theft offense(s) was $300 or more; or (E) dangerous ordnance or a deadly weapon was actually used in the incident, or its use was attempted or threatened. _____

4. Culpability

Assess 2 points if one or more of the following applies: (A) offender was engaging in continuing criminal activity as a source of income or livelihood; (B) offense was part of a continuing conspiracy to which offender was party; or (C) offense included shocking and deliberate cruelty in which offender participated or acquiesced. _____

5. Mitigation

Deduct 1 point for **each** of the following, as applicable: (A) there was substantial provocation, justification or excuse for offense; (B) victim induced or facilitated offense; (C) offense was committed in the heat of anger; and (D) the property damaged, lost or stolen was restored or recovered without significant cost to the victim. _____

NET TOTAL = OFFENSE RATING _____

OFFENDER RATING

1. Prior Convictions

Assess 2 points for **each** verified prior felony conviction, any jurisdiction. Count adjudications of delinquency for felony as convictions.

Assess 1 point for **each** verified prior misdemeanor conviction, any jurisdiction. Count adjudications of delinquency for misdemeanor as convictions. Do **not** count traffic or intoxication offenses, or disorderly conduct, disturbing the peace or equivalent offenses. _____

2. Repeat Offenses

Assess 2 points if present offense is offense of violence, sex offense, theft offense, or drug abuse offense, and offender has one or more prior convictions for same type of offense. _____

3. Prison Commitments

Assess 2 points if offender was committed on one or more occasions to a penitentiary, reformatory or equivalent institution in any jurisdiction. Count commitments to Ohio Youth Commission or similar commitments in other jurisdictions. _____

4. Parole and Similar Violations

Assess 2 points if one or more of the following applies: (A) offender has previously had probation or parole for misdemeanor or felony revoked; (B) present offense committed while offender on probation or parole; (C) present offense committed while offender free on bail; or (D) present offense committed while offender in custody. _____

5. Credits

Deduct 1 point for **each** of the following as applicable: (A) offender has voluntarily made bona fide, realistic arrangements for at least partial restitution; (B) offender was age 25 or older at time or first felony conviction; (C) offender has been substantially law abiding for at least 3 years; and (D) offender lives with his or her spouse or minor children or both, **and** is either a breadwinner for the family or, if there are minor children, a housewife. _____

NET TOTAL = OFFENDER RATING _____

PROCEED TO DETERMINATION OF SENTENCE ON BACK

INDICATED SENTENCE

Circle the box on the chart where the offense and offender ratings determined on the previous page intersect. This indicates a normal sentencing package. If the indicated sentence appears too severe or too lenient for the particular case, do not hesitate to vary from the indicated sentence. In that event, however, list the reasons for the variance in the space provided at the bottom of the page.

		OFFENDER RATING				
		0 - 2	3 - 5	6 - 8	9 - 11	12 or more
OFFENSE RATING	6 or more	Impose one of three lowest minimum terms. No probation.	Impose one of three highest minimum terms. No probation.	Impose one of three highest minimum terms. No probation.	Impose one of two highest minimum terms. Make at least part of multiple sentences consecutive. No probation.	Impose highest minimum term. Make at least part of multiple sentences consecutive. No probation.
	5	Impose one of three lowest minimum terms. Some form of probation indicated only with special mitigation.	Impose one of three lowest minimum terms. No probation.	Impose one of three highest minimum terms. No probation.	Impose one of three highest minimum terms. No probation.	Impose one of two highest minimum terms. Make at least part of multiple sentences consecutive. No probation.
	4	Impose one of two lowest minimum terms. Some form of probation indicated.	Impose one of three lowest minimum terms. Some form of probation indicated only with special mitigation.	Impose one of three lowest minimum terms. No probation.	Impose one of three highest minimum terms. No probation.	Impose one of three highest minimum terms. No probation.
	3	Impose one of two lowest minimum terms. Some form of probation indicated.	Impose one of two lowest minimum terms. Some form of probation indicated.	Impose one of three lowest minimum terms. Some form of probation indicated only with special mitigation.	Impose one of three lowest minimum terms. No probation.	Impose one of three highest minimum terms. No probation.
	0 - 2	Impose lowest minimum term. Some form of probation indicated.	Impose one of two lowest minimum terms. Some form of probation indicated.	Impose one of three lowest minimum terms. Some form of probation indicated.	Impose one of three lowest minimum terms. Some form of probation indicated only with special mitigation.	Impose one of three lowest minimum terms. No probation.

PROBATION AVAILABILITY

Sometimes the above chart will indicate probation when it is forbidden by law in the particular case. Before recommending or imposing sentence in any case, consult the statutes for probationability and check the boxes below if applicable.

[ ] OFFENDER IS A REPEAT OFFENDER OR A DANGEROUS OFFENDER. See RC §2929.01 for definitions. Probation for drug treatment permitted in limited cases under RC §2951.04 (B) (3).

[ ] OFFENSE IS NON-PROBATIONAL PER SE. Includes aggravated murder, murder, rape, felonious sexual penetration, any offense committed while armed with a firearm or dangerous ordnance, and any drug offense in which a sentence of "actual incarceration" is required.

SENTENCE IMPOSED; VARIANCES

ACTUAL SENTENCE IMPOSED

Term imposed each count, and fine if any

_____

_____

_____

[ ] Committed to serve sentence.
[ ] Committed but shock probation possible.
[ ] Other probation granted (describe) - _____

_____

_____

REASONS FOR VARIANCE

If the actual sentence imposed varies from the disposition indicated on the chart in any respect, state the reasons for the variance.

_____

_____

_____

_____

_____

_____

_____

DEPARTMENT OF CORRECTIONS
DIVISION OF PROBATION & PAROLE

Client No. _____ Client Name: _____ Officer No. _____

CLIENT RISK ASSESSMENT	CLIENT NEED ASSESSMENT

CLIENT RISK ASSESSMENT

Instructions: Enter numerical rating in box at right.

1. **TOTAL NUMBER OF PRIOR FELONY CONVICTIONS:**
   (include juvenile ajudications, if known):
   a. None .... Enter 0
   b. One .... Enter 2
   c. Two or more .... Enter 4 ☐

2. **PRIOR NUMBER OF PROBATION/PAROLE SUPERVISION PERIODS:**
   (include juvenile, if known):
   a. None .... Enter 0
   b. One or more .... Enter 4 ☐

3. **PRIOR PROBATION/PAROLE REVOCATIONS:**
   (adult only):
   a. None .... Enter 0
   b. One or more .... Enter 4 ☐

4. **AGE AT FIRST KNOWN CONVICTION OR ADJUDICATION:**
   (include juvenile, if known)
   a. 24 years or older .... Enter 0
   b. 20 through 23 years .... Enter 2
   c. 19 years or younger .... Enter 4 ☐

5. **HISTORY OF ALCOHOL ABUSE:**
   a. No history of abuse .... Enter 0
   b. Occasional or prior abuse .... Enter 2
   c. Frequent current abuse .... Enter 4 ☐

6. **HISTORY OF OTHER SUBSTANCE ABUSE:**
   (prior to incarceration for parolees):
   a. No history of abuse .... Enter 0
   b. Occasional or prior abuse .... Enter 1
   c. Frequent current abuse .... Enter 2 ☐

7. **AMOUNT OF TIME EMPLOYED IN LAST 12 MONTHS:**
   (prior to incarceration for parolees; based on 35 hr. week):
   a. 7 months or more .... Enter 0
   b. 4 months through 6 months .... Enter 1
   c. Less than 4 months .... Enter 2
   d. Not applicable .... Enter 0 ☐

8. **AGENT IMPRESSION OF OFFENDER'S ATTITUDE:**
   a. Motivated to change; receptive to assistance . Enter 0
   b. Dependent or unwilling to accept responsibility .. Enter 3
   c. Rationalizes behavior; negative; not motivated to change .... Enter 5 ☐

9. **RECORD OF CONVICTION FOR SELECTED OFFENSES:**
   (include current offense; add categories and enter total):
   a. None of the following .... Enter 0
   b. Burglary, Theft, Auto Theft, Robbery .... Add 2
   c. Forgery, Deceptive Practices (Fraud, Bad Check, Drugs) .... Add 3 ☐

10. **ASSAULTIVE OFFENSES:**
    a. Crimes against persons which include use of weapon, physical force, threat of force, all sex crimes, and vehicular homicide.

    ☐ Yes   ☐ No

CLIENT NEED ASSESSMENT

Instructions: Enter numerical rating in box at right.

1. **ACADEMIC/VOCATIONAL SKILLS:**
   a. High school or above skill level .... Enter 0
   b. Has vocational training; additional not needed/ desired .... Enter 1
   c. Has some skills; additional needed/ desired ...... Enter 3
   d. No skills; training needed .... Enter 5 ☐

2. **EMPLOYMENT:**
   a. Satisfactory employment for 1 year or longer .... Enter 0
   b. Employed; no difficulties reported; or homemaker, student, retired, or disabled and unable to work ..... Enter 1
   c. Part-time, seasonal, unstable employment or needs additional employment; unemployed, but has a skill .... Enter 4
   d. Unemployed & virtually unemployable; needs training .... Enter 7 ☐

3. **FINANCIAL STATUS:**
   a. Longstanding pattern of self-sufficiency .... Enter 0
   b. No current difficulties .... Enter 1
   c. Situational or minor difficulties .... Enter 4
   d. Severe difficulties .... Enter 6 ☐

4. **LIVING ARRANGEMENTS (Within last six months):**
   a. Stable and supportive relationships with family or others in living group .... Enter 0
   b. Client lives alone or independently within another household .... Enter 1
   c. Client experiencing occasional, moderate interpersonal problems within living group .... Enter 4
   d. Client experiencing frequent and serious interpersonal problems within living group ...... Enter 6 ☐

5. **EMOTIONAL STABILITY:**
   a. No symptoms of instability .... Enter 1
   b. Symptoms limit, but do not prohibit adequate functioning .... Enter 5
   c. Symptoms prohibit adequate functioning .... Enter 8 ☐

6. **ALCOHOL USAGE (Current):**
   a. No interference with functioning .... Enter 1
   b. Occasional abuse; some disruption of functioning; may need treatment .... Enter 4
   c. Frequent abuse; serious disruption; needs treatment .... Enter 7 ☐

7. **OTHER SUBSTANCE USAGE (Current):**
   a. No interference with functioning .... Enter 1
   b. Occasional substance abuse; some disruption of functioning; may need treatment .... Enter 4
   c. Frequent substance abuse; serious disruption; needs treatment .... Enter 6 ☐

8. **REASONING/INTELLECTUAL ABILITY:**
   a. Able to function independently .... Enter 1
   b. Some need for assistance; potential for adequate adjustment .... Enter 4
   c. Deficiencies suggest limited ability to function independently .... Enter 7 ☐

9. **HEALTH:**
   a. Sound physical health; seldom ill .... Enter 1
   b. Handicap or illness interferes with functioning on a recurring basis .... Enter 2
   c. Serious handicap or chronic illness; needs frequent medical care .... Enter 3 ☐

10. **AGENT'S IMPRESSION OF CLIENT'S NEEDS:**
    a. None .... Enter 0
    b. Low .... Enter 1
    c. Moderate .... Enter 4
    d. High .... Enter 6 ☐

Total Score (Range: 0-34) ☐☐

Total Score (Range: 5-61) ☐☐

SCORING AND OVERRIDE

Instruction: Check appropriate block.

SCORE BASED SUPERVISION LEVEL: ☐ Maximum ☐ Medium ☐ Minimum

Check if there is an override: ☐ Override Explanation: _____

FINAL CATEGORY OF SUPERVISION: ☐ Maximum ☐ Medium ☐ Minimum

Date Supervision Level Assigned
MONTH DAY YEAR
☐☐ ☐☐ ☐☐

_____
APPROVED (Supervisor Signature and Date)   Agent

RISK ASSESSMENT SCORING GUIDE

This scale emphasizes behavior while on supervision. The reassessment is based on behavior since the last classification form was completed.

1. Total number of prior felony convictions (include juvenile adjudications if known).

    A. Do not count present offense. The item refers to prior convictions.

    B. Multiple convictions are counted as separate offenses.

    C. For juveniles, this includes only behavior which would be a felony if committed by an adult.

2. Prior number of probation/parole supervision periods. (Include juvenile, if known.)

    A. Revocation hearings which result in a continuance are not counted as a new period of probation/parole.

    B. For juvenile records count only those periods of probation that follow an actual adjudication.

    C. Note: The officer needs only one prior probation/parole in order to move client out of the zero category. It is not necessary to know the total number of revocations which may have occurred.

3. Prior probation/parole revocations - (Adult only)

    A. Disposition of the Court or Board must be revocation, even though the client may later be reinstated or immediately granted a new parole/probation.

4. Age at first known conviction or adjudication, include juvenile if known.

    A. Convictions may be for a felony or misdemeanant.

    B. Exclude routine traffic, such as: speeding, stop sign, parking violations, etc. Include convictions for DUI, Reckless Driving, Careless Driving, etc.

    C. For juveniles, include only those instances where a person has actually been adjudicated for a crime they could be convicted of if they were an adult.

5. History of alcohol abuse.

    A. This item should be interpreted to mean "in the last 36 months".

    B. The officer is not to make a judgment based simply on number of drinks consumed per day or information of that nature; rather, does the client's drinking interfere with his/her ability to function and meet day to day demands. Indications of problems in this area would thus include such things as arriving for work late due to a hangover, frequent drunken quarrels at home or work, excessive expenditure on alcohol etc. Alcohol-related arrests should generally be coded as indications of serious problems.

C. Probationers/parolees being supervisied for a crime such as DUI Man-slaughter should automatically be scored as four.

6. History of other substance abuse.

    A. The officer should interpret this item to mean "in the last 36 months". The scoring of this item is similar to that of the alcohol item with one difference. The officer must bear in mind that drug usage may, in itself, be a violation of the law and thus, is much more threatening to the client's remaining out of legal trouble. The officer should be attuned to other problems stemming from legal drug use as well. In this regard, prescriptions which the client has should be scrutinized in terms of both frequency and duration of usage.

7. Amount of time employed in the last 12 months. (Prior to any incarceration based on 35 hour week).

    A. A person will receive a zero in this category if he has been employed for seven or more months, averaging at least 35 hours per week during the last 12 months.

    A person will receive a score of one if he has been employed four to six months, averaging a 35 hour work week during the last 12 months.

    A client will receive a two if he has been employed less than four months throughout the past twelve months.

    B. Part time employment should be averaged. If a client has been employed for the past twelve months working 20 hours per week, he would receive a score of one.

    C. Students are scored non-applicable, even though they may have been work-ing part time. Use non-applicable if in the officer's judgment, there are valid reasons why the client could not have been employed, as in situations of extended illness, disability, or are retired and receiv-ing a monthly retirement check.

8. Current Living Situations: This area can only be determined after a home visit has been conducted.

    A. A person will receive a zero in this category if his present living situa-tion is stable. There must be an adequate income and no serious family disturbances such as fights, which require law enforcement or outside parties to calm the incident. Takes pride in the appearance of his/her residence.

    B. A person will receive a three if there is an inadequate income in the home, occasional serious arguments, which may require outside assistance to calm and/or cluttered living area.

C. A person will receive a five if any of the following conditions exist: 1) if there is little, if any, income coming into the home; 2) if there are fights which require law enforcement assistance to calm; 3) if there is separation or divorce; 4) if there is dirty cluttered home; 5) if Child Protection has investigated abuse or neglect or any other serious incident which creates disorganization or stress.

9. Agent's impression of offender's attitude.

A. This term is inherently subjective. The officer will find scoring easier if he/she focuses upon the phrase "motivated to change". Does this client recognize the need for change and does he/she accept the responsibility for change. Are there any indications that he/she is beginning to make initial behavior changes? The difference between a score of three or five would be the client's motivation to change.

10. Record of conviction for selected offenses. (Include current offense— Add categories and enter total)

A. This category includes convictions, felony or misdemeanant, during the past five years.

B. The only possible answers are zero, two, three, or five. If the item does not apply, enter zero. The only way to receive five points is to have at least one offense which receives two points plus one which receives three points.

11. Violent or assaultive offenses within the last five years.

A. This category receives no points. If yes is checked, the client may be classified maximum regardless of the number of points acquired.

B. If a client was committed to a treatment for custody, exclude the time spent in those facilities as part of the last five years, unless the client was convicted for a new offense.

C. For parolees, count assaultive offenses occuring five years prior to incarceration.

D. An assaultive offense is defined as an offense against a person which involves the use of a weapon, physical force or threat of force, all forceable felonies, and all sex crimes.

E. The current offense is counted if it is assaultive.

INTRODUCTION:

The needs assessment form has been constructed to provide a standardized information base from which programs may be developed. Its purpose is to serve as a tool in making objective classification decisions.

The items and scores on the instrument are based on agent's time required to deal with the various problem areas and levels. The basic idea behind the scoring of each item is the same - to what extent, if any, is the client's ability to function in the day to day world impaired. The needs assessment instrument differs from the risk assessment instrument in that both positive and negative points are awarded.

The form is designed to indicate areas of programming need and to distinguish among those clients who definitely need programming, those who may require some programming and those that need no programming in each designated area. The needs assessment form has not been designed to make classification a more rigid, mechanical or routine process, nor is its purpose to eliminate client input. In those areas where programming is definitely needed or may be needed, the agent should discuss with the client the various program options and the nature of each program. After reviewing the needed programming and the options available, the probation/parole officer should formulate a supervision plan.

The usefulness and the needs assessment instrument is largely dependent upon the quality of information relied upon.

The goal of the needs assessment instrument is to eliminate subjectivity and the personal interpretation from the classification decision making process. The new classification process will consist of decisions based upon objective criteria. It is believed that this process will be beneficial to both the probation and parole officer who must justify their decisions, and to clients being classified who demand fairness.

1. ACADEMIC AND VOCATIONAL SKILLS.

The item focuses upon functional skills rather than actual academic credentials. Therefore, a skilled craftsman may receive zero even though he or she may have little formal education. The individuals ability to make his or her way in the world is important consideration. College, high school diploma or G.E.D. may not be enough-ability must be shown.

    (a) High school or above skill level (demonstrates ability)... Enter 0
    (b) Has vocational training; additional not needed/desired
        (adequate skills).. Enter 1
    (c) Has some skills; additional needed/desired, low skill
        level, may have high school diploma or G.E.D. but demonstrates difficulty to read and write. Real difficulty
        filling out written reports or job applications. Has
        ability to do better................................... Enter 3
    (d) No skills; training needed, minimal - retarded, special
        education classes or unable to read, write or simple
        mathematical computations............................. Enter 5

2. EMPLOYMENT:

The probation/parole officer must look beyond simple employment/unemployment in rating the item. Under employment should be taken into account as should "unsatisfactory" employment. An example of "unsatisfactory" employment would excessive anxiety or become immobilzed by stress? Ability to cope with day to day life situations is a concern here. The five score would be used for a neurotic client with eight reserved for those with psychotic characteristics.

    (a) No symptoms of instability; no apparent stress, well adjusted...... .... Enter 1
    (b) Symptoms limit, but do not prohibit adequate functioning; neurotic, mild symptoms of depression, anxiety or acting out, occasional abuse of alcohol or other drugs........... Enter 5
    (c) Symptoms prohibit adequate functioning; psychotic, severe symptoms of depression, anxiety or acting out, frequent use of alcohol or other drugs; suicidal................... Enter 8

6. ALCOHOL USAGE (Current):

As on the risk assessment instrument, "interference with functioning" is the key here. Parole/probation officers are to avoid moral judgments regarding alcohol use and focus instead upon the role of alcohol in the client's life. Alcohol related driving offenses receive a seven.

    (a) No interference with functioning, no alcohol abuse........ Enter 1
    (b) Occasional abuse; some disruption of functioning; may need treatment; gets "drunk" by own definition twice a month or more; some disruption in functioning when drinking (whether or not "drunk") with family, work, socially, etc. Minor alcohol related offenses...................... Enter 4
    (c) Frequent abuse; serious disruption; needs treatment; drinks regularly although never or rarely gets "drunk"; has withdrawal symptoms if stops drinking; has physical symptoms of alcoholism; memory lapse, black-outs, passing out; serious disfunctions at work; absenteeism, fired, fights with co-workers or other supervisors or customers; with family; becomes violent, neglectful, abusive towards spouse, children, parents, can't pay bills, separation occurrence, past driving record involving alcohol; present offense or any arrests within the past five years involing alcohol before or during............................. Enter 7

7. OTHER SUBSTANCE ABUSE (Current):

The scoring of this item is to be accomplished in the same manner as the "drug usage" item in the risk assessment instrument. A four score would apply to clients convicted of marijuana possession while the six would refer to present involvement with the drug.

    (a) No interference with functioning, no abuse................ Enter 1
    (b) Occasional substance abuse; some disruption of functioning; may need treatment; convicted of marijuana possession, but no longer using.................................. Enter 4
    (c) Frequent substance abuse; serious disruption; needs treatment; addiction or recent use of marijuana, narcotics, medication as not prescribed; conviction for possession or intent to deliver; deals in selling of drugs...... Enter 6

8. REASONING/INTELLECTUAL ATTITUDE:

This item looks at organic cognitive capacity as opposed to emotional ability, hence the problem level relates to the possibility of retardation. Is the client mentally alert or able to function effectively?

(a) Able to function independently; appears to be of average intelligence. Can't comprehend what is being said in normal conversation. Can't read and comprehend rules of probation/parole.................................... Enter 1
(b) Some need for assistance; potential for adequate adjust-ment; has difficulty in understanding written or verbal communication; has difficulty completing forms without assistance; has difficulty using or reading a clock, ruler, calendar, dictionary; has difficulty in following directions; emphasis on difficulty in comprehension....... Enter 4
(c) Deficiencies suggest limited ability to function inde-pendently; borderline mental retardation; client cannot function independently; client receives SSI Benefits for reason due to developmental disabilities; client is em-ployed in shelter work house...............................Enter 7

9. HEALTH:

The probation/parole officer should take mental health into account (parti-cularly in the case of the substance abuser), as well as the presence of physical handicaps. Alcoholism or drug abuse is automatically two points.
(a) Sound physical health; seldom ill; no problems............ Enter 1
(b) Handicap or illness interferences with functioning on a reoccurring basis; client may have a condition which restricts employment, requires occasional medical atten-tion (high blood pressure, heart condition, epilepsy, missing limb, back problems, etc.)........................ Enter 2
(c) Serious handicap or chronic illnesses; needs frequent medical care; client has a condition which severely re-stricts employment and program participation. He/she requires frequent medical attention and may be on medica-tion (blindness, serious heart conditions, terminal illness, deafness, paralysis, etc.)................................ Enter 3

10. AGENT'S IMPRESSION OF CLIENT'S NEEDS:

This is designed to accommodate the agent's subjective impressions.
(a) None.. Enter 0
(b) Low... Enter 1
(c) Moderate.. Enter 4
(d) High... Enter 6

Chapter 7
Nondirective Counseling: Theory and Practice

Love is the increase of self by means of other.

Spinoza

Robert Martinson's article "What Works? Questions and Answers about Prison Reform" (1974) provided much grist for the mills of those who subscribe to a "lock 'em up and lose the key" philosophy. They were so excited about Martinson's alleged findings that the rhetorical "what works?" was translated into the nihilistic "nothing works." Nevertheless, the Martinson report was interpreted as a justification for terminating all efforts to rehabilitate criminals in favor of punishing them, preferably by long periods of incarceration. Disregarding the fact that to incarcerate all convicted criminals would be financially prohibitive (see Walker's [1985] excellent analysis of the financial waterfall needed to implement this philosophy), to consign all convicted criminals to prison is both morally inhumane and socially insane. Nearly all incarcerated felons will leave prison someday, and they will emerge harder, crueler, more savage, and more bitter than they were before they went in. We already incarcerate more people in the United States than does any other country with humanitarian pretensions. Yet the call for more and more punishment continues to fall on receptive ears.

Before we can determine that something does or doesn't work, we first have to define thresholds. A rehabilitation program is not a machine that either works or doesn't. Where human beings are concerned, nothing works for everybody, or even anybody, 100% of the time. What rate of success is acceptable before we say a program works: 90%, 80%, 50%, 10%? Of the 231 studies that Martinson included in his review, he found that 48% reported some degree of success. If your criterion for success is a demanding 100%, then indeed nothing works. For my part, a 48% success rate (however "success" was defined in the original studies) is cause for optimistic celebration. Walker (1985:170) reports that other reviews of the kind of studies reviewed by Martinson found success rates of between 67% and 77%. Let's then dismiss the pessimism of the "nothing works" crowd and explore counseling theories designed to help those caught up in the criminal justice system to come to grips with their problems.

Counseling

What Is Counseling?

Our first task is to differentiate between the terms *counseling* and *psychotherapy*. Some claim that there is no essential difference between the two terms since their definitions and roles are interchangeable. Further, the theories presented in a text in counseling are the same theories contained in a text on psychotherapy. However, in keeping with my early advice to respect boundaries of expertise, I must stress the differences between the two.

Psychotherapy is practiced by psychiatrists or psychologists with many years of highly specialized training. True, they employ many of the same techniques used by those engaged in counseling, but they have a deeper theoretical understanding of causality pertaining to the conditions they are treating.

The term *treating* delineates another important distinction between psychotherapy and counseling. Psychotherapists operate with a pathology interpretation of their *patients'* problems; counselors are advised to operate with a deficiency interpretation of their *clients'* problems. Psychotherapy differs from counseling in the depth and seriousness of the problems dealt with and in the intensity of the treatment. Psychotherapists attempt to help their patients by a

restructuring of the basic personality over a long period of time. Counselors attempt to help their clients with specific life-adjustment problems and to develop the personality that already exists. Another way of stating this difference might be to say that psychotherapists deal primarily with intrapersonal conflicts, whereas counselors deal primarily with interpersonal conflicts. When a client is obviously in need of treatment that exceeds your capability as a counselor, you shouldn't hesitate to relinquish the further handling of the case to those more qualified to deal with it.

Similarity between interviewing and counseling. Counseling is a series of concerned responses offered to clients who have concerns and problems that adversely affect their functioning. Counseling is essentially an extension of the interviewing process and utilizes the same communication skills and techniques. However, "techniques" are secondary to the warmth, acceptance, and understanding the counselor brings to the task. It has been suggested that good (that is, open, warm, accepting, and empathetic) counselors operating with different theoretical perspectives are more similar to one another than are good and poor counselors with the same theoretical perspective (Lytle, 1964). If you work on improving the quality of the self you bring to the counseling process, then the techniques will come easily to you.

Differences between interviewing and counseling. Although I have said that counseling is an extension of the interviewing process, certain differences between interviewing and counseling in a criminal justice setting should be emphasized. First, you are more likely to encounter client resistance during the counseling process than during the interviewing process. During the PSI interview or parole hearing, the client is fairly anxious to reveal a contrite and cooperative demeanor because he or she knows that you make recommendations. After a case has been disposed of, clients tend to lose some of their motivation to cooperate along with the anxiety about the disposition of the case. This ten-

Lindsey Whitehead is the chief probation officer of the Lucas County Adult Department, Toledo, Ohio, and a Certified Alcoholism Counselor (CAC). He was a probation officer and unit supervisor for seven years before becoming chief. He holds master's degrees in guidance and counseling and public administration.

Getting Back in the Race
Lindsey Whitehead

A few days ago as I was returning from lunch, I saw a young man who looked vaguely familiar to me leaving the probation department. As he approached me, he smiled and asked, "How are you, Mr. Whitehead? You don't remember me, do you?" I wasn't very sure of what the relationship between us had been, but after talking with him for a few moments the memory was clear.

The last time I had seen him was in 1978 when I was his probation officer. He was 18 or 19 years old at the time, and was on probation for his first felony conviction as an adult. He had been convicted of robbing a carry-out store. This young man's social history was very typical of those who find themselves in trouble with the criminal justice system. He was from a broken home, lived in poverty, inadequately educated, unemployed, and his spirit had been demoralized.

During the time that he was on probation he obtained his GED and enrolled in a vocational school to learn welding. Upon completion of training he was immediately hired as a welder by a local company.

"But why is he here at the probation department?" I wondered. "Is he in trouble again?" He explained apologetically that he had been caught with some cocaine and was now serving another term of probation. He further explained that this was the first time that he had been in trouble with the law for nine years and that he was still working as a welder with the same company and trying to be productive.

A few years ago, a young mother of beautiful twin girls was placed on probation for forgery. She had little motivation to do anything to try to improve her pathetic situation. But through the persuasion and leverage of the probation department and the court, she enrolled in the department's GED program. At first she didn't like it, but in time she became enthusiastic and was a willing participant. At the graduation ceremony, as her daughters looked on, she was extremely proud as she walked across the stage to be recognized for having completed her GED. She had come to realize that her efforts could result in positive changes in her life, and that, at the very least, her probation officer considered her worthwhile and cared for her.

There is nothing unique or unusual about these two cases. Similar experiences are repeated daily in probation and parole departments throughout the country. Pencil and paper can no doubt demonstrate a lack of success in the community corrections function, and perhaps this is so. But those of us who are in the trenches often have the opportunity to see the human spirit triumphant over what could have been lost lives. A probation or parole officer cannot run the race for those who have dropped out, or for those who never got into the race in the first place. But it is encouraging, if only occasionally, to see people pick themselves up and get into the race of life through the help of caring and professional probation and parole services.

dency is a good reason to make the best possible effort to establish a working rapport during the initial interview. If you don't establish such a relationship when the client is fairly amenable, you will find rapport much more difficult to develop later on. Don't be disheartened if you do perceive a change in some clients' demeanor following case disposition. Accept it as a professional challenge. Some of my most treasured success stories involved clients of this type.

Second, assuming that you are successful in establishing a working relationship with your clients, you are ready to communicate with them at a deeper level in successive counseling sessions by carefully developing an empathetic understanding of them. You no longer have to gather large amounts of data from them, so you are free to concentrate on specific problem areas. Therefore, counseling differs from interviewing in its depth.

Counseling Theories

With this brief introduction to counseling, we turn to five of the most popular theories of counseling, two in this chapter and three in the next. Important aspects of counseling will be illustrated in the context of the theories that most strongly emphasize those aspects. Special attention will be paid to the processes of generating empathy and dealing with the reluctant/resistant client.

You may view the large number of theoretical orientations to counseling (and there are certainly far more than the five presented here) in two ways. You may consider it to be so much clutter, indicative of a lack of scientific rigor in the field. Alternatively, you may regard it positively as a rich mine of possibilities in which you can dig for counseling gems. No one theory is applicable to all problems and concerns with which you will deal, and no one theory exhausts the uniqueness of each client. I am reminded of a profound statement, the originator of which I have long forgotten: "Each person is like all other persons, like some other persons, and like no other person." It follows that certain insights from

one counseling theory may be universally applicable, be applicable only some of the time, or not be applicable at all on some occasions. The more theoretical insights you have in your repertoire, the better you will be able to respond successfully to the diverse clients and problems you will encounter. Loyalty to any one theory may severely limit your effectiveness by leading you to stretch everything to fit it and/or to ignore whatever won't. By developing an eclectic approach, picking and choosing those elements that fit your style and serve your needs, you will begin to discern some of the common threads woven into all theories. It is my contention that the agreement of greatest importance among all theories is the vital necessity of all human beings to love and be loved.

The present chapter focuses on psychoanalysis and client-centered therapy, which we group separately from transactional analysis, rational-emotive therapy, and reality therapy. Psychoanalysis and client-centered therapy are nondirective forms of counseling. By this I mean that they put great faith in their clients' ability to discover their own capabilities and find their own directions. The counselor plays a relatively passive role and is reluctant to impose his or her values on clients and provide them with direction. Psychoanalysis and client-centered therapy are rarely used in a correctional setting, primarily because they are too nondirective, and also because the terminology and concepts are too abstruse and the methods are difficult for the nonspecialist to apply. They have been included nonetheless because of certain unique aspects, which we will outline as we go along.

Psychoanalysis

Although I have said that psychoanalysis is beyond the boundaries of expertise for the nonpsychiatrist or nonpsychologist, I include it because it contains some very useful insights into the nature of human beings. Whereas the other four theories focus primarily on the present, psychoanalysis puts great emphasis on the role of the past in shaping current behavior. Since so many emotional and behavioral difficulties stem to a large degree from past experiences, I feel that it is important to be aware of and explore a client's past as a vehicle for understanding his or her present.

According to Fine, "The technical task of psychoanalysis has been to elucidate the nature of love" (1973:16). Freud himself has stated that happiness exists in "the way of life which makes love the center of everything, which looks for all satisfaction in loving and being loved" (1961:29). The psychoanalyst explores the patient's childhood to uncover underlying reasons for his or her inability to love. We will relate what follows to the life history of Bill Bloggs as recounted in his PSI report. Again, we refer to the Bloggs case for illustration, not validation, of the theory.

The psychoanalytic theory of the tripartite structure of the personality—the id, ego, and superego—is too well known to warrant repeating here. Suffice it to say that its value lies in the recognition of both the "beast and angel in man" (Wrong, 1968). The bestial side of humanity is the side that most concerns the criminal justice worker. As a criminal justice worker, you are striving to assist the client in understanding himself or herself and to enlist that understanding in the task of strengthening the ego (the rational part of the personality) "so that it can appropriate fresh portions of the id [the irrational and impulsive part]. Where id was, there shall ego be" (Freud, 1965:80).

Psychosexual Stages

Psychoanalysis stresses the great importance of the so-called *psychosexual stages* involved in early character development. There are three such stages: oral, anal, and phallic. Each stage represents the child's first encounters with external restraints on natural urges. These encounters generate negative feelings in the child, such as hostility, hatred, anger, and destructiveness. Since the display of these feelings invites negative reactions from other people, the child learns to repress them, resulting in a later inability to accept and express his or her real feelings. This

barrier to self-knowledge must be breached in any counseling session.

Oral stage: From birth to age 1. The oral stage encompasses the first year of life, which, according to modern neurophysiology, is the critical period for the laying down of the neuronal pathways. This is the period of life in which the child learns love and security and in which the template for the child's basic personality is formed. At the mother's breast, the infant satisfies its hunger and needs for tactile stimulation. These are unconditioned needs (needs that don't have to be learned), the satisfaction of which the infant "loves" because they are intrinsically rewarding. When the infant identifies the source of its pleasure, it develops a love for that source that is stronger than the love of the pleasures the source affords. In this sense, then, love for mother is a sort of conditioned response due to the continual associations made between her and the pleasures she provides.

Negative behaviors, such as acquisitiveness and aggression, may develop as a result of not having these needs adequately met. According to this theory, these behaviors are substitutes for what the individual really needs—love. Such individuals feel unworthy, unwanted, and unaccepted and are mistrusting and rejecting of others. They cannot accept either themselves or others because they have not experienced acceptance. Early love experiences are a safeguard against this kind of negativism. This does not mean, of course, that all people who exhibit these negative characteristics have experienced an unloving childhood or that individuals who did experience an unloving childhood will necessarily exhibit them. The theory merely asserts that negative adult behaviors are more likely to characterize those individuals who experienced a childhood marked by a lack of love than to characterize those individuals who didn't.

As an exercise in understanding, reread the early life experiences of Bill Bloggs in the PSI report. Can we not see his extreme materialism and bursts of aggressive behavior as stemming from his lack of love during the oral stage of his life? It was plain that he was an unwanted child from the start. Wasn't he, by his own admission, quite socially isolated, and didn't he seek to win Susan's love by purchase?

Anal stage: Ages 1 through 3. In the anal stage the child first encounters discipline. The child has received a series of admonitions prior to this stage, such as "Don't touch that oven!" or "Stop biting the cat!" But the child encounters "real" discipline in the anal stage. He or she learns disciplined self-mastery by learning to control bodily functions through toilet training. Toilet training is given such importance in psychoanalytic theory because it is the first time that the child has to suppress natural urgings until they can be satisfied in the appropriate way and in the appropriate place. Although the child tends to rebel against the unnaturalness of toilet training, when the training is completed, he or she takes pride in the accomplishment of mastery. Parents should encourage this sense of mastery by allowing the child to explore and to make mistakes. They should emphasize that it's OK to make mistakes if one learns by them. If parents are constantly critical of mistakes the child makes, the child will be reluctant to explore and expand. If parents show exaggerated concern and do everything for the child, the child will not develop a sense of independence and autonomy. The children of such parents may forever be stuck in a "no-can-do" mode, lacking the self-confidence to expand their horizons and possessing poor self-concepts.

It is easy to view Bill's parents, especially his father, as being hypercritical of him during his formative years, given their personality portraits as painted by Officer Corrick. Bill's whole life seemed to revolve around doing things to please his father. He didn't leave home until he met Susan, indicating a strong sense of dependency. His hanging of the kitten, his bursts of extreme temper, and, not the least, his shooting of a policeman point vividly to his inability to express his feelings appropriately.

Phallic stage: Ages 3 through 5. The phallic stage is a period of early development of con-

science and sex-role identification. During this stage, the child becomes aware of his or her genitals. Masturbation is commonly begun during this stage, and parental response to the discovery of this activity can have serious consequences. If parents are overly moralistic, defining masturbation as something that "nice boys and girls don't do," they are setting the stage for the overcontrol of the superego. Such a rigid conformity to puritanical morality may also preclude the enjoyment of intimacy with others later in life because of inadequate sex-role identification.

We have no information about Bill's experiences during this stage in his life, but it takes no great flight of imagination to see Bill's father as being a real authoritarian moralist where the behavior of others was concerned. Bill did have a great deal of difficulty forming intimate attachments with others, and perhaps his belief that he was a woman in his "previous existence" is indicative of sex-role ambiguity. Bill's later forced incestuous experiences would have seriously conflicted with any early development of a moralistic conscience. The relaying of highly incongruous prescriptive and proscriptive messages to children is the basis of the so-called double-bind theory of schizophrenia because it undermines the child's foundations of reality (Bateson, Jackson, Haley, & Weakland, 1956). Bill did have, to say the least, a quite unusual view of reality, and he was deemed to be in the early stages of schizophrenic reaction.

Defense Mechanisms

The identification of a patient's defense mechanisms is an important part of the psychotherapeutic process. Defense mechanisms, which operate at an unconscious level (the individual is unaware of them), function to protect the ego from a threatening reality by distorting it. Defense mechanisms are not necessarily pathological. We all use some of them to some extent, and they can even be psychologically adaptive. It is only when they become an integral part of a pattern of life leading one to avoid facing reality that they become matters of great concern. There are numerous defense mechanisms listed in the psychoanalytic literature. Any comprehensive listing of them is beyond the scope of this book. We will discuss only those that I feel are most commonly seen in a criminal justice setting.

Denial is the blocking out of a portion of reality that is threatening to the ego. Sexual feelings and activities are often subject to this defense mechanism. Otherwise quite respectable child molesters will often attempt to deny to themselves that the incident ever occurred. This is not simply "forgetting" (*repression*), but rather refusing to recognize that it happened. Bill's denial of his enuresis may be seen as an attempt to deal with the residual anxiety felt about being "hog-tied" and whipped when he wet his bed, and his statement that his incestuous experiences were "no big deal" can be seen as an attempt to divorce himself from the possibility that he could have welcomed them.

Rationalization is the process of providing oneself with acceptable reasons for one's behavior or one's experiences in order to soothe a damaged ego. This is a definite favorite of criminal justice clients. Bill recited a litany of experiences to make Corrick understand "some underlying reason(s) for my behavior," thus creating the impression that he was more wronged than wrong. Rationalization helps us to maintain an acceptable self-image by downplaying our own badness and/or inadequacies; we parcel out blame or disvalue what we may want but can't get ("I didn't get the job because this is a racist society and I'm black. Who wants that stupid job anyway?").

Fixation is being immobilized at an earlier stage of personality development because the more appropriate stage is fraught with anxiety. Many criminal justice clients have a childlike attachment to the present because stepping into the future is stepping into the great unknown. Many have developed a pattern of helplessness through their dependence on the welfare system, which is the only financial "parent" many have ever known. To go out and expand one's capacities and explore one's potential is not one of the lessons imparted by the culture of poverty. As a criminal justice helper, you are charged with

helping your clients to develop a realistic orientation to the future by attempting to enlarge their sense of self-worth and their sense of the possible.

Displacement is the transference of feelings about someone or something onto another person or object because the original person or object is either inaccessible or too powerful. Anger or aggression is often displaced onto the innocent. Wife and child battering is frequently displaced aggression generated by others too powerful to attack directly. All too often one finds that criminal justice clients have much pent-up anger, the source of which they find difficult to identify. Further, they haven't learned to express their feelings in appropriate ways, so they vent them on "safe" targets. Bill's explosive temper and the hanging of the kitten would be interpreted by the psychoanalyst as a displacement of the anger he felt toward his father onto nonthreatening targets.

Intellectualization is a defense mechanism that some of the better-educated criminal justice clients use with accomplished skill, often attempting to assail legal reality by intellectualizing their crimes away. The marijuana dealer who launches into a monologue accusing society of hypocrisy, the petty forger who cites chapter and verse on white-collar crime, and the thief who discourses plausibly on corporate irresponsibility are all examples of people trying to avoid the reality of their own malfeasance. You may certainly accept the legitimacy of their position, but you must also impress on such clients that the issue is their behavior and not that of others and that they cannot avoid confronting their behavior by trying to refocus the discussion elsewhere.

Projection is the mechanism by which people attribute to others the feelings they refuse to see in themselves. One is often most troubled by the behavior of others when it mimics one's own repressed urges. The rough treatment of child molesters in prisons may be viewed as an attempt by other inmates to convince themselves that they couldn't possibly harbor such evil urges themselves. Clients who feel that no one understands or likes them, who harbor hostility toward others, are projecting onto others their negative feelings about themselves to others, thereby protecting the ego by confusing self with other. So many expressions of hostility and hatred of the world by criminal justice clients are really expressions of self-hatred. If you can aid clients to develop more positive feelings about themselves, you will find that they will develop better attitudes toward the world.

Lessons and Concerns

The primary usefulness of psychoanalytic theory for the criminal justice worker is that it provides insights that lead to a better understanding of clients' struggles with themselves and with the outside world. An understanding of the defense mechanisms is particularly useful in understanding client resistance to the helping process.

A little knowledge, it has been said, is dangerous. The criminal justice helper lacks the depth of training necessary to put the techniques of psychoanalysis into practice. To attempt to do so could result in negative consequences. What's more, it is too time consuming and involved. Many psychiatrists themselves have turned to more simplified methods to deal with the problems presented to them by the typical client—methods that have generally been found to be more productive of change because few clients require total personality restructuring. Sometimes the use of psychoanalysis for relatively minor life-adjustment problems is like swatting flies with a baseball bat. This is not, however, to belittle the often profound theoretical insights into human nature provided by this theory.

Client-Centered Approach

Carl Rogers developed his client-centered approach to counseling in response to the deficiencies he perceived in psychoanalysis. Being an existentialist/humanist thinker, he rejected the determinism of Freud's psychoanalytic theory in favor of self-determination and the natural goodness in humankind. Rather than viewing individuals as being driven by irrational biological impulses (which Rogers saw as an intimation that humans were basically antisocial), this approach sees human beings as basically good, self-driven, and possessing an innate capacity for self-actualization (the tendency to become all that they are able to become). Self-destructive behavior and attitudes arise from faulty self-concepts and an inability to grasp the fundamental truth that we are free agents in charge of our own destinies. Although I tend to find this kind of thinking somewhat Pollyannish in that it refuses to see the beast in man, it is ennobling in its enunciation.

Client-centered therapy eschews searching for causes and the teaching of counseling techniques in favor of asserting the absolute primacy of the nature of the client/counselor relationship. What the counselor brings to the relationship in terms of the quality of the self is far more critical than what he or she does within it in terms of technique. The absence of loving human relationships is the basic reason that isolated, alienated, lonely, and self-destructive clients require the counselor's assistance. It follows that the client must form such a positive relationship with at least one other person if anything meaningful is to be accomplished. That one other person is the counselor. Although the burden of discovering the true goodness of the self is placed squarely on the shoulders of the client in this essentially nondirective form of counseling, the burden of establishing the kind of relationship in which it may be accomplished is placed on the counselor: "If I can provide a certain type of relationship, the other person will discover within himself the capacity to use that relationship for growth and change, and personal development will occur" (Rogers, 1961:33). The counselor functions as a kind of midwife, wresting out of the client the goodness that is already present and awaiting birth.

The only techniques of client-centered therapy are those we talked about before (Chapter 4): active listening, clarification, paraphrase, and reflection of feelings. Rogers is much more concerned with the client/counselor relationship and the personal attributes of the counselor than with techniques. The three main attributes that the counselor must bring to the relationship are unconditional positive regard, genuineness, and empathy.

Unconditional Positive Regard

According to Rogers, many negative self-feelings and psychological problems develop because others place conditions on their acceptance of us. They like us or love us "if" we are or "if" we do what they would like us to be or do. Since we all want to be liked, loved, and accepted, we tend to conform to these conditions. Our conformity to the expectations of others leads us to an inauthentic self-image. In order to function as psychologically healthy people, we must set our own standards of behavior and self-acceptance. We have the ability to be fully authentic human beings, but we must first experience this unconditional positive regard from at least one person. For Rogers, the counselor fills that role.

Unconditional positive regard occurs when the counselor communicates to the client a full and genuine acceptance of his or her personhood, warts and all. Acceptance must be uncontaminated by judgments of the client's attitudes, feelings, or behavior as being wrong or bad. This doesn't mean that the counselor approves or accepts illegal or immoral behavior; it means that the client's essential humanity is accepted and valued in spite of his or her attitudes and behavior. This acceptance allows clients to be free to examine their own behavior in a nonthreatening setting. Thus they may themselves arrive at the conclusion that their attitudes and behavior are self-defeating. Officer Corrick appears to have had a positive feeling about Bill Bloggs while at the same time soundly condemning his behavior in the PSI report.

Let's be clear that "unconditional positive regard" is an ideal to be striven for and that it is not an all-or-nothing requirement. It is most unrealistic to think that you can develop this kind of relationship with all of your clients, or even most of them. Any relationship between two people is a chemical mix that may blend or explode.

Some clients are downright determined to make your life as difficult as possible, and they will read only weakness or patronization into your efforts to establish a positive working relationship. Most, however, will respond to your warmth with warmth of their own. The degree to which you can achieve the kind of positive regard that Rogers talks about is largely the degree of success you will achieve in your efforts to turn your client's life around. At the very least, you should respect the basic humanity of the client. Be cautious, however, that the relationship doesn't become one of client dependence on you and that you don't use the relationship possessively to fulfill your own needs for positive regard.

Genuineness

The counselor must be genuine (be completely himself or herself) with the client. The counselor must accept and deal with all feelings, whether positive or negative, generated by his or her interaction with the client. In short, the counselor must be authentic in the presentation of self to the client. Pretensions, game playing, and facades must be avoided at all costs. The displaying of false fronts means that the counselor feels a lack of congruence between the real and the ideal self, which is, according to this perspective, precisely the vulnerable state the client is supposed to be in. Since it is the task of the counselor to help the client become more aware of internal incongruities, it is highly desirable that the counselor present an integrated self to the client. The ultimate aim of self-disclosure exercises for the neophyte counselor is to develop an authentic and congruent sense of self. The goal is that the counselor's transparent and authentic self should permeate freely into the client.

I don't want to give you the impression that only a "fully authentic" counselor can effectively counsel clients. Human genuineness or authenticity exists only on a continuum and must be developed. It is interesting to note the agreement among the giants of the human sciences on this subject of human authenticity. Freud, Marx, and Maslow, despite radically different ideological/

theoretical orientations and concerns, all agree that the ability to love and be loved is the key to human authenticity (Walsh, 1986).

Empathy

Empathy is the counselor's capacity for participating in the feelings of the client. Empathy implies more than an intellectual understanding of the client's feelings. It goes beyond cognitive knowledge about the client to fuse with the client, causing the counselor to experience the client's feelings as if they were the counselor's own. This implies the kind of gut-level subjective understanding that is granted only to those who have walked in similar shoes. Mayeroff (1971:41–42) describes the empathetic ability thus:

> To care for another person, I must be able to understand him and his world as if I were inside it. I must be able to see, as it were, with his eyes what his world is like to him and how he sees himself. Instead of merely looking at him in a detached way from the outside, as if he were a specimen, I must be able to be with him in his world, "going" into his world in order to sense from the "inside" what life is for him, what he is striving to be and what he requires to grow.

This definition of empathy is like the definition of unconditional positive regard—beautiful in its conceptualization but probably impossible to attain in any absolute sense. Yet many books on counseling contain statements such as "Respond to the client with empathy." This gives the beginning counselor the mistaken impression that "getting into" a client's frame of reference is not much more difficult than following instructions such as "Place block A on block B and push." This could be dangerously misleading and falsely reassuring.

Developing accurate empathy. Is empathy possible between persons of different races, social strata, and educational backgrounds? For example, can a white, middle-class, college-educated corrections worker really "participate" in the mind-set of a black, semiliterate street person? I believe that it is possible, but only in a limited sense. Such an ability doesn't come naturally or easily. You must work very hard to develop it, both by examining your own values, prejudices, and stereotypes and by assimilating as much knowledge as you possibly can about the causes and reasons why offenders live and behave the way they do. Your ability to empathize with your clients will increase in direct proportion to the time you spend in these endeavors. Even then, it may be counterproductive to convey to clients that you "understand" their problems until you have had a number of sessions with them in which you have actively listened to what they have to say. It was for this reason that empathy was not stressed in the chapter on interviewing, but listening was: active listening is the essential prerequisite to empathy.

Egan (1982) distinguishes between what he calls *primary* and *advanced* empathy, both kinds of which he subsumes under the general term *accurate empathy.* Primary-level empathy "means communicating initial basic understanding of what the client is feeling and of the experiences and behaviors underlying these feelings" (p. 87). For instance, anger, depression, and anxiety are common to all people, regardless of their unique experiences.

Advanced-level empathy "gets at not only what clients clearly state but also what they imply or leave only half stated or half expressed" (Egan, 1982:89). This is exactly what Reik (1956) means by "listening with the third ear." However, we should distinguish between its use in an initial interview setting and in a counseling setting. In an interview setting your primary task is the assessment of clients, and your secondary task is to prepare the groundwork for future counseling sessions. You are listening to what clients are implying or leaving half expressed in order to gain the best initial understanding you can of where they are coming from. In the initial interview it is simply too early in your relationship to challenge clients about what you think they are implying or half expressing. You have very limited knowledge of clients at that point, trust is not established, and, let's face it, you could be completely wrong in your judgments and interpretations. Even if you are right, clients may not be ready to verify your insight at this time and may deny it. Once some facet of a client's deeply private self has been denied, it becomes more difficult for him or her to admit it at some later date. It is threatening and frightening to be forced to confront a negative feature of the self that has formerly been repressed. Don't risk making erroneous assumptions or provoking the client's denial by premature attempts at advanced empathy.

Empathy, then, is a series of responses rendered by the counselor with a developed sensitivity to the client's unique set of feelings about the world and his or her place in it. You are, in effect, thinking with your clients rather than about them. Let's look at some responses using both forms of accurate empathy in a criminal justice counseling session.

Examples of empathetic responses. It is important to remember that your responses are never neutral; they are either constructive or destructive. This is particularly important for criminal justice clients since they are stuck with you, for better or worse, during this period of correctional supervision. Constructive responses are those that involve clients in self-exploration so that they may arrive at solutions to their troubles themselves. Fully involving clients means accepting the reality of their problems and reflecting them back on them. For example, suppose that Tony comes to you and states that he finds his job (let's say he's a factory assembler) boring, unsatisfying, and unsuitable for his talents and ambitions. Furthermore, he tells you that he wants to quit. You want him to keep his job, knowing that jobs are difficult to find, that he has financial obligations, and that "the devil finds work for idle hands." You respond by saying, "Tony, you feel that your job makes you feel depressed and less than worthy and productive. I can understand that because I've had jobs that made me feel that way too. What is it in particular about your job that makes you feel depressed, Tony?"

What have you accomplished in these three sentences? First, you have recognized the reality of Tony's problem and the fact that it is a genuine

concern for him. Second, you have reflected his feelings about the problem, thereby making him aware that you have correctly understood him. Third, you have shown empathy by self-disclosure of your similar experiences. This reinforces Tony's perception of your acceptance of the reality of the problem and gives him a feeling of commonality with you. This will also make Tony more receptive to the plan of action you will decide upon together, since you have modeled the plan in your own life experience. Fourth, you have probed further by the use of an open-ended question, asking Tony to identify specific conditions, circumstances, or situations that arouse his negative feelings. Your response has generated a positive atmosphere, which will facilitate further discussion and exploration, leading, you hope, to a mutually acceptable plan of action for dealing with the problem. In short, you have made excellent use of accurate primary empathy.

Contrast the positive response to Tony's concern with the following negative response: "Tony, you're always complaining about something. This business about your job is all in your head, it does you no good to dwell on it. How can you expect a better job with your education? Besides, you can't quit without my permission, so relax and forget it, buddy."

What have you accomplished here? First, by responding from your frame of reference rather than Tony's, you have denied the reality of the problem and of his feelings about it. Second, you have denigrated him by calling him a complainer and belittling his education. Third, you have distanced yourself from him by (1) showing a lack of concern and understanding, (2) emphasizing differences in educational levels, and (3) emphasizing the relationship of authority that exists between you. Furthermore, by telling him to "relax and forget it" you have guaranteed that he won't. Instead, you will have exacerbated his negative feelings and left him to deal with them in a possibly destructive manner. You can bet that he won't come to you again with his concerns. In short, Tony will be influenced by the second response just as he would be influenced by the first. The second response, however, generates feelings in Tony that will be destructive to your relationship with him. Your lack of professional concern will make your job more difficult and demanding and may well lead Tony to quit his job despite your warning that he cannot. This, in turn, may lead to a technical violation or further criminality. The golden rule of counseling is "Treat your clients as you would wish to be treated."

Suppose Tony responds to your primary-level empathy with the following statements and nonverbal behaviors. Tony is sitting with his folded hands resting on his thighs and looking at you (a nondefensive, open, and trusting demeanor).

"Well, Joyce, I didn't mind the job so much when I was on days. It's this night shift stuff."

Tony now straightens up, looks away, and raises his voice slightly (some defensiveness, embarrassment, and anger creeping in).

"My wife complains that I don't spend enough time with her. We used to go out dancing once or twice a week, but now I either can't because I'm working, or I'm too damn tired on the weekend."

Tony sits up straight and grasps the arms of his chair. His face reddens a little, and his speech becomes faster and louder (a strengthening of his defensiveness, embarrassment, and anger).

"She goes by herself, though. I don't like that, and I tell her so. We've had quite a few arguments about that crap."

You now come to realize that Tony's job is not the real cause of his depression. His more substantial concern is his wife's dissatisfaction, and his statement contains some significant intimations that he is concerned about the possibility that she may be doing more than just dancing with other men. You might engage in the following dialogue with Tony.

COUNSELOR: Are you saying that it is not the job itself that you want to quit but, rather, you would like to get off the night shift? (*Clarification.*)

TONY: Yes, I think things might be better if I went back on days.

COUNSELOR: The night shift leaves you without much time or energy to devote to your wife, and this is causing some friction between you. (*Paraphrase.*) You are angry and upset because she goes to the dance by herself. (*Reflection.*)

TONY: You bet I am! I've told her that it's not right for a married woman to go dancing by herself.

COUNSELOR: Tony, I can understand your annoyance with your wife, and I know that the two of you have talked about it. Why do you think she continues to go when you have told her that you dislike it? (*Probe.*)

TONY: I don't know. We get so mad at each other when we talk about it that I think she does it out of spite. (*Angry arguments do have a way of leading one of the participants to act in uncharacteristic ways in order to "get back."*)

COUNSELOR: What do you think she would do if you let her know your feelings without getting upset? (*Open-ended question designed to get Tony to think about his wife's possible reaction to a rational discussion of the problem rather than an emotional confrontation.*)

TONY: I don't really know. We don't argue that much about other things. I don't mind her having some fun, but dancing? My wife's an attractive woman—I see the way that men look at her. (*Tony's reply indicates that, except for this one issue, quarreling is not a major feature of his marriage. He quickly disposes of your question and gets down to his real concern.*)

COUNSELOR: You like your wife to enjoy herself, but you find it unsettling for her to do it in this way because she is in the company of other men. (*Paraphrasing and reflecting.*) Am I hearing you say that you are concerned that one of her dance partners may make a play for her? I wonder if she realizes that she is hurting you this way. (*Clarifying your perception of Tony's underlying feeling and using advanced empathy.*)

TONY: I guess I am kind of jealous. I really love Carla, and it eats me up inside to think that she might be playing around behind my back. I haven't admitted this to myself before today. I suppose I wasn't too eager to think about it. What do you think I should do, Joyce? You've made me realize that I don't really want to quit my job—it pays good money and I have my restitution and fine to finish paying—but I don't want to lose Carla. *(Tony is now asking for your advice, which up until now you have resisted giving. He will be more receptive now that he has explored the problem himself and has explicitly requested advice. You have also led him to identify for himself what he was feeling—jealousy. This is much better than simply coming out and asking him, "Do you feel jealous?" He may well have denied the embarrassing feeling if you rather than he had approached the issue directly.)*

COUNSELOR: I don't think it's a question of either quitting your job or losing Carla. I might suggest two courses of action for you to think about. First, you could speak with your boss at work to see if there is any possibility at all of getting back on days, even it if means a different job. Regardless of whether or not this is possible, you could discuss your feelings openly with Carla as you have done with me. Do this without any hint of accusation or anger, and you will find that she will more than likely respond the same way. Since you seem to enjoy dancing yourself, try to arrange it that the two of you can go together at least once a week. What do you think about these suggestions, Tony?

This exchange illustrates both primary and advanced-level empathy. You went beyond the initial problem that Tony presented to you and probed for a deeper concern. You skillfully led him to explore feelings that he was reluctant to admit to himself, and you offered him, at his request, some helpful suggestions for dealing with them. It took a great deal more time than it would have taken to tell him to stop complaining, but you may have gone a long way in helping Tony to save his job and his marriage. What's more, you have probably actually saved yourself time and trouble in the long run.

What accurate empathy is not. Now that you have a good idea what accurate empathy is, it is important to understand what it is not. Empathy doesn't mean that you should condone wrong behavior. If Tony were to tell you, for example, that he goes out and gets drunk because he can't stand Carla's imagined infidelities, nagging, and denigration of him and asks you what you would do in a similar situation, he has put you in something of a spot. He is asking for your sympathy, understanding, and self-disclosure. It is a poor kind of empathy to reply, "I guess I'd do the same thing," even if, in fact, you think you might do so. That answer would imply that you are condoning his behavior.

But if you reply that you certainly wouldn't do so, Tony will perceive you as being critical and judgmental. It would be better for you to say, "I'm sure that your wife's behavior makes you feel terrible. I'm not sure what I would do myself. I think perhaps I would seek marital counseling. Do you think that's a possibility for you?" This reply relieves you of the appearance of condoning the client's behavior while at the same time recognizing his feelings and offering a constructive alternative to the bottle.

Lessons and Concerns

The primary reason for including the client-centered approach in this discussion is its emphasis on the client/counselor relationship. It goes without saying that we all attend more to the concerns of those whose good graces we value than of those about whose judgments we don't care. Objective understanding and special techniques and stratagems are not necessary to bring about change in the kind of relationship Rogers emphasizes.

Although client-centered counseling can be fruitfully applied in some counseling settings, we have to ask ourselves if it is fully practical in the criminal justice setting. It seems to me that unconditional positive regard, genuineness, and empathy as described here are the qualities we manifest only in a very real intimate love relationship with people who are truly special to us. If we are not "in love" with our clients, isn't there a major conflict between being genuine and expressing to clients that we accept them unconditionally? Isn't there also a real danger that we will avoid necessary confrontation with a client in order not to upset the close relationship deemed to be so important? Don't we need to set conditions on our acceptance?

As a criminal justice counselor, you must allow positive regard for your clients to be conditional. This does not mean that you refuse to accept the basic humanity of your clients or that you pass unnecessary judgment on their past behavior. What it does mean is that you must place unambiguous conditions on their future behavior and not be afraid to confront them and let them suffer the consequences when they fail to meet those conditions. Empathy, too, must be guided in responsible directions.

Nevertheless, establishing a positive working relationship with clients is important. Unconditional positive regard, genuineness, and empathy are, please recall, continuous variables that you present to your clients in varying degrees. The degree to which you do present them depends on the quality of your concept of self in interaction with the self-concepts possessed by your clients. It is true that you cannot always be your "genuine self," but you should not suffer a sense of personal failure if you feel a lack of acceptance of the client or an inability to empathize fully with his or her view of the world.

A final point about the powerful influence of establishing positive relationships with clients comes not from criminal justice or counseling research but from medical research. Dr. William Knaus and his colleagues at the George Washington University School of Medicine set out to discover what variable is most important to survival of patients in intensive care units (ICUs). Using advanced statistical techniques, they looked at such variables as technological sophistication, levels of professional expertise of physicians and nurses, prestige of hospital, research funding, and patient/caregiver ratio. Their examination of 5030 ICU patients in a variety of hospitals across the United States over a period of five years found that none of these nominated variables was the crucial one. The crucial variable was the *quality of the relationships* that existed between doctors and nurses and between nurses and patients. The hospitals that allowed nurses to function semiautonomously and to interact with patients at an emotional level (what nurses call *primary-level nursing*) were the hospitals with the best ICU survival rates (Holzman, 1986:56). The researchers expressed their surprise at this finding; Carl Rogers would have responded with a knowing smile.

Summary

Counseling differs from psychotherapy primarily in the depth and intensity of treatment. Psychotherapists attempt to restructure the basic personalities of patients who have intrapersonal conflicts, whereas counselors deal with interpersonal conflicts and problems of everyday living. You should be alert to those clients whose problems go beyond your professional ability.

There are similarities and differences between interviewing and counseling. Many of the techniques they use are the same. The quality of the self—your warmth, acceptance, and understanding—is the most important ingredient in both situations. In essence, counseling is an extension of the interviewing process. Counseling requires communication with clients at a deeper level about more specific issues. You will accomplish this more easily if you have developed a positive relationship with them during the initial interviews.

Freudian psychoanalysis is a theory that offers some profound insights into human nature. It emphasizes the importance of the psychosexual stages of development, especially the importance of love at the earliest stages. The identification of defense mechanisms is useful in criminal justice, particularly denial, rationalization, fixation, displacement, intellectualization, and projection. You will never use the techniques of psychoanalysis in your dealings with clients in the same way that you will use the techniques derived

Perspectives from the Field

Love Is Not a One-Way Street
by a Probation and Parole Counselor

This job involves working with people with low IQs, low educational backgrounds, poor work records, and low incomes. The people I work with are very manipulative. I have to be very direct, quick to assess what I think they should do and not hesitate to tell them to do it. If you are planning to do correctional work, you should be aware that this job involves many failures and that you can't help everyone. Sometimes when you can't help them adjust to the community, then the best help you can give them is to keep them out of the community—by holding them in jail.

Most of the people that I work with have no great desire to see me. They feel that probation is not an opportunity. It is just an obligation they must complete for the court or the parole board.

Many of them do not trust me and never will. And I must say that many of them I cannot trust either. A lot of my job involves verifying, through other sources, what my probationers and parolees have told me. I have found that the best way to develop rapport in dealing with these people is to be stern, not let them manipulate you, and above all be fair.

Did my counselor education program prepare me for working in the field of corrections? Sure, it did. It helped me to communicate with the people I deal with by being concrete and truthful in what I say to them and by making me a more active listener. It helped me to know how to show my feelings and concerns in dealing with people. It also helped me to know how to write concise, meaningful reports and understand the results of tests I must verify. It did not prepare me for the people I work with. Being warm,

accepting, and trusting won't work with people who haven't learned self-acceptance and a sense of social responsibility. You've got to start them at another level and try to work them up to the other ones. Love is a two-way street, and if you don't believe it, you'll break your neck and maybe your heart too.

I don't get much sleep, but I sleep sound. Counselors, no matter where they work, are responsible to lots of people, not just their counselees. We're responsible to our profession, to ourselves, and to our society. So I'd stack my kind of counseling against all the rest when it comes to measuring up to responsibility. Sure, my kind of counseling may lose a few counselees along the way, but just count up how many others we saved.

Reprinted with permission from Gressard and Hume (1983).

from other theories. Its usefulness to you as a criminal justice worker lies in its illumination of human nature.

Client-centered therapy shares with psychoanalysis its passive and nondirective approach. This theory asserts the absolute primacy of the client/counselor relationship. Client-centered counseling rests on three attributes, which the counselor must possess and offer to clients: unconditional positive regard, genuineness, and empathy. Since many psychological problems are the result of conditions that others attach to their acceptance of a person's self-worth, it is vital that the counselor accept his or her clients unconditionally as individuals of worth.

The counselor must also be genuine (be completely himself or herself). Pretensions, dishon-

esty, and game playing must be avoided at all costs. The counselor's authenticity will provide a model for the client to emulate. The counselor should always strive to improve his or her own authenticity.

The final necessary attribute is empathy. It is very difficult to achieve because it implies the ability to participate actively in the mind-set of another, to actually walk in the person's shoes. Primary empathy is the communication to the client of an initial basic understanding of what he or she is saying. Advanced empathy implies a deeper understanding, a reading between the lines. Empathy is something that is developed only by experience, by learning all you can about human behavior, and by really caring about what the client is trying to communicate.

References and Suggested Readings

Bateson, G., D. Jackson, J. Haley, and J. Weakland (1956). "Toward a theory of schizophrenia." *Behavioral Science,* 1:251–264.

Egan, G. (1982). *The Skilled Helper.* Pacific Grove, CA: Brooks/Cole.

Fine, R. (1973). "Psychoanalysis." In R. Corsini (Ed.), *Current Psychotherapies.* Itasca, IL: F. E. Peacock.

Freud, S. (1961). *Civilization and Its Discontents.* New York: Norton.

Freud, S. (1965). *The New Introductory Lectures on Psychoanalysis.* New York: Norton.

Gressard, C., and K. Hume (1983). "Special populations." In J. Brown and R. Pate, Jr. (Eds.), *Being a Counselor.* Pacific Grove, CA: Brooks/Cole.

Holzman, D. (1986). "Intensive care nurses: A vital sign." *Insight,* 56 (December).

Lytle, M. (1964). "The unpromising client." *Crime and Delinquency,* 10:130–134.

Martinson, R. (1974). "What works? Questions and answers about prison reform." *The Public Interest,* 35:22–54.

Mayeroff, M. (1971). *On Caring.* New York: Harper & Row.

Reik, T. (1956). *Listening with the Third Ear.* New York: Grove.

Rogers, C. (1961). *On Becoming a Person.* Boston: Houghton Mifflin.

Walker, S. (1985). *Sense and Nonsense about Crime: A Policy Guide.* Pacific Grove, CA: Brooks/Cole.

Walsh, A. (1986). "Love and human authenticity in the works of Freud, Marx, and Maslow." *Free Inquiry in Creative Sociology,* 14:21–26.

Wrong, D. (1968). "The oversocialized conception of man in modern sociology." In S. McNall (Ed.), *The Sociological Perspective.* Boston: Little, Brown.

Chapter 8
Directive Counseling: Theory and Practice

To love and to be loved is as necessary as the breathing of air. Insofar as we fail in loving we fail in living. The most important thing to realize about the nature of human nature is that the most significant ingredient in its structure is love.

Ashley Montagu

The theories we examined in the last chapter could be described as passive and nondirective: the counselor helps clients to give birth to their own solutions for what ails them. The theories presented in this chapter are very active, directive, and didactic, with equal involvement of counselor and client. These theories—transactional analysis, rational-emotive therapy, and reality therapy—were all formulated by traditionally trained psychotherapists who were dissatisfied with the passive methods of traditional psychoanalysis and the extraordinary length of time required for that kind of treatment. All three theories were designed to identify and deal with problem areas quickly. They are oriented toward cognitive rather than emotional approaches. The creators of the theories realized that most clients, especially criminal justice clients, must be actively assisted in their endeavors to become rational, responsible, whole individuals.

Transactional Analysis

Transactional analysis (TA) is the brainchild of Eric Berne, a psychiatrist best known for his book *Games People Play* (1964). A *transaction* is simply what happens between two or more people when they interact; *analysis* refers to the process of exploring and explaining transactions. It shares with psychoanalysis the assumption that human behavior is rather profoundly influenced by the events of early childhood, particularly events that told the child that he or she was loved or unloved.

Berne feels that the greatest strength of TA lies in its use of colloquial, simple, and direct terms that are easily understood by all. As Berne himself put it (1966:214): "Transactional Analysis because of its clear-cut statements rooted in easily accessible material, because of its operational nature, and because of its specialized vocabulary (consisting of only five words: Parent, Adult, Child, Game, and Script), offers an easily learned framework for clarification."

Scripts

Scripts are "memory tapes" that we all carry around with us in our heads. The most important scripts were recorded in early childhood because children tend to accept messages unquestioningly, lacking the maturity to do otherwise. The messages communicated by our parents during this critical period contribute strongly to our future evaluations of ourselves as worthy ("OK") or unworthy ("not OK") people. By the time we become mature enough to question verbal and nonverbal messages regarding our OKness, any questioning is directed and influenced strongly by the powerful scripting we received in our most impressionable years. If the preponderance of messages told us that we were loved, respected, and appreciated, we will see ourselves as OK. If the preponderance of childhood messages were in the opposite direction, we will see ourselves as not OK. These evaluations of OKness will tend to persist throughout our lives, regardless of the messages we receive in later life, because of the deeply etched early recordings.

Related to these early recordings is the intense human need for what Berne calls *strokes*. People hunger for strokes, to be touched both physically and emotionally. If they do not receive these strokes—think back at this point to our earlier discussion of love deprivation in Chapter 2—they will not develop into psychologically healthy human beings. According to Berne, much of our time is structured around the pursuit of positive strokes (or, as I would put it, seeking assurances that we are loved). Positive strokes lead to positive scripting tapes, and negative strokes lead to negative ones.

There are four basic life positions that issue from our scripting and that act as backdrops throughout our lives in our interactions with others.

1. *"I'm not OK; you're OK."* This is a position commonly found in children. When they are punished for some transgression they often feel "not OK." But their godlike parents, upon whom they depend, are naturally OK in their little minds. You will find this life position in many of your clients, especially in substance abusers. They are frequently depressed and will have what Glasser calls in reality therapy a *failure identity.* At least a client with this life position will consider you OK, so you can concentrate on building up his or her own OKness.

2. *"I'm not OK; you're not OK."* This is the scripted life position of an abused child who was led to question the OKness of his or her parents rather early in life. A person like this views the world as a hostile and futile place, for the person is unloved and unloving. Such a person may withdraw into the fantasy world of schizophrenia (see the case history of Greg in Chapter 12).

3. *"I'm OK; you're not OK."* This too is the position of abused children who have questioned the OKness of their parents. However, they have somehow come to view themselves as OK from their own circumscribed perspective of OKness. They tend to be loners and to project blame for all their problems and actions onto others. The psychopath operates from this life position in its extreme.

4. *"I'm OK; you're OK."* This is the life position from which correctional workers must operate. To do your job adequately you must be convinced of your OKness; to do it well you must strive to generate your clients' OKness. The goal of transactional analysis is a relationship between counselor and client with mutual convictions of "I'm OK; you're OK."

Games

Transactional analysis views *games* as exchanges of strokes that are inauthentic because they have ulterior motives. Games are the result of individuals' interacting with one another from one of the first three life positions. The ultimate payoff in a game-playing relationship in which one's time is structured around getting strokes (or giving them to those in positions of authority) is a storehouse of bad feelings that serve only to reinforce negative life scripts. It is only from an authentic "I'm OK; you're OK" position that individuals can engage in a meaningful, game-free interpersonal relationship.

Games are very much a part of criminal justice supervision and counseling. You must quickly learn to identify and expose them, for they are dishonest and destructive. You might even find yourself playing games with your clients. We have already mentioned one that officers might play in their law enforcement role in the section on interrogation: they play "Now I've got you, you son-of-a-bitch" when they are using clients for power strokes. Another one often heard is "I'm only trying to help you," used by those gentler souls seeking acceptance strokes. Both of these games, of course, issue from an "I'm OK; you're not OK" position.

Offenders are very good at playing games— they've had lots of practice. You will quickly find out that they are much better at it than you are (take that as a compliment). A real value of TA for the correctional worker is the ability it gives him or her to expose them. Games that you will run into with frequency are "Poor me" (scratching for sympathy and "understanding"), "If it wasn't for ..." (ditto), and "Ain't it/I awful" (false remorse). Corrections workers who are acceptance seekers or are ineffectual will easily fall for KIUD ("Keep it up, doc"). Such workers are suckers for clients who tell them that they are doing a great job while continuing to behave irresponsibly. The payoff for KIUD clients is that their counselors will probably let them get away with an awful lot of misbehavior in exchange for their dishonest strokes.

Yet another game, often seen in prison settings, is HDIGO ("How do I get out of here?"). Clients soon learn to tell the counselor just what they think he or she wants to hear. They learn the latest social science explanation for their behavior and spew it back while shaking with "self-understanding" and "remorse." Of course, self-understanding and remorse are very much a part of your goals for each offender in your charge. But it is imperative that they learn to distinguish the real goods from self-serving manipulation of the counseling setting. It is easy, and very human, to accept the game as the real thing because it gives you a feeling of success and a verification of your effectiveness as a counselor. Don't fudge the data for quick and easy self-strokes. If you accept the game as the real thing, the client will have won the battle but will lose the war against his or her criminality.

Parent, Adult, Child

We'll take the last of Berne's five easy terms together. *Parent* (P), *Adult* (A), and *Child* (C), or *PAC,* are ego states: three distinct systems of feelings related to behavior patterns. We all slip into and out of them as we engage in our various transactions.

The Parent is critical, controlling, and moralizing, just like Freud's superego. There is a good side to the Parent, though. The good Parent is the Nurturing Parent who reacts to others with care, dignity, and respect and makes demands that are not overbearing. The Critical or Examining Parent is domineering, self-righteous, and authoritarian. The person who always operates in the parental mode (the Constant Parent) excludes the realism of the Adult mode and the playfulness of the Child. Freud would call such a person neurotic. You will probably not find the Constant Parent represented much among your clients. If you do, they will almost inevitably be sex offenders against children.

The Adult is logical, realistic, and objective. He or she is much better able to judge the appropriateness of when to allow the less characteristic ego states their expression than is either the Parent or the Child. Like the Parent, though, the Constant Adult will enjoy little feeling or spontaneity. You will not, almost by definition, find the Adult among criminal justice clientele. You will, I trust, find many among your colleagues.

The Child is spontaneous, fun-loving, and irresponsible. Many of your clients will be of this type. It is perfectly OK to be an Adapted Child, one who enjoys fun and laughter in appropriate ways and in appropriate settings. The problem is the Constant Child, one who consistently excludes the Adult and Parent and refuses to grow up and behave responsibly. The exclusion of these restraining influences means the exclusion of conscience, the total absence of which is psychopathy.

One or another of these ego states predominates in each individual. The apparent equivalence of the ego states to the Freudian id (Child), ego (Adult), and superego (Parent) has been denied by Berne (1966). Berne's ego states are aspects of only the Freudian ego. Further, he states that whereas the id, ego, and superego are "theoretical constructs" (inferred entities not amenable to observation), his ego states are "phenomenological realities" (amenable to direct observation). Let's see how we can go about making these direct observations.

Structural Analysis

The process of making these observations is known as *structural analysis*. Structural analysis is a tool used by TA counselors to make clients aware of the content and functioning of their ego states. TA seeks as a goal that every client become an expert in analyzing his or her own transactions. If clients become adept at identifying their characteristic ego states, they can better understand their options for change.

Ideally, the Parent, Adult, and Child should be distinctly separate states with clear-cut boundaries, as they are in part 1 of Figure 8-1. Like the Freudian ego, the Adult holds the executive position but admits the Parent and Child when appropriate. Two types of problem arise in personality structure as viewed in structural analysis: exclusion and contamination.

Exclusion occurs when ego-state boundaries are so rigidly drawn that free movement across them at appropriate times does not occur. The fundamentalist puritan who views all kinds of sen-

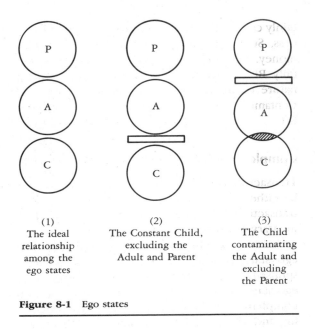

(1)
The ideal relationship among the ego states

(2)
The Constant Child, excluding the Adult and Parent

(3)
The Child contaminating the Adult and excluding the Parent

Figure 8-1   Ego states

suous enjoyment as sin, or who lives out his or her life bound by unexamined rules and strictures, is an example of the Constant Parent excluding the Child and the Adult. But we don't worry much about puritans in our business. We do have to worry about the Child who excludes the Adult and Parent. He or she is the complete opposite of the Constant Parent, doing everything that the Constant Parent would not and doing nothing that the Constant Parent does do. Exclusion is illustrated by part 2 of Figure 8-1.

Contamination occurs when the content of one ego state gets mixed up with the content of another ego state. We think of contamination in terms of the intrusion of either or both of the parent or child states into the rational boundaries defining the Adult state. Contamination of the Adult by the Parent often involves assumptions left over from our early scripting that distort objective thinking. In the chapter on interviewing I related how my prejudices regarding proper behavior for women intruded into my Adult when I interviewed the woman charged with sex crimes against children. This contamination ruined the effectiveness of my interview and my subsequent relationship with her. Bill Bloggs's Adult was certainly contaminated by his Child. He wanted success, Susan, a grandiose wedding, and lots of money. Not too much wrong with that, I suppose, only Bill wanted it "right now!" The childlike nature of his actions hardly needs belaboring. Contamination is illustrated in part 3 of Figure 8-1.

Complementary and Crossed Transactions

Transactions between and among individuals can be either complementary or crossed. The ideal transaction is a complementary one. A complementary transaction occurs when a verbal or non-verbal message (the stimulus) sent from a specific ego state is received and reacted to (the response) from the appropriate, or complementary, ego state of the receiver. In TA communication, complementary transactions occur when stimulus and response lines on a PAC diagram are parallel.

The lines representing a crossed transaction in a PAC diagram are not parallel. Crossed transactions occur when a stimulus sent from one ego state meets a response from an ego state other than the expected one. Crossed transactions usually cause trouble in our interpersonal relationships. However, crossed transactions are sometimes called for and are beneficial if the unexpected ego-state response leads the stim-

ulus sender to adjust his or her ego state to a more appropriate one. Figure 8-2 illustrates some complementary and crossed transactions.

In part 1 we have Parent–Parent communication. This might be two new probation officers discussing the "ignorance" and "immorality" of "welfare mothers cheating on the system." The Adult may never enter into their conversation to explore the whys of the behavior. If one of the officers suddenly shifts into the Adult mode (indicated by the dotted line), the conversation may not be as congenial as when they were transacting at the same level. However, the shift may bring the conversation to a more appropriate Adult–Adult state, at which point the ego states are again complementary. Don't engage in complementary transactions just for the sake of congeniality when you know that some other ego state is more appropriate. As Rogers would say, "be genuine, be yourself."

Part 2 represents Adult–Adult communication. This could involve a prison counselor and his or her client discussing a problem that the client may be experiencing from a mutual "I'm OK; you're OK" position. The counselor does not contaminate the Adult by talking down to the inmate from the Parent ego state nor make light of the problem by joking about it from the Child ego state. These problematic crossed transactions are illustrated by the dotted lines.

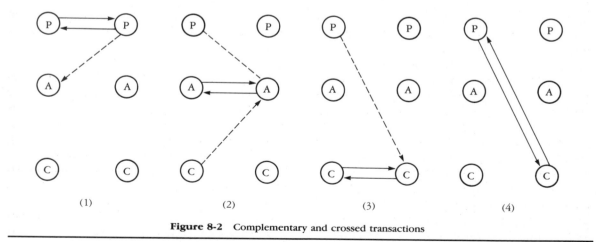

Figure 8-2 Complementary and crossed transactions

Part 3 illustrates a Child–Child transaction. An example of this would be you and your colleagues planning a Christmas party. Obviously, you should never interact with your clients at this level unless the occasion is something innocuous, such as sharing a joke. A crossed transaction in this context could be something like refusing to take part in the office festivities because they are "frivolous," or responding to the client's well-meaning attempt at levity with a cold stare. These responses would both reflect a Critical Parent ego state intruding on what should have been an appropriate Child–Child transaction.

Part 4 illustrates a complementary transaction even though the parties are interacting from different ego states (the lines are still parallel). An example of this type of transaction would be a parole officer chastising a client about some instance of irresponsible behavior. The officer confronts the client from a parental ego state, and the client responds as a child might when caught with a hand in the cookie jar: "You're always picking on me." This transaction is complementary because a Parent–Child stimulus has evoked a Child–Parent response. Had the officer confronted the client from the Adult ego state and asked him or her simply to explain the behavior in question, and had the offender responded from the child state, the transaction would have been crossed.

Remember, any crossed transaction can lead to difficulties in interpersonal relations unless the crossover is purposely designed to shift the transaction to a level that is more appropriate to the immediate situation. In general, crossed transactions usually follow when one party or the other in the transaction operates from one of the first three life positions, which include various combinations of negative "not OK" attributions.

Lessons and Concerns

The beauty of transactional analysis for me is the way it simply and effectively illustrates the consequences of feelings one has about the self or about others in everyday transactions. Berne's genius was his ability to transform complex ideas into colloquial language and easy-to-follow diagrams. These ideas can be relayed with relative ease to clients so that they may analyze their own feelings and behaviors. The emphasis on manipulation and game playing is especially useful for criminal justice workers. Finally, TA nicely describes in a neat linear fashion how early love deprivation leads to poor self-concept, how a poor self-concept usually leads to a negative image of others, and how these negative feelings lead to poor interpersonal relationships. If I had a dollar for every client of mine whom I could identify as having experienced this developmental sequence, I would be rich indeed.

On the other hand, transactional analysis may possess all the vices of its virtues. There is a danger that an inexperienced counselor may simply see counseling as an intellectual exercise consisting of identifying life positions and doing structural analyses. The very simplicity of the theory invites this kind of truncated counseling. It is too easy to hide beneath covers stitched from nifty diagrams and clichéd phrases such as "strokes" and "games." You have to involve your clients' emotions and feelings in the counseling process as well as their heads.

This is one of the reasons that I advise an eclectic approach to counseling. All the theories have something to offer. Although some offer more than others, none of them offers everything. Used in conjunction with client-centered therapy's emphasis on the nature of the client/counselor relationship, transactional analysis could prove to be a powerful counseling tool for you when you finally hit the CJ trenches.

Rational-Emotive Therapy

Rational-emotive therapy (RET), founded by Albert Ellis, takes issue with the assumptions and practices of both psychoanalysis and client-centered therapy. Psychoanalysis is concerned with the darkness of the unconscious mind and nonrational biological drives. Client-centered therapy zeroes in on the emotional rapport of the client/counselor relationship. RET fully recognizes that we share biological drives and emotional states with other species, but relegates them to minor importance in favor of cognition, a unique quality of humankind. Problem behaviors arise from faulty thinking and irrational beliefs, and they can be corrected by helping the client to understand and acknowledge that his or her beliefs are at odds with logic. It follows from this assumption that the RET counselor takes a very active role in the counseling process and considers the quality of the client/counselor relationship to be secondary to what takes place within that relationship. RET counseling is highly directive, didactic, challenging, and often confrontive and painful for the client.

The A-B-C Theory of Personality

RET counseling revolves around Ellis's A-B-C theory of personality. A is the experience of an objective fact, B is the subjective interpretation of or belief about that fact, and C represents the emotional content accompanying the meaning (B) that the experience of the fact (A) has for the individual. The important point is that A is not the direct cause of C, but rather that B, the individual's belief about A, causes C. As Shakespeare put it in *Hamlet,* "There is nothing either good or bad, but thinking makes it so."

Problems of living result from illogical and negative thinking about experiences, which the client reiterates in a self-defeating monologue. He or she is reluctant to let go of irrational beliefs because they serve to protect a fragile ego. This process resembles the Freudian defense mechanism of rationalization. It is the counselor's task to strip away such self-damaging mechanisms by attacking them directly and challenging the client to reinterpret experience in a growth-enhancing fashion. Empathizing with the client's definition of reality in the Rogerian manner only serves to reinforce faulty thinking and is counterproductive. Passive listening to a client's monologue, as in psychoanalysis and client-centered counseling, is replaced by an active and assertive dialogue between counselor and client. Counseling is not a warm relationship of relating partners; it is more akin to a teacher/student relationship, complete with lectures and homework assignments.

MUSTurbations

Ellis has identified 11 ideas that he considers to be pervasive in our society, highly irrational, and leading to "widespread neurosis." He calls these ideas *MUSTurbations* and sums them up thus: "I now see that I have given up any addiction to MUSTurbation many years ago—to thinking that I must do well; that others must treat me considerately or fairly; and that the world must provide me with the things I want easily and quickly" (1982). Most of us are addicted to certain of these MUSTurbations to some degree or another. An examination of some of these ideas will help to identify self-defeating "musts," "shoulds," and "oughts" in both your own thinking and that of your clients. I have listed six of these ideas, adapted from Ellis's delightful little book *A New Guide to Rational Living* (1975). These six are especially applicable to criminal justice clients (and sometimes to criminal justice workers as well).

1. *It is essential that one be loved or approved by virtually everybody.* We would all like our desires for universal approval to be satisfied, but we do not really need them to be. You would hardly be human if you did not derive intense satisfaction from the positive judgments of others, but preoccupation with your own demands for love and approval prevents you from seeing the lovable traits in others. Put otherwise, by not concentrating on your demands that you be loved, you free your psychic energies so that you are able to love. Furthermore, if you believe that you are not a worthy person unless you are universally liked, you guarantee that you will be an insecure and self-disvalued person because you are chasing an unattainable rainbow.

2. *One must be perfectly competent, adequate, and achieving to be considered worthwhile.* This is a trap into which the beginning criminal justice counselor often falls. You have taken on a very difficult task. A fair percentage of your clients will reoffend regardless of all your efforts to rehabilitate them. If you regard that circumstance as a personal failure, you denigrate yourself and your clients' capacity to be responsible for their own lives. As long as you have done

your best, you are a worthwhile person. We must all develop the courage to be imperfect and not to experience failure as catastrophic.

3. *Unhappiness is caused by outside circumstances over which we have no control.* We allow ourselves to be emotionally upset about outside circumstances by our mental interpretations of them. Some outside circumstances constitute such a powerful assault on our lives that it is unreasonable not to expect a negative emotional consequence. However, other circumstances are only as defeating as we let them be. The rational person avoids exaggerating unpleasant outside circumstances and looks for the growth potential in them. Many criminal justice clients find themselves overwhelmed by relatively innocuous unpleasant experiences and turn to the chemical comforts of the bottle or the pill.

4. *It is easier to avoid personal responsibilities than to face them.* You can hide from your responsibilities only for a short while. When your head does emerge from the sand, the responsibility is still there and may well have grown. The rational person knows that it is less painful to attend to a responsibility than it is to deny or avoid it. The criminal justice client is a master at avoiding his or her personal responsibilities because he or she all too often lacks the self-confidence to attend to them. It is the counselor's task to make the client see the logic of the rolling-snowball effect of nonattendance to responsibility.

5. *One must have someone stronger than oneself on whom to depend.* Many criminal justice clients are in a dependency mode. They lack the self-reliance to live a responsible, self-motivated life. An overdependence on others (including a dependence on chemical substances) places the individual at the mercy of life's crutches. The rational person, while he or she may occasionally depend on others, minimizes other-dependence and takes charge of his or her own life.

6. *Past experience determines present behavior, and the influence of the past cannot be eradicated.* Although it is true that our values are largely programmed by our past experiences and that it is difficult to overcome their influence, our behavior is not bounded by them. We have the capacity to transcend our experiences by accepting and analyzing the effect they have on us and by refusing to be determined by them. The typical criminal justice client has not recognized his or her capacity for self-directed change and allows himself or herself to be blown hither and thither by past and present environmental conditions. It is your job to encourage your clients to examine their past experiences, make them realize how they have influenced their negative attitudes and behavior, show them that those past experiences are not acceptable as excuses for present behavior, indicate that they possess the human capacity to break the chains of experience, and activate them toward the goal of self-responsible behavior.

Lessons and Concerns

I chose to include RET in this book because it emphasizes that problems arise from the faulty operation of that which is unique to humankind: the capacity to think. Illogical thought processes are doubtless more easily identified and dealt with by the counselor than are emotions per se or the vagaries of biological drives. You must ask yourself, however, if emotional problems are so easily assuaged by pointing out that they are the result of faulty thinking. One philosophical wag opined that the sole function of the neocortex (the thinking brain) is to justify and rationalize the emotions and behaviors generated by the mammalian and paleo cortices (the emotional and instinctual centers of the brain, respectively). Freud himself was said to believe that his "talking cures" were effective only with educated, middle-class patients having well-developed capacities for rational thought. This is not an apt description of the typical criminal justice client.

Are cognitions really more basic and potent than emotions, as Ellis seems to think? How often have you realized how utterly stupid it was to feel a certain way, wished very much that you didn't, but continued to do so anyway? Is rational thinking always to be identified with the middle-class, law-abiding perspective of the counselor? The insights provided by anomie and differential association theories indicate that under certain circumstances criminal behavior is rational behavior.

Nevertheless, Ellis feels, and I agree, that the counselor's values and attitudes are legitimate therapeutic tools. Many clients, but by no means all, can learn valuable self-insights from an active and didactic counselor. This is especially true if the counselor also draws lessons from client-centered therapy and establishes a warm relationship before attempting to confront the client. Finally, RET, with its teacher/student relationship, is more realistic and genuine than client-centered therapy in a criminal justice setting, provided that teacher is not confused with preacher.

Reality Therapy

Reality therapy, founded by William Glasser, has become a favorite counseling approach among those who work in community and institutional correction. I find this approach highly compatible with my personal philosophy because it takes what I consider to be the outstanding features of the other approaches we have examined and integrates them into a single theory. In agreement with psychoanalysis, reality therapy recognizes that people have basic needs that must be met for healthy functioning. It also agrees that these basic needs are love and a sense of self-worth.

However, reality therapy does not dwell excessively on these deficiencies. Rather, in common with RET, it moves the client away from bemoaning past privations and concentrates on present self-defeating behavior while teaching the client how to become a more lovable and worthwhile person. It is also similar to RET in that it is didactic, concerned with the present, and action oriented. Unlike RET, however, it recognizes the problems inherent in calling antisocial behavior "irrational" and substitutes "irresponsible." This is not just a semantic disagreement. Rationality is seen in terms of positive or negative consequences of an individual's behavior for himself or herself. In contrast, responsibility is seen in terms of positive or negative consequences of

an individual's behavior both for himself or herself and for others. As we have seen, one can be rational and engage in criminal activity; one cannot be responsible and do likewise. The reality counselor will not hesitate, however, to point out self-defeating irrational thinking, just as the RET counselor will not hesitate to point out irresponsible behavior.

It follows that the reality counselor shares with the RET counselor a hard-nosed, no-nonsense approach to clients. But, in common with client-centered counseling, reality counseling recognizes the importance of developing a warm, sensitive, and open relationship with the client as a prelude to effective counseling. Positive regard (not "unconditional"), genuineness, and empathy are stressed without the somewhat syrupy and abstruse connotations attached to them by client-centered therapy.

Theoretical Backdrop

William Glasser believes that those who engage in any kind of self-defeating behavior, including criminality, suffer from the inability to fulfill basic needs adequately. If these needs are not met, the person will fail to perceive correctly the reality of his or her world and will act irresponsibly (in speaking of *reality* Glasser means that the individual realistically perceives not only the immediate consequences of his or her behavior but also the remote consequences). To act responsibly, clients have to be helped to face reality, and to face reality, they must be helped to fulfill their basic needs. These basic needs are the need to love and to be loved and the need to feel that we are worthwhile to ourselves and to others. Glasser goes on to describe how these two needs are interrelated: "Although the two needs are separate, a person who loves and is loved will usually feel that he [or she] is a worthwhile person, and one who is worthwhile is usually someone who is loved and can give love in return" (1975:11). The person who has these needs met develops a "success identity" and the person who does not develops a "failure identity," which results in irresponsible behavior.

Glasser's theory nicely ties in at the psychological level with the sociological insights of Hirschi's control theory. The lack of a loving relationship with significant others (attachment) leads to a generalized lack of concern for the expectations and values of the larger society. This unconcern leads to a lack of commitment to a prosocial lifestyle, failure in school and in the job market, and a failure identity. Lacking this commitment, the individual is not involved with enough people with success identities who could model responsible behavior patterns for him or her. Rather, he or she is involved with others with failure identities who justify themselves and their behavior by developing a set of beliefs that are contrary to conventional morality. If early deprivations are severe enough, the individual may develop a psychopathic personality.

Although reality therapy refers to causes of behavior, it stresses that the causal understanding of behavior should not be viewed as excuses for that behavior. Reality therapy agrees with the client-centered and RET perspectives that the individual is ultimately responsible for his or her own "identity." In common with client-centered therapy, reality therapy asserts that there is a "growth force" within us all that strives for a success identity. Reality counseling attempts to activate that force by helping clients to learn who they are, how to interact with others in a responsible fashion, and how they can be accepted more fully by others. It charges the counselor to be a continuing model of personal responsibility for the client. This means, once again, that the counselor must work on himself or herself with the objective of becoming the best kind of person he or she is capable of becoming.

In a recent interview with Evans (1982), Glasser enumerates seven steps that the counselor must take to effect meaningful changes in a client's behavior. These are paraphrased below:

1. Get involved with clients, develop warm rapport, show respect.
2. Understand clients' personal histories, but deemphasize them in favor of what they are doing now.
3. Assist clients to evaluate their attitudes and behavior, and help them to discover how they are contributing to their failure identities.
4. Explore with them alternative behaviors that may be more useful in developing a success identity.
5. After decisions have been made regarding alternatives, get a commitment in writing to a plan of change.
6. Once the commitment has been made, make it clear that excuses for not adhering to it will not be tolerated. Emphasize that it is the client's responsibility to carry out the plan.
7. Do not be punitive with clients, but allow them to suffer the natural consequences of their behavior. Attempting to shield clients from these natural consequences reinforces their irresponsibility and denies the self-directedness of their actions.

The Reluctant/Resistant Client

The attitudes and techniques of reality therapy are particularly useful in counseling reluctant and/or resistant clients. Most counseling theories assume a voluntary client who has actively sought out help with various problems, although studies indicate that most clients, even self-referred ones, exhibit some reluctance or resistance at times (Paradise and Wilder, 1979). Some authorities even consider voluntary and welcomed interaction with the counselor as an essential prerequisite to the helping process. Reality therapy makes no such assumption. It recognizes that the majority of criminal justice clients are inclined to demonstrate resistance to various degrees, and it hardly needs to be said that none of them is in your office by choice.

Recognizing reluctance and resistance. Client resistance can range from a sullen silence, through game-playing by telling you only what they think you want to know, to outright hostility. Most verbal resistance does not take the form of angry name calling and challenges. It is more often a series of responses like "I don't know," "maybe," "I suppose," and "you're the boss." Nonverbal resistance can reveal itself in frequent finger and foot tapping, negative headshakes, smirky smiles, and arm folding (a gesture of defiance and barrier erection). This kind of verbal and nonverbal behavior can be very disconcerting to the beginning counselor who "only wants to help" and who is desperately trying to be liked.

Since the counselor's intentions are good, and he or she is doing all the right things learned in Counseling 101 to establish rapport, he or she finds it very difficult to accept the client's reluctance and negativism. All of us enjoy positive feelings, and few of us are very good at dealing with negative feelings, either our own or those of others, because it requires confrontation. Rather than acknowledging and dealing with negative feelings, the beginning counselor often tries to deny, downplay, or redirect them. The negative feelings must be acknowledged and worked through with the client. The process requires extra effort on the counselor's part; it is all too easy to coast and avoid uncomfortable issues. A counselor with a strong and integrated self-concept is not afraid to encounter negativism and confrontation.

Reasons for resistance. Why do criminal justice clients resist well-meaning attempts to help them? For one thing, you are a symbol of something that many clients have spent a good proportion of their lives resisting: authority. To cooperate with you may well be an admission of weakness, to their way of thinking, and they are not overly anxious to admit weakness, especially to a representative of "the system." Resistance is a form of defense mechanism designed to protect the ego from the disconcerting feeling of loss of autonomy. They also may not want to cooperate because what you want and what they want are two totally different things. You want them to act responsibly and obey the law; they want to get out of your office and out of your life. The very fact that clients are in your office involuntarily is enough to generate resistance. The principle of psychological reactance tells us that whenever people's sense of autonomy is threatened by forcing them in some way to do something, even if they would otherwise have done it voluntarily,

their natural inclination is to resist. Finally, you should ask yourself why clients should want to surrender themselves to a person whom they do not yet trust and to a condition they see as manipulative, for purposes with which they do not, at least for the present, agree.

Dealing with resistance. The first thing you must do with resisting clients is to acknowledge their feelings by reflecting them back and giving clients the opportunity to vent them. You need not share a client's views of you or "the system" in order to acknowledge the client's right to hold them. Arguing back and forth with clients at this point will only serve to strengthen their resolve. You may even inform them that you don't particularly mind if they feel the way they do as long as they behave responsibly.

Clients must be reminded that probation or parole (if this is the setting for the relationship) is a conditionally granted privilege and that they cannot be allowed to abuse it. You can inform resistant clients that you understand their desire to get out of your office and out of your life and that you share this desire with them. That joint objective provides a mutually agreeable starting point. You can then begin to delineate the conditions under which your mutual goal can be successfully achieved. Emphasize that you are responsible for implementing the conditions of probation or parole and that noncompliance will not be tolerated. You should also state that both of you have a vested interest in successful completion of probation or parole, that it should therefore be a cooperative endeavor, and that a negative and/or hostile attitude could seriously impede your mutual goal: "Let's help each other out."

This approach is the one that the reality counselor would take. He or she has not punished the client by returning hostility for hostility, but has let it be known that the client will be allowed to suffer the consequences of behavioral noncompliance. The counselor has been strong enough to deal with negative feelings in a constructive way by a judicious use of authority. He or she has been straight with the client without being overly authoritarian. The client has been allowed the dignity of possessing and expressing attitudes contrary to the counselor's but has been told up front that nonapproved—that is, irresponsible—behavior is not permitted. It has been my experience that criminal justice clients much prefer and respect directness rather than sweet-talking and beating around the bush. The counselor has enlisted the client's help to accomplish a goal desired by both parties. Involving the client in a shared purpose gives meaning to the relationship. The ability to involve clients in their own rehabilitation is the major skill of doing reality therapy (Glasser, 1975:25).

This area of general agreement between yourself and your reluctant or resistant client is then channeled to specific areas of concern by the implementation of a concrete plan of action. Initial plans should be microscopic in their breadth so as to maximize the probability of successful completion. They should also be formalized in writing and signed by the client and by yourself—a step that says to the client, "Your signature attests to your commitment to achieve this goal, and mine attests to my commitment to support you in your endeavor." Adherence to such a plan begins the process of the development of a "can do" success identity and engenders a sense of responsibility for living up to agreements. Moreover, keeping the expectations of the action plan modest often overcomes a client's reluctance to comply.

Treatment and Supervision Plans

Balance. In order to minimize reluctance, resistance, and probability of failure, treatment and supervision plans should be balanced with your clients' present coping resources. These resources—intelligence and educational levels, financial situation, self-concept, strength of interpersonal relationships, and so on—are known to you from previous interviews and the needs assessment scale. Similarly, you should be aware of problem areas to be addressed in the treatment and supervision plans. Balanced plans are plans whose demands on your clients should neither undertax nor overtax the resources they have

available to implement them. The principle of balanced plans is illustrated in Figure 8-3.

The diagram is divided into three sections: one balanced and two unbalanced. The upper-left triangle represents an unbalanced condition in which high coping resources are paired with low treatment expectation. The lower-right triangle represents the opposite condition. Sam is in the undertaxed section because he has high coping resources and because low demands have been placed on his resources. Sam will be quite happy and content for you to allow him to slide right along without having to do anything toward correcting problems that led to his criminal behavior. Of course, Sam may be a first offender who needs no treatment plan and who is best left alone. But if there are clear problem areas that may lead him to reoffend, you must take advantage of whatever strengths are represented by his relatively high coping resources for his growth toward responsibility.

Nick's situation is the opposite of Sam's. Heavy treatment demands have been made on his limited coping resources. The dilemma here is that Nick's low level of resources is the very reason that more intense treatment is required. That is, Nick's coping resources are low. Therefore, heavy demands are made on him to correct the deficit. But the lack of resources indicates that he probably won't be able at present to meet those demands. Thus, Nick is in a kind of "Catch-22" situation. If you insist on maintaining Nick's pres-

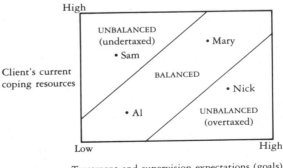

Figure 8-3   Balancing treatment goals

ent level of treatment you will be setting him up for resistance and failure and the consequences that go with them. Present treatment demands on Nick must be lowered so that they are commensurate with his present capacities to cope with them. As his capacities increase you may then renegotiate more demanding treatment goals with him.

The treatment goals set for Al and Mary are balanced with their present coping resources. Mary is considered to have coping resources equal to Sam's, but she is being challenged to use them for personal change and growth. Al has extremely low coping resources and thus probably needs a higher level of treatment than Mary. However, his present resources are not sufficiently strong to allow for the same level of treatment. As his resource strength increases (that is, as he slowly builds up a success identity), so may the demands that you negotiate with him increase. Do not undertax or overtax your clients' coping resources. Rather, move them slowly toward the ultimate goal one simple step at a time.

Simplicity. The main ingredients in a good plan are designed to change a failure identity to a success identity. A good plan should be

1. uncomplicated, simple, unambiguous, concrete, to the point: "Attend AA tonight at 6 o'clock."
2. active—something to do, not stop doing: "Attend AA tonight at 6 o'clock," not "Stop drinking alcohol."
3. something that can be done as close to "right now" as possible: "Attend AA tonight at 6 o'clock."
4. entirely dependent on client's actions for fulfillment, not contingent on the actions of others: *not* "Attend AA tonight at 6 o'clock if your wife/husband lets you off doing the grocery shopping."
5. something that can be done every day, or as often as possible: "Attend AA tonight at 6 o'clock, and every Tuesday and Thursday at the same time and place for the next month."
6. specific as to what, where, when, how, and with whom it is to be done: "Attend AA tonight

at 6 o'clock at St. Anthony Church on Pine Street. You (the counselor) will pick me up at my home for the first meeting to introduce me to other members."

The first plan need not be quite so active as this example. It can be something as simple as being on time for the next appointment. Whatever the plan may be, get it in writing and signed by both you and your client.

Orientation toward progress. Subsequent plans should be designed to build on the client's strengths rather than on his or her obvious weaknesses. Again, the idea is to build a success identity. Too early an emphasis on major weaknesses creates too great a chance of failure, thus reinforcing the client's failure identity and generating further reluctance and resistance. For instance, if JoAnn lacks a high school diploma and all indications are that she could successfully complete a GED program, show her that you have confidence in her capabilities and try to secure an agreement from her to enroll in such a program. Don't forget, though, that this goal must be balanced with her capacities. Do not insist that she commit herself if she is overly reluctant. You might instead persuade her at least to take a placement test. She may well be more receptive to the entire program if the test shows that she could do well. A recent study comparing rearrest rates between probationers enrolled in a GED program and a matched group of probationers not enrolled found that those enrolled in the program were significantly less criminally involved over a three-year period. Notice the "success identity" theme in the paper's conclusion (Walsh, 1985:76):

> The sense of personal accomplishment, the sense of participating in a socially valued endeavor, the anticipation of legitimate employment, and the idea that the "system" finds one worthy enough to make an investment in time and resources to provide one with a second chance, may be sufficient to put the scotch to an incipient criminal life-style.

The secret of counseling in criminal justice is, then, to temper your necessary authority in order to direct your clients' actions along acceptable

Perspectives from the Field

Roman Peña received B.A. and M.P.A. degrees from Idaho State University. He spent four years with the Utah Department of Corrections as a correctional counselor at a half-way house. He is currently a probation and parole officer with an intense supervision caseload.

When Cultures Clash: Resistance and Persistence
Roman C. Peña

I had only been in the intensive supervision program for three weeks when I was notified that I would be getting a new parolee called "Casey Jones." Reviewing Casey's inmate file and conversing with various sources, I became aware of Casey's Aryan Brotherhood affiliation. The Aryan Brotherhood is a white supremacist group that is very active and powerful within prison walls. Well, here's Roman, very much a non-Aryan, going to be this racist's parole officer. Although Casey's involvement in the Brotherhood was minimal, just the fact that he chose to identify with this group and their values was enough for me. Hence, I immediately contrived ways of defending myself in the event of a confrontation.

Sure enough, seated across the interviewing table the next day was Casey. His face and mannerisms displayed hate and anger. I knew that he knew about me from his own sources. As I asked him the required questions and advised him of his responsibilities, he'd respond with abrasiveness and sarcasm. It was tempting to retaliate, but I knew that it was necessary to maintain a professional demeanor.

The first two months of continual daily face-to-face visits were uneventful. Casey's attitude didn't improve, and I often hoped that he would abscond supervision. Nevertheless, he was content in doing as little as possible in most areas of concern, and he managed to stay within the "gray zones" of behavior and attitude. His welcoming remarks to me at home visits were, "Ya, what do you want?" and "Not you again!" His acquisition of a guard dog (which once nipped the back of my leg) became an object in our power struggle. Casey enjoyed watching my approach to the front door, as I tended to proceed with some trepidation. His enjoyment was short-lived as the dog befriended me.

Two more months passed until Casey experienced the setback of being laid off from his job. I couldn't help feeling that his negativism was a factor in his layoff. Casey started showing signs of worry. Christmas was only three weeks away and the job market was stagnant. One day an employer from a local mobile home factory called me up and asked me if I knew of someone who'd like a job installing mobile home windows. I quickly went and notified Casey. He got the job. From that point on he began to be more friendly. He'd even greet me at the door with a friendly "Hello!" He began to share personal problems. I listened intently and offered guidance when possible. He thought I was "one of a kind." Casey completed his six-month intensive parole period and was transferred to regular parole supervision.

Casey's new parole officer was—are you ready for this?—a Mr. Rodriguez. Mr. Rodriguez was firm yet fair with Casey. He told him that there would not be any sidetracking on cultural issues. Compliance to supervision standards was to be the priority.

Casey agreed to cooperate with him the best that he could. One day Casey called Mr. Rodriguez on the telephone. Mr. Rodriguez's face showed concern and empathy as he consoled Casey on the death of his newly born son. This was a major turning point in Casey's life. He became increasingly receptive

to assistance and cooperative in matters of supervision.

As I now submit Casey's final recommendation for discharge to the parole board, I remember our first two months in the program together. I've witnessed a miracle in human relations, not only in Casey but also in myself. Casey's

departing comments to me were, "You know, you're not so bad after all—for a Mexican. Thanks for everything." For some reason his Aryan values and my Mexican culture seemed so insignificant.

---

avenues while always being aware of, and showing a concern for, their basic humanity. Try to view client resistance as a normal response to coercion, perhaps even a psychologically healthy one. Examine your own resistance to self-growth and development, and examine your own behavior with clients to see if you are perhaps doing something to generate resistance. For instance, you may be a little too directive, too authoritarian, or in too much of a hurry to accomplish your goals. Especially examine the possibility that your goals for the client are not balanced with the client's present level of coping resources. As Newman has put it (1961:38):

> One of the first major accomplishments of treatment comes about when the offender becomes aware, both intellectually and emotionally, that the officer represents not only authority with the power to enforce certain restraints and restrictions but that he [or she] is also able to offer material, social and psychological adjustment aids.

Lessons and Concerns

I have no reservations about the application of reality therapy in the criminal justice setting. It is a relatively simple method of counseling that stresses responsible behavior, and it can be fruitfully applied by professionals outside the mental health field. Its "one small step at a time" approach to developing clients' success identities is, I strongly feel, particularly useful. Also very useful is its directive and confrontive stance within a no-nonsense, but warm, client-involved relationship. Its assertion that, at bottom, the origin of many clients' problems lies in early and pro-

tracted deprivation of love is consistent with my own beliefs. Finally, a number of studies have concurred with Rachin's (1974:53) conclusion that "Correctional clients who have proven least amenable to conventional treatment methods respond well to reality therapy."

The only point on which I take issue with Glasser is a theoretical one. His dismissal of mental illness as merely "irresponsible behavior" is overly facile. I think we are coming more and more to the realization that much of what we have termed *mental illness* does have origins in chemical and endocrinal imbalances. To treat individuals with such problems as merely irresponsible when they are demonstrably ill does them a disservice, to say the least. The criminal justice counselor must learn to recognize when his or her clients are behaving "irresponsibly" due to no real fault of their own and refer them to a mental health specialist.

Summary

This chapter has outlined the three counseling approaches most often used in criminal justice settings. These theories have found a place in corrections because they are relatively easy to understand and apply, emphasize the clients' own responsibility for change, and include equal involvement of client and counselor.

Transactional analysis is built around five simple words: *Parent, Adult, Child* (the ego states), *game,* and *script.* Much of our behavior is a playback of scripts laid down during infancy and childhood. The kind of scripts we have in our heads depends on the quantity and quality of the strokes (love) we received early in our lives. Our scripting leads to the four basic life positions from which we carry out our transactions with others: "I'm not OK; you're OK," "I'm not OK; you're not OK," "I'm OK; you're not OK," and "I'm OK; you're OK." The large majority of your clients will be operating from one of the first three life positions. We must strive to conduct all of our transactions from the "I'm OK; you're OK" life position.

Parent, Adult, and Child are three distinct ego states we slip into and out of during our various transactions. Criminal justice clients tend to operate mostly from the Child ego state. Many of them exclude the Parent altogether, and their Adult states are frequently contaminated by the intrusion of the Child. When interacting with clients, you should be operating from the Adult ego state. You should also strive to get your clients more involved with their Adults.

Rational-emotive therapy emphasizes that most of the problems of living we experience are the results of irrational thinking. It is not facts, events, or situations per se that cause us emotional problems. Rather, it is what we allow ourselves to think about those happenings. If only we could think more rationally we would have far fewer emotional problems. The counselor's task is to expose and strip away the client's negative, self-defeating thinking.

Ellis identifies eleven irrational ideas that are pervasive in our society. From these I adapted six that I consider to be particularly applicable to clients and workers in criminal justice. You will find it useful and rewarding to reread and assimilate these six ideas into your everyday operating philosophy.

Reality therapy views self-defeating behavior as being the result of not having one's basic needs adequately met. These interrelated needs are the need to love and be loved and the need to feel worthwhile. People who do not have these needs met tend to develop a failure identity. Your task is to assist your clients to develop success identities by becoming actively involved with them.

Reality therapy is especially useful in dealing with resistant and reluctant clients. You will often run into this type of client in the criminal justice field. Clients resist your help because you are a symbol of authority, and they have spent much of their lives resisting authority. They also resist because they are not in voluntary association with you. You must recognize and confront their resistance rather than ignoring or downplaying it. Allow them the dignity of their opinions, but make it clear that behavioral nonconformity simply will not be tolerated. Indicate that you will allow them to suffer the natural consequences of nonadherence to the conditions of their supervision.

In order to minimize resistance, and in order to develop clients' success identities, treatment plans must be balanced with their present coping resources. You should neither overtax nor undertax your clients' coping resources. Overtaxing invites resistance, and undertaxing is not growth producing. Treatment plans should be as simple and as concrete as possible, and they should be made in writing and signed by both parties.

◐ Exercises in Counseling

Practice in Primary and Advanced Empathy

The exercise in interviewing emphasized practice in listening to what your partner had to say. In these exercises in counseling you will be taking a more active part. Not only will you be intensely listening to your partner but you will be communicating to him or her that you understand where he or she is coming from. You will use all the techniques outlined in the chapter on interviewing, including paraphrasing, clarification, and reflection of feelings. Don't be content with vague statements from your partner; nail him or her down to specifics.

If you are the student being counseled, choose for discussion a topic that is of concern to you. It should be one with emotional content, such as the loss of a loved one, the breakup of a romantic relationship, the inability to get along with someone of importance to you, or a perceived personal defect. Such topics make for realistic counseling sessions for both partners. You will gain experience of a client's feelings when revealing intimate information, and the counselor will gain some experience in attempting to pull out deep feelings that the client may be reluctant to express. However, please do not feel obligated to choose a topic that is too painful to discuss with an inexperienced counselor. This exercise should be both productive and relatively safe. You should, therefore, be given ample time to decide on a topic.

After you have been through a short counseling session, you and your partner should put your heads together and try to identify strategies for understanding and/or amelioration of the problem discussed. Perhaps you could do some structural analyses on the client's important relationships. Do you see a pattern of crossed transactions? What is the client's typical ego state? Does the client agree? Is his or her usual state consistent with what Berne would predict from the client's history of strokes? How about irrational ideas that he or she may be harboring? If the counselor didn't identify them, maybe you can now do it together as a team. Finally, can you together define a simple plan to work on

eliminating the problematic behavior or feelings experienced by the client? You should find these exercises fun if approached from a mutual "I'm OK; you're OK" position.

Counseling "Real" Clients

If you have written PSI reports as interviewing and assessment exercises, your instructor may wish to use them as the basis for providing practice in counseling with a criminal justice flavor. The student who initially wrote the PSI can again team up with the same partner to explore more fully the problems and concerns discovered during the PSI process. These problems are many: alcoholism, child molestation, drug abuse, negative self-concept, anger and aggression, and so forth. The student counselor should determine what referrals, if any, might be beneficial for the client. Explore these problems in turn from each of the three counseling perspectives in this chapter, and then devise some simple "success identity" plans appropriate to your client.

If you are role-playing the client, then prior to the counseling session you should think deeply about being in the offender's shoes (empathy) so that you can present a realistic challenge to your partner's developing counseling skills. Much of your partner's success in this exercise will depend upon how well you are able to capture the feelings of the offender. An added bonus for you will be a greater ability to view the world from the offender's perspective.

References and Suggested Readings

Bateson, G., D. Jackson, J. Haley, and J. Weakland (1956). "Toward a theory of schizophrenia." *Behavioral Science,* 1:251–264.

Berne, E. (1964). *Games People Play.* New York: Grove Press.

Berne, E. (1966). *Principles of Group Treatment.* New York: Oxford University Press.

Brown, J. and R. Pate, Jr. (Eds.) (1983). *Being a Counselor: Directions and Challenges.* Pacific Grove, CA: Brooks/Cole.

Ellis, A. (1975). *A New Guide to Rational Living.* Hollywood: Wiltshire.

Ellis, A. (1982). Entry in *Who's Who in America,* 1982 edition.

Evans, D. (1982). "What are you doing? An interview with William Glasser." *Personnel and Guidance Journal,* 61:460–462.

Glasser, W. (1972). *The Identity Society.* New York: Harper & Row.

Glasser, W. (1975). *Reality Therapy: A New Approach to Psychiatry.* New York: Harper & Row.

Lytle, M. (1964). "The unpromising client." *Crime and Delinquency,* 10:130–134.

Newman, C. (1961). "Concepts of treatment in probation and parole supervision." *Federal Probation,* 25:34–40.

Paradise, L., and D. Wilder (1979). "The relationship between client reluctance and counselor effectiveness." *Counselor Education and Supervision,* 19:35–41.

Rachin, R. (1974). "Reality therapy: Helping people help themselves." *Crime and Delinquency,* 20:45–53.

Vriend, J., and W. Dyer (1973). "Counseling the reluctant client." *Journal of Counseling Psychology,* 20:240–246.

Walsh, A. (1985). "An evaluation of the effects of adult basic education on rearrest rates among probationers." *Journal of Offender Counseling Services & Rehabilitation,* 9:69–76.

Chapter 9

Prison Classification and Assessment

by J. Arthur Beyer

Through its diagnostic and coordinating functions, classification not only contributes to the objective of rehabilitation, but also to custody, discipline, work assignments, officer and inmate morale, and the effective use of training opportunities.

Presiding Judge in *Morris* v. *Travisono* (1970)

Classification is nothing more than a management tool. It is a technique used by virtually everyone to provide an orderly method of relating to or dealing with objects, situations, or people. For example, we classify the weather as warm and sunny or cloudy and cold, thus permitting us to make reasoned decisions as to our day's clothing and activities.

We classify people as well. We call them Republicans, Democrats, conservatives, liberals, alcoholics, criminals, and so on. We may subjectively classify individuals and groups on the basis of our personal experiences, perceptions, and prejudices. Regardless of the methods we use to arrive at our classifications, we tend to respond to the objects classified in a manner consistent with our classifications.

Professional practitioners within their respective disciplines have developed elaborate systems of classification relating to the phenomena of their disciplines. These practitioners have gone beyond subjective methods to embrace more objective ones. For instance, psychologists and psychiatrists classify various systems of behavior

This chapter was written by J. Arthur Beyer, M.P.A. Mr. Beyer is a former sergeant with a city police agency in Idaho. He was also a housing unit counselor, in which capacity he was involved in classification of inmates, and later a security lieutenant at the Idaho State Penitentiary. Currently a probation and parole supervisor for the intensive supervision program, he previously supervised a special sex-offender caseload. Mr. Beyer has published a number of papers on juvenile delinquency.

in a manual called the *Diagnostic and Statistical Manual of Mental Disorders* (DSM-III). This multiaxial system allows for the classification of individuals' characteristics in terms of clinically important factors. It provides a common bond of understanding within the family of mental health professionals. Management of caseloads and the implementation of treatment modalities are therefore greatly facilitated.

Unfortunately, the classification of institutionalized offenders is not yet quite so neat and tidy, although the causes and treatment of criminal behavior have been important items on the criminal justice agenda since it was first suggested that there might just be alternatives to flogging, mutilation, and torture.

Historical Overview

To understand and appreciate client classification as it is practiced today, it is important to have a basic knowledge of historical developments in penology that are related to classification. Early attempts at classification consisted simply of separating men from women and children within prisons. In the late 1700s, the Walnut Street Prison in Philadelphia inaugurated a classification process to separate serious offenders from others. Those classified as serious offenders were placed in isolation and were not allowed to work or interact with other prisoners (Lewis, 1967:17). Some 15 years later, in 1804, the Charlestown Prison in Massachusetts established a trilevel system of classification based on prior convictions of offenders. Each of the three groups was identified by distinctive uniforms, and groups were segregated from one another. On the basis of this classification, offenders were assigned quarters, prison work, and differential access to various amenities. First-time offenders were given the best quarters, job assignments, and food. Second-time offenders were allowed only two meals per day and performed the less desirable work. Third-time, or habitual, offenders did the most menial tasks and received the worst food (Lewis, 1968:71).

In the early 1800s, prison administrators experimented with a variety of new custodial and classification systems. One such system, which was to provide the model for most prison construction for the next 150 years, was the Auburn Prison, opened in New York in 1819 (Allen and Simonsen, 1981:37–38). Prisons based on this model were invariably maximum-security facilities with harsh conditions of confinement. Little effort was extended to establish inmate classification as an integral part of prison administration.

In 1959, criminologists Richard Korn and Lloyd McCorkle (1959) provided a broad classification of crime and criminals according to legal designation, personality types, life organization, and offense types (such as sex offenses and drug offenses). This text set the scene for later and more sophisticated typologies. But it was the intervention of the courts as much as anything else that provided the impetus toward better classification systems.

As late as 1966, the courts generally avoided interfering in specific classification decisions, recognizing "that discipline and the general management of such [penal] institutions are executive functions with which the judicial branch will not interfere" (*Cohen* v. *U.S.,* 252 F. Supp. 679 [N.D. GA., 1966] at 688). However, as a result of a court action in Rhode Island in 1970, the Federal District Court issued the first order that a meaningful, nonarbitrary classification system be designed and implemented. The court further recognized that inmate classification is a management tool that enables the prison administrator to allocate scarce resources to areas where the greatest good may be achieved. The court stated (*Morris* v. *Travisono,* 310 F. Supp. 857 [1970] at 965):

> Classification is essential to the operation of an orderly and safe prison. It is a prerequisite for the rational allocation of whatever program opportunities exist within the institution. It enables the institution to gauge the proper custody level of an inmate, to identify the inmate's educational, vocational, and psychological needs, and to separate nonviolent inmates from the more predatory....

Thus, the courts have charged correctional administrators with the task of minimizing the risk of injury to the public, to inmates, and to the correctional staff. This is to be accomplished while placing each offender in the least restrictive setting consistent with these goals and with the needs of the offender. As you may well imagine, inmate classification is perhaps the most involved and all-encompassing aspect of inmate supervision.

Security and Custody

As you will note from Table 9–1, *security levels* are of a physical nature. They refer to the envi-

ronmental factors of perimeter security and use of towers, patrol, and other detection devices. *Custodial levels* (Table 9–2) refer to the degree of supervision the inmate/client receives. Programs are the activities that are provided, such as educational and vocational opportunities, counseling services, and recreational and hobby activities. Figure 9–2 makes it clear that access to jobs and programs is an inherent function of custodial classification.

Table 9–1 Physical security designations

	Community	Minimum	Medium	Close	Maximum
Perimeter:					
None	X				
Nonsecure: designated by single fence or other boundary.		X			
Secure: walls and/or multiple fences with razor wire, security patrol dogs, and other detection devices.			X	X	X
External armed patrol:					
None	X				
Intermittent		X			
Regular			X	X	X
Housing:					
Single room	X	X	X		
Multiple occupancy	X	X	X		
Dormitories	X	X			
Outside cell: wall or window of cell on outside of building. Escape from cell may allow escape from building.			X	X	
Inside cell: all cells are confined within a cellblock with perimeter walls on four sides. If cell security is breached, the inmate is still confined in the building.				X	X

Source: Standards for Adult Correctional Institutions (2nd ed.), January, 1981, and *Standards for Adult Community Residential Services* (2nd ed.), August, 1980. College Park MD: American Correctional Association.

Table 9–2 Custodial designation

	Community	Minimum	Medium	Close	Maximum
Movement within the facility					
General Unrestricted	X	X	Daylight		
Staff observation			Night	Daylight	
Check out/check in				Night	
Escorted				X	
Escorted in restraints					X
Meals Unrestricted	X	X			
Staff observation		X	X		
Escorted and with staff supervision				X	
In cell or cell block					X
Supervision Periodic, as appropriate to activity	X				
Group supervision or hourly contact		X			
Frequent observation			X		
Continuous				X	X
Escorted (always)					X

Classification Data

Standards and Principles of Classification

Classification of behavior in the DSM-III provides an organized, systematic, and established procedure for assessing client characteristics. This classification in turn allows for differential treatment modalities. In institutional corrections, not all criminals exhibit the same behavior or present the same risk to security. However, we have not normally observed differential approaches; rather, we have tended to treat all inmates in a similar manner.

Our parent discipline, sociology, explores environmental factors to explain aberrant behavior. It tends to downplay individual differences that are not explicable in terms of environmental variation. Sociology, according to Jeffery (1979:113), assumes *equipotentiality,* meaning in effect that we all have the same potential for both good and evil. What we eventually become is the product of variation in the environment, with individual differences being constant. Psychology, although not discounting environmental influences, appeals to the individual's mental processes to explain "acting out" behavior. Each of these opposing perspectives on criminal behavior has had its turn at predominance in corrections. The exchange of orientations and goals in the cyclical exchange of sociological and psychological perspectives has led to pessimism and a "lock 'em up" attitude.

Criminology, as an emerging discipline, is beginning to develop new ways of examining corrections. Jeffery (1979) feels that by drawing on chemistry and biology, as well as the work being

Table 9–2 *(continued)*

	Community	Minimum	Medium	Close	Maximum
Absence from the facility					
Unescorted	X	X			
Escorted			X		
Armed escort			X	X	X
Furlough	X	X	X		
Partial restraints			X	X	
Full restraints				X	X
Access to programs, activities and jobs					
Unrestricted access, including community-based programs, activities, and employment.	X				
Selected community-based programs and activities. Staff-supervised jobs outside the perimeter.		X			
All programs, jobs, and activities inside the perimeter.		X	X		
Selected programs and activities inside the perimeter. Jobs inside the perimeter during daylight only.				X	
Selected cell activity. No access to jobs.					X

Source: Standards for Adult Correctional Institutions (2nd ed.), January, 1981, and *Standards for Adult Community Residential Services* (2nd ed.), August, 1980. College Park MD: American Correctional Association.

done on nutrition, and incorporating sociological and psychological insights as well, we will arrive at a greater understanding of criminal behavior, and thus a greater understanding of the correctional process.

To facilitate and standardize inmate classification on a national level and to address court mandates, the American Correctional Association (ACA) has established a set of standards for classification. The "Principles of Classification," which appear in the Appendix to this chapter (pp. 169–174), were developed by the National Institute of Corrections (NIC), U.S. Department of Justice, on the basis of the research conducted by professional practitioners.

Reception and Diagnostic Unit

Following a sentence of imprisonment, offenders are transported to the designated facility. For offenders being sentenced to prison for the first time, this is very likely the most frightening experience of their lives. Consider for a moment the confusion and fear that the offender must be experiencing as he or she tries to come to grips with the consecutive ordeals of trial, conviction, sentencing, and arrival at the "big house."

Upon arrival at the institution, all offenders are considered close custody inmates pending initial classification. The function of the security staff at this point is to instill the reality of prison security in the newly committed inmate. Armed guards are present, orders are given, and immediate compliance is demanded. Inmates are stripped naked, all property is seized, and a "strip search" is conducted. The strip search is very likely the greatest intrusion of one's privacy known. Inmates are then ordered to shower, with instructions to apply a delousing agent to all areas of body hair. At no time is an inmate allowed out of sight of a member of the correctional staff. Following the shower, inmates are issued a drab prison uniform and a number. All vestiges of individuality are removed. The inmate has effectively become a nonentity, totally vulnerable and dependent upon his or her keepers. Although I agree that this process is demeaning, I make no apology for it. It is unfortunately necessary as both a security and a sanitation precaution.

Inmates stay at the reception and diagnostic unit from two to three weeks, during which time they will be closely observed by security and programming staff. Observations of adjustment and behavior are forwarded to the classification committee for inclusion in their assessments and evaluations.

During the reception and diagnostic period, inmates will be seen by medical staff and will be tested in accordance with the policies of the particular state or institution. These tests may include the Nelson Reading Skills Test, the General Aptitude Test Battery (GATB), the Wechsler Adult Intelligence Scale (WAIS), the Minnesota Multiphasic Personality Inventory (MMPI), the Human Synergistics Lifestyle Inventory, (HSLI), and the Myers-Briggs Type Indicator (MBTI). Let's take a brief look at each of these tests.

Tests

Nelson Reading Skills Test. The simplest of these tests in terms of student understanding is the Nelson Reading Skills Test. It is designed to evaluate the client's reading grade level and vocabulary level.

General Aptitude Test Battery. The General Aptitude Test Battery is often administered by governmental employment services and is designed to measure aptitudes that have been found to be significant in many occupations. Developed in 1947, the GATB is not normally administered to anyone who does not read at least at the sixth grade level. Although it was designed to test adults and high school seniors, conversion tables have been devised for converting scores obtained by those reading at less than twelfth grade level.

Areas for which scores are obtained are presented below. Combining specified scores provides a composite score, which is then cross-referenced with specific occupational areas, indicating a general aptitude for that field.

1. *General learning ability (G).* The ability to understand instructions and underlying principles; the ability to reason and make judgments.
2. *Verbal aptitude (V).* The ability to understand meanings of words and the ideas associated with them, and the ability to use them effectively. The ability to comprehend language, to understand relationships among words, and to understand meanings of whole sentences and paragraphs.
3. *Numerical ability (N).* The ability to perform arithmetic operations quickly and accurately.
4. *Spatial ability (S).* The ability to comprehend forms in space. Frequently described as the ability to visualize objects of two and three dimensions.
5. *Form perception (P).* The ability to perceive pertinent details in objects or in pictorial or graphic material.
6. *Clerical perception (Q).* The ability to perceive pertinent details in verbal or tabular material.
7. *Motor coordination (K).* The ability to coordinate eyes, hands, and fingers rapidly and accurately in making precise movements with speed.
8. *Finger dexterity (F).* The ability to move the fingers and manipulate small objects with them rapidly and accurately.
9. *Manual dexterity (M).* The ability to move the hands easily and skillfully.

Combining the G, V, and N scores provides a score related to cognitive abilities. A functional "performance" score is obtained by combining the S, P, Q, K, F, and M scores. Although comparing results from instruments designed for different purposes is a risky business, it is interesting to note the similarity of criminal profiles obtained by the GATB and Wechsler IQ tests. As we remarked in the section on psychopathy, criminal samples tend to score significantly higher on the performance test of the WAIS than on the verbal test. Similarly, inmates tend to score significantly higher on the functional than on the cognitive sections of the GATB. These significant differences are not reported when either the GATB or the WAIS is administered to noncriminal samples.

Wechsler Adult Intelligence Scale.

The Wechsler Adult Intelligence Scale consists of eleven subtests, six of which are verbal and five of which are nonverbal. Three IQ scores are obtained from the WAIS: verbal, performance, and full-scale. The verbal scale reflects cognitive skills, the performance scale reflects skills on tasks such as puzzle solutions and design reproduction, and the full-scale score is a combination of the two subscales.

Minnesota Multiphasic Personality Inventory.

The MMPI, developed in the 1930s, is one of the most widely used personality inventories in corrections. It consists of 550 affirmative statements to which the test taker responds with "true," "false," or "cannot say."

The MMPI has ten scales relating to ten different clinical disorders:

1. Hypochondriasis (Hs)
2. Depression (D)
3. Hysteria (Hy)
4. Psychopathic deviate (Pd)
5. Masculinity–femininity (Mf)
6. Paranoia (Pa)
7. Psychasthenia (Pt)
8. Schizophrenia (Sc)
9. Hypomania (Ma)
10. Social introversion (Si)

Three additional control scales are built into the inventory. The Lie (L) scale is designed to assess the person's tendency to try to "look good." The Validity (F) scale is intended to reveal confusion and carelessness. The Correction (K) scale is more subtle than the L or F scales. A high K score tends to indicate that the respondent either is highly defensive or is attempting to "fake good." A low K score is indicative of either an attempt to "fake bad" or a tendency to be overly self-critical.

Human Synergistics Lifestyles Inventory.

The Human Synergistics Lifestyles Inventory, developed by Dr. Clayton Lafferty, is another self-report test. People taking the HSLI test are asked to select which statement of two is more descriptive of them. A series of paired statements is presented to the respondent. Each statement is repeated often, with alternative pairings. A profile is developed of individual lifestyle preferences from the responses. Here are brief descriptions of those preferences.

1. *Humanistic.* Enjoys helping, developing, and teaching others. Regards people as inherently good and accepts them unconditionally. Likes people and understands them. Needs to establish and maintain open, warm, and supportive relationships.
2. *Affiliative.* Cooperative, friendly, and open with others. High need for relationships with many friends. Wants to like and be liked.
3. *Approval.* Overly concerned with being liked. Bases own opinion of self and things on what others think.
4. *Conventional.* A conformist, takes few risks, covers mistakes, and follows rules.
5. *Dependent.* Does what is expected without question. Compliant and eager to please. Highly influenced by others.
6. *Avoidance.* Tendency to stay away from any situation that may pose a threat. Needs to protect self-worth rather than experiencing life and growth.
7. *Oppositional.* Needs to question things, including resisting authority. Critical tenden-

cies may be a reaction against the need to be close to others. Behavior can be antagonistic, causing defensiveness in others.

8. *Power.* Tends to be hard, tough, bossy, and aggressive. Needs to gain influence and control over others to maintain personal security. Authoritarian and dictatorial as a leader.

9. *Competitive.* Self-worth based on winning. Turns many situations into contests. Strong need for commendation and praise. Can be self-defeating because failure is unacceptable.

10. *Competence.* Driven need to appear independent and confident. Selects high expectations for self to the point that they are unreasonable. Failure to meet perfectionist standards results in self-blame.

11. *Achievement.* Feeling that personal effort makes the difference in the outcome. Needs to set own standards of excellence and pursue set goals. Willing to take some risks if they may produce positive results.

12. *Self-actualizing.* Concerned with personal growth and development. Responsible, confident, relaxed, and unique. Motivated by internal need to accomplish set goals. Perceptive and understanding of others, and accepts life in all its fullness.

High scores in a specific series can provide a composite of specific traits. Individuals scoring high in areas 1, 2, 11, and 12 tend to have a realistic view of self. Such people are extremely rare within prison walls. Individuals scoring high in areas 3, 4, 5, and 6 are insecure, but mask it to gain approval. They avoid risks and are easily influenced. High scorers in areas 7, 8, 9, and 10 tend to keep people at a distance and show an inability to deal with their feelings and emotions. They have a strong distrust of others. This group is heavily represented in institutional settings.

The Lifestyles inventory not only is designed to generate personality profiles but also is useful in identifying oppositional aspects of respondents' personalities. If an individual scores high on opposing lifestyle areas (for example, Humanistic/Oppositional, Affiliative/Power, or Approval/Competitive), he or she is attempting to meet competing and incongruent needs. Such attempts will probably result in debilitating intrapersonal conflicts and stress.

Myers-Briggs Type Indicator. Developed in 1962, the MBTI is based on psychoanalyst Carl Jung's theories of judgment and perception. Jungian theory proceeds from the premise that, from an early age, people are predisposed to react to the world in different ways. These preferences of interaction will tend to direct the use of judgment and perception and will influence both what people direct their attention to and the conclusions they draw from their interactions.

The MBTI identifies four separate preference categories. The interaction of the preference categories provides 16 separate groupings or "types" of individuals. These are the four categories.

1. *Extroversion–Introversion (EI).* This category reflects the individual's basic orientation. An extrovert is oriented to the outer world and tends to focus perceptions and judgments on people and things. An introvert is oriented inwardly and tends to focus judgments and perceptions on concepts and ideas.

2. *Sensing–Intuition (SN).* The SN category indicates the individual's perception preference. The sensing process is dependent on observable objects and occurrences, which are processed through the senses. Intuition is based on "gut feelings" about relationships, things, and occurrences and is beyond the scope of the conscious mind.

3. *Thinking–Feeling (TF).* The TF category is the judgmental index. Thinking allows the individual to reflect on the probable consequences of choices made. Feeling, in contrast, will provide the basis of personal or social values.

4. *Judgment–Perception (JP).* This category relates directly to the extroverted function of a person's life—how he or she deals with the outer world. A person who prefers to use judgment in these dealings will assign either the thinking or the feeling process to situations. However, if the individual reports a percep-

tion preference, the perceptive functions of sensing and intuition will dominate in relating to outer-world activities. The purpose of the JP category is to identify the tertiary (meaning "third most important") and inferior functions of the type indicator.

Each of the sixteen possible groups, referred to as *types,* is derived from factor analyses of the category scores. Each type has particular characteristics associated with it, depending on which of the bimodal attributes are dominant, auxiliary, tertiary, or inferior functions.

For example, an ENTP profile indicates an individual who is an extrovert (E) who relies on intuition (N) to make decisions most of the time. When that person's intuition factor is overly challenged, the auxiliary function T (thinking) will be brought into play. The perception factor (P) identifies the tertiary function as F (feeling) and the inferior function as sensing (S), the opposite of the dominant function N.

This summation may be translated into a client profile that depicts the client as quick, ingenious, and good at many things. ENTP clients are normally stimulating company, alert, outspoken, and quick to argue either side of a question for the sheer pleasure of arguing. Although they are resourceful in solving new and challenging problems, they tend to neglect routine assignments and flit from one new interest to another. They are also skilled in finding logical reasons for what they want, which may be used to justify their actions.

Any further explanation of the MBTI is beyond the scope of this book. I can say, though, that I have found it to be very helpful in identifying and understanding clients' personalities. Once this understanding is achieved, the counselor can assist the client to develop the tertiary and inferior functions of his or her personality in a wholesome direction, enhancing the development of the client's personality. For example, the counselor can assist ENTP clients to deal with routine assignments until they are completed and help them to identify flaws in the logic they use to justify aberrant behavior.

The results of all of this testing, in conjunction with information extracted from the presentence investigation report, reports submitted by custodial and other staff, and the client's criminal history, are consolidated by the classification committee to provide a comprehensive profile of the inmate.

Risk and Needs Assessment

Once all the data have been gathered and consolidated, a classification interview is arranged for the new inmates. The factors that establish the inmates' risk and custody level are explained to them. The psychological, educational, and vocational needs that have been identified during the assessment period are also explained. Inmates are told about available programs and how to get into them.

The final step is the establishment of any override considerations. An *override* means that unusual factors not addressed in the classification instruments are considered to be important enough to override the custody level determined by them in favor of some other custody option. Areas of concern related to security and maintenance of order include any gang or organized crime affiliations. Areas of concern related to custodial safety include consideration of any suicidal gestures, protection of any inmates known to be informants, and protection of those inmates whose crimes make them targets for abuse, such as child molesters.

The override option provides for both objective and subjective considerations not addressed in the classification instruments. Care must be exercised in the use of overrides, and the chairperson of the committee should be required to justify in writing the reason for the override action. If the classification instrument is overridden with some frequency, either the classification committee is not properly using the instrument or the instrument itself is defective and thus invalid. Either condition may result in judicial action to correct the problem.

In the years following the Morris decision, several classification models have appeared. The *ac-*

tuarial prediction model summarizes statistical data in an effort to predict future behavior. *Consensual classification* is an incremental process, conducted by prison administrators, that weighs classification criteria for implementation with individual inmates. *Clinically based* systems employ psychological test data as predictors of behavior and adjustment. *Decision tree* models are sequential. Each decision is based on the evaluation immediately preceding the current choice. Figure 9–1 illustrates the decision flow. We haven't extended it to provide the ultimate decision, but you can see the beginnings of the decision flow and progression. "Further decisions" are based on the criteria met at each level and will lead the decision makers to the custody level appropriate for the individual inmate. The *additive* models combine both actuarial and statistical data to provide cut-off scores along a continuum.

A common feature among models is the relative simplicity of the instruments used to deal with a complex problem. The issues they address are of the utmost importance, first and foremost being the risk that an inmate presents to society and the institution, as well as the needs of the inmate, which should be met to minimize that risk.

The risk and needs models discussed below offer you a closer look at the classification process. They are the National Institute of Corrections Proposed Classification Model for Custody and Need and the Adult Internal Management System (AIMS).

The NIC Model

The instrument developed by the National Institute of Corrections and presented in its publication *Prison Classification: A Model Systems Approach* is reproduced in the Appendix to this chapter, pp. 175–178.

Custody classification. The "Initial Inmate Classification: Custody" identifies eight areas of assessment that, when properly scored, provide for objective custodial placement. To assess the new inmate accurately, the classification committee needs to refer to the detailed classification manual that accompanies the instrument. After becoming

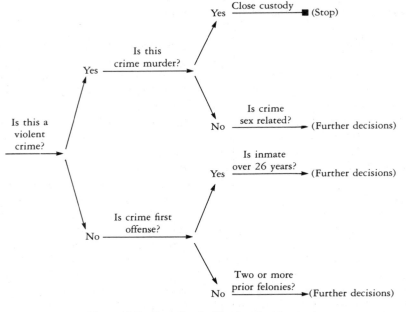

Figure 9-1   Custody classification decision tree

thoroughly familiar with the manual and instrument, committee members need to refer to the manual only periodically to verify adherence to and use of appropriate criteria. For our present purpose, a brief explanation is sufficient. As we go through the custody classification sections, we will apply them to Bill Bloggs using the information contained in his PSI report in Chapter 5.

1. *History of Institutional Violence.* Assault and battery is defined as any overt act toward another person, including another inmate, in which contact was made and injury attempted. If a weapon was used or serious injury occurred, this section is scored 7. In the event of two similar offenses, only the more serious is scored.

Bill Bloggs had no previous institutional history. Therefore, unless he assaulted someone at the reception center, he would have a score of 0.

2. *Severity of Current Offense.* A severity of offense scale is provided on the reverse side of the instrument (see p. 176). Although an inmate may be committed for several offenses, only the most severe is scored, for a maximum of 6 points.

Turning to the severity of offense scale, we see that Bill would get 6 points assessed against him because he committed armed robbery.

3. *Prior Assaultive Offense History.* This section reflects the offender's propensity for frequent violent behavior. Attempts to commit battery (simple assault) are scored regardless of the degree of contact or injury. Maximum score is 6.

Bill's assaultive history is minimal in terms of frequency. However, shooting a police officer to avoid capture is extremely serious and indicates that Bill can be dangerous when cornered. An assessment of 6 or 4 points is rather discretionary. In light of the seriousness of his assault, I would assess Bill 6 points.

4. *Escape History.* Any documented escape or attempt within the time framework provided is scored. It is noted that any adjudication by an institutional disciplinary hearing committee is sufficient for assessment regardless of any court prosecution. Maximum score is 7.

Bill has no escape history. Assess him 0 points.

The preceding four areas are the primary indicators of the risk that an inmate presents to the security of the institution and the welfare of other inmates and staff. A maximum score of 26 may be obtained. A score of 10 or more requires that the inmate be initially classified to close custody supervision. A score of 9 or less on the first four classification criteria requires that the last four areas be scored.

Bill has had 12 points assessed against him. Thus, he will be placed initially in maximum custody. We will assume for the purposes of the exercise that he had 9 or fewer points and score him on the following.

5. *Alcohol/Drug Abuse.* Abuse causing occasional legal and social adjustment problems is defined as any abuse that has resulted in five or fewer misdemeanor convictions, or interruption of employment within the last three years. Six or more alcohol or drug convictions during an offender's lifetime, or commitment to jail or treatment facilities within the last three years for substance abuse, is considered serious abuse. Maximum score is 3.

Bill has no history of drug or alcohol abuse causing him legal and social adjustment problems. He gets 0 points here.

6. *Current Detainer.* A detainer is a legal hold that another jurisdiction has placed on an inmate. Prior to releasing the inmate on parole or at the expiration of sentence, the institution notifies the jurisdiction that holds the detainer so that the agency that issued the detainer can make arrangements to transfer the inmate to its jurisdiction. Maximum score is 6.

Bill has no current detainers. He gets 0 points here.

7. *Prior Felony Convictions.* A simple summation of prior felony convictions. Do not include the current offense. Maximum score is 4.

Again, Bill is not assessed any points since the current offense is his first.

8. *Stability Factors.* Each item should be verified prior to scoring. This is the only area in which the scores are cumulative, thus resulting in a possible score of − 4.

Bill would receive the maximum points for stability factors. He was 26 or over at the time of his offense (− 2), he is a high school graduate (− 1), and he had been employed for more than six months at the time of his arrest (− 1). If this section were scored regardless of the custody score, Bill would have a total of $12 − 4 = 8$ points. This would place him in medium rather than maximum custody. The classification committee might well decide to override the custody classification score and place him in medium custody.

After sections 1 through 8 of the instrument have been completed, the scores are summed to provide a score used to determine custody level. Recall that a score of 10 or more points in sections 1 through 4 results in close custody classification. If the score in sections 1 through 4 was 9 or less, the score is totaled with the scores in sections 5 through 8. If the final score is 7 or more, the inmate will be assigned to medium custody. If the score is 6 or less, the assignment will be to minimum custody.

Needs classification. Identification of inmate needs is based on all gathered data, plus the inmate's own perceptions of his or her programming needs. During initial assessment interviews and testing, staff should elicit from inmates their ideas of what they need in order to become productive citizens. Areas of primary concern are educational, vocational, and medical needs, mental abilities, psychological problems, and substance abuse problems. The instrument reflects the fact that an individual's perceptions of his or her needs are somewhat subjective. For this reason, it is imperative that a high-quality classification interview be conducted by personnel thoroughly trained in the process (see "Initial Inmate Classification: Assessment of Needs" in the Appendix).

Following the risk and needs classifications, the classification committee will summarize the findings. Included in the summary will be the custody level and score, any override considerations and justifications for them, a final custody level assignment, and program and job assignment recommendations (see "Initial Classification Summary" in the Appendix).

Adult Internal Management System

Herbert C. Quay has developed a classification system that differs substantially from the NIC model. Dr. Quay's model relies on observable behavior patterns as assessed by correctional staff and integrates the documented behavioral history addressed by the NIC model. This system of classification was adapted from an earlier model designed by Dr. Quay for use in the Florida juvenile corrections system, and the Federal Prison System, as well as some states, has used it in the form discussed here.

The AIMS model establishes five groups based on the behavioral characteristics of inmates (see Table 9–3). These groups are identified as Groups I and II ("heavy"), Group III ("moderate"), and Groups IV and V ("light"). The terms *heavy, moderate,* and *light* allude to prison argot that describes a degree of perceived risk, threat, or the propensity to victimize other inmates or to be victimized. The basic idea behind the AIMS model is that classifying inmates according to behavioral characteristics can greatly enhance differential treatment modalities.

Under the risk classification model we have already examined, we may find all five of the AIMS groups represented in each custody level. The unspoken assumption behind custody classification based on type of crime is that those who commit similar crimes are similar in terms of more general behavioral traits. Those of us who have been employed "behind the walls" can attest to the fact that at each custody level there is a wide variety of behavioral types. At each level there are those who are victimized and those who victimize. The vast majority of inmates, however, are found between these extremes. Also, within each custody level, it is necessary to provide programs that are duplicated at other levels. AIMS classification is an attempt to discriminate more meaningfully among prisoners so that mixing victimizers and victims does not occur and so that programs are not unnecessarily duplicated. This should result in a reduction of prison violence and an increase in program effectiveness.

Correctional Adjustment Checklist. Dr. Quay has devised two very simple checklists (the "Correctional Adjustment Checklist" and the "Checklist for the Analysis of Life History," both shown in the Appendix, pp. 179–180) that, when trans-

Table 9–3 Characteristic behaviors by group

I ——————— Heavy ——————— II		III —— Moderate	IV ——————— Light ——————— V	
• Aggressive	• Sly	• Not excessively aggressive or dependent	• Dependent	• Constantly afraid
• Confrontational	• Not directly confrontational	• Reliable, cooperative	• Unreliable	• Anxious
• Easily bored	• Untrustworthy	• Industrious	• Passive	• Easily upset
• Hostile to authority	• Hostile to authority	• Do not see selves as criminals	• "Clinging"	• Seek protection
• High rate of disciplinary infractions	• Moderate-to-high rate of disciplinary infractions	• Low rate of disciplinary infractions	• Low-to-moderate rate of disciplinary infractions	• Moderate rate of disciplinary infractions
• Little concern for others	• "Con artists," manipulative	• Concern for others	• Self-absorbed	• Explosive under stress
• Victimizers	• Victimizers	• Avoid fights	• Easily victimized	• Easily victimized

ferred to appropriate score sheets (also shown in the Appendix, pp. 181–184), provide a raw classification score. The raw score is then converted through the use of conversion tables into what statisticians call T-scores (p. 183). This is not the place to go into detail about the derivation of T-scores. Suffice it to say that they are raw scores that have been mathematically standardized in order to achieve comparability of scores from distributions of raw scores that are dissimilarly shaped. In Quay's own words (1984:34): "The intent of the checklist is to cover as adequately as possible the domain of behaviors that might forecast adjustment and program participation in correctional settings."

To develop the Correctional Adjustment Checklist (CACL), Dr. Quay solicited behavioral descriptions from professional correctional practitioners and from mental health professionals with correctional experience. He also incorporated descriptions developed from his own research with juveniles. The checklist contains 41 behavior descriptions. The CACL tends to identify behavioral extremes of aggressiveness or submission.

In practice, line correctional personnel—that is, the staff that has the most contact with inmates—complete the CACL. The form is then submitted to the classification staff for scoring.

The scores place inmates in either the "aggressive-manipulation" group (Groups I and II) or the "passive-inadequate" group (Groups IV and V). Group III inmates are not identified by the CACL instrument, inasmuch as their behavior is generally acceptable within prison environment.

Checklist for the Analysis of Life History. The source of data for the Checklist for the Analysis of Life History (CALH) is the presentence investigation report. Dr. Quay asserts that the descriptions that should be readily available from the PSI report and from the casework interview can be used to gauge the degree of institutional adjustment and program participation of the inmate (1984:36). The classification staff completes the CALH and assigns inmates to groups on the basis of their scores.

After completing both the CACL and the CALH raw-score forms, the classification committee transfers the data to the "Classification Profile for Adult Offenders" (see Appendix, p. 184) and converts the raw scores to T-scores. The T-scores are then combined to provide a final classification of the inmate.

As a correctional practitioner, I feel that the AIMS classification method provides an excellent management tool for the differential assignment of inmates to programs. Studies have shown that it discriminates very well among inmate behavioral types. Group I inmates are involved in serious disciplinary problems more often than those in other groups, and Group III inmates generally are not involved in violent disturbances and present fewer management problems overall. However, I would be loath to substitute it entirely for the risk classification tools provided by the NIC model.

For example, an inmate convicted of homicide, having no prior contact with the criminal justice system, would be classified as a close custody inmate under the NIC model. However, it is conceivable that the same inmate could qualify as a Group III inmate (which is equated with minimum custody level) solely on the basis of the AIMS criteria. Given the current public mentality regarding incarceration, it is extremely doubtful that we could justify placing a convicted murderer in minimum custody at initial classification.

Figure 9–2 is a diagram summarizing the process of classification, starting with the presentence report and ending with the initial

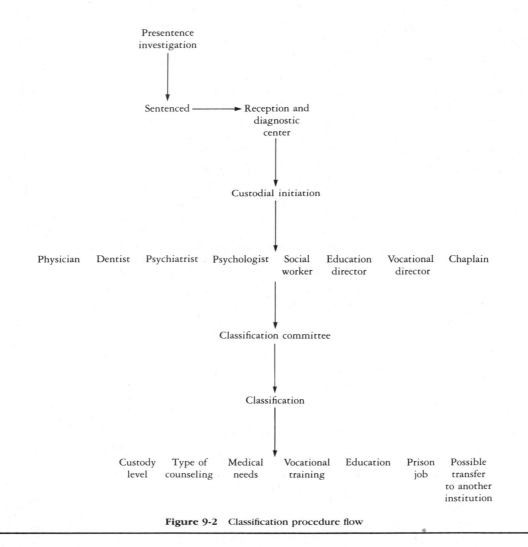

Figure 9-2   Classification procedure flow

Perspectives from the Field

Charles L. Miller spent six years as a police officer before entering the corrections field. His corrections experience includes supervision of maximum security and death row sections and command of a SWAT team at the Idaho State penitentiary. He holds an M.S. degree in human relations from Abilene Christian University, Texas.

On Rules and Crisis Intervention
Charles L. Miller

The supervision of a high-security prison unit will provide numerous opportunities to practice and experiment with different aspects of crisis intervention. A crisis may occur at any time and for any reason. The key to good crisis intervention in an institutional setting begins long before a crisis ever occurs. The counselor involved with the crisis intervention must have developed a great deal of credibility with the inmates. He or she must demonstrate a willingness to enforce the rules of the institution consistently, equally, and fairly, and at the same time demonstrate a genuine concern for the welfare of the inmates.

My experience leads me to the belief that inmates have an unrecognized desire to be controlled. While they try all sorts of devious things to circumvent the rules, and may even riot when rules become too oppressive, they desire some sort of structure. A great many of them desire rules to make up for the self-control that they personally lack. Lack of self-control probably got them into prison in the first place. They lack the controls necessary to live within the boundaries established by society and its laws. Many come to see the prison rules as a sign of caring on the part of those who enforce them.

I remember a young man I dealt with when I was a street cop. Ted had served time in a juvenile facility and had been released to live with his sister. His sister lacked the ability or desire to enforce any rules. Ted soon found himself in all kinds of trouble with the law again. The funny thing is that it seemed as though he wanted to be caught. He either turned himself in or made it extremely easy for us to catch him. The upshot was that he was returned to the juvenile facility.

About nine months later I was sitting in a coffee shop on a break when Ted walked in with a friend who had been incarcerated with him. They sat down with me and we talked about a number of things. I asked Ted if he hadn't been trying to get caught for his crimes and returned to the institution nine months before. He proudly explained that he was. I asked him why—wasn't it a prison? I'll never forget his answer: "I liked it there because the people there cared enough about me to tell me what I could and couldn't do." His friend chipped in "Ya, that's right." It appeared that Ted had become institutionalized at an early age—unable to function in open and free society as a result of his juvenile incarcerations.

Ted proved me wrong for a while. He had married an older woman who kept him in line. But she left him, tired of playing mother as well as wife, after he came home stoned one day.

I next saw Ted as an inmate in prison. He was a model prisoner who never caused any trouble. Ted is on parole now and seems to be doing well. What will happen when he is no longer supervised will be interesting.

Another way that a person demonstrates a genuine caring is through the art of listening. Far too often we see counselors acting before they have really listened.

Perspectives from the Field *(continued)*

When a crisis threatens, we often see them taking strong security actions or opening their big mouths to make matters worse. We could all be more effective and demonstrate more caring if only we would listen.

Listening is a skill that must be worked on. It is more than simply hearing what a person says. The listener must demonstrate that he or she understands the implications of what is being said. I have always tried to be a listening supervisor. I have found that at those times when I have

not taken the time to really listen, the level of tension on the tier increases. I have never been an inmate, but I can understand how their frustrations and impotence to change their environments can lead to violence. Many potentially dangerous crisis situations can be averted by empathetic listening.

To sum up. Crises in prison occur with disquieting frequency. They occur when inmates are thrown off emotional balance by the various frustrations of inmate life. The best way to deal with

crises is to anticipate them by being sensitive to precipitating conditions and by listening empathetically to complaints. When they do occur, remain calm and project self-confidence. Listen to the complaint and examine with the inmate(s) what can be done about it. However, never promise anything you can't produce, and produce what you have promised. Through conscious efforts to show a caring attitude, a great number of potentially major incidents can be defused.

---

classification of an inmate to custody level, job assignments, and various programs aimed at his or her institutional adjustment and personal improvement.

Summary

In this chapter we have briefly looked at what prison classification is, why we classify prisoners, and how it is accomplished. Classification of prisoners is the differential assignment of people to varying levels of security: maximum, close, medium, and minimum. The determination of custody level is influenced primarily by the risk that the prisoner presents to the safe and orderly operation of an institution. Custody classification is related to security classification, and the classification level affects an inmate's access to various counseling, educational, vocational, and recreational programs. A general observation is that program access varies inversely with security and custody levels—as security is increased, program access is decreased.

Professional organizations such as the American Correctional Association and the National Institute of Corrections have been influential in the development of classification standards and of models for implementing those standards.

Modern classification procedures have been influenced by the judiciary and by the various human sciences. These influences have resulted in some classification procedures that go beyond the concern for institutional security. Various testing and assessment tools have been developed that can be used by correctional administrators to evaluate prisoners in terms of their personalities, needs, and potentialities. We briefly examined the GATB, WAIS, MMPI, HSLI, and MBTI instruments.

There are numerous classification methods in use, most of which are hybrids of the two models (NIC and AIMS) presented here. As new data become available through research, we will see the development of more efficient and effective classification systems, just as evolution occurs in the more advanced fields.

References and Suggested Readings

Allen, H., and C. Simonsen, (1981). *Corrections in America.* New York: MacMillan.

American Correctional Association (1981). *Classification* (monograph, series no. 1). College Park, MD: Author.

American Correctional Association (1982). *Classification as a Management Tool: Theories and Models for Decision-Makers.* College Park, MD: Author.

American Correctional Association (1984). *Standards for Adult Correctional Institutions.* College Park, MD: Author.

Jeffery, C. (1979). *Biology and Crime.* Beverly Hills, CA: Sage.

Korn, R., and L. McCorkle, (1959). *Criminology and Penology.* New York: Holt, Rinehart & Winston.

Lewis, O. (1968). *The Development of American Prisons and Prison Customs, 1776–1845.* Montclair, NJ: Patterson-Smith.

Myers, I., and M. McCaulley, (1985). *Manual: A Guide to the Development and Use of the Myers-Briggs Type Indicator.* Palo Alto, CA: Consulting Psychological Press.

National Institute of Corrections (1981). *Prison Classification: A Model Systems Approach.* Washington, DC: Author.

Quay, H. (1984). *Managing Adult Inmates.* College Park, MD: American Correctional Association.

Chapter 9 Appendix

Principles of Classification

The foundation of classification is a *system*—the organized and established procedure for combining an interdependent group of events into a unified whole. A system entails the coming together of all components to produce a product: *classification*. The type of system that exists will determine the type of classification that exists. The *process* by which classification is effected is an integral part of the product. If the process (embodied in the policy and procedure manual) changes, then the classification decisions will change.

Any classification system must operate on the basis of valid principles; those presented below describe the factors necessary for a classification *system* to exist (Solomon, 1980). (In addition, the 14 principles listed below make up the criteria for a classification system assessment tool for evaluating basic system functioning. Specific methods for use of the principles as an assessment tool are discussed in Section 5, *Prison Classification: A Model Systems Approach*.) It is important to note that the following principles must apply to the *entire* prison system, including women and youthful offender institutions and programs.

1. **There must be a clear definition of goals and objectives of the total correctional system.**

   Traditionally, security and custody have been the primary goals and objectives of correctional systems. While most also have rehabilitation as a goal, it is secondary to security and custody, as the latter comprise the primary public mandate to corrections. Humane care and treatment, however, should be integral to all systems.

   Prior to attempting to design a classification process or other system-wide program, the Department of Corrections must be very clear as to its own goals and objectives (its function, purpose, and priorities). These should be realistic and understandable to both staff and inmates.

   Within these goals, a classification system can be developed to sort those prisoners whose identified needs fall within the agency's objectives. Only after conceptualizing its own goals can a correctional system develop a rational classification process.

2. **There must be detailed written procedures and policies governing the classification process.**

   An essential component for a classification decision-making model is a policy statement that sets forth the Department of Corrections' goals, objectives, and purposes for the new classification system. For example, when developing its new classification system in 1979, the Minnesota Department of Corrections based the system on eight departmental "principles" regarding classification. These principles, in order of importance to Minnesota's Department of Corrections, are:

   • Minimize risk to the public;

   • Minimize risk to other inmates and institution staff;

   • Minimize breaches of security;

   • Minimize system risk;

   • Minimize security levels;

   • Maximize fairness (similar offenders treated in a similar manner);

   • Maximize the objective and quantitative nature of all classification criteria; and

   • Maximize inmate understanding of the classification system and inmate participation in program decisions.

Policies such as Minnesota's should be included in a comprehensive departmental classification policy manual. The American Correctional Association (ACA) *Manual of Standards for Adult Correctional Institutions* (1977) calls "essential" (Standard No. 4373) a ". . . classification manual containing all the classification policies and detailed procedures for implementing policies; this manual is made available to all staff involved with classification and is reviewed at least annually and updated as necessary."[*] The manual must be written clearly and concisely, and *must* be understood by classification personnel. The policies contained in the manual should deal with such classification issues as:

- Initial inmate classification and reclassification;

- Instructions regarding the makeup of classification committees, units, and teams, and the full responsibilities of each;

- Definitions of various committees' responsibilities for custody, employment, and vocational/program assignments;

- Instructions concerning potential changes in an inmate's program;

- Procedures relating to inmate transfer from one program to another and from one institution to another;

- Content of the classification interview; and

- Method of documentation of decisions made.

Since classification policies must be dynamic, constantly subject to change and revision as the classification process is continuously evaluated, the classification manual should be prepared in such a manner as to provide for easy update. (An important caution here is that the length of the manual is not necessarily correlated with its quality.)

3. **The classification process must provide for the collection of complete, high-quality, verified, standardized data.**

The classification system must define the data needed and the format in which it is to be collected and analyzed. High-quality, standardized data is essential to a valid statistical base for classification decision-making and for correlation of prediction and need factors.

Complete and verified data permits:

- Equitable determinations based on particular factors of individual cases;

- Similar decisions among individual classification analysts on roughly comparable cases; and

- Quantitative analysis of trends in classification decision-making for individual facilities or the Department of Corrections as a whole.

Through its technical assistance projects, NIC has found that the quantity and quality of offender data (criminal history, personal and family background, etc.) available to teams when the classification decision must be made are frequently less than adequate, and sometimes entirely unusable. Forms often are incomplete, some data collected are of questionable relevance, and much information is subject to broad interpretation because of its qualitative (narrative) nature.

---

[*]This standard has since been superseded by Standard 2-4399, which states: "There is a written plan for inmate classification which specifies the objectives of the classification system, details the methods for achieving the objectives, and provides a monitoring and evaluation mechanism to determine whether the objectives are being met. The plan is reviewed at least annually and updated if necessary." *Standards for Adult Correctional Institutions*, Second Edition, 1981.

In many of the systems studied, NIC found that no specific guidelines were given to field staff regarding the collection of offender background data necessary for a valid classification decision. Without specific and objective guidelines, field staff are not likely to prepare reports sufficiently comprehensive and reliable to be used in an empirically valid statistical analysis.

4. **Measurement and testing instruments used in the classification decision-making process must be valid, reliable, and objective.**

The numerous legal grievances filed by prisoners in recent years charging that classification decision-making processes are discriminatory, biased, or invalid, point up the necessity to ensure that any tests administered to inmates have been validated for reliability as predictors of custody and/or program needs. In addition, correctional departments must be able to demonstrate that testing processes are objective, logical, and fundamentally fair, and are designed to meet the needs of both the prisoners and the institution. By the same token, tests designed for other purposes should not be used to classify inmates (I.Q. tests, personality inventories).

In mid-1979, NIC sponsored a national survey of screening and classification processes, which assessed the current state-of-the-art in the design and utilization of classification instruments for decision-making (American Justice Institute, 1979). The survey found that correctional agencies have been shifting from subjective judgments to standardized instruments for classification decision-making. The instruments being used are printed forms containing a fixed set of weighted criteria that provide an overall offender summary score. Considerations of this score in the process assists the classification team in making more uniform and consistent decisions that are less subject to legal challenge. (North Carolina and Minnesota submitted their instruments for legal review prior to implementation.) In some states, the forms are used both for custody and needs decision-making.

5. **There must be explicit policy statements structuring and checking the discretionary decision-making powers of classification team staff.**

A corrections department must establish clear guidelines governing the discretionary decision-making powers of classification team staff. Otherwise, the department leaves itself open to allegations of unfairness, arbitrariness, and bias.

Discretionary powers of classification staff remain unstructured in too many systems. One example of the resultant problems was provided by a state corrections department in a grant application to NIC: "There is a very broad range of subjective and informal criteria used by those responsible for the classification of inmates; each person involved in the classification process has internalized his own set of significant variables, has established the relative importance of each of these variables according to his own value scale, and applies these standards in the classification decision on a case-by-case basis."

While discretion cannot and should not be completely eliminated, steps can be taken to designate boundaries within which classification decisions will be made, thus eliminating too broad discretionary power of individuals. A system in which the classification processes, rules, policies, findings, and reasons are open to scrutiny can further serve to check discretion.

Structuring and checking discretion is the responsibility of the Department of Corrections' central office. This responsibility is carried out by:

- Direction and supervision of the classification process by high-level central office personnel;

- Establishment of procedures for inter-institutional transfer, including review by central office staff and an appeal procedure and administrative review of difficult cases;

- Establishment of procedures for central office monitoring and evaluation of the classification process to ensure that it is operating according to policy;

- Establishment of procedures for consideration of mitigating or aggravating factors in decision-making;

- Initiation of policy pertaining to classification, inmate programs/treatment, and casework, including a classification manual; and

- Selection, training, and supervision of counselors and other classification staff members.

6. **There must be provision for screening and further evaluating prisoners who are management problems and those who have special needs.**

This necessary function, also the responsibility of the Department of Corrections' central office, must be included in any model classification system.

Prisoners who are management problems and require special considerations in placement and programming fall into several categories:

- Those who require protection and separation because they may be in danger from other prisoners;

- Those who, by reason of their offense, criminal record, or institutional behavior, require particularly close supervision; and

- Those who received unusual publicity because of the nature of their crime, arrest, or trial, or who were involved in criminal activities of a sophisticated nature, such as organized crime.

The most dangerous inmates must be separated from the less violent individuals; thus, the classification process, by necessity, needs to include procedures to determine which prisoners are potentially dangerous, such as those who have a history of assaultive or predatory behavior.

In additon to screening and further evaluating inmates who are management problems, the correctional system's central office must provide for prisoners who have special needs. Those individuals who, through effective screening, are shown to require special program assignments and monitoring include, but are not limited to, the aged and infirm, the mentally ill and retarded, and those with special medical problems.

7. **There must be provisions to match offenders with programs; these provisions must be consistent with risk classification needs.**

This process involves the establishment of clear, operational definitions of the various types of offenders and available institutional programs. But risk as well as need factors must be considered when decisions are being made.

Thus, NIC recommends that the classification process be directed toward:

- Identifying and evaluating the factors underlying each prisoner's needs;

- Recommending programs and activities for prisoners according to their *specific* needs and the availability of resources; and

- Developing and recording the necessary data to support services and long-range program planning.

To fulfill these tasks, it is necessary to identify and utilize *all* programs that are available to each individual prisoner. This function can be accomplished through a systematic classification of the offender and subsequent development of a program plan specifically designed for him/her.

8. **There must be provisions to classify each prisoner at the least restrictive custody level.**

This model classification system component targets the prevalent problem of overclassification. Eliminating overclassification is among the most significant objectives of new classification systems being designed and implemented in Minnesota, Tennessee, New York, and other states.

The first step involved here is developing specific criteria for differential custody assignments. Equally crucial is the second step of ensuring that both staff and prisoners are aware of these criteria.

NIC recommends that clearly understandable custody definitions and supervision guidelines be applied system-wide. At a minimum, definitions should be given for: (1) the traditional levels of custody — maximum, close, medium, and community; and (2) the different uses of segregation (especially disciplinary segregation). A basic premise is that *every* prisoner should be in the *lowest* custody believed suitable for adequate supervision and warranted by his/her behavior.

9. **There must be provision to involve the prisoner in the classification process.**

   Each new prisoner should be provided with a copy of the custody criteria; a written explanation of the classification process; and a written explanation of the health care, employment, vocational training, education, transfer, and special programs available, including the selection criteria for each.

   In addition, the correctional system should provide for classification teams at each institution so the prisoner can participate in the classification decision-making process. ACA Standard No. 4374 [Standard 2-4403, Second Edition, 1981] calls for "maximum involvement of inmates in their classification reviews." The prisoner should be present except, perhaps, during deliberations of the classification team.

10. **There must be provisions for systematic, periodic reclassification hearings.**

    Providing for reclassification on a regularly scheduled basis is another "essential" standard (No. 4376) [Standard 2-4404, Second Edition, 1981] recommended by the ACA. Periodic review and reclassification is a cornerstone of any model classification system.

    In reporting on its study of the classification process at the Tennessee Department of Corrections, NIC suggested the adoption of the following reclassification guidelines:

    • Review/reclassification within two weeks following the prisoner's transfer from another institution within the system;

    • Review every three months for prisoners serving terms of 18 months or less;

    • Review every six months for prisoners serving terms of 18 months and one day to five years; and

    • Annual review for prisoners serving terms of five years or more. (NIC now recommends review every six months.)

    If suitable manpower is available, reviews can be conducted on a more frequent basis. Optimally, prisoners should be permitted to initiate reviews of their progress, status, and programming (ACA "important" Standard No. 4379) [Standard 2-4407, Second Edition, 1981].

11. **The classification process must be efficient and economically sound.**

    An empirically based classification system should enable the Department of Corrections to handle large numbers of offenders efficiently through a grouping process based on needs and risks. This can be accomplished by using modern technology to assist in the storage, correlation, and retrieval of data, although use of a computer should not be essential.

    An efficient, economically sound classification system also makes effective use of other components of the criminal justice system, as well as social service agencies, for the provision of offender data (such as information obtained for pre-sentence reports).

    The development of a model classification system should involve cooperating with other agencies to devise a standardized reporting format for offender information , preferably one which elicits quantitative data insofar as possible.

12. **There must be provisions to continuously evaluate and improve the classification process.**

Any true process continuously strives to improve itself through feedback, evaluation, and action to correct deficiencies. Thus, the model classification system, if it is to be effective, must be able to continuously improve to meet the changing needs of the inmate population and the correctional system as a whole. It must be responsive to emerging knowledge and professional understanding of the classification process. The system must also be responsive to staff and inmate input.

13. **Classification procedures must be consistent with constitutional requisites.**

The central office must keep abreast of litigation applicable to its jurisdiction in order to ensure the continued legality of its classification policies, procedures, and decisions. Most state Departments of Corrections have a legal section that can be of assistance in this area.

14. **There must be an opportunity to gain input from administration and line staff when undertaking development of a classification system.**

In summary, *the hallmark of classification is the non-capricious assignment of individuals.* In order to accomplish equity in custody, security, program and treatment determination, and placement, a system reflecting the above principles must exist. Furthermore, it must be utilized.

A basic tenet of classification takes the idea of non-capricious placement a step further. As stated earlier, classification seeks to determine the placement of individuals in accord with their various correctional needs. Each of these outcomes may be accomplished separately, but it is only when they are combined into a comprehensive process that strives for equity and objectivity that we define it as *classification*. Since equity and objectivity are goals, principles and procedures should be employed that reflect these aims.

Initial Inmate Classification
Custody

NAME _____   NUMBER _____
      Last   First   MI

CLASSIFICATION CASEWORKER _____   DATE _____ / _____ /

1. HISTORY OF INSTITUTIONAL VIOLENCE
(Jail or Prison, code most serious within last five years)

                                              score

None 0
Assault and battery not involving use of a weapon or resulting in serious injury 3
Assault and battery involving use of a weapon and/or resulting in serious injury or death 7

2. SEVERITY OF CURRENT OFFENSE
(Refer to the **Severity of Offense Scale** on back of form. Score the most serious offense if there are multiple convictions.)

                                              score

Low 0
Low Moderate 1
Moderate 2
High 4
Highest 6

3. PRIOR ASSAULTIVE OFFENSE HISTORY
(Score the most severe in inmate's history. Refer to the **Severity of Offense Scale** on back of form.)

                                              score

None, Low, or Low Moderate 0
Moderate 2
High 4
Highest 6

4. ESCAPE HISTORY (Rate last 3 years of incarceration)

                                              score

No escapes or attempts (or no prior incarcerations) 0
An escape or attempt from minimum or community custody, no actual or threatened violence:
    Over 1 year ago 1
    Within the last year 3
An escape or attempt from medium or above custody, or an escape from minimum or community custody with actual or threatened violence:
    Over 1 year ago 5
    Within the last year 7

CLOSE CUSTODY SCORE (Add items 1 through 4)
(If score is 10 or above, inmate should be assigned to close custody. If score is under 10, complete Items 5 through 8 and use medium/minimum scale.)

☐

5. ALCOHOL/DRUG ABUSE

                                              score

None 0
Abuse causing occasional legal and social adjustment problems 1
Serious abuse, serious disruption of functioning 3

6. CURRENT DETAINER

                                              score

None 0
Misdemeanor detainer 1
Extradition initiated - misdemeanor 3
Felony detainer 4
Extradition initiated - felony 6

7. PRIOR FELONY CONVICTIONS

                                              score

None 0
One 2
Two or more 4

8. STABILITY FACTORS
(Check appropriate box(es) and combine for score.)

                                              score

    Age 26 or over .... -2
    High school diploma or GED received .... -1
    Employed or attending school (full or part-time) for six months or longer at time of arrest .... -1

MINIMUM/MEDIUM SCORE (Add items 1 through 8.)

TOTAL SCORE

MEDIUM/MINIMUM SCALE:
Medium Custody 7-22
Minimum Custody .... 6 or less

SEVERITY OF OFFENSE SCALE
(from Massachusetts Superior Court Sentencing Guidelines Project, 1979)

6 POINTS

Armed assault in a dwelling
Armed robbery while masked
Armed robbery
Arson in a dwelling place, night, occupied
Burglary, being armed
Kidnapping to extort
Murder*
Rape
Robbery
Stealing by confining or putting in fear

5 POINTS

Extortion
Incest
Kidnapping
Manslaughter
Mayhem

4 POINTS

Arson (Note: not Arson as listed above)
Breaking and entering, nighttime
Burglary, not being armed
Burning to Defraud
Burning Insured Property
Burning Real Property
Carrying a Firearm†
Common Receiver
Indecent A&B Child under 14
Mfg., dist. or poss. with intent to dist., Class A&B

3 POINTS

Assault and battery to collect a loan
Assault and battery with a dangerous weapon
Assault with intent to murder, maim
Assault with intent to rob while being armed
Attempt to murder by poisoning
Breaking and entering in the daytime

Attempt or Accessory before the Fact of an offense receives the same score as the substantive offense.

*Score only if prior offense.

†If present offense, score only if not most serious offense.

Initial Inmate Classification
Assessment of Needs

NAME_____

        Last   First   MI

NUMBER_____

CLASSIFICATION CHAIRMAN_____

DATE_____ / _____ / _____

TEST SCORES:

_____
I.Q.

NEEDS ASSESSMENT: Select the answer which best describes the inmate.

_____
Reading

_____
Math

HEALTH:

1 Sound physical health, seldom ill.

2 Handicap or illness which interferes with functioning on a recurring basis.

3 Serious handicap or chronic illness, needs frequent medical care.

_____
code

INTELLECTUAL ABILITY:

1 Normal intellectual ability, able to function independently.

2 Mild retardation, some need for assistance.

3 Moderate retardation, independent functioning severly limited.

_____
code

BEHAVIORAL/EMOTIONAL PROBLEMS:

1 Exhibits appropriate emotional responses.

2 Symptoms limit adequate functioning, requires counseling, may require medication.

3 Symptoms prohibit adequate functioning, requires significant intervention, may require medication or separate housing.

_____
code

ALCOHOL ABUSE:

1 No alcohol problem.

2 Occasional abuse, some disruption of functioning.

3 Frequent abuse, serious disruption, needs treatment.

_____
code

DRUG ABUSE:

1 No drug problem.

2 Occasional abuse, some disruption of functioning.

3 Frequent abuse, serious disruption, needs treatment.

_____
code

EDUCATIONAL STATUS:

1 Has high school diploma or GED.

2 Some deficits, but potential for high school diploma or GED.

3 Major deficits in math and/or reading, needs remedial programs.

_____
code

VOCATIONAL STATUS:

1 Has sufficient skills to obtain and hold satisfactory employment.

2 Minimal skill level, needs enhancement.

3 Virtually unemployable, needs training.

_____
code

Initial Classification Summary

1 Override Considerations—Custody Classification   _____
    1. None   code
    2. Inmate Needs Protection
    3. Temporary Placement—Pending Investigation
    4. Temporary Placement—Punitive Isolation
    5. Temporary Placement—Suicide Threat   score
    6. Other, Specify: _____

                                         I.Q.

2. Custody Level Assignment: _____
    1. Community   code   score   Reading
    2. Minimum
    3. Medium   Math
    4. Close
    5. Maximum
    6. Protective Custody
    7. Other, Specify: _____   code

                                         score

3. Facility Assignment: _____   code
    (See attached Code List)   code

4. Program Recommendations   score
    (In order of priority)

                                         code

	Program Code	Enrollment Code*
_____	____	____
_____	____	____
_____	____	____
_____	____	____

                                 [ ]   code

                                 score   code

5. Work Recommendations:

	Work Code	Inmate Skills	Skill Code
_____	____	_____	____
_____	____	_____	____
_____	____	_____	____
_____	____	_____	____

                                 score   code

                                 score   code

                                 score

                                 =====
                                 TOTAL SCORE

*Enrollmend Code
Program available = 1
Program currently at capacity/unavailable = 2
Program needed but does not exist at required
   custody level = 3
Inmate refuses program = 4

Correctional Adjustment Checklist (CACL)

Name and number of inmate _____

Name of person completing this checklist _____

Your position _____ Date completed _____

Instructions: Please indicate which of the following behaviors this inmate exhibits. If the behavior describes the inmate, circle the "1." If it does not, circle the "0." *Please complete every item.*

0	1	1. Worried, anxious
0	1	2. Tries, but cannot seem to follow directions
0	1	3. Tense, unable to relax
0	1	4. Socially withdrawn
0	1	5. Continually asks for help from staff
0	1	6. Gets along with the hoods
0	1	7. Seems to take no pleasure in anything
0	1	8. Jittery, jumpy; seems afraid
0	1	9. Uses leisure time to cause trouble
0	1	10. Continually uses profane language; curses and swears
0	1	11. Easily upset
0	1	12. Sluggish and drowsy
0	1	13. Cannot be trusted at all
0	1	14. Moody, brooding
0	1	15. Needs constant supervision
0	1	16. Victimizes weaker inmates
0	1	17. Seems dull and unintelligent
0	1	18. Is an agitator about race
0	1	19. Continually tries to con staff
0	1	20. Impulsive; unpredictable
0	1	21. Afraid of other inmates
0	1	22. Seems to seek excitement
0	1	23. Never seems happy
0	1	24. Doesn't trust staff
0	1	25. Passive; easily led
0	1	26. Talks aggressively to other inmates
0	1	27. Accepts no blame for any of his troubles
0	1	28. Continually complains; accuses staff of unfairness
0	1	29. Daydreams; seems to be mentally off in space
0	1	30. Talks aggressively to staff
0	1	31. Has a quick temper
0	1	32. Obviously holds grudges; seeks to "get even"
0	1	33. Inattentive; seems preoccupied
0	1	34. Attempts to play staff against one another
0	1	35. Passively resistant; has to be forced to participate
0	1	36. Tries to form a clique
0	1	37. Openly defies regulations and rules
0	1	38. Often sad and depressed
0	1	39. Stirs up trouble among inmates
0	1	40. Aids or abets others in breaking the rules
0	1	41. Considers himself unjustly confined

Source: Herbert C. Quay, Ph.D.

Checklist for the Analysis of Life History Records of Adult Offenders (CALH)

Name and number of inmate _____

Name of person completing this checklist _____

Your position _____ Date completed _____

Instructions: Place a checkmark before each behavior trait that describes this inmate's life history.

_____ 1. Has few, if any, friends
_____ 2. Thrill-seeking
_____ 3. Preoccupied; "dreamy"
_____ 4. Uncontrollable as a child
_____ 5. Has expressed guilt over offense
_____ 6. Expresses need for self-improvement
_____ 7. Socially withdrawn
_____ 8. Weak, indecisive, easily led
_____ 9. Previous local, state, or federal incarceration
_____ 10. Tough, defiant
_____ 11. Irregular work history (if not a student)
_____ 12. Noted not to be responsive to counseling
_____ 13. Gives impression of ineptness, incompetence in managing everyday problems in living
_____ 14. Supported wife and children
_____ 15. Claims offense was motivated by family problems
_____ 16. Close ties with criminal elements
_____ 17. Depressed, morose
_____ 18. Physically aggressive (strong arm, assault, reckless homicide, attempted murder, mugging, etc.)
_____ 19. Apprehension likely due to "stupid" behavior on the part of the offender
_____ 20. Single marriage
_____ 21. Expresses feelings of inadequacy, worthlessness
_____ 22. Difficulties in the public schools
_____ 23. Suffered financial reverses prior to commission of offense for which incarcerated
_____ 24. Passive, submissive
_____ 25. Bravado, braggart
_____ 26. Guiltless; blames others
_____ 27. Expresses lack of concern for others

Source: Herbert C. Quay, Ph.D.

Raw Score Form: Correctional Adjustment Checklist (CACL)

Name and number of inmate _____

Name of person completing this checklist _____

Your position _____ Date completed _____

Instructions: For each "1" circled on the Correctional Adjustment Checklist, place a checkmark on the line corresponding to the item number. Add the checkmarks to obtain the Raw Score for each group.

Group

I	II	IV	V
			1. _____
		2. _____	3. _____
		4. _____	5. _____
6. _____		7. _____	8. _____
9. _____			
10. _____			11. _____
		12. _____	
13. _____		14. _____	
15. _____			
16. _____		17. _____	
18. _____	19. _____		
20. _____			21. _____
22. _____		23. _____	
	24. _____	25. _____	
26. _____			
27. _____	28. _____	29. _____	
30. _____			
31. _____			
32. _____		33. _____	
	34. _____	35. _____	
36. _____			
37. _____			38. _____
39. _____			
40. _____	41. _____		

Total (Raw Score) _____ _____ _____ _____

Source: Herbert C. Quay, Ph.D.

Raw Score Form: Life History Checklist (CALH)

Name and number of inmate _____
Name of person completing this checklist _____
Your position _____ Date completed _____

Instructions: For each item checked on the Checklist for the Analysis of Life History Records of Adult Offenders, place a checkmark on the line corresponding to the item number. Add the checkmarks to obtain the Raw Score for each group.

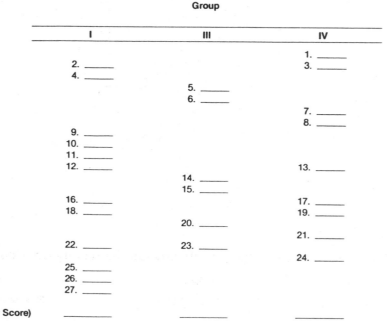

Group

I	III	IV
		1. _____
2. _____		3. _____
4. _____		
	5. _____	
	6. _____	
		7. _____
		8. _____
9. _____		
10. _____		
11. _____		
12. _____		13. _____
	14. _____	
	15. _____	
16. _____		17. _____
18. _____		19. _____
	20. _____	
		21. _____
22. _____	23. _____	
		24. _____
25. _____		
26. _____		
27. _____		
Total (Raw Score) _____	_____	_____

Source: Herbert C. Quay, Ph.D.

Raw Score to Normalized T-score Conversions for Correctional Adjustment Checklist (CACL)

Scale I		Scale II		Scale IV		Scale V	
Raw score	T-score	Raw score	T-score	Raw score	T-score	Raw score	T-score
0	41	0	44	0	40	0	39
1	49	1	54	1	47	1	46
2	53	2	59	2	51	2	50
3	56	3	62	3	54	3	54
4	58	4	65	4	56	4	57
5	59	5	70	5	59	5	61
6	60			6	61	6	65
7	61			7	63	7	71
8	62			8	65		
9	63			9	69		
10	64			10	73		
11	65			11	78		
12	66						
13	67						
14	68						
15	69						
16	71						
17	73						
18	76						

Raw Score to Normalized T-score Conversions for Life History Checklist (CAHL)

Scale I		Scale III		Scale IV	
Raw score	T-score	Raw score	T-score	Raw score	T-score
0	35	0	39	0	39
1	43	1	47	1	47
2	47	2	52	2	53
3	51	3	58	3	58
4	55	4	64	4	62
5	58	5	70	5	66
6	61	6	76	6	70
7	64			7	74
8	67			8	82
9	71			9	90
10	75				
11	82				

Classification Profile for Adult Offenders

Name and number of inmate _____
Name of person completing this profile _____
Your position_____ Date completed_____

	Scale	Raw score	T-score
1. Correctional Adjustment Checklist (CACL)	I	_____	_____
	II	_____	_____
	IV	_____	_____
	V	_____	_____
Checklist for the Analysis of Life History Records (CALH)	I	_____	_____
	III	_____	_____
	IV	_____	_____

2. Combined Scores	Scale	CACL T-score		CALH T-score		Final T-score
	I	_____	+	_____	÷ 2 =	_____
	II	_____			=	_____
	III			_____	=	_____
	IV	_____	+	_____	÷ 2 =	_____
	V	_____			=	_____

3. Assignment

____ Group I   ____ Group III   ____ Group IV

____ Group II   ____ Group V

Instructions:

1. Transfer Totals from Raw Score Forms onto appropriate Raw Score lines.
   Using the appropriate conversion table, convert each Raw Score to a T-score.
   - If two CACLs are used per inmate, convert all Raw scores to T-scores; then add the T-scores obtained for each scale and divide the sum by 2.
2. List the final CACL and CALH T-scores on the appropriate lines in the Combined Scores section.
   - For Scales I and IV, add the T-scores and divide by 2.
3. Use the highest Final T-score to make the final assignment.
   If two scores are tied, use the following tie-breaker rules:
   - If Group I and Group II are tied for highest,
     —and there is one housing unit for *both* groups, assign to Heavy.
     —and there is one housing unit for *each* group, assign for the best balance or use of available housing.
   - If Group IV and Group V are tied for highest,
     —and there is one housing unit for *both* groups, assign to Light.
     —and there is one housing unit for *each* group, assign for the best balance or use of available housing.
   - If Group I *or* Group II are tied with any other group, assign to Heavy.
   - If Group IV *or* Group V are tied with Group III, assign to Light.

(**Note:** Before using any tie-breaker rules, recheck all scoring and calculations.)

Chapter 10
Group Counseling in Institutional Settings

When the prison gates slam behind an inmate, he does not lose his human quality, his mind does not become closed to ideas, his intellect does not cease to feed on a free and open interchange of opinions; his yearning for self-esteem does not end; nor his quest for self-realization conclude. If anything the needs for identity and self-esteem are more compelling.

Justice Thurgood Marshall

The Power of the Group

In the Prison Community

Jails and prisons are not very nice places. They were never meant to be, and they never can be. They exist to punish lawbreakers and to separate them from "decent" society. They are prime examples of what Goffman (1961) has called *total institutions*. Total institutions can be mental hospitals, army training facilities, or any other institution where large groups of people live together under tightly restricted and scheduled circumstances and under the control of a central authority. Total institutions are divided into "managers," who control, and "subjects," who are controlled. It is the function of the managers to restrict social interaction between the subjects and the outside world. The consequence of such an authoritarian and coercive situation is the development of two antagonistic subcultures within the institution. Social distance between the controllers and the controlled is great, and each group tends to develop hostile attitudes toward the other.

The inmate code. The hostility toward the managers is expressed in an informal set of rules known as the *inmate code*, which includes the game playing we discussed in the section on transactional analysis. One of those rules is "Don't be a sucker," a rule that warns inmates against granting overt respect and prestige to prison guards and staff and against trusting them. This rule does not mean that inmates should openly defy prison officials and regulations, because overt acts of defiance may bring down the wrath of the managers on the entire group. Rather, it means never being openly friendly to officials unless you can use them for your own ends, never cooperating at a level beyond that which is necessary to avoid trouble, never volunteering for anything simply for the good of the institution, and never showing subservience. Unfortunately, the noncooperative inmate code extends to noncooperation with those members of the prison staff whose function it is to counsel and help inmates. No wonder it has been said that trying to rehabilitate criminals in prison is like trying to help alcoholics maintain sobriety in a brewery. Institutional counseling is therefore the ultimate challenge for the criminal justice helper.

Origins of the inmate code. When we discussed differential association theory we noted that many criminals develop a set of values and attitudes in opposition to lawful behavior through the frequency, duration, priority, and intimacy of their associations with individuals of like mind. The individuals with whom they most associate, either by choice or of necessity, become their reference group, the group around which they orient their lives, and against whose standards they evaluate themselves. When criminals are incarcerated, the power of the reference group over their lives increases considerably because it is now the only group with which they are able to associate. Within this closed community, antiestablishment values are refined and reinforced. In prison, compliance with antiestablishment values and attitudes can become much more of a survival imperative than it ever was on the outside.

Prisonization. Not all inmates enter prison with a ready-made set of antisocial attitudes. However, new prisoners, like new immigrants, face a painful process of assimilation into a new culture from which it is difficult to remain aloof. The process of assimilating the norms and values of the prison subculture has been termed *prisonization* by Clemmer (1958). The basic premise of prisonization is that people who share a common experience, especially one imposed upon them, develop a sense of "we-ness" buttressed by a set of legitimizing attitudes that are in opposition to those of "them" who imposed the experience upon them. The first steps in the prisonization process are simple acts of behavioral conformity. This behavioral conformity occurs regardless of how the inmate feels about performing it. The inmate watches and follows the examples of other inmates because conformity makes life easier, avoids conflicts, and enables the inmate to fit in without being conspicuous. Before the inmate knows it, he or she is speaking the language of fellow inmates and beginning to define the inmate world in their terms. As Clemmer (1958:299) points out, it requires only a subtle and minute change to make a stated attitude become a "taken-for-granted perception."

Although all prisoners have to conform behaviorally, not all, perhaps not even most, will conform attitudinally in the sense that they will internalize the inmate code as right and proper. Ways to avoid attitudinal assimilation suggested by Clemmer are shorter sentences and more frequent contact with the outside world. Prisoners with strong personalities and those who actively strive to remain aloof from the prison subculture do not succumb to prisonization to the same extent that more pliable individuals do. Some take on the values and attitudes surrounding them only as a measure of convenience, being fully aware all the time that their conformity is a temporary condition of their confinement (Hawkins, 1976). We can help these individuals to counteract the insidious process of prisonization, and even perhaps those who have already succumbed, by well-run group counseling sessions.

In Group Counseling

Group counseling. A major obstacle to effective institutional counseling is the oppositional stance of the inmate code. Inmates do attend counseling sessions, Alcoholics Anonymous (AA) and Narcotics Anonymous (NA) meetings, and vocational and educational programs. Attendance at these sessions is not a violation of the inmate code. Indeed, much banter is heard in prisons about the necessity to "get into a program." Unfortunately, the concern for getting into a program is more often than not motivated by efforts to impress the parole board than a genuine concern for self-improvement (Berne's "HDIGO"). If the possibility of the ultimate reward for participation, that of early release, were not a reality, inmates who attended such sessions would be violating the inmate code and branded as "suckers" or "ass kissers." Consequently, inmates who attend sessions aimed at reforming criminal behavior patterns may spend a great deal of time telling other inmates how they are exploiting the sessions for their own ends.

Group counseling is an effective way to combat the negative group pressures that hinder rehabilitative efforts. Group counseling may be viewed as a kind of intellectual jujitsu in which the strength of the group is used against itself. Group counseling uses group peer pressure to combat the criminal attitudes and values that many of the group members hold as individuals. The differential association theory of crime stresses the power of peer group pressure to lead the individual into conformity with antisocial values. Why not use the same pressure for the opposite purpose? As Cressey has put it, "If the behavior of an individual is an intrinsic part of groups to which he belongs, attempts to change the behavior must be directed at groups" (1955:117).

Let's not be so naive as to imagine that this is an easy task. How does one change the criminal attitudes of individuals in a group that, with the exception of the group leader, consists of criminals? Although it is extremely difficult, and realistically you can expect at least as many failures as successes, it is not impossible. Think about the gratifying success rate of Alcoholics Anonymous groups. Do you think it is more difficult to rehabilitate the typical alcoholic or the typical criminal? It seems to me that objectively the alcoholic presents the more difficult case. After all, there is no biological urge to commit crimes in

the same sense as there is for the alcoholic to drink. The criminal who desists from committing crime does not suffer painful physical withdrawal symptoms that are alleviated only by committing one. Criminals are not physiologically punished for stopping their activities the way alcoholics are. On the contrary, they run the risk of punishment for continuing with the activity.

Many criminals enjoy the thrills and excitement of the criminal lifestyle just as alcoholics enjoy drinking. But neither alcoholics nor criminals like the negative consequences of their respective activities. Significant emotional events in their lives, the loss of jobs, spouses, and self-respect, and the loss of long periods of freedom constitute powerful motivations for change.

Whatever motivations exist for change must be brought into full consciousness and sharply focused. They must then be carefully cultivated and nurtured. In other words, dissonance and tension must be generated in the minds of those whose attitudes are to be modified by forcing them to confront the reality of their behavior. Many criminals are so present-oriented that they fail to consider what five years in prison actually means. It is the group counselor's task, with the cooperation of the group, to bring each member to the realization that powerful motivations for change do exist in every one of them. Specific strategies for achieving this in a group setting are presented later in this chapter. If AA can achieve respectable success rates in groups consisting of members who have all experienced the pleasures and the pains of alcohol, there is no reason to feel that groups consisting of those who have experienced the pleasures and pains of crime could not enjoy similar success.

Group pressure. George Homans has defined a group as "a number of persons who communicate with one another often over a span of time, and who are few enough so that each person is able to communicate with all others, not at secondhand, through other people, but face-to-face" (1950:1). The prison community is not a group in this sense, but merely an aggregate of people in the midst of which the individual could feel terribly alone. None of us likes to feel alone, and we will often go to great lengths to become part of a group. We are, as they say, very social animals. Group counseling takes advantage of this human need for social interaction by offering inmates a constructive alternative to the antisocial cliques that form in prisons.

Groups possess dynamics of their own that are relatively independent of the sum of the individual attributes of their members. Much of sociology and social psychology revolves around issues of how group life affects individual behavior. Numerous studies attest to the ability of groups to generate a general conformity to their norms, even among reluctant members. Here we can't consider in detail the question of why groups possess powers that appear to be greater than the sum of their constituent parts. Suffice it to say that group conformity is more likely if goals are shared, and goals are more likely to be shared if they are democratically determined. As the group leader, meaning the person who initiates the process and who gives the initial direction and initial suggestions, the counselor is in a position to strongly influence the nature of the goals. Inmates realize, of course, that the ultimate goal is to reeducate them into conformity with society's standards and expectations. Therefore, they are not likely to choose topics that they perceive as being too directly related to this end. As a group counselor, you must make haste slowly. If inmates are to learn new values and unlearn old ones, they will do so only by the process of self-exploration that is of their own choosing.

Planning for Group Counseling

Goals and Operating Philosophy

The first task in the planning of group counseling is to formulate in your own mind the specific aims and goals that you want the group to pursue. Your operating philosophy should be something like that of a professor who has a certain core content of knowledge to impart to the class but who remains flexible enough to let the students dictate the pace of the class. Much student interest and participation is lost in classes where professors refuse to follow a train of thought brought up by a student because "We have to finish Chapter 10 by Thursday." Group interest and participation can be similarly stifled if you do not maintain an attitude of structured flexibility.

Selection of Members

Your next task is the selection of group members from the pool of volunteers. For various reasons, there is rarely any lack of volunteers for group counseling in prisons (Juda, 1984:48). You should not simply throw people together to see what will happen, an all-too-frequent practice in prison settings (Rizzo, 1980:29). Rizzo suggests a "loose homogeneity" in such settings (1980:29). An examination of the offenders' classification scales and of the psychological profiles will obviously aid you in this endeavor. Needless to say, if the group is to be centered around a specific problem, such as alcoholism, drug addiction, or sexual offenses, then inmates are selected on the basis of problems they have in the specific area rather than on other considerations.

Each prospective member of the group should then be given an individual screening interview. This practice is laid down as one of the ethical guidelines of the Association for Specialists in Group Work (ASGW). This section of the ASGW guidelines states (1980:1):

> The group leader shall conduct a pre-group interview with each prospective member for purposes of screening, orientation, and, in so far as possible, shall select group members whose needs and goals are compatible with the established goals of the group; who will not impede the group process; and whose well-being will not be jeopardized by the group process.

Corey (1983:102) indicates that the following questions concerning suitability can be explored in about a half-hour interview with each candidate:
1. Why does this person want to join the group?
2. How ready is the person to become actively involved in the process of self-examination that will be a part of the group?

3. Does the candidate have a clear idea about the nature and purpose of the group? Does he or she have a view of what is expected?
4. Are there any indications that the person might be counterproductive to the development of cohesion in the group? Might this group be counterproductive to the person?

Such a screening interview not only allows you to choose group members who you feel will strengthen the group's possibilities of success but also allows you and individual clients to become acquainted with one another. Moreover, it gives clients the opportunity to decide for themselves whether or not they want to be part of your group after all. Thus you have a double screening process, yours and theirs. Without the dual check-out process, you and your clients are on a blind date. I think we all know how disastrous blind dates can sometimes turn out to be.

Components of Group Counseling

The best definition of group counseling that I have come across is that of Gazda, Duncan, and Meadows (quoted in Mahler, 1973:101):

> Group counseling is a dynamic, interpersonal process focusing on conscious thought and behavior and involving the therapy functions of permissiveness, orientation to reality, catharsis, and mutual trust, caring, understanding, acceptance, and support. The therapy functions are created and nurtured in a small group through the sharing of personal concerns with one's peers and the counselors. The group counselees are basically normal individuals with various concerns which are not debilitating to the extent of requiring extensive personality change. The group counselees may utilize the group interaction to increase understanding and acceptance of values and goals and to learn and/or unlearn certain attitudes and behaviors.

Let's cut this rather long definition into its component parts in order to get a feeling for the process of group counseling, what it is and how it should be conducted.

"Group counseling is a dynamic, interpersonal process" alerts you to the fact that the process is active, productive, forceful, and energetic. It is not static, but full of continuous verbal movement toward purposeful goals. It can be dynamic only if real concerns and problems are put before the group for open evaluation and discussion by members of the group.

"Interpersonal" means that it is an activity that takes place between or among two or more people. Advocates of group counseling feel that members learn and/or unlearn attitudes, values, and perceptions better in a group setting because it is more similar to their natural interpersonal world. Relating to peers is more consistent with normal socialization experiences than relating to a counselor in a situation that can be reminiscent of the teacher/student relationship. Most of all, "interpersonal" means sharing.

"Focusing on conscious thought and behavior" indicates that the topics explored are attitudes and behaviors of which the group members are fully aware and which are problematic. Group counseling is not group therapy. *Group therapy* is more likely to deal with unconscious motivations, and it is usually conducted by individuals with advanced degrees in psychiatry, psychology, or psychiatric social work. The difference is analogous to the distinction we made earlier between psychotherapy and individual counseling. Like psychotherapy, group therapy goes into great depth, and it is a process that may last months or years. Group counseling is very short by comparison and may be conducted by individuals with minimal specialized skills. Remember, the most successful group counseling in the world is conducted by the concerned amateurs of Alcoholics Anonymous. Remember also that the personal attributes of the counselor are more important to success than the depth of the counselor's knowledge of the complexities of mental health.

"Permissiveness, orientation to reality, catharsis, and mutual trust, caring, understanding, acceptance, and support" are attributes that the counselor must strive to foster in the group. This is no easy task with a prison group! Permissiveness does not mean that the group is allowed to act out, to bully weaker members, or to be otherwise disruptive. It means that the group

should be democratic in its choice of problems to discuss, that no one member be allowed to monopolize the floor, and that no relevant topic be denied a hearing.

Neither does "permissiveness" mean that the group is run without some basic ground rules. As in formulating treatment plans in community corrections, the rules should be determined in concert with the group. However, group counseling is a guided group experience. Accordingly, during the initial screening interview, the counselor will indicate a series of expectations about what will go on in the group. The counselor basically wants group members to examine their impulses' in an atmosphere of acceptance to help them make connections between those impulses and their criminal behavior. Groups function much more effectively if each member is aware of the expectations and has been given an opportunity to participate in their formulation. A democratically determined group structure outlining purposeful goals goes a long way toward developing a feeling of "we-ness" in the group. The essential elements of group interaction—each individual "I," the "we" of the group, and the "it" of the goals—must form an integrated "I-we-it" triangle if the process is to be useful (Anderson, 1984:13–15).

Take care, however, that democratically derived decisions regarding group topics and issues are not at odds with institutional requirements, are not socially unacceptable, and are not unfit for some individual members of the group. Neither group nor counselor pressure should be used to cajole individual members into conformity. As Bennett, Rosenbaum, and McCullough put it (1978:89): "We cannot continue to coerce offenders into conformity. We must provide those experiences necessary to individual adjustment and a meaningful life. For most people this comes through opportunities for intellectual and emotional growth. Why not for offenders?" Why not indeed?

"Orientation to reality" refers to an awareness on the part of all group members that the goals of the group are directed toward the rejection of unrealistic and irresponsible values and behavior

and the substitution of realistic and responsible values and behavior. *Realistic* and *responsible* here are consistent in meaning with Glasser's usage in his reality therapy. The general goals of a prison group are improved self-awareness, genuine problem sharing, an awareness of the self-defeating nature of a criminal lifestyle, improved coping skills, and an understanding of the benefits and possibilities of the straight life. Specific goals are determined by the makeup of the group (for example, alcohol abusers, exhibitionists, and so forth).

"Catharsis" refers to the release and ventilation of repressed emotions associated with painful experiences. Psychoanalysts feel that much guilt, anger, aggression, and hostility are the result of repressed emotions. If these pent-up emotions can be liberated—that is, brought into consciousness and explored—then much of the negativism they generate will dissipate.

"Mutual trust, caring, understanding, acceptance, and support" are attributes conspicuously absent among prison inmates at anything beyond a superficial level. However, they should not be considered impossible to generate in a prison-setting. By and large, inmates do not possess these attributes because they have rarely encountered them in their lives. If you, by your example, can foster such an environment, if you can demonstrate acceptance, understanding, and caring, chances are that some of it will rub off. Here is one inmate's report of her experience in group counseling: "I have felt needed, loving, competent, furious, frantic, anything and everything, but just plain loved. You can imagine the flood of humility, release that swept over me. I wrote with considerable joy, 'I actually felt loved.' I doubt that I shall soon forget it" (quoted in Jarvis, 1978:197–198).

"The therapy functions are created and nurtured in a small group" says that the size of the group is an important consideration. A group of too few members, say three, is comfortable for the group leader to handle, but it is not very practical in terms of the efficient management of time and resources. Groups this small also have the disadvantage that inevitably seems to occur,

that of two members forming an alliance against a third. Having too many members renders the group unmanageable for the leader. The group begins to act like a class in school, directing communications primarily at the group counselor. This tendency defeats the whole purpose of being in a group. The more people there are in a group, the easier it becomes for some members to hide and avoid discussing their problems. Even if no one wanted to hide, there is just so much "air time" to go around, and the multiplicity of topics may prevent focusing where it is desirable. A generally accepted optimal group size is between four and eight members (Ohlsen, 1970:58).

Even a group of this size can be intimidating and difficult to manage for the new counselor. In a one-on-one situation the counselor has the feeling of being in control, because he or she has only one individual to attend to. It is not unusual for inmate groups to test the new counselor by ganging up on him or her. Having something of a vested interest in maintaining current self-concepts, in demonstrating independence and noncooperation, and in displaying bravado, group members often feel that the best defense is offense. The confident and self-assured counselor recognizes and deals with this obvious game playing by indicating to the group that he or she knows what is going on and asking the members why they feel that they have to do it. He or she should never go on the defensive, but should rather toss the ball right back at the group, without emphasizing his or her moral or authoritative superiority over the group. The self-confident bull rules his pasture without snorting and bellowing.

"*Through the sharing of personal concerns with one's peers and the counselors*" points to the exchange of self-disclosure and feedback among members of the group. This is the essence of group counseling. The success or failure of the group depends almost entirely on the meaningfulness of the self-concerns disclosed and the nature of the feedback.

But prison is a place where it is often necessary to shut off one's emotions, where inmates are supposed to "do their own time," and where to reveal personal concerns is to open oneself up to possible abuse, derision, or even blackmail. Consequently, inmates in a group session may go to great lengths to lead the group communication away from themselves and toward others, or to general topics. Such ploys may be in evidence in any group setting, but they are especially so in the prison setting. You must learn to identify them and confront members with them, at the same time recognizing the motivations behind them. A prison group is not an encounter group for which members have paid considerable sums of money to seek "self-actualization." You will be setting yourself up for disappointment and failure if you fail to empathize with the special concerns about self-disclosure within a prison setting.

There are several ways to handle the lack of self-disclosure within the group. I feel that it is wise not to expect or to attempt to facilitate self-disclosure at all during the first session. Simply give the group members an opportunity to warm up to intergroup communication by venting general nonthreatening concerns. Inmates must sense at least a modicum of trust and acceptance before they will risk self-disclosure.

I am in agreement with Nicholson (1981) that an excellent institutional counseling strategy is to begin the first session with an explanation of Berne's theory of structural analysis. Its easy terminology and simple diagrammatic presentations of PAC interactions provide a useful shared framework from which all participants can analyze what will go on during future sessions. The various ego states and their transactions can be drawn and explained on the blackboard. You will be surprised how much more easily group members will pick up on game playing and how it will quickly facilitate understanding when you use this very powerful anchor of shared discourse.

After one or two "getting acquainted" sessions, you may make a statement to the group something like the following: "You know, we've been talking for quite some time together now, but I haven't heard any of us touch on the topics of 'self' or 'I' yet. Will somebody volunteer to explore the question 'Who or what am I?' with us?"

The first attempt at self-disclosure should be positively reinforced by the use of nonthreatening and nonjudgmental feedback from the counselor. Feedback should reflect the feelings of the discloser, making sure that the reflection is based on accurate perceptions rather than on inferences. If, for instance, Frank responds to your request to explore the question "Who am I?" with the response, "I suppose that by society's standards I am a failure, a no-good screw-up," he is making a statement about his perceptions of how others on the outside view him. You should not infer that he perceives himself that way by asking him why he is a "screw-up." Instead, you should ask him if he agrees with that perception and why he does or does not. Such feedback could lead to an animated group discussion of values and attitudes held by group members.

As a member of the group, the counselor should be prepared to model self-disclosure for the group. Needless to say, the counselor must feel that he or she is fair game in any session and must be prepared to answer uncomfortable questions in an honest and forthright manner. It is not unusual for inmates to test the counselor by asking pointed questions such as "Did you ever steal anything?" Everybody has stolen something at one time or another, even if it was only a candy bar or a company pen. You must not attempt to give the impression that you are a "goody two-shoes" by denying that you have, thereby modeling dishonesty for the group. You could take advantage of such a question by describing how guilty you felt afterwards and asking other members of the group how they feel when they steal and how they themselves have felt when others have stolen from them. You can also use the opportunity to describe your ideas of responsibility, emotional maturity, and respect for self and others, and how your values have enabled you to lead a basically happy life. Again, this should not be delivered in a preachy style calculated to impress the group with your moral superiority.

"The group counselees are basically normal individuals with various concerns which are not debilitating to the extent of requiring extensive personality change" is a reminder to respect the humanity of the group members. Do not think of them as being sick, evil, beyond help, or radically different in any way from yourself. They are basically unloved individuals with deficiencies that prevent them in one way or another from functioning in a socially acceptable way. Inmates who do have crippling and debilitating concerns do not belong in group counseling. You should think of all group members as possessing wholesome potentialities that need only to be recognized and developed. The distortions of reality you encounter are the result of faulty thinking rather than pathological blockages. Your basic task is to reeducate toward responsibility, not to psychoanalyze.

"The group counselees may utilize the group interaction to increase understanding and acceptance of values and goals and to learn and/ or unlearn certain attitudes and behaviors" simply restates the goals of any counseling session, group or individual. It is a guided effort to change a failure identity into a success identity through self-disclosure and feedback. The only difference emphasized here is that group counseling makes use of peer feedback and modeling.

Some Specific Topics and Strategies for Group Counseling

The goal of group counseling is to guide your clients toward change by exploring and assessing their values, attitudes, and behaviors. What follows are some specific strategies for getting the ball rolling.

Counting the Cost of a Criminal Lifestyle

We have seen that from the perspective of some criminals crime may be considered a rational pursuit, in the sense that there is a logical fit between the attainment of ends and the means used to achieve them. In other words, it gets them what they want at a price they think they can afford. This group exercise is designed to challenge that perception of rationality. From any objective viewpoint (that is, going beyond the subjective perception of immediate rationality), for all but the "kingpins" of crime, crime simply does not pay in the long run.

You can help your group members discover this for themselves by having them make out an inventory of their estimated criminal gains (assuming property offenders) obtained for the crime(s) for which they are doing time. You might go even further by asking them to list their gains from undetected crimes committed during the period between the current arrest and any previous arrest. The list should contain actual cash gains and the "fenced" value of any property taken. A list compiled by an offender who did 40 months in prison for three burglaries is presented below. This individual also included in his inventory 10 other break-ins for which he was not caught.

Cash	$ 400
Stereos	150
TVs	75
Jewelry	200
Tools	20
Miscellaneous	180
Total	$1025

After these lists are completed, you should divide the monetary gains from crime by the amount of time spent in prison (take along a calculator). For instance, the person in this example received a "paycheck" from his criminal activity of $1025, for which he did 40 months in prison. Therefore: $1025/40$ months $= \$25.62$ per month, $0.82 per day, or $0.10 per hour. You'll be surprised at just how surprised the group members will be when they discover how much they've been "working" for per hour! Few of your clients, if any at all, have ever thought along these lines. You may then proceed with what should be an animated discussion of just how smart it is to work for 10 cents per hour.

You can drive the point home by calculating the possible gains if that person had spent his 40 months in noncriminal activity. Ask each individual to speculate about what portion of his or her prison sentence he or she could reasonably have expected to work at a regular job on the outside. If our individual doing 40 months stated that he would have worked only about one-quarter of the time, multiply this time by the take-home pay he would have received at minimum wage (about

$400 per month). Thus, $400 times 10 months $= \$4000$. Add to this approximately $100 per month he could have received in welfare during his periods of unemployment, and we reach a total of $7000. Hardly a princely sum, but considerably in excess of $1025. Even if you add the fruits of a criminal lifestyle in the form of prison wages (an average of about 35 cents per hour) for those lucky enough to have a prison job, the contrast will only be slightly diminished.

Other, less tangible but sometimes more important, costs and benefits associated with a criminal lifestyle can be discussed in the group. To start this discussion rolling, have each member divide a sheet of paper into two equal sections. Have them label one column *Benefits* and the other *Costs*. Rather than doing this on an individual basis, you might consider dividing the group into two sections, one to brainstorm about the benefits of crime and the other to do the same about the costs of crime. They might arrive at a set of costs and benefits like that shown in Table 10-1.

Other costs and benefits are possible, but you will almost invariably find that members will be able to think of a lot more costs than benefits. Discuss this discrepancy with them, as well as the inconsistency of such items as "being free to be my own man," on the one hand, and having every movement dictated by the "screws" on the other. You may go even further and invite them to rate each item on a scale of 1 through 10 according to how positive they consider each benefit of crime and how negative they consider each cost of crime. They can then sum the columns to arrive at their own numeric evaluation of the costs and benefits of their lifestyles. Since they will have listed the items themselves, as well as deciding what numeric score to assign to them, this exercise can be a powerful tool in getting your group members to realize how destructive to themselves their lifestyles are.

Role Reversal and Empathy Training

Criminals rarely think of the feelings of their victims. One of the ways to encourage such thought

Table 10-1 What do I gain and lose from a life of crime?

Benefits	Costs
Lots of leisure (not working)	No regular paycheck, little money to spend
The excitement and thrills	The boredom of sitting in a cell
The street reputation	The worry caused to my parents
Doing what I want, being free to be my own man	Having the screws decide almost all I do and when I should do it
Lots of girls think I'm cool	No women in the joint
The laughs	Police hassle and arrest
Putting one over on the system	Can't get a job because of record
Money for nothing	The whole prison experience
	Appearing in court and paying fines
	This prison is a long way from home, so I rarely see my parents
	My wife divorced me and married another guy while I was away

is to ask them to compile a list of feelings that they think the victims of their latest crimes may have experienced as a consequence of those crimes. The lists may contain such feelings as anger, revenge, fear, and outrage. Ask the group members if they feel that these responses of the victims are justified. This exercise should not be conducted in the spirit of "How would you like it . . .?" Most members will have long ago been inured to such moralizing.

It is highly likely that most group members will have been victims of crimes themselves in the past. Ask them to recall the feelings that they had about their victimizers on those occasions. Also have them explore feelings they had when family members or close personal friends were victimized. Such a discussion should lead to the general conclusion that even criminals value justice and "law and order" when the offender/victim roles are reversed.

Sentencing Exercises

Without being explicit, you can further emphasize their belief in conventional morality by engaging in the kind of sentencing exercises you have been asked to do as students. That is, you could provide the group with hypothetical criminal cases and have the group decide on appropriate penalties for them. You will find that inmates

will present arguments similar to those of probation officers at sentencing staffings (meetings at which officers decide together on an appropriate sentencing recommendation) and that they can often be considerably more punitive in their sentencing decisions! What group members will be doing implicitly in these exercises, without fully recognizing it for the moment, is revealing and reflecting upon some of their anticriminal and prosocial values.

Reattributing Responsibility and Increasing Self-Esteem

Criminals share with the rest of us a penchant for systematically biasing causal attributions of responsibility for what happens to them. It is generally true that when something good or praiseworthy happens to us, we locate the causal agent in ourselves: "I was able to accomplish this goal because I'm a pretty dependable and neat kind of person." When something bad or blameworthy happens to us, we tend to attribute it to circumstances beyond our control: "I'm branded a criminal because I was never given a chance. My parents beat me and never took an interest in me. Nobody'll give me a job, so I have to steal." In the first instance, we take a free-will perspective by offering "reasons" located within the self for having accomplished a goal. In the second instance, we tend to take a determinist position by offering "causes" external to ourselves that guarantee "it could not be otherwise."

Such attributions of responsibility are normal. They function as defense mechanisms to protect our self-images. Like all other defense mechanisms, however, they can become pathologically destructive if we deny all responsibility for the negative things that happen to us. Unfortunately, many criminals are remarkably creative in inventing and exaggerating the power of circumstances deemed beyond their control to justify their criminal behavior and their inability to follow the straight and narrow. Your task is to demonstrate the irrationality and lack of responsibility inherent in this attitude. We are not dead leaves blown hither and thither by environmental winds. We do have a hand in what happens to us, and we do possess the capacity to bring those events under our control.

In order to explore this way of thinking with your group, ask them to draw a large four-celled square like the one in Figure 10-1. Instruct them to list in the windowed cells (1) what good things in their lives are the results of their own actions, (2) what good things in their lives are the results of circumstances outside their control, (3) what bad things in their lives are the results of their own actions, and (4) what bad things in their lives are the results of circumstances outside their control.

The odds are that you will see the great majority of responses in the upper-left and lower-right cells of the square. You might begin the discussion by asking members to volunteer reasons why they have placed a given event in a given cell and then open up those reasons for discussion. You can steer the discussion around to the concept of human autonomy, guided by the insights of Ellis's rational-emotive therapy. Emphasize that the subjective reality of free will is extremely useful for individuals if they are to believe that they are capable of initiating actions that will lead to self-improvement. Individuals who insist that they are the directors of their own lives, that they alone are responsible for what they will become, and that they can overcome almost anything through sheer acts of will, are people who will achieve far more than their less active peers who seek excuses for their failures outside themselves.

Of course, things do happen to us that are beyond our personal control. Individuals who blame themselves for events that are clearly outside their power to influence suffer from low self-esteem (Ickes and Layden, 1978). The objective of this exercise is not to move everything into the top two cells. It is rather to explore ways in which

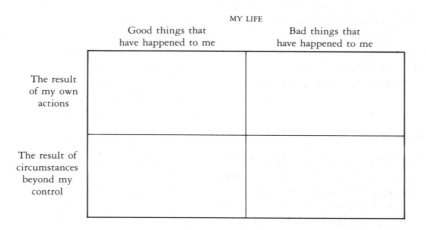

Figure 10-1   Reattribution of responsibility   (*Adapted from McGuire and Priestly, 1985.*)

some of the bad events could have been brought under the individual's control. The exercise is also designed to enhance the self-esteem of those who masochistically attribute all negative events to themselves and who may tend to attribute the positive events in their lives to outside influences. The idea is expressed in Reinhold Niebuhr's so-called Serenity Prayer: "God grant me the serenity to accept the things I cannot change, courage to change the things I can, and wisdom to know the difference."

Difficult Group Members

Despite the screening process designed to gather together a relatively homogeneous group, and despite all the other things you have done to assemble a smooth-running group, you will probably run into members who will be disruptive and/or uncooperative in one way or another. Their behavior may not necessarily be intended as disruption or noncooperation. In order to prevent such members from hindering the progress of the other members of the group, you must quickly identify and deal with disruptive behavior. Even if noncooperative behavior affects only the person not cooperating, you should also identify and deal with it. Some of the more usual types of difficult members are described below. Although we begin with the resister as a separate type, you should realize that all other types are also resisters in one or more respects.

The Resister

Since all group members have volunteered and all have had the opportunity to screen themselves out of the process, you can assume that the resister is experiencing ambivalence about the process. He or she has made a commitment in theory to explore himself or herself but finds it difficult to do so in practice. Since we have dealt at some length with resistance in Chapter 8, we will not explore it in detail here. Most authorities on group counseling feel that resistance is easier to deal with in a group setting than it is in an individual setting. This will be particularly true if you have

provided the group with a common discourse for identifying resistance, such as TA's structural analysis. For instance, Bry (1951:112) states:

> The first and most striking thing in handling of resistance in groups is that frequently resistance does not have to be "handled" at all, at least not by the therapist. The group is remarkably effective in dealing with this phenomenon. Early in the experience of each group considerable effort is directed toward demonstrating what resistance is and how to become sensitive to its appearance in others as well as oneself. The group members as well gradually develop ideas as to how to deal with resistance and how to use it productively. In cases of protective talking, sooner or later a group member usually gets sensitive to its resistance character and starts complaining about the "beating around the bush."

The "Expert"

The "expert" in a group knows the answer to everyone's problems in the group and is not above liberally dispensing advice on how to deal with them. This behavior can be intimidating to the group leader if the advice giver really is an expert, or if everyone believes him or her to be. I once had a physician in a group of child molesters who knew what was wrong with everyone but himself. Since he was an M.D. and I had only a master's degree at the time, I was somewhat awed. I soon felt myself relinquishing the group direction to him. Rather than trying to understand his motivations, I eventually confronted him with a reminder that I was the group leader and he was an offender, and that I had dealt with "hundreds" of sex offenders. In other words, I reduced myself to his level by puffing up my sense of importance as an "expert" in my own right. This was a very poor way of handling the situation; I was a bull bellowing that this was my pasture.

I should have recognized instead that this man's conviction as a child molester had severely damaged his self-respect and that he was trying to regain some of it by demonstrating his superiority. An empathetic recognition of this would have led to a more sympathetic and understanding resolution to the problem he posed to the group. It is highly likely that he used advice giving also to divert attention from his own problems, from letting others help him to face and cope with his painful situation. Perhaps he even genuinely felt that his advice would be helpful to his fellow members.

We all know how unwelcome unsolicited advice is. The group is not meeting for exchange of advice but for self-exploration. When a group member offers advice to another member, you might say something like this to the advice giver: "Charlie, it is obvious that John's problem is of concern to you, and you are concerned enough to offer some suggestions about what he might do." Without pausing, you could then address John as follows: "John, when you have difficulty in coping, do you like to have someone who cares enough to suggest what you might do?" "Do you feel that Charlie's suggestion could be of use to you?" These responses indicate to Charlie that you have interpreted his offered advice as a genuine attempt to help John with his problem; you have not put him down. You have also given John an opportunity to respond to Charlie's advice giving, plus a chance to explore his problem further. John will probably put Charlie in his place if he feels he needs to; that's part of the group process of getting feelings out into the open. It is important that any necessary putting down be left to the group members rather than to the group counselor. Only after "experts" are confronted with the unacceptability of their behavior will they start to explore their own problems.

The Monopolizer

The monopolizer shares many of the characteristics of the resister and the expert. He or she tends to be a self-centered recognition seeker who wishes to rule the group pasture. Motivations for monopolizing the group discussion are very similar to the motivations of the expert. The monopolizer may really feel that he or she is the only one present with anything meaningful to contribute. However, the monopolizing may be a conscious tactic to steer the group away from discussing uncomfortable topics and toward topics of the monopolizer's choosing: "the best form

of defense is offense." Either way, the negative effects on the group are the same.

Bry's statement about the resister is likely to be applicable here. Sooner or later someone will pipe up with "Why don't you give somebody else a chance to speak?" When a statement such as this emerges, you can say something like the following to the protester: "Debbie, you feel angry at Sue because you feel that she is not interested in what others have to say and that she may be avoiding topics that are not comfortable for her. Am I right?" If Debbie indicates that you have accurately reflected her feelings, you might go on to say to Sue: "Sue, do you see yourself as monopolizing the conversation? Wouldn't you really like to listen to what others have to say and perhaps learn more about yourself and about others?" Monopolizers lack the important skill of listening. They need feedback from the other members about how their behavior is affecting others, even if the feedback results in a temporary sullen withdrawal from group participation.

The Withdrawn Member

The withdrawn group member either is engaging in what might be termed passive resistance or may be lacking in confidence and/or the verbal skills to express himself or herself effectively. He or she hides in the group and is quite content to let the monopolizer, or anyone else, have the limelight. The group counselor should resist putting such a person on the spot by calling on him or her as a teacher calls on a student in a classroom. As part of the group, however, the withdrawn member is fair game for other members to call on. You should be ready to help the person out on such occasions so that being on the spot does not become too painful.

You might decide that you have made a mistake in allowing the withdrawn person to participate in the group or that the person has made a mistake in deciding to participate. The fact that that person is present, however, can be taken as a sign that he or she desires some form of counseling. You can determine this by the use of a session evaluation form containing the question: "Would you like an individual session with me?" If the answer is yes, that person can withdraw from group counseling and enter individual counseling. If it is no and he or she continues in the group, every effort must be made to include that person in the discussions.

The Masochist and the Sadist

Masochists are persons with low self-esteem and ingrained dependency needs who purposely set themselves up as targets for the displaced aggression of others. They doubt their ability to be loved, respected, or accepted by others. Since they desire companionship and relationships, however, they feel that the only strategy available to them is to put themselves into the hot seat, where they are the victims of bullying, teasing, bad jokes, and sarcasm. They often become welcome targets for sadistic members of a group, and others may quickly follow the sadist's lead to avoid personal exploration.

Both the masochist and the sadistic bully should be quickly identified by the group leader. The feelings of both parties should be reflected so that other group members can suggest better methods for each to relate to others. Under no circumstances should you allow a group member to be set up as a constant target for unproductive criticism and hurtful comments. When other group members realize that such bullying is not acceptable to you, they will rally to the defense of the masochist. They can be relied on to put the offending party down. Allow them to do this for as long as seems useful—he or she needs it. However, if fisticuff's threaten to replace the spoken word, as they may well do with an individual who relies on bullying to get his or her way, you must bring the put-down to an end. You may offer the offending party an "out" by suggesting that he or she perhaps really didn't mean to be hurtful: "Isn't that true, Mike?"

Advantages and Disadvantages of Institutional Group Counseling

There are, then, a number of theoretical and practical reasons why group counseling may be con-

sidered superior to individual counseling in an institutional setting. It will not be preferable for all clients, for some clearly benefit more from private individual sessions. Likewise, many corrections workers are more comfortable conducting private rather than group sessions. I have summarized below the major advantages and disadvantages of group counseling in an institutionalized setting.

Some Advantages

1. Time constraints and personnel shortages make it an efficient method of counseling a number of individuals with similar problems at the same time.
2. Groups with prosocial purposes offer inmates a constructive alternative to antisocial inmate cliques that form in response to the need of human beings for social interaction.
3. Because of the sharing of problems with the group, members learn much about alternative coping strategies.
4. Inmates can learn these alternative strategies, which can also be tried out in the abstract by involved discussions with those others who have experienced them.
5. Well-led and democratically run groups tend to develop a feeling of togetherness and "we-ness."
6. This sense of belonging can enable group pressure to change the attitudes of individuals in the direction of the group's purposes—to change antisocial attitudes into prosocial attitudes.
7. Unlike one-on-one counseling sessions with a representative of "the system," group counseling lessens the possibility that an inmate will be intimidated by a perceived authoritarian relationship.

Some Disadvantages

1. Some offenders may be reluctant to explore intimate feelings in the company of peers, although they may desperately want to. There are those who feel much more comfortable

speaking in private with an authority figure. You can handle this by passing out evaluation forms that contain a question such as "Would you like to arrange an individual session with me?" Concerns that have surfaced in the offender's mind during a group session can then be given voice in private.

2. A lot of time can be wasted pursuing meaningless topics. The snag here is that we can realize that they are meaningless only after they have been fully expressed. Only experience will tell you when to cut off such topics and redirect the session along more meaningful avenues. However, this lost time is more than compensated for by the time saved in counseling a number of individuals at one time.

3. Closely allied to point 2 is the danger that the means become accepted as the goals. If the group counselor succeeds in generating discussion without reference to where the discussion is leading, nothing much is accomplished. The discussion is the means, not the goal. Group counseling must always be geared to realistic goals.

4. Some group members may take advantage of the numbers in the group to hide. We are all aware of students who select large classes and then sit at the back of the room to avoid class participation. They are missing out on much of the educational experience by doing this. Likewise, the offender who hides misses out on much of what could be meaningful to him or her. By the use of the same evaluation form, the counselor can determine if a given person is merely a hider or one who really wishes to address problems but who is shy in groups.

Institutional Victimization and Caring: August's Story

I end this chapter on institutional counseling with a story that is both tragic and inspiring. It is tragic because it illustrates the profoundly debilitating effects of extreme institutionalism and bureaucratic bungling. It is inspiring because it illustrates how change can take place, even for someone as mentally disabled as August, given a loving environment in which one's basic human-

ity is recognized and nurtured. August's is an extreme case. As a criminal justice helper, you will not encounter individuals with problems of the same magnitude as August endured. However, the story is all the more compelling for its extremity, and the lessons imparted are valuable for anyone contemplating a career in criminal justice. This story is reproduced with the kind permission of Dr. Taylor. It was previously published in *Institutions, Etc.,* vol. 7, 1984, and in the *Academy of Criminal Justice Sciences Today,* May, 1986.

Summary

Time and cost considerations make group counseling in institutionalized settings attractive. This doesn't mean that group counseling is "second best" to individualized counseling. Group counseling can actually be more beneficial for some clients than individual counseling. Group counseling uses the power of the group to achieve its aims. It offers inmates a constructive alternative to the antisocial cliques that develop in prisons and can function to offset the power of the inmate code. Through the process of sharing, inmates can learn about alternative coping strategies from others who have "been there." A properly run group can develop a feeling of "we-ness," which is not always possible in individual counseling.

A number of exercises derived from the insights of TA, RET, and reality therapy were presented as discussion topics. I think you will find that the "counting the costs" exercise will be particularly beneficial. It is important that you include predetermined topics like this in your counseling strategies. It is too easy to mistake animated discussion on irrelevant topics for progress. Group counseling must have a goal to aim toward. However, any relevant topic raised by a group member should be explored. And don't forget, you as a member of the group are fair game for discussion.

In almost any group setting there will be members who are disruptive. You can minimize their effect through the proper selection of members based on assessment information and one-on-one interviews with prospective members. But disruptive members, intentional or otherwise, will

Perspectives from the Field

Dr. Taylor is the Director of the Center on Human Policy and professor of special education and sociology at Syracuse University, New York.

A Man Called August
Dr. Steven Taylor

This is a story—a true one—about an ugly institution, an amoral bureaucracy, personal tragedy, and the indefatigability of the human spirit. It is the story about a man named August.

I first met August in March 1979. He was living then at a place called Craig "Developmental Center," an institution for the so-called mentally retarded in Sonyea, New York. Sonyea is a road sign found on a stretch of highway located between Auburn and Attica prisons in Upstate New York. August had lived there since 1941.

August seemed to be the kind of fellow who gave severely and profoundly retarded people a bad name. He was certainly one of the most retarded people I had ever met. He couldn't speak, use the toilet, dress himself, or do much of anything at all. He also had quite a few troubling behaviors. Staff at the institution variously described him as "aggressive," "regressive," the "worst case," and "the most severe behavior problem." In short, August was the prototypical "wild man," a lost member of the human family.

August wasn't always this way. We'll probably never know August's side of the story. But the institution's side is well-documented in volumes of case records, ward logs, and professional evaluations maintained over the past 40 years.

Born in New York City in October, 1936, August's early years had been far from trouble-free. Doctors suspected that he had suffered brain injury at birth, and at 9 months of age he incurred a severe head injury in a

fall from his crib. As bad as all of this might seem, his real troubles were only starting. In the fall of 1940, his 26-year-old mother was killed as she attempted to rescue August from the path of an on-coming truck. One year later, August, scarcely 6 now, found himself at what was then Craig State School, hundreds of miles away from his New York City home.

August's first several months at the institution were rather uneventful, at least from the institution's perspective. An entry from the ward notes on October 31, 1941, reads: "On ward in good condition. Gets along well with other boys." Then something happened.

By mid-January of 1942, August was striking out at his peers on the ward. By 1948, he was digging his rectum and smearing feces, and by 1949 he was continually ripping off his clothes.

Remember the 1950s and 60s? August's memories of the period are probably hazy at best: ". . . he is constantly under heavy sedation."

The drugs took their toll. By 1958, August began to experience "extrapyramidal disorders," a drug-induced pseudo-Parkinson's disease involving twitches, tremors, difficulty ambulating, and loss of balance. To this day, August walks with an unsteady gait. Yet, the drugs did not do what they were supposed to do: namely, control his behavior, reduce his aggression, or eliminate his untidy personal habits.

So the institution turned to a time-proven device for controlling unruly inmates, the straight jacket, euphemistically called the camisole. August spent the 50s and 60s in restraint: ". . . occasionally, pt. (patient) has days and short periods of time out of restraint."

By the early 1970s, the man seemed to have been broken, a real-life R. P. McMurphy. He lost weight, looking "emaciated and run-down," became "dull and lethargic," and began "falling frequently." He still occasionally assaulted fellow inmates and staff. However, he slowly turned inward, becoming asocial rather than antisocial, isolating himself.

They extracted his infected teeth around this time. And he lost one ear to the surgeon's knife. The records don't say much about this. What is it about institutions that we can find out more about a man's bowel than how he lost his ear?

Sometime around the spring of 1972, they say August took a liking to the shower room on his ward. The records don't say a lot about this either; 3 months' worth of ward notes for this period are missing completely. August spent the next 7 years of his life in the shower room.

The advocates got August out of the shower room. I'm sure you know the type: naive and idealistic, smug and self-righteous, pushy and arrogant. Advocates seemed to be getting their way back in 1979.

The day I first met August was his second day out of the shower room. August looked like what they called the "living dead" at Auschwitz and Treblinka. He lay on the floor, grunting and groaning, with an agonized look on his face. He didn't seem to be interested in having visitors, no eye contact, no sign of recognition.

Within days, August became a plaintiff in a federal law suit against Craig's Director and the Commissioner of New York's Office of Mental Retardation and Developmental Disabilities. After fighting the suit for 5 years, the

state finally agreed to settle the case this past April. It probably just wasn't worth all the time and embarrassment.

I saw August last August, for the fifth time. He's out of the institution now.

August lives in a small home with six other people. It's not perfect. The house is located not far from Craig and formerly was the groundkeeper's residence. It's not part of the community, but it's not the institution either.

August spends his days at the Medicaid-funded "day treatment center." He sits at a table sorting blue and yellow pieces of paper, putting pegs in a pegboard, and otherwise wasting his time. For doing this day in and day out, August gets oyster crackers and some kind words.

August is a changed man. I knew this when he reached out his hand to shake mine.

August will never receive a college diploma. He's developed some skills and never causes any trouble, though. He's toilet trained, eats with a fork and spoon, and not only keeps his clothes on, but dresses himself.

Perhaps the biggest change in August is his sociability. He never used to smile at anyone else. Now he thrives on human contact. This wild man, this aggressive and then asocial individual, spent the better part of an hour holding my hand, patting me on the back, and taking my hand and stroking the side of his head with it. The supervisor of August's home says that everyone likes working with August: ". . . he's loving, kind, and gentle."

A lost member of the human family has come home.

So, what are the lessons of August's story? The first has to do with what sociologists call the self-

fulfilling prophecy. If we view people as animals and treat them that way, then surely they will act like animals. This goes for people we label mentally retarded as well as juvenile delinquents and even hardened criminals.

The second lesson is that all people, even the so-called profoundly retarded, can learn to grow if given the opportunity. August was the "worst case," the "most severe behavior problem," at the institution. If August can learn skills and live in a small home, then no person need live in an institution for the mentally retarded.

The next lesson relates to the nature of change. August's life did not improve because the bureaucracy became more humane or just. To be sure, some decent people made changes in August's life possible. Yet, the bureaucracy resisted change at every step. It took a law suit to get August out of the shower room.

The last lesson is a more sobering one. It concerns the endurability of institutions. Craig was not always an institution for people labeled mentally retarded. Before that, it was a facility for people with epilepsy. We no longer put people with epilepsy in institutions. One hopes that the day when we will stop segregating people with mental retardation is not far away.

The place called Craig seems to be a dying institution. While one building is earmarked for the mentally retarded, most of the institution is being converted to the Groveland Correctional Facility.

As retarded as they say he is, August knew it was a prison all along.

remain. Group members themselves will take care of much of the disruption, but you retain the ultimate responsibility of recognizing and dealing with disruption. Disrupting members should be dealt with in a dignified and caring manner. It is possible that disruption is a clear signal that the person doing the disrupting should not be in the group. You should approach that person with an offer of individual counseling with you. Finally, the story of August illustrates how even the most intractable of individuals can improve significantly if dealt with in a warm and caring fashion.

◑ Exercises in Group Counseling

One of the best exercises for getting the feel of group counseling is to repeat the exercise in reattribution of responsibility. Since social psychologists tell us that almost everybody has the tendency to systematically bias causal attributions, this exercise will be more realistic for you than exercises such as counting the cost of a criminal lifestyle because you will be dealing with real issues rather than role-playing criminals.

The instructor may wish to act as the group leader, or he or she may wish to assign this task to someone. Just as in a real group situation, the group leader can begin the process by asking one of the other members to volunteer to explain a life event and to state where he or she has placed it in the 2 × 2 square. The discussion among group members can then begin to explore whether or not that event (good or bad) could have been brought more under the control of the individual.

This is obviously a time-consuming exercise, and it is likely that not everyone in the class will have the opportunity to offer a life event or serve as the group leader. Given the time constraints, I feel that it is preferable to go into some depth with one or two individuals rather than to try to cover everybody superficially. Therefore, the instructor may wish to examine everyone's summary of life events prior to commencing the exercise, select one or two of the more interesting ones, and ask those people to volunteer.

References and Suggested Readings

Anderson, J. (1984). *Counseling through Group Process.* New York: Springer.

Association for Specialists in Group Work (1980). *Ethical Guidelines for Group Leaders.* Falls Church, VA: Author.

Bennett, L., T. Rosenbaum, and W. McCullough (1978). *Counseling in Correctional Environments.* New York: Human Sciences Press.

Bry, T. (1951). "Varieties of resistance in group psychotherapy." *International Journal of Group Psychotherapy,* 1:106–114.

Clemmer, D. (1958). *The Prison Community.* New York: Holt, Rinehart & Winston.

Corey, G. (1983). "Group Counseling." In J. Brown and R. Pate (Eds.), *Being a Counselor: Directions and Challenges.* Pacific Grove, CA: Brooks/Cole.

Cressey, D. (1955). "Changing criminals: The application of the theory of differential association." *American Journal of Sociology,* 61:116–120.

Goffman, E. (1961). *Asylums.* Garden City, NY: Anchor.

Hawkins, G. (1976). *The Prison: Policy and Practice.* Chicago: University of Chicago Press.

Homans, G. (1950). *The Human Group.* San Diego: Harcourt Brace Jovanovich.

Ickes, W., and M. Layden (1978). "Attributional styles." In J. Harvey, W. Ickes, and R. Kidd (Eds.), *New Directions in Attribution Research* (vol. 2). Hillsdale, NJ: Lawrence Erlbaum Associates.

Jarvis, D. (1978). *Institutional Treatment of the Offender.* New York: McGraw-Hill.

Juda, D. (1984). "On the special problems of creating group cohesion within a prison setting." *Journal of*

Offender Counseling, Services and Rehabilitation, 8:47–59.

Mahler, C. (1973). "Group Counseling." In J. Lee and C. Pulvino (Eds.), *Group Counseling: Theory, Research, and Practice.* Washington, DC: American Personnel and Guidance Association.

McGuire, J., and P. Priestly (1985). *Offending Behaviour: Skills and Strategems for Going Straight.* London: Batsford Academic and Educational.

Nicholson, R. (1981). "Transactional analysis: A new method of helping offenders." In P. Kratcoski (Ed.), *Correctional Counseling and Treatment.* Pacific Grove, CA: Brooks/Cole.

Ohlsen, M. (1970). *Group Counseling.* New York: Holt, Rinehart & Winston.

Rizzo, N. (1980). "Group therapy: Possibilities and pitfalls." *International Journal of Offender Therapy and Comparative Criminology,* 24:27–31.

Chapter 11
Dealing with Substance Abusers

*If you treat an individual as he is, he will
stay as he is. But if you treat him as if he
were what he ought to be, he will become
what he ought to be and could be.*

Johann Wolfgang von Goethe

Although we might talk in very broad and general
terms about causes of criminal behavior, all theorists should acknowledge that their nominated
causes are all subject to the deadening qualification "all other things being equal." It is true,
but not very helpful, to describe criminal behavior as irresponsible. It is also true that such irresponsible behavior is highly associated with the
lack of warm reciprocal love attachments to others, and this deficiency can be, in most cases,
traced back to early emotional deprivation. But
criminal behavior is located somewhere in a dense
and messy causal maze, and many are the specific
pathways trodden by those who arrive at the
criminal justice helper's office. Many clients have
substance abuse problems, a few have chemical
imbalances, some are normally responsible individuals who succumbed to the pressures and
urges of the moment. Without these specific in-
tervening variables functioning as *proximate*
causes (assumed determinants most immediately
preceding an event), the more general hypoth-
esized *ultimate* causes (determinants that are
fundamental and usually the furthest removed
from the present) may have remained dormant.
Although proximate causes may be quite difficult
to work with, they are certainly more amenable
to identification and treatment than are ultimate
causes, whatever they may be considered to be.

This book does not offer an exhaustive typology of the characteristics of various offender types
such as the murderer, the robber, the check forger,

and so forth. A good treatment of such typologies, very useful for the criminal justice helper to have access to, can be found in Clinard and Quinney (1973). We are concerned here with general patterns of behavior and/or personal characteristics that may dispose different people to commit any number of different crimes. I have chosen to examine the five problem areas that either are the most frequently encountered or present the greatest treatment challenges in corrections. In this chapter we will explore alcoholism and drug abuse, the two problems most commonly found among criminal justice clients. Substance abuse problems are problems that "normal" clients largely bring upon themselves by choosing to take behavior-altering substances into their bodies. The next chapter deals with clients whose problems are within themselves rather than within a pill or a bottle: the sex offender, the schizophrenic, and the intellectually deficient. In the appendix at the end of this chapter there is a glossary of terms related to alcohol and drug abuse.

Alcohol Abusers

It has been estimated that 55% of all arrests and up to 92% of all arrests for violent crimes are associated with alcohol abuse (Taylor, 1984: 107–108). Alcohol is at the same time the most deadly and the most popular of chemical comforters. We drink to be sociable, to liven up our parties, to feel good, to sedate ourselves, and to anesthetize the pains of life. A definitive 1976 study of alcohol consumption estimated that of 122 million drinkers in the United States, 12 million were problem drinkers and 6 million were alcoholics, 83% of whom were males (Keller & Gurioli, 1976: 4–12). The cost of alcohol abuse to society in terms of crime, health, and family and occupational disruption is nothing less than staggering.

Alcohol is a depressant drug that affects our behavior by inhibiting the functioning of the higher brain centers, the locus of our rational thought processes (the conscience, or the superego). As we ingest more alcohol, our behavior becomes less and less inhibited as the rational neocortex surrenders control to the emotions of the more primitive limbic system. Raw basic emotions are then allowed expression without benefit of first being channeled by rational consideration. With the superego brake released, husbands beat up wives, fathers molest their daughters, young men demonstrate their bravado by assaulting strangers and breaking into gas stations, and friends sometimes kill one another. The rate at which this surrender to raw emotionality occurs depends on a number of variables such as the alcohol content of the drink and the amount, the speed with which it is drunk, the weight of the drinker, the amount of food in the stomach, and even the time of day.

The Problem Drinker and the Alcoholic

The difference between a problem drinker and an alcoholic is not an easy one to discern. Certainly, both types drink themselves into a stupor with regularity, and the negative consequences to themselves and to others are equally serious. One way of differentiating them might be in terms of their motivation to drink. Problem drinkers are not physically addicted to alcohol; they drink to achieve the euphoria that enables them to escape a threatening reality. Problem drinkers may or may not become alcoholics (physically addicted to alcohol) after a number of years of excessive drinking. The roots of their problem are seen as psychological and/or social in origin, but they certainly have a psychological dependence on alcohol.

Full-blown alcoholics have a physical dependence on alcohol. *Physical dependence* means that the body has developed a metabolic demand for a particular substance and rebels violently when it is denied that substance. Alcoholics are not necessarily or normally using alcohol as a means to assuage psychological pain, but as a means to avoid the terrible physiological pains of withdrawal (alcohol withdrawal can be more life threatening than withdrawal from narcotics). You will often meet alcoholics whose social and psychological difficulties followed from their alcoholic condition rather than having caused it. For the problem drinker, the causal sequence appears to be invariably that life's problems led them to seek solace in the bottle. Approximately 10% of those who drink become alcoholics.

Alcoholic Stages

Jellinek's (1960) authoritative series of studies suggests that alcoholism is a progressive disease that occurs in fairly predictable stages. We will concentrate on four primary stages, although each one can be broken down more minutely.

1. The first stage is the *prealcoholic symptomatic stage.* This stage begins with the first drink, taken for social or any number of other reasons. Drinkers may occasionally overindulge and make fools of themselves, but they find it a small price to pay for the pleasure they experience. Not only does drinking give them pleasure, but they find that it increases their confidence and sociability and diminishes their tensions. Unfortunately, many of us come to view alcohol as a magical tonic to which we turn with greater and greater frequency as a morale booster and a tension reducer.

2. The *prodromal stage* begins when heavy drinkers suddenly begin to experience amnesic or "blackout" episodes. They often wake up the morning after a bout of drinking without the ability to recall what they did the night before. This stage also marks the onset of secret drinking, a preoccupation with planning for the next drink, and the gulping rather than sipping of drinks. Drinkers in this stage show some signs of anxiety about their growing reliance on booze, which they quickly submerge in a sea of more of the same. Their drinking increasingly becomes more of a private than a social activity.

3. In the *crucial stage,* individuals begin to lose their grip on alcohol as it tightens its grip on them. They are still able to control when they will drink but not how much they will drink once they start. They have progressed from being social drinkers to being antisocial drinkers. Faced with impaired efficiency on the job and in the bedroom, they begin to experience occupational and marital problems, even dismissal and divorce. The threat of such impending problems may lead drinkers to foreswear drinking for long periods

of time, for they still have the ability to exercise their willpower at this point. However, they are still psychologically predisposed to turn back to drink and easily revert with minimal prodding.

If they do turn back to the bottle at this stage they have probably crossed the line from psychological to physical dependence. They now engage in frequent and prolonged drinking binges, known as "benders." They become oblivious to their responsibilities, to their personal health safety, and to the welfare of their families. Their lives become an all-consuming quest for alcohol.

4. The *chronic stage* is the stage in which the drinker "hits bottom." This stage is characterized by almost continuous drinking. The drinker's physiology will be so altered at this point that he or she requires only about half the amount of alcohol previously needed to maintain the drunken stupor and cannot stop drinking once having started. At this stage, drinkers drink mainly to avoid withdrawal symptoms such as nausea, vomiting, hallucinations (the "pink elephant"), and delirium tremens ("the DTS," or the "shakes"). Among the many health problems the alcoholic will certainly risk in this stage are hepatitis, gastritis, anemia, pellagra, cerebellar degeneration, the Wernicke-Korsakoff syndrome, and cirrhosis of the liver. In short, the chronic alcoholic is a physical and psychological mess.

It should be emphasized that the above stages are another example of the "ideal type" method of examination and exploration. Jellinek's stages proceed in predictable fashion from the social drinker to the Skid Row bum. However, it is estimated that only about 5% of alcoholics go all the way to Skid Row (Stencel, 1973: 989). Most alcoholics have families and jobs and may have little or no contact with the law. It would appear that there are social and psychological differences between those alcoholics who maintain a fairly conventional lifestyle and those who do not. In a statement with which control theorists and reality therapists would heartily concur, the President's Task Force on Drunkenness concluded that these differences were that the chronic drinker "has never attained more than a minimum of integration in society. . . . he is isolated, uprooted, unattached, disorganized, demoralized, and home-less" (1967: 11–13). We do not know to what extent these differences are consequences rather than causes of chronic alcoholism, but the task force report once again emphasizes the tremendous importance of reciprocal love relationships for healthy human functioning. It is this type of alcoholic with whom you are most likely to come into contact in corrections work.

Causality

The task force's conclusion points to possible so-cial-psychological percursors of alcohol abuse. Such an explanation fits nicely into anomie theory, discussed in Chapter 1. We can think of alcoholics who get into trouble with the law as anomic retreatists from the American goal of materialistic success. Such people may have been denied access to the means of attaining it, or perhaps do not possess the fortitude to take advantage of the opportunities that they have had. Winick (1986: 355) points out that Native Americans represent a group of people with high anomie and high rates of alcoholism, whereas Jews have both low anomie and low rates of alcoholism.

As well as viewing alcohol as a self-prescribed remedy for the anxiety and bitterness that accompany a lack of social mobility in a competitive society, Reichman (1978) views it as a tool that assists the drinker to deal with identity conflicts. The drinker feels more confident and "successful" with an alcoholic booster. Thus, success identity needs are being met, albeit destructively. Think of the stereotypical themes of success, masculinity, and sensuality implicit in the names of some of our popular alcoholic concoctions, such as Manhattans, pink ladies, Margaritas, piledrivers, and boilermakers.

Recognizing some of the reasons that people take to excessive drink does not tell us why some become alcoholics while others do not. Accumulating research appears to be pointing more and more to the conclusion that physical addiction to alcohol, as opposed to psychological dependence, is genetic and related to differential enzyme functioning (Rosenfeld, 1981). Enzymes are protein molecules that serve as catalysts in the chemical conversion of molecules into other types of molecules. In the body, ethanol alcohol is broken down by enzymes into a molecule called acetaldehyde (AcH). AcH produces unpleasant reactions to drinking, such as nausea and headaches, if it is not itself converted by other enzymes into other molecules that are excreted in the urine. Those people who metabolize alcohol rapidly will quickly be sensitized to its unpleasant effects if they ingest it in quantity, and that "punishment" for doing so makes them less likely to overindulge in the future. AcH, as the first metabolite of alcohol, is thus a built-in guardian against alcoholism. In fact, disulfiram (Antabuse) is used as a treatment for alcoholics because it functions to maintain high levels of AcH in the body by retarding further metabolic reactions. The use of Antabuse is a form of aversive conditioning whereby physical discomfort is associated with drinking. Aversive conditioning is used to eliminate a behavior by pairing the behavior with an unpleasant consequence.

In alcoholics, it appears that enzymes convert AcH into a morphinelike substance called tetra-hydropapaveroline (THP), which is highly addictive. This biophysical line of inquiry could lead to the explanation of why the vast majority of those who drink over a lifetime never become addicted. Perhaps alcohol itself is not inherently addictive, but rather the biosynthetic by-products of alcohol, which are produced differentially in individuals according to the functioning of their metabolic systems. This is not the complete story of the etiology of alcoholism. It only states that among those who do turn to drink, there are some with an inherited predisposition to become addicted. More complete explanations of this interesting line of thought are contained in Applewhite (1981) and Taylor (1984).

Assessment, Treatment, and Counseling

In view of the high social and financial costs of alcoholism and problem drinking, it is imperative that you make every effort to identify clients with these problems. It has been my experience that most alcoholics and problem drinkers will not admit to having a problem. Nearly all of the clients

I have confronted with the possibility that they do have an alcohol problem have felt that they could control their drinking. Those who deny their problem do so because they do not wish to admit, even to themselves, that they have relinquished control of their lives to alcohol. Alcoholics have the choice of either rejecting alcohol or rejecting reality. They often choose to reject reality in order to maintain consistency between their evaluation of themselves as being in control of their lives and their continued use of a substance that they find so rewarding. In contrast, some clients will overemphasize their drinking, hoping that you and the judge will regard it as a mitigating factor when considering sentencing alternatives.

Identifying alcoholics. The ability to identify the alcoholic and the problem drinker is an art that all criminal justice counselors should strive to acquire. The most obvious indicator of a drinking problem is an arrest record of alcohol-related offenses (drunk driving, drunk and disorderly, and so on). You should also inquire into the client's drinking patterns. The frequency and amount of alcohol consumed on a weekly basis, the frequency of legal problems due to drinking, and the amount of time and money spent on drink are all indications of the depth of the problem. If you discover such patterns, you have an ipso facto case to present to the client showing that he or she does have a drinking problem. Point out to the client that to continue to deny it in the face of such evidence is irrational and unacceptable to you. On no account must you discuss alibis designed to convince you that factors other than drinking are responsible for irresponsible behavior. To do so will result in an argument over the merits of the alibi, thus possibly reinforcing the alibi, since the more a person defends a position, the more difficult it becomes to relinquish it.

There are a number of screening tools that you can use to help to identify the alcoholic client. One frequently used tool is the Michigan Alcoholism Screening Test (MAST), reproduced in the Appendix to this chapter. This 24-item questionnaire should be used only as a corroborative diagnostic aid. By no means should you rule out alcoholism if the scale score is negative for alcoholism. Clients can certainly lie on the questionnaire, and verbal and nonverbal cues, such as alcohol-related arrests (which you will know about independently of client responses), may be more valuable with clients reluctant to disclose the requested information. The questionnaire is best administered in the presence of the criminal justice worker so that he or she can clarify the items if necessary. Each question is answered yes or no.

The client's general appearance and behaviors during the interview provide some useful cues for identifying an alcoholic. An emaciated figure with a swollen abdomen, a flushed or sallow complexion, sunken eyes, dilated pupils, and generally poor hygiene are markers of the insomnia, poor nutrition, frequent sickness, and dehydration that frequently accompany alcoholism. Behaviors to look for are tremors of the face and hands, poor concentration, memory impairment, and confabulation (the tendency to invent names, places, and stories to cover up memory loss). The more serious the drinking problem, the more obvious these signs will be. The absence of these symptoms, or your failure to perceive them, does not mean that the client has no drinking problem. If the client has a record of alcohol-related offenses, and/or the present offense is alcohol related, he or she has a problem that must be addressed.

Treating alcoholics. Treatment for the alcoholic or problem drinker is a complex affair that may include both medical treatment and psychosocial counseling. Much will depend on the level of the client's drinking at the time that you first meet him or her. If the client is in the chronic stage of alcoholism, hospitalization for detoxification ("drying out") will be necessary. It is most likely, however, that detoxification took place in the jail or at a hospital after the client's arrest, and you will not have to concern yourself with it. If it did not, you should make every effort to secure in-patient medical treatment for your client. Detoxification in a medical environment is a necessary prerequisite to any future treatment. If the client does not have insurance that provides for such treatment, or if welfare authorities cannot provide it, organizations like the Salvation Army and the Volunteers of America are often successful in securing the necessary treatment. Although these organizations do not accept clients for detoxification (not being medical facilities), they both run valuable in-house programs for recovering alcoholics on a free or sliding fee basis. Detoxification is not a treatment of alcoholism, which is a long and difficult process; it is a treatment for intoxication preparatory to treatment for alcoholism.

Perhaps the best nonresidential program for alcoholics is Alcoholics Anonymous. This organization of recovering alcoholics is a very supportive group whose members will go to great lengths to assist one another. They will nurse fellow members through hangovers, depressions, and periods of craving for alcohol, and they may even provide room and board for them. However, there are those who assert that AA can be of little use to individuals who refuse to admit their problem and who are not motivated to do something about it. This assertion, they believe, is implicit in the first of AA's famous Twelve Steps (to recovery): "We admitted we were powerless over alcohol—that our lives had become unmanageable." Voluntary affirmation is obviously a plus, but it doesn't necessarily mean that you should dismiss AA as a treatment option if your client refuses to recognize the problem or is unmotivated. You can make attendance at AA meetings a condition of probation or parole. Experiencing the warm support and caring of fellow travelers may well turn the reluctant client into a motivated client. Insisting that the client attend AA is another instance of the constructive use of authority.

An alternative to AA meetings outside the probation or parole office is an in-house alcohol program. The advantage of an in-house program is that officers can closely monitor attendance, participation, and progress. In-house meetings and group counseling sessions are best led by volunteer members of AA and/or community corrections workers who are thoroughly versed in alcohol counseling. The department where I worked never experienced any problems in obtaining AA volunteers for biweekly sessions. We also found it beneficial to invite spouses and other concerned parties to these meetings once per week with the realization that they are psychologically involved with the client's drinking problem.

Counseling alcoholics. Alcoholic group counseling has certain advantages over individual counseling. Each member of the group, including the AA volunteer group leaders, knows where all other members are coming from. All the requisites for successful counseling outlined by Carl Rogers are, or are potentially, present in a gathering of similarly situated individuals. Positive regard for fellow members is an integral part of the quasireligious philosophy of AA. Alcoholics are led to the "conversion" experience in a fellowship of individuals like themselves who are in various stages of alcoholic recovery. There is no saint like the reformed sinner, or so the saying goes.

Empathy is also present in the Rogerian sense. There can be no skirting of the issue in such company. Alcoholic clients cannot reasonably tell their "bottle-wise" compatriots that they "just don't understand," the way they could their non-alcoholic corrections counselors. Fellow AA members will provide your clients not only with support but also with visions of the possible. They are role models whose presence serves to emphasize much more strongly than the counselor could that recovery is possible. Methods of dealing with specific alcohol-related problems are discussed by drawing on the various experiences of those who may have successfully dealt with them in their own lives. When the solution to a problem is offered by a peer, it is more likely to carry weight than if it is posed by "the Man."

Genuineness is another Rogerian principle that is a hallmark of AA treatment. The AA program insists that its members honestly confront their problems, their shortcomings, their responsibil-

Perspectives from the Field

Sandra Tebbe is a probation officer who specializes in working with alcoholic clients. She holds master's degrees in both sociology and rehabilitation counseling, and she is also a Certified Alcoholism Counselor. In the past Ms. Tebbe was a specialist in counseling compulsive gamblers on probation.

Tough Love and Alcoholics
Sandra Tebbe

Alcoholics usually will not recognize that they have a drinking problem. Many don't want to recognize it because they enjoy their alcoholism and find satisfaction in the "loving" concern of those around them. They use this "love" as a means of manipulating their way through a drunken lifestyle. The alcoholic's skillful maneuvers and manipulations do not stop when he or she commits a crime. Most alcoholic probationers come under supervision expecting the same "loving" concern and the same ignoring, overlooking, and excusing they are accustomed to.

To help the alcoholic offender you have to be willing to be rejected. That's what "tough love" is all about, caring enough about clients to hold them totally responsible for their behavior, regardless of whether they like you or not. Tough love is making each decision carefully to assure that you are not enabling the probationer to continue his or her drinking. This will not make you popular, and it certainly won't make you loved. It's all too easy to ease up a little, to give some slack, so they will like you. But you are not the issue. You demonstrate your love for them by holding them responsible for the defeat of their alcoholic conditions.

I started working as a probation officer three years ago. For the past year and a half I have coordinated a special state-funded in-house alcohol program. This program provides one of the highest levels of supervision in community corrections and provides for strict and unambiguous

correctional consequences for every misbehavior. It has been a good program to learn what tough love is all about.

I am often asked, "How can you spend so much time working with alcoholics without getting burned out?" I entered the probation profession at a young age and with idealistic attitudes. It didn't take me long to learn how to adapt and survive. Counseling alcoholics means learning how to let go. It doesn't mean that you stop caring, it means that you must learn that you can't do it for someone else. It's the realization that you can't control another person's life or fix its defects. Only they can do that. You have to respect their capacity for control and choice, and allow them to learn from the natural consequences of their behavior.

Most alcoholics have had someone to enable, or make possible, their drinking behavior from the very start. This is one of the reasons that the alcoholic's family, and most everyone else influenced by him or her, becomes "sick." Enabling is usually in the form of continually making excuses for and rescuing the alcoholic from distress. Unfortunately, it is not until alcoholics experience the real pains of their disease that they get around to making a decision to change their lifestyles.

You can easily fall into rescuing behavior with your alcoholic clients, but you are not doing them any favors if you continue with the enabling patterns they have come to expect. You are not being "nice," "neat," or "loving" to those who need tough love by allowing them to manipulate you and to continue to ruin their lives.

Confront them, challenge them, educate them, help them!

Alcoholics will almost always deny their alcoholism. Take Jim, a high-risk probationer of mine. He had been in prison for threatening the life of his baby when police arrived at his home on a domestic dispute call. During the alcohol screening period, Jim stated over and over that he was not an alcoholic: "I don't have to wake up to a drink every day like the drunks on the street. I'm not a weak man. There's lots of times I don't drink."

Jim's defensiveness was a reaction to the many myths associated with alcoholism. Many people think of alcoholics as weak, low-class moral degenerates who lack willpower. My job as his probation officer was to educate him about his disease so that he would open up his mind to treatment. Jim learned through my efforts and through mandatory participation in AA that alcoholism is primarily a physiological disease and that he became addicted because his body is incapable of processing alcohol normally. He also learned that alcoholism is a disease that affects all classes and races. Jim's many family and financial problems did not cause his alcoholism. Rather, his alcoholism undermined his ability to cope, and this inability then exacerbated his problems.

Once Jim learned about his disease he was better able to deal with it. Jim had to realize that to admit his alcoholism was not to admit that he was a weak or bad person. Through small-group participation and AA attendance, Jim found comfort and support from others with the same problem. These folks "tough loved" Jim into sobriety. Jim has been sober for two years now. He has chosen a new life for himself. Although all of his other problems have not disappeared, he is learning how to cope with them without alcohol.

Jim was relatively easy to deal with, as alcoholic probationers go. Often I find that supervising alcoholic probationers means long periods of time waiting for them to "hit bottom." "Hitting bottom" means that the alcoholic comes to realize that he or she has gone about as low as he or she can go, and that he or she must change or be forever lost. A few months ago, one of my probationers hit his bottom while sitting in the county jail. John was doing 30 days for his second probation violation, a violation which I could have easily ignored. He had continually denied having a drinking problem, refused to go to AA meetings, and was resentful of authority. This time, however, something was different about John when I visited him in jail. For the first time he didn't attempt to rationalize his behavior or blame it on someone else. He was physically sick from withdrawal, homeless, and his wife had left him (a natural consequence of his behavior) because she couldn't handle his drinking anymore. With a broken spirit, John started to take a hard look at himself and finally asked for help. John now is doing something about his problem. He is one of the several sober probationers in the program. John is one of the many probationers who have learned to love and respect themselves through an officer's use of tough love.

---

ities, and their realities. Manipulation and game playing are quickly recognized and rejected: "You can't con the cons." Members are encouraged to share with the group their fears, anxieties, hopes, and self-evaluation. This self-disclosure provides the client with the opportunity to share genuine feelings with others and to build self-esteem and a group identity, qualities sorely lacking in the lives of alcoholics.

I would urge that all alcoholic or problem drinkers caught up in the criminal justice system be prodded into involvement with AA. It has been estimated that half of those who regularly attend AA meetings with serious intent are rehabilitated (Chafetz and Demone, 1972). Although no figures are available specific to criminal justice clients, one would not expect their success rate to be this high. When all is said and done, client motivation remains a crucial variable. You can only help by doing your best to generate this motivation.

Antabuse treatment. Antabuse treatment, as a kind of aversion therapy, can be a very useful adjunct to other treatment modalities. Antabuse treatment, administered under medical supervision, is begun after detoxification. The drug is usually given to the client for several consecutive days along with small doses of alcohol. The unpleasant feelings that accompany drinking alcohol while AcH level is high act as negative reinforcers. It is hoped that these highly unpleasant consequences associated with alcohol ingestion will be sufficiently aversive to condition the patient from future abuse. Realize, however, that Antabuse treatment is voluntary on the patient's part; you cannot require it as a condition of supervision. A client who does make the voluntary decision to take Antabuse is taking his or her treatment seriously because he or she has, in effect, also made the decision not to drink during the period that this highly aversive drug remains effective. In fact, some alcoholics take it for extended periods of time as a medicine rather than merely as a conditioning agent.

Like most other conditioned responses, however, the effects of Antabuse will be extinguished with the passage of time. It does provide a strong and immediate reason not to drink and thus buys time for the implementation of other types of treatment. It appears to be quite successful when used in conjunction with psychosocial counseling. Billet (1974) reports that 64% of a sample of patients who were administered Antabuse in addition to undergoing a comprehensive psychosocial rehabilitation program showed "marked improvement." Only 31% of those who were in the same program but who did not receive Antabuse showed a similar level of improvement.

Drug Abusers and Addicts

Although alcohol is a mind-altering drug in common with the other drugs we will examine below, we discussed it separately because of the attitude of American society toward alcohol in comparison with nonalcoholic drugs. Alcohol is a legal and socially acceptable form of drugging oneself; marijuana, heroin, LSD, cocaine, and so on are not. Respectable middle-class people drink, but criminals, long-hairs, street people, and ghetto-types take drugs. Contrast the rather positive names that we give to "our" booze with the negative tags ("weed," "acid," "scag," and the generic "dope") attached to "their" drugs. Drug abusers and addicts carry the additional burdens of the illegality of their chemical comforters and of the criminal activity they frequently engage in to obtain them. Estimates of the number of individuals addicted to just one drug (heroin) range from 200,000 to 900,000 (Walker, 1985:200). The relationship between addiction and crime is evident in the finding that arrest rates per 100 drug-addicted individuals prior to their addiction was 3.1, but during their addiction the rate was 35.1 (Walker, 1985:203).

Drugs affect brain functioning in one of four ways: (1) they inhibit or slow down the release of chemical neurotransmitters, (2) they stimulate or speed up their release, (3) they prevent the reuptake of transmitters after they have stimulated neighboring neurons, or (4) they break down the transmitters more quickly. Depending on the type of drug taken, then, the individual's behavior and/or feelings are speeded up or slowed down, intensified or reduced, or stimulated or mellowed.

People turn to drugs for the same reasons that people turn to booze. They take them initially to be "with it," to be sociable and to conform, to induce pleasure, to escape psychic stress or to escape chronic boredom. They abuse them and become dependent on them because they find little pleasure, comfort, solace, or meaning in their lives. People who confront more pain than pleasure in their daily lives tend to pursue all the artificial comfort they can get. Addicts become emotionally attached to their substances the way most of us become attached to other people because, generally, their experiences have not prepared them for intimate relationships with people. As Chein, Gerhard, Lee and Rosenfeld put it (1964:273), "In almost all addict families, there was a disturbed relationship between the parents, as evidenced by separation, divorce, open hostility, or lack of warmth." Lacking this inner sense of warmth, addicts think of their pharmacopoeia of fake happiness not in terms of what it does "to" them, but rather in terms of what it does "for" them. We have to break through all their rationalizations, projections, and denials to make them understand the profound difference between *for* and *to.*

Jellinek's four stages of alcoholism are applicable to the process of moving from casual drug usage to full-blown addiction. Some drugs are physically addictive and some are only psychologically addictive, meaning that there are no painful physiological symptoms associated with withdrawal. Don't take this somewhat artificial distinction between physical and psychological addiction as necessarily implying that the former is more serious than the latter. For instance, the various barbiturates, such as Seconal® and phenobarbital, are considered physically addictive, but cocaine is not. Yet cocaine addiction is probably the most difficult of all types of addiction to treat successfully. Regardless of the type of drug we are talking about, addiction is not an invariable outcome of drug usage any more than alcoholism is an invariable outcome of drinking. The danger of addiction, however, is considerably greater.

Classification of Drugs

As a criminal justice counselor, you should become familiar with all types of illegal drugs and their effects. However, our mission here precludes any attempt at an exhaustive treatment. What follows is a brief description of the different classes of drugs, with an emphasis on heroin and cocaine. These are perhaps the two drugs that cause the most problems in terms of their association with crime, in terms of treatment, and in terms of the frequency with which they are encountered in the criminal justice setting. A fairly comprehensive listing of many of the drugs and their street names is presented in the Appendix to this chapter.

Depressants. The depressants include the barbiturates/sedatives and the narcotics/opiates. All drugs in this category have the potential for physical and psychological dependence, and all produce tolerance (the tendency to require larger and larger doses to produce the same effects after

the body adjusts to lower dosages). Depressants range from the relatively mild analgesic sedatives to the insidious narcotics such as heroin. This class of drugs tends to appeal to individuals whose characteristic coping style leans toward isolation, withdrawal, and indifference.

Taking one of the stronger varieties in this category, such as heroin or Dilaudid, a cheaper and increasingly popular substitute, wafts the individual into a euphoric state of sweet indifference, a state that heroin users describe as the "floats." Intravenous injection of heroin ("mainlining") is the most popular method of administering the drug among hard-core addicts. This produces the famous "rush," a warm skin flush and orgasmic feeling. After the initial rush, the addict drifts off into a private carefree world for anywhere from three to twelve hours. Needless to say, the problems are still around after the effects wear off, not the least of which is the problem of securing the next rush. I once supervised a heroin addict who had a $300-per-day habit and who challenged my characterization of him as lazy. He said, "Man, we addicts work harder than anybody you know. You try to hustle the streets to come up with that kind of bread every day."

This "hustle" is the main reason for heroin addiction's close association with criminal activity. The euphoric state achieved under the influence of heroin is not conducive to effort, criminal or otherwise. Narcotics users are significantly less likely to commit violent crimes than are users of alcohol or amphetamines, particularly methamphetamine. In fact, Hartman (1978:404) reports: "In those countries where free narcotics are supplied to habitual abusers, the crime rate is said to be lower for this group of people than for the general population."

Heroin is a derivative of morphine, a powerful painkiller. It has been reliably established that the brain has its own pain-killing substances, the so-called endorphins (for "endogenous morphine-like substances"). The presence of these naturally occurring analgesics provides clues to the addictive process. It has been suggested that some individuals become heroin addicts because they have insufficient endorphins in the brain to anesthetize naturally the pains of life (Applewhite, 1981:132). In other words, it is not that heroin addicts experience more pains of living than the rest of us but that they have less endorphins. Lacking normal amounts of nature's "tonic" precipitates a search for artificial substitutes to make up the deficit.

This assumption is deceptively similar to the AcH explanation of alcoholism. However, the evidence relating AcH and alcoholism is compelling, whereas the evidence for an endorphin-deficiency theory of opiate addiction is practically nonexistent. For one thing, whereas alcoholism tends to be fairly evenly distributed across class lines, heroin addiction tends to be concentrated at the lower levels of the class structure. If there were a hereditary predisposition to become drug addicted, one would expect it to appear at about the same rate among the various class strata, assuming that experimental usage is itself not class based.

Restak offers what is perhaps a more plausible biological explanation of heroin addiction. He feels that the frequent injection of heroin affects the body's natural capacity to release endorphins in much the same way that giving individuals too much thyroid extract will eventually cause the body to cease its own production of the thyroid-stimulating hormone, thus turning them into "thyroid junkies." An addict's assumed lower level of natural endorphins is therefore considered a consequence rather than a cause of addiction (Restak, 1979:344–355).

Stimulants. The stimulants, primarily amphetamines and cocaine, have effects opposite to those of the depressants. They mimic the activity of the sympathetic division of the autonomic nervous system, meaning that they increase arousal and a sense of well-being. They seem to be the drugs of choice for individuals who seek excitement and adventure, the bored, the driven, and the chronically underaroused. This class of drugs includes everything from the $3.95 over-the-counter diet pills to $100-per-gram cocaine. In my six years as a probation officer I never had a heroin addict who was a professional person, or even a middle-class person. My cocaine clients, on the other hand, tended to be almost exclusively middle-class and professional people (physicians, lawyers, businessmen). This class-based usage appears to be changing of late as we see a dramatic leap in cocaine's popularity. The Drug Enforcement Agency (DEA) states that about 5000 new people each day try cocaine. The magic of the free market system has apparently combined with the glamor of cocaine's association with the rich and powerful to steadily democratize its use. Along with the depressant alcohol, the use of amphetamines and cocaine has the most immediate association with violent criminal behavior (Hartman, 1978:412).

Cocaine is the powdered derivative of the South American coca plant. Although officially classified as a narcotic, it is actually a very strong stimulant. Cocaine users, who collectively spend about $30 billion a year for the drug, have about a fifty-fifty chance of becoming addicted (compare this with the approximately 10% chance for frequent drinkers of becoming alcoholic). Whether or not one becomes addicted appears to be a function of the frequency and amount of intake rather than any biological predisposition.

Cocaine works by blocking the reuptake of the neurotransmitters dopamine and norepinephrine at the synaptic neuroterminals, thus keeping the body in an extended state of arousal. Being highly soluble in fatty tissue, coke is taken up by the brain quickly, producing the familiar euphoric rush. When cocaine is taken intravenously, the rush takes only about 15 seconds. The strongest and fastest rush comes from smoking "freebase" (the cocaine alkaloid is freed from its acid salt to produce pure cocaine).

A new form of smokable cocaine, known as "rock" or "crack," has been hitting the streets with a vengeance over the past few years. Crack is manufactured by combining cocaine, baking soda, and water. This mixture is then heated, allowed to cool, and broken into tiny pieces resembling gray slivers of bar soap. Without the elaborate and sometimes dangerous preparations necessary to produce freebase cocaine, crack produces the same sort of high, and its relatively low price makes it attractive to those who formerly resisted the more expensive powdered cocaine. Crack is smoked though a water pipe, and the high, which lasts about 15 minutes, comes within 10 seconds. With all these "advantages" associated with this new menace, probation and parole officers can expect an increasing number of clients on their caseloads who are smoking crack, a drug that many predict will become the most abused drug in the United States.

Cocaine addiction is extremely difficult to treat because use of the drug is so rewarding. Addicts who have been involved with other kinds of drugs will tell you that cocaine is by far the most desirable. I once had a client who spent nine days locked in her room living on only cocaine and water. Her nine-day cocaine holiday cost her $5000, which she had obtained by trafficking the stuff among her quite middle-class friends. Cocaine addiction is also very difficult to treat because its nonuse after prolonged use produces a devastating "crash." This is a period of intense anxiety, irritability, and depression that lasts about four days.

It is generally thought that although the amphetamines and cocaine quickly produce tolerance, requiring increasingly greater amounts to obtain the same effects, they do not produce physical dependence. Psychological dependence is very strong, however. The depression and fatigue resulting from the overstimulation of the nervous system create a tremendous desire for more cocaine to counteract these effects. Since smoking cocaine produces a quicker and stronger high than snorting it, its effect is of shorter duration and the crash is more devastating. If more cocaine is not immediately available, addicts will resort to taking barbiturates to help ease the crash.

Methamphetamine (speed). Methamphetamine or "speed" is the most dangerous of all drugs in terms of its association with violence. It was a favorite with the hippie subculture of the sixties, but it is still very much around. It operates on the limbic system to accentuate and accelerate the visual, tactile, auditory, and olfactory impulses. The intensification of these senses was tailor-made for the free-love philosophy of the hippie generation, for it generates hypersexuality.

When "speed freaks" become "wired," they have boundless energy, are super alert, and feel on top of everything. The effects feel so good that they often go on what is called a "run." A run consists of several days on speed without pausing for sleep. Speed is considerably less expensive than cocaine, so a run of five days will cost only about $150. The price to be paid for the run is that the longer it lasts, the more the feelings of well-being turn to hyperactive aggressiveness. The accentuated sensitivity to stimuli, intermixed with fatigue, can very easily produce psychoticlike reactions. This is especially true if the run is being conducted, as it usually is, with several others, all of whom are similarly hypersensitive. Love and beauty and clever conversation will become paranoia, ugliness, hostility, and violent disagreement. This result becomes increasingly more likely as the run is extended and as the available supply of speed peters out.

Speed freaks are especially dangerous after the run is over. They find themselves in deep post-high depressions, their nerves are badly frayed, and they are in desperate need of sleep. They become very argumentative and are susceptible to explosive violence. Any confrontation worsens the depression and leads them on a desperate search for more speed to alleviate the feeling. They will do almost anything to get the next fix and start the vicious cycle spinning again.

Hallucinogens. The hallucinogens are mind-altering drugs such as marijuana and lysergic acid diethylamide (LSD). The smoking of marijuana is so pervasive today that we pay little attention to it. I would hazard a guess that nine out of ten criminal justice clients under 40 years of age have tried it or continue to smoke it. Its quasiacceptance can be discerned by reading PSI reports that frequently contain such statements as "With the exception of marijuana, the defendant denies any drug usage." I have never heard of any client being ordered into treatment for a marijuana habit. It appears that most criminal justice workers consider it to be a relatively innocuous habit.

Those who consider it to be merely a "simple natural weed" akin to tobacco fail to realize the greater potency of the modern product. Whereas the marijuana of the sixties and early seventies contained about 5% of the mind-altering cannabinoid THC, today's product contains about 25%. Unlike alcohol, which is water soluble and quickly metabolized and excreted from the body, cannabinoids are fat soluble. They penetrate the fatty areas of the body—notably in the brain and the gonads—and remain there for long periods of time. Since only about 10% of the THC crosses the blood–brain barrier to produce the marijuana "high," one shudders to think of the damage that the other 90% of this powerful chemical is doing to the body. Marijuana is anything but harmless. It has a wide range of subtle, insidious physical and psychological effects, many of which are still to be discovered.

LSD is a more immediately dangerous form of hallucinogen. In its unadulterated form, LSD is a clear, odorless, and tasteless liquid. It is sold soaked in sugar cubes, in tiny pills, or on saturated blotting paper (microdots). LSD has been termed a *psychomimetic* drug because its effects sometimes mimic psychosis. In a very few cases (I personally recall only one), LSD usage produces a psychotic break. It could be, however, that these few people were predisposed and that LSD functioned as an immediate catalyst.

After a period of decline, LSD's usage appears to be increasing again. Today's LSD, however, is only about half as potent as it was during the hippie period. It is a drug primarily favored by those who seek intellectual adventure, the inward-lookers who seek to increase awareness rather than escaping it. It causes hyperawareness and a greatly enhanced appreciation of stimuli in the user's perceptual field. Among the lower classes and habitants of the ghettoes, where drug use is seen as an attempt to decrease the awareness of the reality of life, LSD has found little acceptance. LSD does not cause physical dependence, but psychological dependence may occur, and the drug produces tolerance rapidly.

Drug Abuse Treatment

Everything I have said about alcoholism treatment has general application to drug treatment. Attempts to rehabilitate drug abusers have been impeded by the pessimistic attitude "once an addict, always an addict." This attitude may be partly a function of society's more negative perceptions of drug addicts in relation to its perceptions of alcoholics. The corrections worker should not share these attitudes.

Like alcoholics, drug abusers and addicts are reluctant to admit that they have the problem unless they feel that you may consider the problem to be a mitigating factor. If drug abusers don't admit their dependency during the initial interview, they will tend to do whatever they can to hide it while under supervision. It is important that you identify any existing drug problem at your first contact. There are several signs that can assist you in this endeavor.

The most obvious first step is to check the record for a history of drug-related arrests or previous drug treatment. Ask the client to explain involvement with drugs at those times. This may lead into an admission of current usage. The chronic drug abuser tends to have a disheveled appearance similar to that of the alcoholic because his or her personal hygiene and nutritional habits are likewise subordinated to the habit. If you suspect narcotics usage, look for tracks on their hands and arms, which they conceal, even in summer, by wearing long sleeves. Does the client wear sunglasses to your office to conceal constricted and fixed pupils? Is the client drowsy and "laid back" during visits? If the client's nose is frequently running or eyes watering, it may indicate that he or she is late in getting a fix. Does the client scratch himself or herself and complain of frequent sickness? Does the client have difficulty concentrating and frequently arrive late or miss appointments?

The abuser of stimulants is somewhat harder to detect by behavior in your office. As opposed to the narcotics addict, the stimulant abuser may display an excited, hyperactive, and talkative demeanor, which may sometimes degenerate into hostility and irritability. This behavior will be particularly in evidence if you tell the client that you suspect him or her of drug abuse and order the client to go to a clinic for a urinalysis. Nevertheless, all clients whom you suspect of drug abuse should be made to undergo urinalysis.

Addicts have the same range of treatment options open to them as alcoholics. They can obtain detoxification and initial counseling in an inpatient setting, or they can be part of the communal living of a half-way house surrounded by models of recovered and recovering addicts. Finally, they can avail themselves of antagonistic drugs.

Narcotics Anonymous is a group therapy program modeled on AA. It too is usually staffed and run by ex-addicts. Half-way houses provide comprehensive social, psychological, educational, and vocational programs aimed at helping the client to reenter society as a more responsible individual. The assumptions and dynamics of these programs are the same as those addressed in the section on alcoholism. Unfortunately, drug addicts are more difficult to deal with in such settings than are alcoholics, especially during the first few crucial days when the drugs are still in the system. Addicts feel anxious, fearful, and paranoid during this period. They need a calm, quiet, and supportive environment, and they should be isolated as much as possible from outside contacts at this time. Any phone contact from fellow users on the outside can trigger the urge to run from the facility and back into the arms of drugs.

Among the various drug therapies, the best known and most widely used is methadone maintenance. Some authorities feel that this method should be used only after psychotherapeutic methods have been tried and failed because methadone creates its own dependence, and methadone-related deaths have been reported (Brown, Benn, & Jansen, 1975). However, it is extremely successful in blocking the withdrawal pains of heroin wihout producing any rewarding euphoria or rush of its own. Methadone also comes with withdrawal symptoms, but they are not nearly as severe as heroin withdrawal symptoms and they do not appear for about 24 hours after the last dose, as opposed to about 5 hours for heroin. Best of all, the heroin addict on a methadone program can function normally in the community. Although addicts retain their physical dependence on a narcotic (methadone), they defeat their psychological craving for heroin and no longer have to engage in criminal activity to avoid withdrawal.

If psychological craving for heroin exists, narcotic antagonists such as Cyclazocine and naloxone are available to offset the craving. These antagonists block the desirable effects of heroin and, like Antabuse, should be used in conjunction with intensive counseling.

Disipramine is a new drug that has been used experimentally in the treatment of cocaine addicts. It has a claimed success rate in keeping addicts from craving the drug for up to nine months. This is quite an advance over the use of other methods, which have reported records of only fifteen days (Hazleton, 1984). You should be familiar with medical facilities that dispense these antagonistic drugs in the event that you are faced with a particularly intractable client with whom all else has failed.

Don't be put off by arguments that these drugs "only treat symptoms, not the cause." The symptoms are precisely what we are most immediately concerned with. Much of medicine is concerned with "treating symptoms" while the body's natural defenses get marshaled to attack the cause. In fact, apart from the infectious diseases, medicine has very few "cures." Ailments such as heart disease and arthritis, just like alcoholism, are never cured. Drugs designed to alleviate these medical problems minimize the destructive effects of the symptoms associated with the problem on people's lives; they help them to cope.

Further, do not be disheartened by those who tell you that it is practically "impossible" to wean substance abusers successfully from their problems, or by those who will assert that voluntary acquiescence on the part of the client is "absolutely necessary" for successful treatment. Peel has written that 90% of all soldiers who served a tour in Vietnam and in whom heroin use was detected were able to give up their habits without undue discomfort. Once they were back in the United States "removed from pressures of war and once more in the presence of family and friends and opportunities for constructive activity, these men felt no need for heroin" (Peel, 1978:65). This is an instructive statement about the power of attachment, commitment, and involvement to generate responsible behavior.

Of the second pessimistic assertion, it should be said that the majority of chemically dependent people who have been successfully treated were somehow forced into treatment against their wills. They did not necessarily want to discontinue their chemical usage, but certain crises in their lives forced them to accept help. Certainly, being involved with the criminal justice system because of substance abuse should be crisis enough to generate the beginnings of motivation in the client.

Summary

This chapter addresses the two most common problems you will encounter in corrections: alcoholism and drug abuse. We differentiated between the alcoholic and the problem drinker in terms of the physiological dependency of the alcoholic. Jellinek's four stages of alcoholic progression—prealcoholic, prodromal, crucial, and chronic—are not universally experienced by all problem drinkers. Only about 5% of all alcoholics ever "hit bottom" and arrive at Skid Row.

The latest scientific evidence on the cause of alcoholism points strongly to the role of the production and metabolism of acetaldehyde (AcH). Antabuse, a drug used in treating alcoholism, functions to maintain high levels of AcH in the blood stream. This causes the alcoholic to experience the "punishing" physical feelings associated with high alcohol intake. Antabuse is administered to chronic alcoholics in association with intensive psychosocial counseling.

The most successful program for counseling alcoholics is Alcoholics Anonymous. You should endeavor to place every client with a drinking problem in this wonderful organization. It provides members with all the components of a successful counseling relationship as outlined by Carl Rogers: positive regard, genuineness, and empathy.

Looking at drug abuse and addiction, we noted that drug users bear the additional burden of the illegality of their practices and that crime is associated with drug addiction largely because of the high cost of drugs. Many more drug users become addicted than do users of alcohol.

The depressants such as heroin tend to be used most by those people who desire an escape from the pains of life. It is extremely difficult to overcome the heroin habit, but Peel's statement regarding the soldiers who used heroin in Vietnam but who kicked it on their return to the United States is a powerful one about the value of attachment, commitment, and involvement.

The stimulants have the opposite effect. Whereas the users of depressants are "laid back," the stimulant users are hyperaroused and sensitive to their environments. Methamphetamine users are especially prone to violence when they are "wired." Cocaine appears to be the most popular and rewarding drug of all, and the emergence of crack in recent times has removed class boundaries from the use of cocaine.

The hallucinogens, such as marijuana and LSD, are not quite so problematic for the corrections counselor. Their relative cheapness does not necessitate criminal activity for their acquisition, and their effects do not ordinarily make their users prone to violence.

The assessment and treatment of drug addicts is much like that of alcoholics. Narcotics Anonymous functions in much the same way as AA, and there exist narcotic antagonistic drugs that are analogous to Antabuse. Methadone (for heroin addiction) is the best known of these drugs. Don't fall for the "only treating symptoms" or the pessimistic "once an addict, always an addict" arguments. The symptoms of alcoholism and drug addiction are what we are most immediately concerned with, and pessimism has a way of becoming a self-fulfilling prophecy.

References and Suggested Readings

Applewhite, P. (1981). *Molecular Gods: How Molecules Determine Our Behavior.* Englewood Cliffs, NJ: Prentice-Hall.

Billet, S. (1974). "Antabuse therapy." In R. Cantanzaro (Ed.), *Alcoholism: The Total Treatment Approach.* Springfield, IL: Charles C Thomas.

Brown, B., G. Benn, and D. Jansen, (1975). "Methadone maintenance: Some client opinions." *American Journal of Psychiatry,* 132:623–628.

Chafetz, M., and H. Demone. (1972). *Alcoholism and Society.* New York: Oxford University Press.

Chein, I., G. Gerhard, R. Lee, and E. Rosenfeld. (1964). *The Road to H: Narcotics, Delinquency and Social Policy.* New York: Basic Books.

Clinard, M., and R. Quinney. (1973). *Criminal Behavior Systems: A Typology.* New York: Holt, Rinehart & Winston.

Glasser, W. (1975). *Reality Therapy.* New York: Harper & Row.

Hartman, H. (1978). *Basic Psychiatry for Corrections Workers.* Springfield, IL: Charles C Thomas.

Hazleton, L. (1984). "Cocaine and the chemical brain." *Science Digest,* 92:58–66.

Jellinek, E. (1960). *The Disease Concept of Alcoholism.* New Haven, CT: Hillside Press.

Keller, M., and C. Gurioli. (1976). *Statistics on Consumption of Alcohol and on Alcoholism.* New Brunswick, NJ: Rutgers Center of Alcohol Studies.

Liebowitz, M. (1983). *The Chemistry of Love.* New York: Berkley Books.

Peel, S. (1978). "Addiction: The analgesic experience." *Human Nature,* 1 (September):61–66.

The President's Commission on Law Enforcement and Administration of Justice (1967). *Task Force Report: Drunkenness, Annotations, Consultant's Papers, and Related Materials.* Washington, DC: U. S. Government Printing Office.

Reichman, W. (1978). *Alcoholism and Career Development.* New York: Baruch College, CUNY.

Restak, R. (1979). *The Brain: The Last Frontier.* New York: Warner.

Rosenfeld, A. (1981). "Tippling enzymes." *Science,* 81, 2:24-25.

Selzer, M. L. (1971, revised 1980). "The Michigan Alcoholism Screening Test (MAST): The quest for a new diagnostic instrument." *American Journal of Psychiatry,* 127:1653–1658 (1971).

Stencel, S. (1973). "Resurgence of alcoholism." *Editorial Research Reports,* 2 (December) 990–991.

Taylor, L. (1984). *Born to Crime.* Westport, CT: Greenwood.

Walker, S. (1985). *Sense and Nonsense about Crime: A Policy Guide.* Pacific Grove, CA: Brooks/Cole.

Winick, C. (1986). "The Alcohol Offender." In H. Toch (Ed.), *Psychology of Crime and Criminal Justice.* Prospect Heights, IL: Waveland Press.

Chapter 11 Appendix

TERMS ASSOCIATED WITH ALCOHOL AND DRUG ADDICTION

AA Alcoholics Anonymous

alcoholic paranoia a delusional system suffered by some alcoholics; feelings of being persecuted and plotted against

alkie alcoholic

acid LSD

acid head user of LSD

angel dust PCP

bad trip unpleasant experience after taking a drug

bag or **baggie** small packet of drugs, usually marijuana

barbs barbiturates

big D LSD

big chief mescaline, a hallucinogen

black beauties black capsule containing caffeine and phenylopropanolamine, often sold as **speed**

black tar about 50% pure heroin; looks like chunk of tar

blaze LSD or acid

blackout temporary loss of memory from drinking alcohol

bummer unpleasant experience after taking a drug, not as unpleasant as a bad trip

buzz minor degree of euphoria after taking a drug

chasing the dragon smoking cocaine

coke cocaine

connection drug peddler

confabulation pseudomemory associated with alcoholism; the person reminisces about things that never occurred

cook up a pill to smoke opium

cooker spoon used for dissolving heroin over a flame

crack ready-to-smoke, freebased cocaine (also known as **rock**)

crash to come down hard from a drug experience

crystal methamphetamine

cut to adulterate drugs with another substance such as milk-sugar

detox detoxification, the process of ridding the body of toxicants

dexie Dexedrine, a stimulant

double trouble Tuinal, a sedative

downers all kinds of depressants—alcohol, barbiturates, etc.

dried out withdrawn from alcohol or drugs

drivers amphetamines

DTs delirium tremens, extreme bodily tremors experienced by alcoholics withdrawing from alcohol; often accompanied by terrifying hallucinations

dynamite mixture of heroin and cocaine

fix a dose or shot of a narcotic

flash sudden euphoria after injection of heroin or methamphetamine

freak out temporary psychotic reaction after using hallucinogens

freebase process of freeing cocaine from its "cut." Purifying and smoking cocaine

fruit salad taking a mixture of different kinds of pills, often with alcohol as a chaser

hash hashish, most potent source of THC, pure resin of the cannabis plant

high   under the influence of drugs

hit   dose of drugs or drag on a marijuana cigarette

hooked   addicted

horse   heroin

jolly beans   pep pills

joint   marijuana cigarette

joy pop   injecting drugs under the skin

junkie   narcotics addict

key   short for kilo; 2.2 pounds of any drug

kick   break the drug habit

lid   street measure of marijuana; makes about 40 joints

lude   methaqualone, a depressant drug

mainlining   injecting drugs directly into the veins

Mexican brown   high-grade marijuana from Mexico

microdot   small round pill of LSD

pep pills   amphetamines

pink ladies   Seconal, a barbiturate drug

pot   marijuana; **pot, hay, grass, weed, reefer, tea, maggies,** and **Mary Jane** are all street synonyms

red devils, or **reds**   Seconal, a barbiturate drug

roach clip   any device used to hold a marijuana cigarette

rush   warm euphoric feeling after injecting heroin

rush   Amyl/Butyl/Nitrate, an inhalant that produces a hallucinogenic effect

scag   heroin

score   buy drugs

score   buy drugs

schroom   psilocybin mushroom, a hallucinogen

seccy   Seconal, a barbiturate

shakes   beginning stages of the DTs

shoot up   inject drugs

shooting gallery   place to shoot up drugs

snow   cocaine

stoned   under the influence of drugs

STP   a synthetic hallucinogen: "serenity, tranquility, peace"

THC   tetrahydrocannabinol, the active ingredient in hashish and marijuana

tracks   collapsed veins from frequent drug injections

trip   an experience with a hallucinogenic drug

wasted   heavily under the influence of alcohol or drugs

water pipe   pipe used to smoke drugs

Wernicke-Korsakoff syndrome   a condition associated with alcoholism and thought to be due to extreme Vitamin B deficiency. The syndrome is characterized by amnesia, distortion of memory, and disorientation of time and place. Sometimes called **Korsakoff psychosis.**

wet brain   neurological condition of a long-term alcoholic; sometimes used inaccurately as a synonym for Wernicke-Korsakoff syndrome

wired   high, especially on methamphetamine

THE MICHIGAN ALCOHOLISM SCREENING TEST

Points		Yes	No
	0. Do you enjoy a drink now and then?	—	—
(2)	*1. Do you feel that you are a normal drinker? (By normal we mean you drink less than or as much as other people.)	—	—
(2)	2. Have you ever awakened the morning after some drinking the night before and found that you could not remember a part of the evening?	—	—
(1)	3. Does your wife, husband, parent, or other near relative ever worry or complain about your drinking?	—	—
(2)	*4. Can you stop drinking without a struggle after one or two drinks?	—	—
(1)	5. Do you ever feel guilty about your drinking?	—	—
(2)	*6. Do friends or relatives think you are a normal drinker?	—	—
(2)	*7. Are you able to stop drinking when you want to?	—	—
(5)	8. Have you ever attended a meeting of Alcoholics Anonymous (AA)?	—	—
(1)	9. Have you ever gotten into physical fights when drinking?	—	—
(2)	10. Has your drinking ever created problems between you and your wife, husband, parent, or other relative?	—	—
(2)	11. Has your wife, husband, or another family member ever gone to anyone for help about your drinking?	—	—
(2)	12. Have you ever lost friends because of your drinking?	—	—
(2)	13. Have you ever gotten into trouble at work or school because of drinking?	—	—
(2)	14. Have you ever lost a job because of drinking?	—	—
(2)	15. Have you ever neglected your obligations, your family, or your work for 2 or more days in a row because you were drinking?	—	—

Points			Yes	No
(1)	16. Do you drink before noon fairly often?		—	—
(2)	17. Have you ever been told you have liver trouble? Cirrhosis?			
(2)	**18. After heavy drinking have you ever had delirium tremens (D.T.'s) or severe shaking or heard voices or seen things that really weren't there?		—	—
(5)	19. Have you ever gone to anyone for help about your drinking?		—	—
(5)	20. Have you ever been in hospital because of drinking?		—	—
(2)	21. Have you ever been a patient in a psychiatric hospital or on a psychiatric ward of a general hospital where drinking was part of the problem that resulted in hospitalization?		—	—
(2)	22. Have you ever been seen at a psychiatric or mental health clinic or gone to any doctor, social worker, or clergyman for help with any emotional problem, where drinking was part of the problem?		—	—
(2)	***23. Have you ever been arrested for drunk driving, driving while intoxicated, or driving under the influence of alcoholic beverages? (If yes, how many times? ———)		—	—
(2)	***24. Have you ever been arrested, or taken into custody, even for a few hours, because of other drunk behavior? (If yes, how many times? ———)		—	—

Scoring system: In general, five points or more would place the subject in an alcoholic category, four points would be suggestive of alcoholism, and three points or less would indicate the subject was not alcoholic.

Source: M. L. Selzer, 1971–1980.
  *Alcoholic response is negative.
 **Five points for delirium tremens.
***Two points for each arrest.

Chapter 12

Dealing with Offenders Having Personal Disorders

Our task now is to begin to understand that the causes of mental health problems are as varied as their manifestations. Some are physical. Some are emotional. Some are rooted in social and environmental conditions. Most are a complex combination of these and other factors, some of which are unknown.

President's Commission on Mental Health

Sex Offenders

Sexual offenses encompass such a wide range of behaviors that you may reasonably question the wisdom of placing all of them in a single category. After all, the exhibitionist is as different from the rapist as the check forger is from the armed robber. If you live in a state that has antisodomy laws, you might even be guilty of felonious behavior for which you could be imprisoned if you engage in certain sexual acts, even with your consenting spouse. However, we will be concerned just with those sexual offenses that involve a true offender/victim relationship, such as rape and child molesting; that is, behavior that is almost universally considered to be a serious breach of lawful behavior rather than relatively mild deviations from sanctioned behavior.

Sex and American Society

The sex offender and his (sex offenders are almost invariably male) behavior have to be viewed in the context of his culture. Few things interest Americans more than sex. The culture is shot through with sexual themes. Billions of dollars are spent every year on cosmetics, hair styling, breath mints, health spas, and so forth, to make us appear sexually attractive. Ears are pierced, lips painted, underarms sprayed, necklines lowered, and skirts raised, and young men advertise their wares by pouring themselves into shrunken jeans. Goaded on by the wizards of Madison Avenue, many of us have fallen prey to the notion that we are less than good Americans if we are not supremely sexual beings.

Counteracting this pressure toward sexual expression is the highly puritanical strain that exists in American culture. It has been somewhat exaggeratedly said that, with the exception of John Calvin's Geneva, the United States has the most moralistic criminal code that the world has ever seen (Morris & Hawkins, 1969:15). The sensitivity of the American legal system to sexual behavior, extending even into the marital bed, is made evident by Robertson (1977:196): "The laws [pertaining to sex] have few parallels in the modern world outside of the Soviet Union and some of its satellites. Western European nations have generally abandoned similar legislation, in some cases as long as a century ago." Thus, Americans are simultaneously pushed toward sexual expression by a permissively erotic market and then pulled back again by a restrictive code of sexual morality. It is against this background that the sex offender is defined and punished.

The Public Image of the Sex Offender

We Americans don't like sex offenders very much. We are convinced that the sex criminal is "insane or mentally retarded; that he is brutal, depraved, immoral and oversexed. He is a social isolate who spends his time reading dirty books or haunting dirty movies; a godless, brainless fellow, a 'dirty old man,' crippled or disfigured, dope addicted, and incurable" (Cohen & Boucher, 1972:57). Put otherwise, the general public sees the sex offender as an inhuman "species apart," either a "super male" in an interminable state of tumescence or a pathetic and evil old man searching for sparks of sensuality in the unwilling arms of a child. Although such characteristics are occasionally true, the criminal justice worker must not harbor such stereotypes.

No common denominator distinguishes all sex offenders. A sex offender can be everything from a sexual sadist who uses his penis to defile and degrade his victim to the gentle and unassuming church deacon who "playfully" touches a neighborhood child where he shouldn't. There are cer-

tainly differences between the sex offender whose passion for his new date exceeds her expectations and the rapist who attacks with equal intensity the nubile homecoming queen and the octogenarian cripple—differences that will affect your recommendations and treatment strategies. Likewise, we should not treat equally the father who, because of some extreme circumstances, sexually molests his daughter on a single occasion and the father who feels that he has the lordly "right of the first night" with a succession of his offspring.

Rape and Rapists

Forcible rape is defined in the FBI's Uniform Crime Reports as "the carnal knowledge of a female forcibly and against her will" (FBI, 1986:15). According to this report, there were 87,340 reported rapes in 1985, up 3.7% from the previous year. Rape is perhaps the most underreported of all crimes, probably because of the fear and embarrassment suffered by its victims. There is no doubt that rape is an excruciatingly traumatic event for its victims, the effects of which may last long after any physical scars have healed.

The views of the rapist in the professional literature run the gamut, with many of the opinions being strongly colored by such nonobjective factors as personal morality and sexual politics. Each view, of course, fits some rapists, but no view fits all rapists. There are those who regard rape as being symptomatic of some dark psychological disturbances and others who see it simply as part of a complex of cultural values that emphasize macho masculinity, aggression, and sexual violence. The first of these views is exemplified by the work of Drzasga, who explains rape as an act performed by "degenerate male imbeciles" seeking to satisfy "sadistic and aggressive desires for sexual dominance" (1960:57). In this perspective rape is a violent rather than a venereal act in which the penis is substituted for the gun or knife.

This view may be accurate in some unknown percentage of rape cases, but to ascribe such motivations across the board is to commit what philosophers call the logical fallacy of *affirming the consequent.* "Affirming the consequent" means that having observed the consequences of an action we infer that they were the motivations of the actor. Thus, we observe that the rapist asserts his dominance over his victim and in doing so humiliates, defiles, and degrades her. It is unwarranted, however, to assume that this outcome necessarily constituted his motivations for attacking her.

In relation to this point, we often hear the assertion that "there is nothing sexual about rape." In fact, if intercourse was accomplished, the sexual component of the attack is the only component of which we can always be sure—everything else is conjecture. We have no direct access to a rapist's motivations; perhaps he himself doesn't really understand what they were. Many rapists in prison will eventually respond to a counselor by saying that their motivations were to degrade and defile their victims. But do they do this because those were indeed their motivations, or do they do it because they have learned that the way to obtain parole points is to tell officials what they think officials want to hear? Is it really only coincidence that sophisticated criminals always seem to explain their behavior in accordance with the contemporary academic explanation? I think not.

All this is by way of saying that I believe that the majority of rapes are motivated by misdirected and misguided sexual needs rather than by dark, sadistic, and disturbed psychological motivations far removed from sex. It is readily granted, however, that male dominance feelings are an integral part of sexual relations, whether consensual or otherwise. Perhaps rape is best viewed as a fusion of sex and aggression, with sex being primary in some cases and aggression in others. As a criminal justice worker, you will be doing your clients a disservice if you succumb uncritically to pat interpretations that sound esoteric but may well be empty.

The other dominant interpretation of rape, more sociological in orientation, is exemplified by the position of Ploscowe. He sees rapists as "men who are simply following the pattern of racial and cultural behavior with which they are familiar" (1968:205). This view is supplemented by the writing of feminist theorists Clark and Lewis, who view rape as indicative of a general hatred of women that characterizes the behavior of "normal" adult men (1977:140). Although this is a somewhat gratuitously harsh view of all men in general, and of lower-class males in particular, it is one that sees rape as little more than an occasional and unfortunate manifestation of a general principle defining the relationship between the sexes.

Having dealt with hundreds of sex offenders both in the field and as a researcher, I find that Ploscowe's view comes closest to my experience. Most rapes involve offenders and victims who are acquainted with one another. In *general* terms, many men I dealt with who were convicted of rape under these circumstances were indeed enamored of traditional masculine values. They valued sexual prowess and tended to hold the "whore/madonna" image of women. They had difficulty understanding how their victims could be so ungrateful as to accuse them of rape. They felt that once a woman's initial protestations have been overcome in a forceful "masculine" way, just like the style of the romantic heroes in the movies, then she should just melt into their arms. After all, in the world of veiled sexual messages it is common knowledge to them that no really means yes.

Here is an excerpt from a PSI report in which the processing officer is commenting on the statement of a defendant convicted of raping his sister-in-law. This defendant came home drunk one night (rape is often associated with alcohol), dragged his 17-year-old sister-in-law into his bedroom, told his sleeping wife to get up and get out, and proceeded to rape his victim.

It is clear from the defendant's explicit statement that he does not deny the charge. On the contrary, one almost gets the impression that he rather enjoyed writing his statement, which depicts him as an accomplished lover and mentor to the sexually naive. "How can this be rape?" he asks in an aggrieved tone of voice. He believes that his amorous designs were pursued fully in accord with the rules of the game; i.e., in the "masculine" way of his subculture. For him the crime was little more than an "assault with a friendly weapon." It strains this officer's imagination to think of the defendant as venting his sexual passions on an unwilling girl whose mother was in the next room fully aware of what was going on. Not only that, he had the audacity to ask his wife to vacate her bed so that he could do his thing in comfort.

Rapists such as this young man use aggression as a means to an end, not as an end in itself. Many of them might not have gone on to complete the act if they did not harbor stereotypes of women as sexual playthings who "really" want to "be taken," even if they do put up a little token resistance. Many date rapes and acquaintance rapes would not occur if males who engage in this kind of behavior rid themselves of such stereotypes. Females would also do well to divest themselves of their own stereotypes of femininity. Talking to many victims of date and acquaintance rape often reveals that they tend to be passive, nonassertive types with traditional views of the relationship between the sexes. Counselors at rape crisis centers will frequently state that many rapes can be avoided if women forcefully assert their rights to their own bodies.

There are those rapists who do become more sexually aroused when victims fight back. They may prefer violent to consensual sex, and their primary motive may well be to defile and humiliate. Such rapes tend to be stranger rapes and are thus more terrifying and physically injurious to the victim. Rapists of this type tend to have marked feelings of inadequacy and inferiority (Hartman, 1978:230) and powerlessness (Thio, 1978:139), and, unlike the typical date or acquaintance rapist, tend to have histories of other violent crimes (Adler, 1984:163).

Most studies of rapists concentrate on the violent rapist. We do know with relative certainty that among these subjects violence is an important component of the sexual excitement they obtain from their crimes. This pattern is determined by comparing penile responses of convicted rapists with those of nonrapists when exposed to sexual stimuli with a strong violence content. Penile response is measured by a device

called a plethysmograph, which is rather like a blood pressure gauge. The plethysmograph measures the pressure of blood in the penis to ascertain how sexually excited subjects become when exposed to auditory and/or visual stimuli depicting violent sexual situations. Violent rapists become significantly more aroused than nonrapists or nonviolent rapists when exposed to this material (Barbaree, Marshall, & Lantheir, 1979; Quinsey & Chaplin, 1982).

Such findings do seem to indicate that the violent rapist is "sick" in that he apparently needs violence in order to complete the sexual act. Strangely enough, rape is not listed as a sexual deviation in the DSM-III of the American Psychiatric Association (APA). The APA apparently doesn't see any clearly defined syndrome associated with rape that could be called *rapism* in the same way that they identify conditions like exhibitionism and pedophilia (Hartman, 1978:279). Violent rapists may simply be violent men who take what they want, whether it be money or sex. Their sexual offenses appear to be part of a pattern of violent criminality. My personal opinion is that the criminal justice worker's primary concern should be the safety of the public. Accordingly, individuals who exhibit patterns of violent behavior should be placed in custodial care for as long as the law allows.

A statistical look at stranger versus date/acquaintance rape. My data on sex offenders reveal some remarkable differences between stranger and date/acquaintance rape (Walsh, 1983). Victims of stranger rape were significantly older, ranging in age from 15 to 71. The age range of victims of date/acquaintance rape was much smaller (14 through 44). Stranger rapists had significantly more serious prior records, were of significantly lower class, and were significantly younger (an average of 22 years versus an average of 31). Eighty percent of the victims of stranger rape were physically harmed, as opposed to 33.3% of the date/acquaintance category; 73% used some kind of weapon, as opposed to 21% of the others; and 66.7% were drug and/or alcohol addicts, as opposed to 12% of the others. These findings are

Case Study

Portrait of a Sex Offender

Tony was a tall, good-looking man with an IQ of 119. He also had an attractive wife and a five-year-old son. Nevertheless, his work record was extremely poor. He was mainly a casual laborer. He never kept a job very long because he always seemed to get into an argument with his bosses and get fired or quit. After losing a job he would go on short drinking binges. Despite his rather quick temper, his wife said that he was never abusive to her or their young son.

I first met Tony after his conviction for gross sexual imposition. He had been driving around one day in the rain after a minor drinking bout when he came upon two children—a girl age 12 and a boy age 11—standing at a bus stop in the rain. Tony stopped and offered them a ride, which they accepted. The children later said they had accepted because they had just missed one bus, it was raining heavily, and they apparently felt safety in numbers.

After some small talk, Tony took the children into an alley and told them both to take their clothes off. The children refused and started to cry. Tony then called the children "little fuckers" and proceeded to force his hand up the dress of the girl and stick his fingers in her vagina. He also fondled the boy's penis and told them both to keep quiet. The young boy was able to escape and shout for help from a nearby construction gang, who apprehended Tony and held him for the police.

Tony told me that his initial motive was simply to get the children out of the rain. Once the children were in the car, "I felt an overwhelming urge to expose myself to them." He admitted frequently exposing himself to children standing at bus stops in the past, and he had two prior convictions for such behavior. He admitted telling the young girl to remove her blouse: "It gave me a feeling of mastery. But I knew she wouldn't do it because of modesty." He denied touching the girl's vagina or the boy's penis.

My investigation led me to discover a rape conviction in another state that was not on Tony's FBI rap sheet. He reluctantly admitted this conviction to me, but said that he was wrongfully convicted. This turned out to be the truth, much to my surprise. He has been granted a full governor's pardon and $2000 compensation for the three years he spent in prison for his conviction. Tony's wife informed me that he had told her that he had been frequently raped in prison, which he described as "a whore house where the only thing missing was the women." She felt that many of his sexual problems stemmed from his prison experience.

Tony had self-referred himself to a private psychiatrist after his arrest and bail. This psychiatrist wrote that Tony's pedophilia was of recent origin, and that with "intensive psychotherapy it would never reach a stage of chronicity." He felt that Tony's desire to expose himself to children was caused by "deep-seated resentment of his mother's early

rejection of him" (he was essentially "thumbing his penis" at his mother). The psychiatrist recommended that Tony be placed on probation and that the county pay for his therapy.

For my part, I reasoned that Tony had kidnapped, terrified, and sexually molested two young children and that nothing less than incarceration could be justified. The judge reasoned otherwise, and placed Tony on probation on the condition that he continue treatment and spend 60 days in jail. Tony did not continue therapy with his psychiatrist. Instead he opted to attend group counseling at the court diagnostic and treatment center and individual counseling with me.

For a variety of reasons, not the least, I suppose, being his ability to make intelligent conversation, Tony's case fascinated and challenged me. During one session in which we were discussing his prison experiences, he told me that other inmates had ridiculed him about the size of his penis and how this used to devastate him (he never even divulged to his psychiatrist that he had been incarcerated). Further discussion led to his telling me that he had measured his erect penis at five inches.

I then changed directions somewhat to discuss the possibility that his urge to expose himself to children may have stemmed from an exaggerated concern for the size of his penis. To a young child, an erect adult penis seems gigantic. Tony acknowledged that perhaps he was trying to reassure himself about the adequacy of his penis by shocking his victims with its erect enormity to compensate for the cruel hazing he had received about it from his fellow inmates.

Latching onto what I thought might be a crucial piece of information, I assigned Tony some rational-emotive therapy "homework." I instructed him to go to the public library and check out three textbooks on human anatomy and physiology. From these books, he was to look up information on the size of the normal male erect penis. He signed a plan saying that he would do this the following morning. The assignment led to Tony's discovery that 90% of all males have an erect penis of between five and one-half and six and one-half inches, meaning that Tony was just one-half inch short of "normalcy."

This discovery provided for a fruitful evaluation of just how irrational it was for Tony to get himself into so much trouble for the sake of one-half inch of floppy flesh that no one but him and his wife would ever see if he didn't expose himself. He was guided to view his self-esteem in terms of his good looks, his high intelligence, and the love of his supportive wife and dependent child.

Over the next few months, Tony reported that he had experienced urges to expose himself again. However, he had not done so because he reminded himself of the irrationality of the act and of his responsibilities to his family. Tony successfully completed three years of probation without further trouble with the law. I monitored the daily arrest sheet for the two remaining years I spent in probation without ever seeing his name on it. I ran into his wife one day at a shopping center. She told me that everything was going fine, that Tony had been at his job for over a year, that he had drastically cut down on his drinking, and that there didn't seem to be any residual sexual problems. Tony's was the kind of case that made me feel glad and proud to have been a probation officer, and, for once, glad that my recommendation to the court had perhaps been wrong.

---

consistent with other such studies and emphasize the quantitative differences that can exist among acts of rape and its perpetrators.

Assessment and treatment. The assessment and treatment of sexual offenders is almost always conducted by mental health teams. Treatment for the violent rapist is extremely difficult and the results discouraging. Many treatments such as aversive conditioning (a method of treatment by which an offender is shown sexually arousing pictures in conjunction with some sort of punishment, such as an electric shock) have been drastically curtailed in the United States because of civil rights considerations. Therapeutic castration has been tried in some states (Indiana, for one) but has been discontinued, even if the offender requests it, for the same reasons. It remains to be seen how the courts will ultimately view chemical castration by the use of the drug Depo-Provera®. This drug works by reducing the offender's level of testosterone, the male sex hormone, thereby diminishing his arousal or responsiveness to sexuality and violence. It has been reliably established that violent male criminals have significantly higher levels of testosterone in their bodies than nonviolent male criminals (Kreuz & Rose, 1972). As a corrections worker you will rarely be involved in the treatment of the violent rapist.

Whereas the violent rapist is nearly always incarcerated, the date or acquaintance rapist tends to get probation more often than imprisonment. The treatment of the latter type of rapist while on probation should center around group counseling sessions in which stereotypical images of women are brought out into the open and discussed. Educating males to accept women as equals who have the right to say no can go a long way toward preventing a recurrence. Exercises such as the one concerning the victim experience in the chapter on institutional counseling can be fruitfully used here. Movies can be shown that reveal the psychological trauma that accompanies rape. It is better yet to have a rape victim speak to the group about her experience and about how it affected her life. Select the victim carefully, however. You don't want one who flays the group and denigrates all men because of her experience. Although such a response from a victim is quite understandable, the group will act defensively against her and refuse to take her seriously. Local rape crisis centers usually have a number of strong victims willing to talk to various groups about their experiences in a dispassionate way. Needless to say, if alcohol was involved in the incident, attention to that problem area should also be part of the offender's treatment.

Child Molesters

Our definition of a child molester is consistent with the definition offered by McCaghy (1967:78): a male over the age of 18 who manipulates the genitals of a child of 13 or younger, or has the child manipulate his. A child molester may or may not be a true pedophile (a person who is literally a "lover of children" and whose sexually orientation is toward them). Most individuals convicted of molesting children apparently prefer adult sex but have opportunistically taken advantage of a child. Some child molesters are offenders who take advantage of any form of sexual gratification immediately available to them, regardless of age, sex, or even at times, of species. Child molestation tends to be associated with three age categories: the teen years, the mid- to late thirties, and the midfifties on (Hartman, 1978:213–214).

Teenage molesters tend to be socially withdrawn and of lower intelligence than the average teenager. These young molesters rarely attempt intercourse. Sexual activity tends to take the form of kissing and the manual manipulation of the genitals. The victim is most often known to the offender, and the act can be viewed as a form of sexual curiosity on the part of a teenager who is too self-effacing to attempt to satisfy it with consenting persons of his own age.

Those offenders in their mid- to late thirties are more likely than not to be married. Quite often the victim is a stepchild of the offender. Not in-

frequently, the molestation can go on for quite some time. The offender usually is able to maintain the ongoing "relationship" by telling his victim that the child's mother would get mad if she found out, or that the child would probably be placed in a juvenile detention center or a foster home if the offense became known. The initial act of molestation is likely to occur when the offender finds himself unemployed for an extended period of time, has been drinking, or finds that his normal sex life has soured. My study of child molesters found that 34.3% of them were unemployed at the time of their offense (Walsh, 1985). This is about five times the average unemployment rate for males over a six-year period in the jurisdiction from which the data were obtained.

The molester of 55 and older is usually a man without any prior contact with the law. He may have recently suffered the loss of his wife by death or divorce and finds himself quite lonely. It is extremely rare that such offenders will use any kind of force to gain compliance. They will usually use promises of rewards such as money or candy to persuade victims to do their bidding. As with teenage molesters, but not middle-aged molesters, actual intercourse rarely figures in the sexual activity of this group. They are usually deeply ashamed and remorseful when their activity is discovered, and they are the least likely of all offenders to offend again.

Homosexual molesters tend more to be true pedophiles than are their heterosexual counterparts. My study (Walsh, 1985) found that 34.7% of the homosexual molesters were diagnosed as pedophiles, as opposed to 13.2% of the heterosexuals. They were also more likely to be strangers to their victims (26.5%, versus only 4.8% of the heterosexual offenders). On the one hand, homosexual offenders were much less likely (4.1%) to use force or the threat of force to gain compliance than were the heterosexuals (19.2%). On the other hand, they were more than twice as likely to have a prior conviction for molesting (49% versus 22.1%). However, in 41.6% of those prior "homosexual" molestations, the victims were females. It may be thus more accurate to call these men bisexual pedophiles.

Perspectives from the Field

Tula Starck is a Boise State University graduate in criminal justice. She has field experience in a community services program for offenders, in probation and parole, and as a counselor in a sex abuse program called Sexual Abuse Now Ended (SANE).

Counseling Sex Offenders: The Thoughts of a "SANE" Counselor
Tula M. Starck

Only recently has the problem of sexual abuse been pulled from under the carpet where it had been swept by embarrassed families and law enforcement alike. In response to this belated house cleaning, a comprehensive community-based treatment and prevention program for sex offenders and their victims was instituted in the Third Judicial District of Idaho. This program is called Sexual Abuse Now Ended, or SANE. I like to tell people that I'm a "sane" counselor.

Counseling sex offenders requires unusual people. The capacity for empathy must exist, but a tough outlook, the ability to recognize a con, and the capacity to confront clients are essential. Before beginning with SANE, I spent many months with probation and parole researching sex offenders' case files. I was accepted as part of the agency's family and would often accompany officers on home visits and sit in on their talks with their sex offender clients. I learned to expect anything and be outwardly shocked by nothing. I learned that the sex abuser and the sexually abused could be anyone. He or she can be your neighbor, your doctor, the Skid Row bum, the girl or boy next to you in the church choir, the introvert or the extrovert.

After years of study, numerous lectures on sexual abuse, many research papers, and interviewing both abusers and the abused, I was still not adequately prepared for working with sex offenders on a daily basis. I had not counted on my own emotional involvement. I'd heard countless people make statements about abusers such as "Why not use a .22? It's cheaper!" A part of me used to agree with this "solution," but the bigger part of me believes that there's a salvageable part to every human being.

In my work with SANE I've discovered that there's no typical day. I've seen mothers bring in children from 1 to 18 years of age. All forms of sexual misconduct have been perpetrated on these children. Some of these children react by abusing others, some live in fear, some don't speak. Almost all regard themselves as guilty and worthless. We work with these children in group and individual counseling. There is also counseling for nonoffending spouses. We have found that a high percentage of nonoffending spouses were themselves abused as children.

My main function with SANE is as a cotherapist working with adult male offenders. Each day I go over case files trying to understand the offenders I will be working with. I'm mostly looking for each client's defense mechanisms, the methods by which they deny, fog, or excuse their behavior. Their abilities to negate responsibility for their acts are amazing. Many tend to be powerless and low-self-esteem individuals who seek even more powerless individuals as targets for sexual assault. They use sex as an avenue to boost their feelings of power and control. They drain their victims of self-respect and create a feeling of helplessness in them.

Perspectives from the Field *(continued)*

I feel that group counseling is the best tool we have. New offending clients are confronted not only by the counselor but also by "veteran" clients who have come to recognize warped thinking patterns. New clients in these programs are angry, afraid, and defensive. But the program is working because the offenders have to attend as conditions of their probation or parole. They are given short-term and long-term goals on a daily basis. It's a painful process for them because they have to look at themselves realistically again and again. They must become aware of their responsibility and their dysfunctional thinking and behavior. They are confronted with their needs for instant gratification and excitement. When they lie, they are confronted with that lie. For the first time in their lives they are made aware of their responsibility for their actions and of the consequences those actions have for their victims.

There are many stages that they have to pass through. It is only through successfully passing each of these stages that they can get out of the program. Reading assignments and reports are mandatory. Daily journals are kept. These journals are inspected by the staff and are often read aloud during group sessions. A clarification process is hoped for— a process in which the offender comes to understand his behavior by writing down a description of each act of abuse and why it was perpetrated. If the victim agrees to meet with the offender in the presence of the counselor, the victim shares his or her feelings and questions with the offender. It is hoped that both offender and victim benefit from these meetings—the offender by acknowledging total responsibility, and the victim, by hearing this acknowledgment, ridding himself or herself of guilt.

I hope to make the counseling of sexual abusers and victims my life's work. I have found it so rewarding for two major reasons. First, I'm helping to fight this national ailment through education and counseling. Second, each day and each client present a new challenge. You won't get bored in this business.

Rapists versus Child Molesters

As Groth (1979:151) points out, both rapists and child molesters are threatened by normal adult sexuality. The difference is that the rapist attacks the source of the threat and the child molester retreats from it by turning to safer substitutes. It is not unusual to see cases in which an offender carried on an affectionate "affair" with a child for long periods of time. The emotional investment appears quite often to extend beyond sexuality. However misdirected the attachment, the child is valued as a person and a "lover." In contrast, the target for the rapist is just an object or symbol upon whose body he seeks to satisfy his selfish needs. It is rare that the child molester attempts sexual penetration, whereas such penetration, as the primeval symbol of conquest, is the ultimate aim of the rapist. Only 14% of my sample of child molesters vaginally or anally penetrated their victims, as opposed to 69% of the combined stranger and date/acquaintance rapists. Oral sex (61%) was the primary kind of sexual activity engaged in by the child molesters, with 25% having only manual sexual contact with their victims.

Among other interesting comparisons, the rapists had significantly more serious criminal histories despite being significantly younger (average age 28 versus an average of 37 for the molesters). The child molesters were of significantly higher social class. Occupationally, molesters ranged from laborers to ministers and physicians. The rapists were almost all in lower-status occupations, if working at all. Seventy-two percent of the molesters had been married at some stage in their lives, with 42% being married at the time of their offenses. The identical marriage figures for the rapists were 58% and 30%, respectively. Ninety percent of the child molesters were related to or acquainted with their victims, as opposed to 61% of the rapists, and 63% had had previous sexual contact with their victims, as opposed to 23.8% of the rapists. None of the molesters used a weapon, whereas 30% of the rapists did. These and many other important differences indicate the sharp line that divides the rapist from the child molester.

Most child molesters, child rapists excepted, tend to have a fairly adequate stake in conformity. If the offense was not violent or if the offender has no previous record of similar behavior indicative of an abiding interest in children as sexual targets, he can usually be considered a good probation risk. But given the level of seriousness attached to this kind of behavior, it is imperative that a thorough investigation into the offender's background be conducted prior to making any recommendations to that effect. Needless to say, the findings and recommendations of mental health professionals should be read and considered very carefully.

Schizophrenics

Schizophrenia is the most widespread of the psychotic disorders, affecting perhaps as much as 1% of the population. It is estimated that 170,000 schizophrenics live at home with their families and 120,000 are on the streets without any permanent home (Department of Health and Human Services, 1981:21–22). With an incidence of this magnitude, you can expect to have two or three offenders who have been diagnosed as schizophrenic on your caseload at any one time. Schizophrenics are extremely difficult to supervise in a community corrections setting, and they frequently end up seriously violating their conditions of probation or parole and being consigned to prison. This strikes me as a very inhumane way of dealing with clients whose ability to function conventionally is seriously and quite obviously impaired.

We should not think of schizophrenics as a homogeneous category of individuals. There are various subtypes that need not concern us here. They can also be differentiated by the degree of mental deterioration and by the pathway they took to their condition. The most severely impaired schizophrenics are hospitalized, which means that those with whom you will be dealing

are able to function outside of a mental institution. The most serious form of general schizophrenia is a condition that develops insidiously over a long period of time in so-called *process* schizophrenics. These are individuals whose histories show an early inability to function normally, to make friends, to handle school work, and to behave acceptably. *Reactive* schizophrenics may not have such early histories of psychological and social dysfunction. Their descent into schizophrenia is usually marked by the onset of an acutely stressful experience (Kantor & Herron, 1966). Bill Bloggs's "early stage of reactive schizophrenia" was no doubt related to the stress of his arrest and incarceration (sometimes termed *jailhouse psychosis*).

The "four A's" are used by mental health professionals to identify schizophrenia: *autism* (living in a subjective fantasy world), *ambivalence* (having simultaneous conflicting feelings), inappropriate *affect* (emotions and feelings that are not congruent with the situation), and loose *associations* (the connection of an experience or idea with an unrelated experience or idea). Although schizophrenia is most often diagnosed long before a client is seen by a community corrections worker, you should be on the lookout for evidence of these four A's. If you encounter them, you should make a referral to the local court diagnostic and treatment center.

Causality

The causes of schizophrenia, and even its objective existence, have long been hotly debated. In my undergraduate days, radical environmentalists dismissed it as a myth, or as a diagnostic "grab bag" used against poor people whose behavior we disapproved of. Subsequent hard evidence has shown their dismissal to be as premature as the dismissal of the psychopath as an identifiable entity. The most compelling evidence comes from the radioisotope brain scans utilizing positron emission transaxial tomography (PETT). PETT scans use computer imaging techniques similar to those of the more familiar CAT scans. Whereas CAT scans reveal information about brain structure, PETT scans provide information about brain functioning. Injecting radioactive glucose isotopes reveals a biochemical map of neurometabolism as the glucose is converted into energy. This technique produces distinct neurological maps of normal, schizophrenic, and manic-depressive individuals (Fincher, 1981:142–143). These identifiable differences in brain functioning indicate an objective physical reality corresponding to the condition we call schizophrenia.

An earlier clue to the chemical basis for schizophrenia came with the advent of the antipsychotic drugs such as Thorazine®. Thorazine works by blocking dopamine at the synapses that use it as a neurotransmitter. Schizophrenia as viewed at this level of analysis seems to be a function of one of three possible conditions: (1) an excess of dopamine, (2) a deficiency of an enzyme called monoamine oxidase, which removes dopamine by oxidation after it has performed its excitatory function, or (3) an excess of dopamine receptors in the brain (Clare, 1979). Any one of these conditions would cause the hyperstimulation characteristic of schizophrenics. It has also been noted that high doses of amphetamines can produce symptoms mimicking psychosis by stimulating the secretion of dopamine (Konner, 1982:98). If any of your clients shows schizophrenic symptoms, it may be a good idea to check his or her substance abuse history for excessive use of stimulants and hallucinogens.

As a cause of schizophrenia, an excess of dopamine receptors currently looks like one of the better bets. In comparing the dopamine receptors of 20 deceased schizophrenics and 28 deceased nonschizophrenics, Seeman and Lee (1981) found twice as many dopamine receptors in the limbic systems (the emotional area of the brain) of the schizophrenics as they did in the limbic systems of the nonschizophrenics. This excess capacity allows for a greater sensitivity within the limbic circuitry to the emotional content of the environment.

Linking the schizophrenic syndrome to brain structure and functioning does not preclude strong environmental input. The genetic endowment with which we enter the world (genotype) interacts with the environment to produce the organism we recognize as "me" (phenotype). Genes are not expressed in a vacuum; many require a particular environment in order to be expressed in the direction of their predisposition. Regardless of genetic predisposition, schizophrenia occurs in the brain, and brain structure and function are particularly sensitive to input from the environment. A common developmental picture of schizophrenics found in study after study is that they tend to come from homes lacking in security and love (Wilson and Kneisl, 1983:425). Recall how the Harlows were able experimentally to manufacture schizophreniclike behavior in their love-deprived monkeys.

It very well may be that early childhood experiences change the physical structures of our pleasure and pain centers to determine thresholds for activation and shutdown. Liebowitz (1983:46–47) is among those who think that limbic thresholds for pleasure and displeasure are determined by early experiences. If our early experiences were loving ones, our pleasure centers in the future will be easily activated. In contrast, "People in whom painful childhood experiences are constantly stirred up are experiencing bombardment of their displeasure centers, rendering them more vulnerable and more likely to experience new events as painful as well" (Liebowitz, 1983:47). This analysis certainly fits in with the withdrawal, isolation, depression, and anhedonia (inability to experience pleasure) so characteristic of the schizophrenic, and it again underscores the insidious nature of deprivation of love.

Treatment

The treatment of schizophrenics is primarily a medical concern. The criminal justice worker is involved as a community resource broker and as a medication monitor. Most schizophrenics with whom I have been involved were quite manageable and cooperative as long as they were taking their antipsychotic medication. The difficulty has always been to make sure that they take it. They are quite prone to "forgetting" their daily dose, and some who may be willing to take it one day will be unwilling to take it the next day for fear that they are being "poisoned." This problem is compounded by the fact that you cannot legally require a client to accept medical treatment. You may be able to circumvent your schizophrenic clients' ambivalence about daily pill taking by negotiating an agreement to treatment with the long-acting drug Prolixin®. This drug is injected every two or three weeks and the medication is gradually released over that time. One can usually enlist the help of a family member to drive the patient to the community health clinic for this treatment every two weeks or so.

Again, be cautioned against the old "treating symptoms rather than causes" argument. Drugs no more cure schizophrenia than insulin cures diabetes. But who would deny insulin to the diabetic? Antipsychotic drugs do for schizophrenics what insulin does for diabetics. They stabilize biological functions, and by doing so they help the sufferer to cope. They enable schizophrenics to control desires to act out their delusions. They do not, however, assist them to regain their zest for life or human warmth. Perhaps you can help them to do this.

Sometimes schizophrenics who do not suffer too severely from the disorder are able to stabilize their lives through a supportive marriage and the acquisition of some work skills. You can't play Cupid, but you can try to obtain employment for schizophrenic clients in sheltered workshops. Sheltered workshops provide an opportunity to learn work skills, gather self-esteem, and become somewhat independent in a protective work setting that is not as demanding as a regular work setting. Such work shelters also provide counseling and instruction on such work-related activities as grooming, timekeeping, work habits, following instructions and orders, and getting along with fellow employees. Most cities of any size have at least one such workshop in the community, but the final decision about admissions belongs to their administrators. If you have a client who you feel is a likely candidate for admission to a work shelter, you should accompany the client on a visit so that you can learn about the shelter's program and the administrators' reasons for granting or denying your client a place.

One thing you must remember about schizophrenics is that their perceptions of reality, how-

ever distorted, are real to them. They have withdrawn from the common reality because it is too painful and threatening, so they have a vested interest in maintaining their own. You should not argue with their reality, but this restraint does not preclude your pointing out its disadvantages or comparing it with your own reality in a gentle and reassuring manner. On no account should you validate their reality by pretending to participate in it, and you should not accept their condition as hopeless.

Glasser feels that schizophrenics, like other "deviants," are the way they are because they have not been able to fulfill their basic needs to give and receive love and to feel worthwhile. He also feels that they can be brought back to reality by an involved counselor who works by carefully graded increments to increase the individual's level of responsible behavior. The techniques for "treating" schizophrenia, according to Glasser, are exactly the same as those used with nonpsychotic clients. The counselor must demand responsible behavior from the client regardless of the label attached to him or her: "We have found over and over again that we pay the biggest price whenever we slip on the side of being too undemanding or too accepting of deviant behavior" (Glasser, 1975:163).

The Intellectually Deficient

By *intellectual deficiency* I do not mean mental retardation. The former term connotes a correctable deficiency in mental functioning; the latter connotes an impairment (possibly organic) of the ability to learn. Clients who are mentally retarded are relatively rare in criminal justice, but clients with intellectual deficiencies are not. Mentally retarded individuals are usually too well protected and too "innocent" in their outlook to engage in criminal activity. The only two mentally retarded (defined as having IQs of 65 or below) clients I can recall were both on probation for sexually molesting children. Those with intellectual deficiencies, however, are somewhat overrepresented on the criminal dockets. These people have the mental capacity to commit crimes but are lacking somewhat in the capacity to forge

Case Study

Portrait of a Schizophrenic

Greg was a frail, good-looking young man of 24 when I first met him. He had two prior convictions for misdemeanor vandalism and was in my office now convicted of felony vandalism. Greg had this nasty habit of throwing chunks of rock through plate glass windows.

He was extremely difficult to interview, for he manifested all the classic symptoms of the schizophrenic. He sat staring at me with flat affect, his hygiene was poor, and he didn't particularly care what I had to say to him. I was able to find out that his life revolved around the TV set, in front of which he spent practically every waking hour. He wasn't fussy about which programs he watched, but he was concerned that whatever channel it happened to be must not be changed. Each of his vandalism charges stemmed from arguments he had had with his mother or some other family member over changing channels. The upshot of those arguments was that his mother would throw him out of the house. When that occurred, Greg would proceed to the closest business establishment with a big glass window, put a brick through it, and sit down among the debris to await the arrival of the police. This tactic yielded him a place to sleep and another TV to stare at.

I took Greg home after the PSI interview since he had just been released from the county jail and was penniless. I also wanted to get a feel for his home environment.

Upon meeting his mother, I soon formed an opinion of her as a dominating, egocentric, and manipulative shrew. She flatly informed me that the only reason that her son was welcome in her house was his $200 monthly disability check.

His four brothers were likewise unfriendly and cruel. Since Greg was much smaller than his brothers, and a "wacko" to boot, he was a convenient target for their verbal and physical aggression. It seemed to me that rather than involving himself with those who rejected him and offered him no love, Greg had withdrawn into a semicatatonic world of dials and plastic people. The characters on the screen could not rebuff him as real people could. I came to view his reactions to channel switching as an attempt to protect somehow the existence of those benign characters on the screen.

I learned that Greg was seeing a psychiatrist at a local center who was prescribing Thorazine for him. Unfortunately, family members never made it much of their business to make sure that Greg took his medication as directed. I was able to persuade his mother to request that his psychiatrist place him on Prolixin if medically advisable, arguing that for a small investment of her time (driving Greg to the center for his injection twice a month) she could enjoy a semblance of peace in the house. And, more important for her, she could be assured of the uninterrupted flow of his disability checks. I also suggested

that to avoid future problems she might consider buying Greg his own TV set.

Greg's mother did both of these things, and peace reigned for about nine months. Greg reported at my office on time twice a month and was fairly agreeable. Visits to his home revealed to me that things were still the same in terms of the family's treatment of Greg. He was still picked on and rejected, even beaten, by other family members, even though his own behavior had improved rather remarkably.

Then I received a call from the mental health center informing me that Greg had missed his last two appointments with them. He was also a week late reporting to me. I decided to go to his home to find out what was going on. I was informed that two weeks prior to my visit Greg had gotten into a fight with his older brother and had stabbed him. Although the wound was superficial and the police had not been called, Greg panicked and fled from the house. I never heard from Greg again. Had he remained in my city, he would surely have been arrested again and I would have seen him. As far as I know, Greg is still out there somewhere among the hordes of loveless and rejected individuals who aimlessly wander the streets of our big cities. Greg's case is an example of how one's best efforts can sometimes come to less than an ideal ending. We have to accept failures as well as successes and learn from them both.

a responsible lifestyle for themselves (or the capacity not to get caught).

The link between IQ and criminal behavior has been a hot issue within sociological criminology, which has tended to avoid the issue or even to consider it a taboo topic (Gordon, 1980). It has been thus avoided because of mainstream sociology's distaste for individual differences (Hirschi & Hindelang, 1977) and especially because of the uneasy suspicion that intelligence may have a heritable component (Jeffery, 1980). A recent review of the literature on genetics and intelligence does, in fact, show across various studies that genetic variability is approximately five times more potent than environmental variability in determining IQ (Plomin & DeFries, 1980).

This finding doesn't mean that the environment does not have a profound effect on intelligence levels. Nutritional deprivation and deprivation of stimulation during infancy have a pernicious effect on intelligence. A study by Lewin (1975) comparing the IQ levels of children from nutritionally adequate and stimulus-enriched homes and children from malnourished and stimulus-deficient homes found an average IQ difference of 19 points between the two groups. This is the difference between "normal" and "superior" intelligence, or the difference between "normal"

and "borderline" intelligence. Perhaps the "rubber band" metaphor offered by Stern best expresses the interaction of heredity and environment in relation to intelligence. He states (1956:53): "Different people initially may have been given different lengths of unstretched endowment, but the natural forces of the environment may have stretched their expression to equal length, or led to differences in attained length sometimes corresponding to their innate differences and at other times in reverse of the relation."

Table 12-1 compares the percentages of convicted felons within seven IQ levels with percentages of the general population within those same levels. The table represents the IQ levels of 376 individuals taken from presentence reports. The small number (IQs were available for only 59% of the sample) precludes any statement about IQ's being a contributory "cause" of crime. The table merely gives some indication of the distribution of IQ levels with which the criminal justice helper can expect to work.

The table provides comfort for those of us who believe in the concept of rehabilitation. Mindful of the limitations of the sample, what conclusions can we draw from it? It is clear that the great majority of crimes were committed by individuals with "normal" intelligence and that high

Table 12-1 Comparison of population norms on IQ with scores of a criminal sample

IQ level	Descriptions and anticipations	Percentage of general population*	Percentage of sample of felons
65 and below	Defective: Needs special education, can function in protected work situation	2.2	0.5
66–79	Borderline: Slow learner, can perform routine work under close supervision	6.7	13.3
80–90	Dull normal: Can function independently but needs vocational training	16.1	25.0
91–110	Normal: Can complete high school and some college level work, has few vocational limitations	50.0	56.6
111–119	Bright: No limitations	16.1	2.4
120–127	Superior: No limitations	6.7	2.1
128 and above	Very superior: No limitations	2.2	0.5

*General population norms adapted from D. Wechsler, *The Measurement of Adult Intelligence* (Baltimore: Williams & Wilkins, 1944).

intelligence (IQs over 110) is relatively incompatible with criminal activity (at least with the kind of criminal activity with which you will be most concerned as a corrections worker). Only 5% of our sample had IQs over 110, whereas 25% of the population have IQs that high. At the other end of the scale, those with IQs less than the normal range were only slightly overrepresented in our sample. They constituted 38.3% of the sample, as opposed to the 25% that we would expect if IQ and criminal activity were unrelated variables. To put it as simply as we can, with the possible exception of the "defectives," all the criminal clients in our sample were found to possess the intellectual capacity to be educable and/ or trainable. This also means that they have the capacity to be taught to act responsibly.

An area of concern relating to low intelligence is its appearance in conjunction with a psychopathic personality. Some recent studies have found that psychopaths functioning at low levels of intelligence are significantly more violent than psychopaths functioning at higher intellectual levels (Heilbrun, 1979; Heilbrun & Heilbrun, 1985). An even more violent combination is the psychopath with low intelligence who has a history of severe love deprivation. Comparing 38 such juvenile delinquents with 218 other delinquents, Walsh, Beyer, and Petee (1987) found that the former group were 4.3 times more likely than the latter group to have been convicted of at least one violent crime.

We should be aware that IQ does not represent in any total sense the individual's true problem-solving capacity. Any person's IQ score, especially at the lower levels, reflects his or her minimal level of functioning, not his or her maximal level. Many variables, such as motivation, test anxiety, attention span, cultural deprivation, and even the previous night's activities, can reduce a person's test score. With a caring, involved, optimistic, and demanding helper, most clients can be taught to behave responsibly and can be motivated to make the best of their innate capacities. If you do not make this belief an integral part of your operational style, then perhaps your talents would be better employed in some other line of work.

Summary

Few kinds of criminals arouse our passion for punishment more than does the sex offender. Sex offenses are perhaps the most underreported of all major crimes. But we should not put all sex offenders into a common basket. The rapist differs dramatically from the child molester, and stranger rapists and acquaintance rapists also differ considerably. The majority of rapists appear to be traditional macho males who hold onto the notion that no means yes. They rarely respect women as autonomous human beings who have absolute rights to their own bodies. There are those rapists (usually strangers to their victims) who do appear to require violence and victim degradation for their perverted satisfaction. You will find this type of rapist to be rare in comparison with the acquaintance/date rapist.

Treatment of rapists in community corrections should center on discussions of sex roles, their images of women, and the victim experience. The violent rapist is usually imprisoned. Treatment there must be more intense and specialized. Such treatment is usually administered by psychiatrists and psychologists.

Child molesters are in the main weak and lonely individuals. Only occasionally will you run into a true pedophile. Child molesters tend to be concentrated in three age categories: the teens, mid- to late thirties, and the midfifties onward. There are usually some special conditions contributing to child molestation, such as mental deficiency, unemployment, and loneliness. Just as there are some major demographic differences between acquaintance and stranger rapists, there are major differences between rapists and child molesters. The biggest differences are the average ages of the two groups and the rapists' greater propensity to use force.

You are likely to get at least one or two individuals who have been diagnosed as schizophrenics on your caseloads at any one time. The "four A's"—autism, ambivalence, inappropriate affect, and loose associations—are used to identify schizophrenics. Schizophrenia can also be identified today by the use of the PETT scan, which reveals the brain's functioning, as opposed to its structure.

At the physiological level, schizophrenia appears to be a function of an excess of various chemical neurotransmitters, or perhaps an excess of receptors for those neurotransmitters. There are also strong indicators that schizophrenics tend to have histories of childhood deprivation of love.

Your job in dealing with schizophrenics is to act as a medication monitor and to put them in touch with various community agencies, such as sheltered workshops and specialized counseling services.

High IQs tend to be relatively incompatible with crime. The mentally deficient commit a slightly disproportionate amount of crime in comparison with those with normal IQs. Low intelligence coupled with a psychopathic personality is a combination highly associated with violence. The good news is that just about all the clients represented in the data were educable or trainable. Don't give up on low-IQ clients. Remember that IQ tests measure only their minimal, not maximal, functioning.

References and Suggested Readings

Adler, C. (1984). "The convicted rapist: A sexual or a violent offender?" *Criminal Justice and Behavior,* 11:157–177.

Applewhite, P. (1981). *Molecular Gods: How Molecules Determine our Behavior.* Englewood Cliffs, NJ: Prentice-Hall.

Barbaree, H., W. Marshall, and R. Lanthier (1979). "Deviant sexual arousal in rapists." *Behavior Research and Therapy,* 17:215–222.

Clare, A. (1979). *Psychiatry in Dissent.* Philadelphia: Institute for the Study of Human Issues.

Clark, L., and D. Lewis (1977). *Rape: The Price of Coercive Sexuality.* Toronto: The Woman's Press.

Cohen, W., and R. Boucher (1972). "Misunderstandings about sex criminals." *Sexual Behavior,* 2:24–35.

Department of Health and Human Services (1981). *Toward a National Plan for the Chronically Mentally Ill.* DHHS publication no. (ADM) 81–1077.

Drzasga, J. (1960). *Sex Crimes.* Springfield, IL: Charles C Thomas.

Federal Bureau of Investigation (1986). *1985 Uniform Crime Reports.* Washington, DC: U.S. Department of Justice.

Fincher, J. (1981). *The Brain.* Washington, DC: U.S. News Books.

Glasser, W. (1975). *Reality Therapy.* New York: Harper & Row.

Gordon, R. (1980). "Research on IQ, race, and delinquency: Taboo or not taboo?" In E. Sagarin (Ed.), *Taboos in Criminology.* Beverly Hills, CA: Sage.

Groth, A. (1979). *Men Who Rape.* New York: Plenum.

Hartman, H. (1978). *Basic Psychiatry for Corrections Workers.* Springfield, IL: Charles C Thomas.

Heilbrun, A. (1979). "Psychopathy and violent crime." *Journal of Consulting and Clinical Psychology,* 50:546–557.

Heilbrun, A., and M. Heilbrun (1985). "Psychopathy and dangerousness: A comparison, integration and extension of two psychopathic typologies." *British Journal of Clinical Psychology,* 24:181–195.

Hirschi, T., and M. Hindelang (1977). "Intelligence and delinquency: A revisionist review." *American Sociological Review,* 42:571–587.

Jeffery, C. (1980). "Sociobiology and criminology: The long lean years of the unthinkable and the unmentionable." In E. Sagarin (Ed.), *Taboos in Criminology.* Beverly Hills, CA: Sage.

Kantor, R., and W. Herron (1966). *Reactive and Process Schizophrenia.* Palo Alto, CA: Science and Behavior Books.

Konner, M. (1982). *The Tangled Wing: Biological Constraints on the Human Spirit.* New York: Holt, Rinehart & Winston.

Kreuz, L., and R. Rose (1972). "Assessment of aggressive behavior and plasma testosterone in a young criminal population." *Psychosomatic Medicine,* 34:321–332.

Lewin, R. (1975). "Starved brains." *Psychology Today,* September.

Liebowitz, M. (1983). *The Chemistry of Love.* New York: Berkley Books.

McCaghy, C. (1967). "Child molesters: A study of their careers as deviants." In M. Clinard and R. Quinney (Eds.), *Criminal Behavior Systems: A Typology.* New York: Holt, Rinehart & Winston.

Morris, N., and G. Hawkins (1969). *The Honest Politician's Guide to Crime Control.* Chicago, IL: University of Chicago Press.

Plomin, R., and J. DeFries (1980). "Genetics and intelligence: Recent data." *Intelligence,* 4:15–24.

Ploscowe, M. (1968). "Rape." In E. Sagarin and D. MacNamara (Eds.), *Problems of Sex Behavior.* New York: Thomas Y. Crowell.

Quinsey, V., and T. Chaplin (1982). "Penile responses to nonsexual violence." *Criminal Justice and Behavior,* 9:372–381.

Restak, R. (1979). *The Brain: The Last Frontier.* New York: Warner.

Robertson, I. (1977). *Sociology.* New York: Worth.

Seeman, P., and T. Lee (1981). "Chemical clues to schizophrenia." *Science News,* 112 (November).

Stern, C. (1956). "Heredity factors affecting adoption." In *A Study of Adoption Practices.* Child Welfare League of America.

Taylor, L. (1984). *Born to Crime.* Westport, CT: Greenwood.

Thio, A. (1978). *Deviant Behavior.* Boston: Houghton Mifflin.

Walsh, A. (1983). *Differential Sentencing Patterns among Felony Sex Offenders and Non-Sex Offenders.* Ann Arbor, MI: University Microfilms International.

Walsh, A. (1985). "Homosexual and heterosexual child molestation: The similarities, the differences, and the societal reaction." Paper presented at the 1985 Annual Meeting of the Idaho Sociology and Political Science Association.

Walsh, A., J. Beyer, and T. Petee (1987). "Violent delinquency: An examination of psychopathic typologies." *Journal of Genetic Psychology,* 148:385–392.

Wechsler, D. (1944). *The Measurement of Adult Intelligence.* Baltimore: Williams & Wilkins.

Wilson, H., and C. Kneisl (1983). *Psychiatric Nursing.* Menlo Park, CA: Addison-Wesley.

Chapter 13

Community Agencies and Volunteers as Treatment Aids

Corrections personnel must do more to discover how community and societal resources can be brought to bear on the problems of offenders, bearing in mind that the community is the corrective aspect of the correctional process ... what helps the offender protects the community.

Louis Radelet

Community Resources

Individual and group counseling of clients is not always enough. The professional criminal justice worker knows that more concrete help for the client is often needed. Attempting to move your clients toward more responsible lifestyles is a difficult task that you need not bear alone. Corrections is a community problem, and you should consider yourself to be in partnership with the various community-supported agencies in the rehabilitative endeavor. Probation and parole departments simply do not have the resources to provide for all the needs of their clients.

It is an unfortunate fact that many criminal justice workers are unaware of the help that is available to their clients (and to themselves) within the community. To make proper use of community agencies, you should gain a thorough knowledge of them and an understanding of their functions before you need them. Only with this knowledge and understanding can you decide on the appropriate referral for the specific need. Mangrum has stated that the corrections worker's ability to provide extended and effective services to clients will be proportional to the scope of his or her knowledge of available resources in the community (1975:258). This kind of knowledge is helpful in the supervision of all criminal justice clients, but it is particularly important for parolees. They have to be integrated back into the community after long absences. Here is a brief overview of the types of community resource agencies available in most cities.

Mental Health Centers

The mental health center is the community resource with which the criminal justice worker is most familiar. Most jurisdictions have a diagnostic and treatment center specifically to deal with criminal justice clients. The center is staffed by social workers, psychologists, and psychiatrists. They deal with competency testing, presentence evaluations, and postsentencing and parole testing and treatment. Specialized individual, group, and family counseling is provided at these centers.

In addition to centers run for and by the courts, there are the more general mental health centers. These centers may be the preferred referrals of the client because they are not a part of the criminal justice system. Whatever the case may be, you must develop the ability to recognize symptoms of mental illness and/or specific diagnostic and treatment needs best dealt with by a referral to a mental health professional. Never underestimate or downplay symptoms displayed by clients that lead you to suspect serious mental problems. You may be right or you may be wrong, but err on the side of caution and refer.

Substance Abuse Centers

Substance abuse centers can be either private or public agencies. They include hospitals, chapters of Alcoholics Anonymous, Volunteers of America, methadone centers, half-way houses, and often residential centers specifically designed for criminal justice clients. For clients who are veterans of the U.S. armed forces, various VA hospitals provide excellent in-patient substance abuse treatment free of charge. Many health insurance policies cover costs of drug and alcohol treatment. If you have clients who have either of these problems and who are lucky enough to still have a job, check out their insurance with them. It's amazing how often this possibility is overlooked by both officers and clients.

Educational and Vocational Guidance

Since most convicted criminals tend to be unemployed high school dropouts, education and vocational training should be high on the list of client needs. Community high schools offer GED preparation classes free of charge, as well as some vocational training for minimal fees. One drawback of GED classes at local high schools is the traditional teaching methods seen there. Students are taught as a group without much attention paid to individual levels of ability. It was with this problem in mind that my department set up its own GED program based on individualized instruction. Students were able to proceed at their own pace without regard to classroom norms. I suggest that all probation and parole departments should start a program such as this. Money to employ a part-time teacher need not come from tight departmental budgets. We were always able to fund the program adequately by small grants from local churches and other concerned organizations.

The Bureau of Vocational Rehabilitation provides many opportunities for vocational testing and on-the-job training. Since this program operates within the prison system as well as in the community, it is sensitive to the special needs of criminal justice clients. It provides clients with counselors who can assist them with job interviewing and other work-related skills. This is a particularly useful agency with which to become fully acquainted.

State employment agencies duplicate, with somewhat less success, many of the functions of the Bureau of Vocational Rehabilitation. Additionally, they maintain lists of currently available employment in the area. In this age of technology, however, it is becoming increasingly difficult to take advantage of the employment office's ever-decreasing job list without adequate vocational preparation.

Welfare Agencies

The local welfare department administers various federal, state, and local welfare programs.

Most criminal justice clients are better acquainted with "the welfare" than are their officers, but many are not aware of the range of programs available. In addition to general relief and food stamps, this agency administers aid to the disabled, medical assistance, aid to the aged, and family counseling, to name just a few programs. It is useful for probation and parole officers to have a contact at the welfare department who will expedite matters when the need for client assistance is acute. Such an occasion may arise when a homeless and penniless client has been released from jail or prison or when a young man has been thrown out of his family home with only the clothes on his back.

Most communities have an agency that specializes in finding accommodations for the homeless. In cooperation with the welfare department, it may provide the client and his or her family with permanent or temporary accommodations. It is also often able to provide the client or spouse

with homemaking skills, such as family planning and balancing a tight budget. Temporary shelter for the real down-and-out can be found at various religious and secular "missions." These places offer meals, counseling, and companionship as well as accommodations.

In and Out Referrals

You will not always be able to determine your clients' needs and problem areas by yourself. Quite often other agencies—the police, courts, prosecutors, ministers, neighbors, family members, and concerned citizens—will provide information regarding their needs and problem areas. Your task is to act as a broker or go-between, matching the complaint or concern referred to you with the appropriate action. The appropriate action will often be a referral of your own to another specialized agency. Figure 13-1 is a flowchart illustrating the in- and out-flow of referrals.

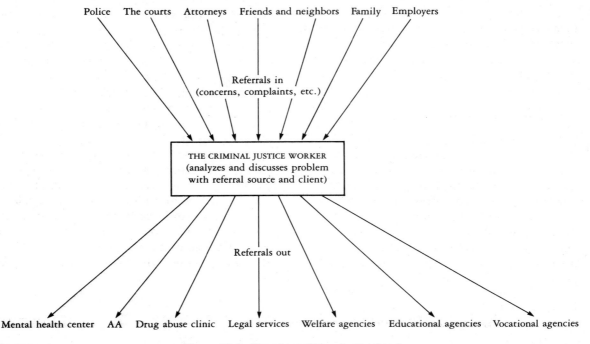

Figure 13-1 Flowchart of in and out referrals

Volunteers

A Community-Resource Volunteer Speakers Program

Some years ago, the probation department where I worked instituted a very successful program aimed at helping clients to deal with various problems of living. It provided some useful services for clients. The program was modeled after the Texas Pre-Release Program, designed to prepare inmates for release into the community. Both the Texas program and ours were based on the recognition that much recidivism could be traced to an inability to cope with what most of us would consider relatively mundane problems. Inability to cope was in turn traced to simple ignorance rather than any lack of native ability or debilitating mental health problems. Consequently, we developed a Citizens' Volunteer Speakers' Bureau to provide probationers with much-needed guidance and advice on matters of daily living. Each volunteer, and we never experienced any difficulty recruiting them, was a specialist in his or her field. Our easy successes in getting concerned speakers points to the vast amount of talent "out there" just waiting to be tapped.

The program worked by first identifying clients with simple problems of living and getting them to agree to attend a four-week cycle (two nights per week) of informal "resource information" talks conducted by the specialists. If such a program is initiated in your department, you should not require or demand that clients attend. Insistence could be counterproductive. You should intimate, however, that you will view their attendance very positively as being indicative of their desire to help themselves. Typical topics and sources of speakers are presented in Table 13-1.

Unfortunately, our program was never formally evaluated for its effectiveness, but the general consensus was that it was extremely helpful to clients dealing with the problems of living addressed by the various speakers. Officers also learned a great deal about the community resources available to help them help their clients. However, the original Texas Pre-Release Program was formally evaluated. According to Clark (1975:240), it significantly reduced recidivism among former inmates of the Texas prison system. It is a system well worth instituting in your department or agency.

Table 13-1 Community-resource information speakers' program

Week	Subject	Speaker or source
1	Job opportunities and employment aids Finding and keeping a job Social Security benefits Unions and employment	Employment bureau Local employers Social Security Administration Union representative
2	Sensible spending and budgeting Sensible borrowing Insurance needs Your welfare department	Financial counselor Credit union representative Insurance representative County welfare department
3	The family Human relationships Responsible citizenship Veteran's benefits	Family counselor Human relations counselor Leaders in civic affairs Veterans Administration
4	Personal health Alcohol and drug abuse Educational and vocational opportunities Mental health and general assistance agencies	State and county health departments AA and NA members Bureau of Vocational Rehabilitation Mental health and Community Chest professionals

Volunteer Officers in Corrections

The practice of probation began with volunteers (unpaid nonprofessionals) and, to a somewhat lesser extent, so did parole (Scheier, 1974). Volunteers in probation and parole can be a tremendous aid to the professional officer, going far beyond filing cases and licking stamps. I began my career in probation as a volunteer before accepting a paid position. With proper screening for suitability, initial and ongoing training, and proper matching of clients and volunteers, volunteers can be a most useful addition to any community corrections endeavor.

What kind of person is a volunteer, or what kind of person should the volunteer be? According to Henningsen (1981:119): "Typically, the volunteer is a sensitive and concerned individual with maturity and control over his or her own life. The volunteer relates well to others and is usually a warm and caring person capable of giving and receiving love." In other words, the volunteer's self must be every bit as much "together" as the professional's. After all, if volunteers are to be used efficiently and meaningfully by professionals, they have to be very much like professionals. A noncaring, nonloving, and immature dilettante is of no use to either you or your clients. If such a person manages to slip through the selection net, he or she won't stay long, but can do a lot of damage in the meantime.

What can you as a professional corrections worker expect to gain from the services of volunteers? According to Scheier (1974), the two biggest gains lie in the areas of amplification of services and diversification of services. The volunteer frees the professional worker from dealing with a number of less problematic cases so that he or she can increase meaningful contact time with the remainder of the caseload. It has been my experience that clients often accept volunteers more readily than they accept professionals because they see volunteers as less threatening. Some may also view volunteers as more concerned precisely because they receive no financial remuneration for their time and services.

Volunteers can be especially well accepted if you do your best to match clients and volunteers according to the needs and abilities of each. For example, an older volunteer who is the "nurturing parent" type could be matched with a young offender who has lacked such a person in his or her own life. Perhaps another client would be more comfortable with an age and sex peer volunteer, who could serve as a role model. Table 13-2 shows the matching criteria employed in a highly successful volunteer probation officer program in Lincoln, Nebraska. Notice that the importance of the criteria varies according to the type of client/volunteer relationship desired. For example, if an adult role model relationship is

Table 13-2 Matching clients with volunteers by type of relationship

Volunteer/client match	Relationship desired by usefulness of match			
	Adult role model	Friend/companion	Supervisor	Counselor
Ethnicity	Essential	Very useful	Useful	Useful
Sex	Essential	Essential	Irrelevant	Irrelevant
Age	Essential	Essential	Useful	Irrelevant
Education	Very useful	Very useful	Irrelevant	Irrelevant
Community contacts	Useful	Useful	Very useful	Irrelevant
Interests	Very useful	Essential	Irrelevant	Irrelevant
Social class	Very useful	Very useful	Irrelevant	Very useful
Counseling skills	Useful	Useful	Useful	Essential

Adapted from Richard Ku, *The Volunteer Probation Counselor Program, Lincoln, Nebraska* (Washington, DC: U.S. Government Printing Office, 1975), p. 48.

desired, matching for ethnicity is considered "essential"; if a friend/companion relationship is desired, ethnic matching is seen as "very useful," but it is considered to be only "useful" if a supervisory or counseling relationship is desired. In contrast, counseling skills are essential if a counseling relationship is desired but only "useful" if any of the other three kinds of relationship is desired. Such a chart may prove valuable to you in matching clients with volunteers.

With respect to the diversification of services, Scheier (1974:263) cites one report that indicated that a court system made use of 50 different types of skill brought to it by citizen volunteers. During my time in probation I recall volunteers from all walks of life who provided clients with everything from spiritual guidance to jogging classes. These valuable services most certainly could not have been supplied by the professional staff. As for the benefit to the department, one retired volunteer with my department, the late Larry Zucker, put in as much time as any of the paid staff for about ten years. He supervised all of the department's welfare fraud cases, as well as supervising a number of other volunteers. This wonderful and caring gentleman was sadly missed on his passing.

Although not all corrections agencies can expect to find their own Larry Zuckers, they are remiss not to recognize and use the tremendous variety of skills available in any community. To use volunteers effectively and efficiently not only magnifies the efforts of professional workers but can also greatly assist the rehabilitative possibilities of the client. Isn't that what it's all about?

A word of warning is necessary at this point. You have to make quite sure that clients are not manipulating volunteers and that volunteers are holding clients responsible for living up to their conditions of supervision. Problems in these areas can arise with some frequency if volunteers are not screened for suitability, if they are not adequately trained and told what is expected of them, or if they are not matched well with clients. You retain the ultimate responsibility for monitoring the client's progress. Thus, volunteers should submit a monthly progress report on each of the clients he or she supervises for you. Volunteers expect and appreciate this. Feedback enables volunteers to improve their services to clients and lets them know that they are being taken seriously.

A Final Word

The professional application of the knowledge, tools, and techniques presented in this book will, I believe, assist you in supervising and helping those unfortunate lives that it may one day be your privilege to touch. It is an awesome responsibility to be charged with helping, befriending, and rectifying the attitudes and behaviors of another human being. Never cease examining and improving yourself or learning everything you can about your profession. Make wise use of the numerous community resources available to aid you in this endeavor.

However, you must never lose sight of the fact that the most important person in the rehabilitative effort is the client. You must not fall into the trap of doing things for and to clients; rather, you should do things *with* them. We wish to foster client responsibility through self-reliance. An overemphasis on providing everything for the client, beyond the initial stage, is not congruent with this aim and tends to encourage client dependence. It is fine if clients lean on you a little, but only if they lean in order to lift themselves up to responsibility.

The experienced worker may be excused for asking how all these concepts, suggestions, and techniques can realistically be put to work, given the constraints imposed by time and large caseloads. The judicious management of caseloads requires organization and a thorough knowledge of clientele. This is best accomplished by proper client classification based on presentence investigation information. Proper classification and risk and needs assessment enable the officer to determine which clients are most in need of his or her attention. Many clients on the average caseload require little, if any, "treatment" beyond occasional reporting and the officer's monitoring of daily arrest sheets. These low-risk/low-needs clients are often "situational" offenders whose

Perspectives from the Field

Dr. McConnell is a professor of sociology at the University of Toledo. His fields of specialty are criminology and social stratification. He began as a volunteer probation officer with Lucas County adult offenders in 1983 and acquired field experience working in a large California prison.

Volunteer Probation Work
Dr. Stephen B. McConnell

Many things are too important to be left to the professionals alone: defense to the Pentagon, medicine to the M.D.s, law to legislators and attorneys. If any truth lies in this observation, there may well be a point for volunteerism in criminal justice. For after all, an array of professional personnel implements correctional policy.

Whatever value volunteer probation officers (VPOs) have, it has minimally to do with saving a jurisdiction money or sparing regular staff even bigger caseloads. The central contribution of VPOs derives from the inclusion of ordinary citizens, albeit civic-minded ones, in the operation of justice proceedings. The professionalism of full-time staff is leavened with the innocence of volunteers.

There is a well-documented tendency for police officers to develop cynicism as an occupational necessity. Similarly, but to a much lesser extent, probation officers can develop a less-than-sanguine view of offenders and rehabilitation. Volunteers who have developed value systems and understandings outside the criminal justice system, for whom criminal cases have not become routinized affairs, can—and occasionally do—challenge the orthodoxy of the prevailing professional views and ideology. In short, volunteers can ask fresh questions, even provide new insights that do not occur to veteran professionals.

So much of corrections work pivots on anticipating which offenders will or will not repeat crime. Predicting human behavior is a crap-shoot at best, and this is especially true concerning criminal recidivism. Some psychologists would have us believe that prediction is a science, but the fact is otherwise. Nobody has a monopoly on predicting what another will do post conviction/post probation-parole. On this count, the VPO whose mature understanding of behavior stems from coping with life itself is on equal footing with the professionals.

The justice system involves a number of somewhat technical and arcane practices that obscure the big picture of the reality of criminal justice. Informed volunteers can demystify and demythologize the system for a public for which such matters are remote and alien. Likewise, volunteers can step beyond the "trained incapacities" (the inability to see beyond the taken-for-granted realities imposed by socialization into a professional role) of professionals-as-professionals.

The motivations of volunteers in criminal justice are very broad. Most of the college students are amassing experience to ease their transition into paid positions upon graduation. Older volunteers have more altruistic and diverse motivations. In my own case, the motivation is twofold: I had been teaching in the city for over a decade and wanted to repay in some fashion the community from which I extract a living. Equally important, I wanted to gain some hands-on experience with offenders, for it is nearly 20 years since I worked in the field. I knew how direct experience contributes

Perspectives from the Field (continued)

so much to the rethinking and refining of the theoretical ideas I teach in my criminology and corrections classes. In brief, I saw the chance to volunteer as a means of keeping fresh in the classroom.

Being a VPO involves a host of qualifications too numerous to recount here. Certainly one learns to listen with the third ear to detect what clients are saying indirectly (or trying to conceal) rather than saying directly.

And since serving as a VPO involves making recommendations, even giving direct orders to clients about intimate aspects of their lives, it behooves the VPO to know as much as he or she can about society. (For this reason, sociology continues to be a valuable study for people in correctional work.) At the broadest level, the VPO comes to see how the U.S. economic system of capitalism creates a permanent underclass from which the huge majority of garden-variety criminal justice clients come. In conjunction, the VPO comes to realize how the occupational structure works, how, for example, a drop in the unemployment rate increases the likelihood of clients' getting minimum wage jobs in, say, the fast food or motel industries.

As well, the VPO comes to understand numerous components of community organization. This information covers everything from local agencies, which may be able to help a poor or alcoholic or drug-addicted client, to understanding the subtleties of the operation of the courts, the police department, and the prosecutor's office.

Thus, for a person to be effective as a VPO, there is a great deal of information to be absorbed. This information can then be passed on to clients for their benefit, and it enables the VPO to understand clients' behavior in a realistic context.

A cautionary note is in order. Corrections work is not for the fainthearted volunteer. Nor is it for people who demand 100% success. Criminal justice clients can be difficult to work with, and on occasion are outright hostile. Not all clients make good on probation or parole: some do commit new offenses and are sent to, or back to, prison. The VPO adapts to the idea that whatever he or she does or doesn't do, much of the eventual outcome for a client lies effectively beyond his or her control. Respect the fact that clients are responsible for their own destinies. Maybe it's fair to say that working as a VPO lends a certain humility to one's perspective.

trip through "the system" can be sufficient to teach them the errors of their ways. The time you save by having minimal contact with these clients can be put to good use by concentrating on more problematic offenders. Knowledge and proper use of community resources, and of the skills and motivations of volunteers, will strengthen your efforts. There is always enough time for organized, efficient, and caring criminal justice workers to do the job they have chosen. Few vocations are more psychologically rewarding and uplifting.

Summary

This chapter has dealt with the very important task of acquainting the corrections worker with the resources, skills, and desires to become involved that exist in the community. Numerous specialized agencies can help clients with their day-to-day problems. You can't be expected to have in your head all the information that these community agencies have gathered. Your task is to recognize client problem areas and to make the appropriate agency referrals if the problems are not within your area of expertise. Your expertise should be that of a broker matching clients with agencies.

You can also provide your clients and yourself with much-needed information by organizing a community resource information speakers' program. Such a program can be run periodically to accommodate new clients. Many clients find themselves in trouble simply because they do not have access to information about the kind of help that exists in the community to aid them with their problems. Speaker programs have proven to be most helpful to clients and corrections workers alike.

Another valuable resource that should not be overlooked is the desire of many individuals in the community to be useful and helpful. These people can be fruitfully incorporated into the correctional enterprise as volunteers. Probation and parole volunteers provide amplification and diversification of services to criminal justice clients. Volunteers must be screened, trained, and matched with clients. Their performance should be monitored by the professional worker to make sure that they are holding clients responsible and that they are not being manipulated by clients.

You have chosen an immensely satisfying career. Your satisfaction will be greatly increased if you learn to use properly the resources available in your community.

◑ Exercises in Using Community Resources

Nearly all communities have a clearing house (sometimes referred to as the Community Chest) where you can obtain information about the various kinds of resources available to help the unfortunate. You should identify the needs of the client on whom you have written a practice PSI report and match them with appropriate agencies. You should then find out if your community has an agency that could deal with your client's particular problem. If your community does not have such an agency, what would your second-best referral or plan of action be?

Devise a resource information speakers' program based on the resources available in your community and on the needs of criminal justice clients as you perceive them. What additional resources not included in this chapter do you think clients would find useful?

Find out if the community corrections agencies located in your community have volunteer programs. If so, call and ask them about their criteria for volunteer selection, about the training offered to volunteers, and if they make attempts to match volunteers with clients. What did the person you spoke with consider to be the most useful attribute of a prospective volunteer?

References and Suggested Readings

Clark, J. (1975). "The Texas Pre-Release Program." In L. Hippchen (Ed.), *Correctional Classification and Treatment.* Cincinnati, OH: Anderson.

Henningsen, R. (1981). *Probation and Parole.* San Diego: Harcourt Brace Jovanovich.

Mangrum, C. (1975). *The Professional Practitioner in Probation.* Springfield, IL: Charles C Thomas.

Scheier, I. (1974). "The professional and the volunteer in probation: An emerging relationship." In G. Killinger and P. Cromwell, Jr. (Eds.), *Corrections in the Community.* St. Paul, MN: West Publishing.

Index